**Corporate Governance
and Managerial Reform in Japan**

Corporate Governance and Managerial Reform in Japan

edited by
D. Hugh Whittaker and Simon Deakin

OXFORD
UNIVERSITY PRESS

OXFORD

UNIVERSITY PRESS

Great Clarendon Street, Oxford OX2 6DP

Oxford University Press is a department of the University of Oxford.
It furthers the University's objective of excellence in research, scholarship,
and education by publishing worldwide in

Oxford New York

Auckland Cape Town Dar es Salaam Hong Kong Karachi
Kuala Lumpur Madrid Melbourne Mexico City Nairobi
New Delhi Shanghai Taipei Toronto

With offices in

Argentina Austria Brazil Chile Czech Republic France Greece
Guatemala Hungary Italy Japan Poland Portugal Singapore
South Korea Switzerland Thailand Turkey Ukraine Vietnam

Oxford is a registered trade mark of Oxford University Press
in the UK and in certain other countries

Published in the United States
by Oxford University Press Inc., New York

© Oxford University Press, 2009

The moral rights of the authors have been asserted
Database right Oxford University Press (maker)

First published 2009

British Library Cataloguing in Publication Data
Data available

Library of Congress Cataloging in Publication Data
Data available

Typeset by SPI Publisher Services, Pondicherry, India
Printed in Great Britain
on acid-free paper by the
MPG Books Group, Bodmin and King's Lynn

ISBN 978–0–19–956363–0

1 3 5 7 9 10 8 6 4 2

Contents

v

Contents

List of Figures and Tables

Figures

Tables

List of Contributors

Takashi Araki Professor, Faculty of Law, University of Tokyo.

John Buchanan Research Associate, Centre for Business Research, University of Cambridge.

Simon Deakin Professor, Faculty of Law and Centre for Business Research, University of Cambridge; Visiting Professor, Doshisha University, Kyoto.

Ronald Dore Associate, Centre for Economic Performance, London School of Economics.

Hisayoshi Fuwa President and Chief Executive Officer, Toshiba Carrier Corporation.

Masaru Hayakawa Professor, Doshisha University Law School.

Takeshi Inagami President, Japan Institute for Labour Policy and Training; Professor Emeritus, University of Tokyo.

Sanford M. Jacoby Howard Noble Professor of Management, Public Policy, and History, UCLA.

George Olcott FME Teaching Fellow, Judge Business School, University of Cambridge.

D. Hugh Whittaker Professor, University of Auckland Business School; Visiting Professor, Doshisha University, Kyoto.

Note: Japanese names throughout this book appear in English order, with the surname last.

Acknowledgements

This book grew out of research collaboration between the Institute for Technology, Enterprise, and Competitiveness (ITEC) at Doshisha University, Kyoto, and the Centre for Business Research (CBR) at the University of Cambridge, UK. We would like to acknowledge the support of both centers, including financial support from the Ministry of Education, Culture, Sports, Science, and Technology (MEXT) 21st Century Center of Excellence Program through ITEC. We thank Yoshifumi Nakata, Jacques Payet, and the staff of ITEC, as well as Alan Hughes, Sue Moore, and the staff of the CBR, for their support, and above all Kate Hansen of the CBR for her editorial assistance. We are also very grateful to our editors at OUP, David Musson, Matthew Derbyshire, and Abigail Coulson, for their encouragement and advice.

1

On a Different Path? The Managerial Reshaping of Japanese Corporate Governance

Simon Deakin and D. Hugh Whittaker

Introduction

The chapters in this book address the state of Japanese corporate governance and managerial practice at a critical moment. They are mostly based on detailed and intensive field work in large Japanese companies and on interviews with investors, civil servants, and policy makers in the period following the adoption of significant corporate law reforms in the early 2000s up to the months just prior to the global financial crisis of 2008. Among the legal changes made during this period were reforms which, with effect from April 2003, allowed firms to opt into a "company with committees" structure based, loosely, on American practice, with provision for an enhanced role for independent directors. At around the same time, several high-profile takeover bids attracted public concern and challenged the perceived wisdom that hostile takeovers were impractical in Japan, giving rise to a series of court rulings and attempts by the industry and justice ministries to generate consensus on guidelines for companies involved in such takeovers. In the decade prior to these developments there had been a steady rise in foreign share ownership, a decline in the cross-shareholdings which had insulated large firms from capital-market

We are grateful to John Buchanan for comments on an earlier draft.

pressures, and the erosion of the practice of bank-led monitoring of corporate performance. Above all, there had been the massive disillusionment of the post-"bubble" years, when a stream of scandals and corporate failures throughout the 1990s and beyond called into question the integrity of Japan's entire postwar system of corporate governance. The time seemed right for Japan to make the final move to a market-driven, "Anglo-American" system of corporate governance.

Almost a decade later, the picture looks rather different. Although listed companies make greater use of external directors than before, few have taken up the company with committees option. The hostile takeover movement has stalled, with firms taking advantage of the evolving state of the law to put in place antitakeover defenses and, in some cases, reconstruct cross-shareholdings. Activist shareholders, both pension funds and hedge funds, have had mixed success and some significant rebuffs. Meanwhile, despite a growth in the numbers of temporary and part-time workers, the practice of lifetime employment (best understood as a nonlegally binding commitment on the part of large firms to providing stable, continuous employment to core workers) has persisted, together with a renewed emphasis on employee voice as an intra-firm mechanism for ensuring managerial accountability.

It is possible to interpret this process as the unnecessary prolongation of a period of transition, which will eventually see Japanese practice converging on what has come to be generally understood as the global template for corporate governance. Alternatively, Japan's experience may be telling us a story about the distinctiveness of national "varieties of capitalism," even in the face of global pressures. The work we will present in this book suggests that neither of these contrasting images of "transition" and "resistance" very well captures what has been happening. The idea of a partial, possibly stalled transition to the Anglo-American model is hard to square with the continuities we observe in terms of the "internal" orientation of Japanese management, its commitment to employment stability for the core workforce, and the relatively limited influence of shareholders. But nor is it the case that large Japanese firms have simply been resisting pressure mounted from outside by investors and corporate governance reformers. On the contrary, shifts in the legal and institutional framework, as well as the competitive environment, have been the trigger for some far-reaching changes to organizational structures and management style. An adjustment, and in some senses a renewal, of the postwar model of the large Japanese corporation has taken place, not in spite of the legal, institutional, and competitive changes of the early 2000s, but, paradoxically, because of them, at least in part. The legal reforms were a catalyst or trigger for changes to corporate practice which helped to reinforce a model that they had been expected (by some, at least) to displace.

The aim of this chapter is to put the subsequent, more detailed case study chapters in context, and to set out the book's main themes and findings. The following section considers the institutional origins of the postwar model of Japanese corporate governance and the next one outlines the pressures for change which operated on that model in the period following the bursting of the "bubble" up to the early 2000s. The section after that, drawing on the chapters contained in this book, looks at specific factors at work in the process of adjustment which large Japanese companies have been undergoing since the start of the period of our study in 2003. The final section offers an evaluation of Japanese developments in a comparative perspective and draws out some of the implications of the Japanese case for the wider understanding of global trends in corporate governance.

Institutional Origins of the Postwar Model

The model of corporate governance which emerged in large Japanese companies in the period of sustained postwar growth that ended with the bursting of the "bubble" at the end of the 1980s was one which appeared to be highly stable, was rooted in specific national practices, and, notwithstanding its distinctiveness, was efficient in the sense of providing a framework for the growth of a corporate sector which was highly competitive in product market terms and successful in generating secure and well-paid employment for a sizable core of employees. This model came to be understood as the result of interaction between a number of complementary institutions. Capital markets were relatively illiquid, with extensive corporate cross-shareholdings, limited voice for external shareholders, and passive institutional investors (Sheard 1994). By contrast, there was a prominent role for mechanisms of so-called relational finance, such as bank-led monitoring, and internal financing channelled through group-level holding companies (Aoki 1994). Within the organizational structure of the "community firm" (Dore 1973; Inagami and Whittaker 2005) labor relations were arranged around lifetime employment, company unionism, and internal promotion of management. In various ways, finance and labor complemented each other to favor the emergence of firms which were strongly growth-orientated, and

3

committed to generating internal capabilities over the longer term. Management had considerable autonomy within a system of "contingent governance" in which banks, holding companies, or, occasionally, government ministries might intervene at points of crisis (Aoki and Patrick 1994), but in which there was little experience of the continuous monitoring through capital-market mechanisms of the kind which were developing in the United States and Britain toward the end of this period, most notably through hostile takeover bids and the growing role within boards of external, independent directors.

One of the most striking features of this model was its apparent lack of visible institutional support. Japan's corporate law during the middle decades of the twentieth century was contained in the Commercial Code of 1899, which had been based on the German civil law of the late nineteenth century. The Code was revised in 1950 under the influence of the policies of the General Headquarters (GHQ) of the Allied Occupation, thereby incorporating a number of elements drawn from the US corporate law of that time (West 2001). The Japanese joint stock company was one in which the ultimate governing body consisted of the shareholders in general meeting; they had the power to appoint and remove directors on a simple majority vote, and to pass special resolutions with a two-thirds majority. The board of directors was the organ vested with executive powers and the responsibility for running the company as a business. Thus the basic legal form of the Japanese firm was (and is) no different from that which prevailed in most other developed economies. It was only distinctive in a few respects. One of these was the institution of the statutory or corporate auditors. This body, which predated the 1950 reforms, was given the responsibility for overseeing the board's conduct of the company's business as well as various accounting matters, and could demand information from the board. The 1950 changes limited its supervisory powers to accounting issues, partly in order to emphasize the board's responsibility for overseeing management. In the mid-1970s, some of the powers of the corporate auditors were restored as a response to high-profile failures and scandals. The corporate auditors can be seen as playing a similar role to the supervisory board in the two-tier structure which is normal in German-origin systems. However, the Japanese structure was not, formally, a two-tier board as the German one was, and the powers of the Japanese auditors were much more limited than those of the German supervisory board. There was no provision for employee-nominated directors or auditors, or, more generally, for labor-management codetermination on German lines. There was also no equivalent in Japanese labor law to the legal support for employee voice through works councils which characterized the German model.

Thus the main elements of the Japanese model – bank-led monitoring, executive-dominated boards and a strong orientation, in terms of managerial style and value, toward the interests of core employees – were in no sense legally mandated, or even very much encouraged by the legal and institutional framework. The legal structure of the Japanese firm was, on the face of it, based on the principle of shareholder sovereignty, admittedly with the delegation of executive authority to the board, but with shareholders no more disadvantageously treated than elsewhere in industrial economies; indeed, in many respects, they enjoyed at least equivalent or possibly superior rights (West 2001). Japanese corporate governance practices were (and remain) "context dependent" (see Chapter 8), that is to say, shaped by the interaction of a number of complementary mechanisms operating beyond the reach of the legal framework, rather than being institutionally underpinned as they are, for example, in the German case.

At the same time, the origins of the postwar system owed much to the particular institutional trajectory of Japanese corporate governance in earlier periods. Between the wars, Japan had had active shareholders in the form of large, mostly family-owned blocks, who were capable of exercising direct control over management, and, for much of the time, a liquid capital market, which listed companies accessed for external financing on a regular basis. This picture began to change with the shift to a planned economy during wartime, when dividend controls were introduced and the authority of company presidents was enhanced at the expense of shareholder influence. These changes were brought about by a mix of legislation (most notably the Munitions Corporation Law of 1943), governmental regulation, and administrative direction which, while not formally bringing about a revision of the Commercial Code, substantially qualified its effects in practice. Executive boards replaced shareholder-dominated ones, and the practice of internal promotion of managers to board level became more widespread. At the same time, the main bank system was taking shape with the development of loan consortia organized under government and central bank auspices. The effects of these changes were that, by the end of the war, "stocks and shares became in effect fixed interest-bearing securities, and profits remaining after the fixed dividend had been paid were distributed among managers and employees in a profit-sharing system" (Okazaki 1999: 120). Laws on corporate restructuring passed during the GHQ period maintained this trend, and even with the more market-orientated Dodge Plan from 1949 onward there was a focus on bank-led monitoring and the integration of core employees into the decision-making structures and values of the firm. The effect was that by the early 1950s, "a pro-growth corporate governance structure had been formed, its major players being growth-oriented lifetime employees and a similarly growth-oriented financing body of investors centred around a main bank" (Okazaki 1999: 138).

The way in which the component parts of the postwar model complemented each other was dependent to some degree on the contingencies and accidental diversions of the historical path which the Japanese economy and society had undergone during the wartime years and the years of allied occupation. However, it was also the case that "the major constituent elements of the Japanese system were deliberately created" in this period (Okazaki and Okuno-Fujiwara 1999: vii), against the background of policy debates which made the suppression of shareholder interests explicit. By the 1960s, formal controls over dividends and restrictions over mergers associated with the postwar reconstruction period had long been removed, and the legal structure associated with the Commercial Code revived. But this legal framework, which was in any event largely facilitative rather than prescriptive, proved to be entirely compatible with the practice of managerial autonomy from shareholder control, at least until the bursting of the bubble in the late 1980s.

Pressures for Change in the 1990s

In the so-called "lost decade" of the 1990s, although there were significant legal reforms relating to share repurchases, stock options, and the use of holding companies, among other things, there were few significant legal changes directly related to corporate governance. However, the component parts of the corporate governance system underwent a number of overlapping and interconnected modifications as the nature of the economic environment changed. There was, first of all, the eclipse of bank-led monitoring, as the rolling over of loans by banks faced with financial distress (both of the companies to which they lent and, increasingly, of themselves) made bank-led intervention in corporate affairs less credible. The weakening of bank-led monitoring may have led client firms to postpone restructuring and helped to stabilize employment during a period of prolonged low growth (Arikawa and Miyajima 2007: 75).

Secondly, cross-shareholdings began to decline, but not uniformly. Their extent decreased most quickly in firms in which bank lending was becoming less significant, but was maintained by firms with continuing links to a main bank. More profitable firms which made greater use of external finance through the capital market, and which tended to have a larger proportion of overseas shareholders, began to unwind previously stable cross-holdings, while less profitable ones tended to keep them (Miyajima and Kuroki 2007).

Thirdly, with growing foreign ownership, there came a shift in investment style and practice. Foreign shareholders, who mostly acquired stakes in larger, export-orientated and higher-performing firms (initially at least), were investing for financial returns, in contrast to traditional Japanese investors who had tended to have relational commitments; institutional investors often had ties to a main bank while corporate pension funds would tend to hold shares in business partners of the company sponsoring the scheme. Foreign holdings were more liquid in the sense of being frequently traded, so that a small stake in nominal terms could acquire a larger significance in terms of its impact on share price movements. Foreign ownership was also associated with downsizing, although the direction of causation was unclear (Ahmadjian 2007: 145): were mainly foreign investors pressing otherwise reluctant firms to pursue strategies of downsizing and asset divestment, or were these investors simply attracted to the kind of firms that had confidence to engage in radical internal restructuring?

Fourthly, the coverage of lifetime employment began to shrink, as temporary and part-time employment grew (see Sako 2006), but the practice of employment stability for core workers continued. The share of wages in national income fell, as elsewhere: in the decade after 1997, dividends rose, cumulatively, by 180 percent but total salaries fell by 10 percent. There was, however, a tendency for employment reductions to be carried out in tandem with dividend cuts: only 2 percent of listed companies taking part in the 2003 METI (Ministry of Economy, Trade and Industry) survey on the corporate system and employment reported cutting jobs but not dividends. Fewer firms engaged in downsizing than in France, Germany, the United States, and Britain in the same period, and downsizing rates fell in the early 2000s. Employment stability was correlated with the presence of insider-dominated boards, but there was no link between lifetime employment practices and foreign ownership (Jackson 2007: 285–9).

This was the context in which the company with committees reform was introduced, in legislation of 2002 which came into force in 2003. In large part thanks to pressure exerted by the principal business association, the Keidanren, the legal changes were only optional, and even when firms took them up they envisaged a limited role for independent directors, who had to constitute a majority of the board committees for audit, nomination, and remuneration, but not of the main board which retained responsibility for strategic decision making. Nevertheless, the reform clearly envisaged the displacement of the traditional, executive-dominated board, by one in which shareholder interests would in future be more clearly represented and articulated. 2005 saw the hostile bid by Livedoor for Nippon Broadcasting System (NBS), and by extension control of the whole of the Fuji Sankei group, which promised to galvanize the market for corporate control. Although the bid for NBS was not successful, and Livedoor's senior management not long afterward became caught up in an (unrelated) false accounting scandal, it marked increased bid activity in a number of sectors and the arrival of activist hedge funds prepared to use the threat of a hostile bid as a way of refocusing managerial priorities. It also gave rise to an intense legal debate, as courts used the litigation around the Livedoor case to clarify the qualified scope allowed for poison pills and takeover defenses under company law, and the Corporate Value Study Group, a body of experts and representatives of industry and finance established with support from the trade and industry ministry METI and (initially) the Ministry of Justice, set about the task of drafting takeover guidelines. These, among other things, suggested parameters for managers' actions in response to a bid situation and spelled out their duty to show a regard, however qualified, for the interests of shareholders.

The changes to the rules and recommended practices governing external directors and hostile takeovers, while in some respects limited in scope, nevertheless served to import into the Japanese context two pivotal institutions of Anglo-American corporate governance. There is a long tradition in developed economies of nonexecutive directors sitting on the boards of companies. However, the idea that external directors should be independent of management, and should act not simply as advisers on matters of strategy but as monitors of managers in the interests of shareholders, is a relatively recent phenomenon (Gordon 2007, 2008). It began to gain ground in the United States in the 1970s following some high-profile corporate failures, most notably the bankruptcy of the Penn Central railroad, "the bluest of blue chip stocks, as disturbing in its day as Enron's a generation later" (Gordon 2008: 10). It was given legal expression even more recently: the formal requirement that boards of American-listed companies should have a majority of independent directors goes back only as far as the changes made to stock exchange (principally, NYSE and NASDAQ) rules under SEC supervision, following the passage of the

Sarbanes–Oxley Act in 2001. Well before that point, however, most US-listed companies had moved over from the insider-dominated boards of the immediate postwar decades to a structure in which the majority of board members, and in some cases all of them with the exception of the CEO, were independent of the company.

In Britain, the Cadbury Committee's report of 1993 marked the equivalent turning point, although the subsequent Combined Code only contained a recommendation for a majority of independent members on the main board after the Higgs report of 2001. Moreover, the Code's definition of independence largely requires companies to police themselves on this matter, in contrast to the strict definitions which now apply in the American context. Nevertheless, as in the United States, a combination of institutional shareholder pressure, a shift of opinion in favor of the shareholder value norm among senior executives, and the standardizing influence of corporate governance codes and associated legal and regulatory reforms has gradually transformed the composition and function of boards of British-listed companies over the course of the past twenty years (see Armour et al. 2003).

The influence of the hostile takeover in the so-called Anglo-American systems has also been substantial. The hostile takeover is the core mechanism by which, in a "market for corporate control," shareholders can not only bring disciplinary pressures to bear on management, but also, in practice, assert the primacy of their interests over those of other stakeholder groups. Hostile takeover activity moves in cycles, and by no means represents a consistent or continuous pressure on the management of listed companies (Cosh and Hughes 2008). However, successive waves of hostile takeovers since the early 1970s have played a part not just in the restructuring of British and American corporations, but also in helping to shift the views of executives and other corporate governance actors on the issue of whose interests management is meant to serve, with a clear move in favor of the shareholder value norm (Deakin et al. 2003; Jacoby 2005). After the initial impact of the first hostile takeover waves, institutional shareholder influence became the functional equivalent of the hostile bid; from the early 1980s, asset disposals, downsizing, high dividend yields, and share buybacks were increasingly relied on by companies to meet shareholder expectations, whether or not they were the immediate targets of bids (O'Sullivan 2001).

The regulatory changes which occurred alongside the rise of the takeover movement had wider implications for corporate governance practice. In the United States, the case law of the Delaware courts allowed listed companies to put in place poison-pill type defenses to takeover bids. Boards, with independent directors playing a central role, had some discretion to oppose bids on the grounds of stakeholder concerns, but they were required to have regard to the fundamental principle of safeguarding shareholder interests, in particular, where multiple bidders were involved and change of control became unavoidable. Hostile takeovers were nevertheless seen as an instrument of last resort, and an increasingly expensive one, and were constrained to some degree by legal changes, including pro-stakeholder statutes at state level. The role of the independent board in the 1990s became one of "providing a solution to a core corporate governance problem: how to maximise shareholder value without hostile bids," which it did by the "benchmarking of management performance to shareholder value through compensation instruments and termination decisions" (Gordon 2008: 15).

In the United Kingdom, the City Code on Mergers and Takeovers went somewhat further in restricting both prebid and postbid defenses, and in focusing the attention of boards on shareholder interests during takeover contests. With few of the legal constraints facing US bidders, hostile takeovers continued to take place on a regular basis, while the shareholder value norm was further reinforced, as in America, by the linking of executive compensation to share price movements and by the dismissal of executives who had underperformed by reference to these criteria (see generally Armour and Skeel 2007, for a comparison of the trajectory of American and British takeover regulation and associated corporate governance changes in this period).

The transplantation of these characteristically Anglo-American institutions into the Japanese context was expected to lead to a significant realignment of Japanese managerial practice. An amalgam of Anglo-American practices and norms drawn from global standards was used as a benchmark for the Japanese reforms. While the changes implied by this approach might not have been intended to bring about a straightforward replication of the American or British models, they were designed to enhance the effectiveness of Japanese corporate governance, on the assumption that the Anglo-American approach represented a model which was better capable of holding management to account and ensuring the efficient allocation of economic resources in response to capital-market pressures (see Ahmadjian 2003). In the early 2000s, the large, insider-dominated boards of the traditional Japanese firm were seen as slowing down decision making and protecting senior executives from appropriate scrutiny, in particular, given the declining influence of the banks in the aftermath of the bubble. More generally, there was a view that a much-needed restructuring of large Japanese corporations was being delayed by the absence of capital-market pressures of the kind which American and British companies were accustomed to facing. As we have already suggested, the outcome has been somewhat at odds with these expectations. Why is this, and what, more precisely, has been the nature of the changes which have occurred since the early 2000s?

The Paradoxical Transformation of Japanese Corporate Governance: Factors at Work in the 2000s

In Chapter 2, John Buchanan and Simon Deakin present an empirical analysis of the implementation of the company with committees law and related changes to the legal framework governing publicly listed companies. Their work takes the form of a longitudinal case study of twenty companies, beginning in late 2003 and ending in January 2008. Most of the companies were visited at least twice, with extended interviews with senior managers taking place on each occasion. Over fifty such interviews were carried out, covering a range of manufacturing, services, and financial sectors. In addition, over forty interviews were conducted with investors (including insurers, pension funds, and hedge funds), civil servants, experts, and policy makers. The chapter traces the origins of the 2002 law in terms of the criticism of "traditional" corporate governance practices which was mounted around the turn of the millennium, and discusses the significance of the adoption by Sony in the late 1990s of a corporate executive officer system with independent directors on a slimmed-down board, which effectively provided a working model for the 2002 law. They trace the extent of take-up of the new law after it was brought into effect in April 2003, noting that while some prominent companies have adopted the company with committees option, the 110 companies which had opted in by July 2008 represented only 4.6 percent of the first and second sections and Mothers market of the Tokyo Stock Exchange.

Their interview data reveal a picture of the law's impact which suggests that while its direct effects have been less far-reaching than the proponents of reform might have hoped, its indirect influence on the listed company sector as a whole has been considerable. In companies with committees, they find that, notwithstanding the formal change in corporate structure which followed from the decision to opt into the law, there was little alteration in the roles played by directors: most boards continued to have a significant executive presence, beyond the CEO, and external directors were treated as advisers and associates, very much as before, rather than as monitors of management or as agents of the shareholders. This could have been because of the limited reach of the law. After all, it was only optional, and, in some ways, not very far-reaching. It did not mandate a majority of independent directors on the main board and its definition of "independence" was loose, enabling corporate groups to place directors from the parent company on the boards of subsidiaries and vice versa, for example. If the intention of the law had been to enable companies which wished to prioritize shareholder value to signal their intention to do so, it was remarkably deficient in meeting this goal (Gilson and Milhaupt 2005).

However, the experience of firms opting into the company with committees structure is only half the story. As Buchanan and Deakin explain, there was a striking continuity between their implementation of the law, and the practice in companies not adopting the committee structure. Although not legally required to do so, many of the latter had increased the representation of external directors and had introduced variants of the corporate executive officer system, in which there is a clearer separation than before between board members and senior executives below the board, and hence between monitoring and execution. Companies of both varieties had used the advent of the corporate executive officer concept to streamline managerial decision making and to put in place more formal internal audit systems, with a prominent role for the board in overseeing internal risk management processes. Thus Buchanan and Deakin argue that while the law has not, a few companies aside, brought about convergence of practice on the Anglo-American model, it has served as a catalyst – or accelerator – for changes in management style and organizational structure which have affected the listed company sector as a whole. Because, in most of the companies concerned, the core of the "community firm" remains intact, not least the commitment to lifetime (or stable) employment, they interpret these developments as a renewal of the postwar model, stressing elements of continuity while acknowledging the model's adaptability in the face of external pressures. At the same time, growing shareholder pressure in a number of contexts, including hostile takeover bids and hedge fund activism, makes some form of accommodation between the organizational priorities of the community firm and shareholder interests highly likely. It is against this background that a new Corporate Governance Study Group, set up by METI in

December 2008, has been given the task of re-examining the company with committees law. Among other things, the Group will consider whether there is a case for making mandatory legal provision for external directors in listed or other companies, with a view to better protecting the interests of shareholders. Thus the policy debate is by no means settled in favor of the current framework.

The evidence from the study by Buchanan and Deakin complements and updates the more quantitative study of the impact of corporate governance reforms carried out by Aoki, Jackson, and Miyajima in the early 2000s (see Aoki 2007; Miyajima 2007; Aoki and Jackson 2008). On the basis of a survey of listed firms which was carried out in December 2002 and the use of a synthetic index to create a "corporate governance score" for each of the respondent companies, they found a strong relationship between corporate governance and firm performance only for those indicators which related to the level of information disclosure by firms. There was no governance–performance link in the case of board structure changes or the introduction of a corporate executive officer category (their data refer to firms which made this move in the period before the 2002 law came into effect). In companies coming under capital-market pressure by virtue of the presence of foreign and/or more liquid shareholdings, they found that a higher degree of employee participation was more likely, not less, to be correlated with governance reform. Governance changes were less likely in firms with a commitment to lifetime employment and seniority pay, and more likely in firms with limited-term employment and ability-based pay; but they also found that "hybrid" firms with long-term employment and ability-based pay were open to corporate governance reform. This is a theme – the possible emergence of hybrid models which combine external monitoring by shareholders with a continuing commitment to the organizational values of the community firm – to which we shall return.

In Chapter 3 in this book, Masaru Hayakawa and Hugh Whittaker focus on the other major legal reforms which took place in the 2000s, those relating to takeover bids. They provide a detailed account of the legal background to the recent increase in hostile takeover bid activity. They show how takeover bids, while formally possible within the framework of company law, were restrained in practice by cross-shareholdings and corporate group structures in the immediate postwar decades, in some cases as a result of conscious corporate planning and with the encouragement or at least tacit consent of government ministries. In the early 2000s the securities laws were amended so as to formalize the conditions for tender offers (publicly disclosed bids for control of listed companies). In the Livedoor case, these rules were avoided, along with regulations governing the disclosure of large stakes, with the company taking advantage of the Tokyo Stock Exchange's after hours trading system to acquire over 30 percent of the share capital of NBS without mounting a public bid. When NBS responded by attempting to issue share warrants to a friendly third party, the courts, in judgments drawing on concepts developed in the Delaware case law, responded with an injunction preventing the move. They held that the board, as the organ of the shareholders, was not entitled to take a step which would have had the effect of radically changing the constitution of the shareholder body, with the primary motive of entrenching the existing management. The Livedoor litigation nevertheless established that defensive action would be permissible, in the context of a bid, in one of four circumstances: where the bidder was a "greenmailer" out to extract cash from the company without any regard for its long-term value; where the bidder planned a "scorched earth" policy of disposing of the company's core assets; where a leveraged buyout was being proposed, replacing equity with debt; and where there was share price manipulation based on asset disposals. In the later Bull-Dog Sauce litigation, which involved a challenge to a dilutive share warrant issue arranged by management in response to a tender offer mounted by an activist hedge fund, Steel Partners, the courts took a more negative view of the bid, deciding that the target company was entitled to defend itself against an "abusive acquirer." This did not prevent Steel Partners from making a substantial return on their investment in Bull-Dog Sauce, as the defense put in place by the target company involved compensating Steel for the dilution of their stake brought about by the issuing of warrants to friendly parties.

Following amendments to the law in 2005, large numbers of listed companies put in place poison-pill type defenses of the kind which had succeeded in preserving the independence of the target company in the Bull-Dog Sauce case. There is a contrast between the Japanese stance on poison pills, which are generally intended to be a genuine deterrent to bidders, and US practice, in which, it can be argued, poison pills more clearly serve shareholder interests, even if they lead to the break-up of the firm at the expense of other stakeholders, let alone the much more bidder-friendly regime under the UK's Takeover Code. This difference is reflected in the development of a discourse around "corporate value" in the judgments of the courts and the guidelines being considered by the Corporate Value Study Group. "Corporate value" appears to be an alternative to the

Anglo-American concept of "shareholder value" which stresses the importance of the organizational continuity of the firm in the face of opportunistic bids. However, Hayakawa and Whittaker point out that, since the Bull-Dog Sauce litigation, the Corporate Value Study Group has expressed its support for shareholder empowerment in the context of takeover bids, while the newly established Corporate Governance Study Group has been considering whether to recommend the adoption of a Takeover Panel or similar mechanism along UK lines. Although Japan has not aligned itself with the shareholder value norm, Hayakawa and Whittaker conclude that there is probably no going back to the pre-Livedoor days of shareholder passivity.

These two chapters (2 and 3), then, present something of the uncertainties and ambiguities surrounding key legal reforms of the 2000s. The subsequent chapters serve to explain why their effects have not been more clear cut, by looking in detail at contextual factors at play in the wider corporate governance environment: the role of institutional investors (Chapter 4), the part played by the principal employers' organizations and trade associations in the debate over corporate governance (Chapter 6), the attitudes of civil servants (Chapter 5) and senior executives (Chapter 7) towards the shareholder value norm, the possible growing role for employee voice within corporate governance (Chapter 8), and the use by management of corporate governance reform as a catalyst for streamlining decision making (Chapter 9). Chapter 10 offers an assessment of the findings of the book as a whole, in the context of the "varieties of capitalism" and of the recent financial crisis.

Sanford Jacoby's chapter is a study of the activities of the Californian state pension fund CalPERS in Japan. Drawing on extensive interviews with pension fund trustees and managers and corporate governance practitioners in America and Japan, he shows how, starting in the 1990s, CalPERS attempted to transplant the activist approaches which it had pioneered in the US to the Japanese context. The initial stimulus for activism in the United States in the mid-1980s was the practice of incumbent managers paying off "greenmailers" (the Texaco and Bass Brothers case). This prompted CalPERS officials to found the Council for Institutional Investors with the aim of coordinating the efforts of pension funds and other institutional shareholders. Another incentive was provided by the nature of CalPERS' holdings: because they held shares in indexed tracker funds, and thereby had a stake in most large listed firms, it made sense for them to try to improve governance standards across the market as a whole. CalPERS accordingly began to press the companies it invested in for wider disclosure, restrictions on takeover defenses, independent boards, and greater acceptance of shareholder resolutions at annual general meetings. This approach was pursued despite a lack of evidence that activism of this kind led to higher returns.

CalPERS' foreign investments began to grow at around the same time (as regulatory constraints were lifted), rising to almost 25 percent by the early 2000s. It began to use its proxy voting rights in Japan to vote against renewal of internal directors, and plans to expand the size of boards; it also attempted to use its influence to raise dividends. This strategy was largely unsuccessful, for a number of reasons which Jacoby sets out on the basis of a close analysis of the institutional context in which CalPERS was operating. Disclosure was limited by US standards, with companies often not publicizing the details of votes. Dividend payouts fell in the 1990s as part of the aftermath of the bubble. Another tactic adopted by CalPERS was to encourage local partners: CalPERS offered encouragement to the Japan Corporate Governance Forum (JCGF) whose principles of corporate governance appeared in 1997, shortly after which CalPERS produced its own standards. The International Corporate Governance Network, which was established with CalPERS' support in 1995, held a meeting in Tokyo in 2001. However, the meeting was used by Hiroshi Okuda, the then Chairman of Toyota, to argue for the continuing distinctiveness of the Japanese approach. In the course of his speech, which senior CalPERS officials interpreted as highly discouraging for their approach, Okuda asserted that a listed company could not be regarded as simply the property of its shareholders. Failing to find a sufficient number of like-minded fellow activists, CalPERS scaled back its activism from 2002 onwards: there were no new major governance initiatives, although some support was given for local "turnaround funds." What then were the long-term consequences of CalPERS' intervention? CalPERS' limited impact implies, Jacoby suggests, that the view of the Keidanren, expressed in the early days of the fund's Japanese investments, that CalPERS's corporate governance recommendations were sub-optimal in the Japanese context, was basically correct.

Ronald Dore looks at the development of attitudes to shareholder value, focusing on the views of civil servants, both publicly and privately expressed, and the experts and industry representatives who make up the membership of the Corporate Value Study Group. He identifies a sea change in attitudes from the 1980s to the present day, and suggests that Livedoor's takeover bid for NBS played a critical role in breaking down an implicit "code of restraint," paving the way for the arrival of activist hedge funds such as Steel Partners and The Children's Investment Fund (TCI).

There is some recognition, Dore argues, that the organizational strength of the Japanese company is threatened by the growing assertion of shareholder interests, and, in particular, by the hedge funds' access to liquidity and by the possibility of high returns that they hold out to investors. He points to skepticism in high circles concerning the role played by hedge funds in a number of the recent high-profile cases: officials and others have been asking what exactly the hedge funds had brought to the companies they invested in, and whether the conditions under which they were compensated for the dilution of their interests were fair to other shareholders. However, the debate over "corporate value" initiated by the Livedoor judgments and the report of the Corporate Value Study Group illustrates, Dore argues, fundamental uncertainty over what the objectives of the publicly listed corporation should be, in place of the clear priority given to organizational values over financial ones as recently as the late 1980s. He concludes that a "silent shareholder revolution" is taking place: an "unshakable orthodoxy" is in the process of forming, in which, notwithstanding the doubts expressed by civil servants, senior industrialists, and others, takeovers are regarded as essential mechanisms for the discipline of managers, with the stock market functioning above all as a market for corporate control.

Takeshi Inagami looks at the evolution of attitudes to corporate governance reform on the part of senior trade and industry bodies since the early 1990s. He argues that there was no clear road map for the evolution of Japanese corporate governance when it began to move towards the shareholder value norm in the early 1990s. In 1994, when the Enterprise Trends Study Group of the Keizai Doyukai (the Japan Association of Corporate Executives) met to initiate debate on corporate governance, it argued for a greater role for independent directors, a move away from the seniority pay system, and the replacement of the "closed" group structures of the keiretsu with more open, flexible capital-market-based financing. The *11th Enterprise White Paper* and the document *Establishing a New Japanese Corporate Governance* were written with certain historical precedents in mind, in particular, the 1947 Keizai Doyukai document, *A Draft on Democratising the Corporation*. Although this text had argued against shareholder primacy in favor of a principle of equality in terms of decision making, profit-sharing and ownership between labor and capital, with unions shifting their perspective from guaranteeing workers' interests in opposition to the enterprise to strengthening managerial efficiency from within, it had also stressed openness to certain aspects of western capitalism, and had argued for striking a balance between the interests of capital and those of society. In the same

way, the members of the Keizai Doyukai study group saw corporate governance reform at the end of the twentieth century as a means of modernizing
Japanese management, while retaining its distinctive essence. The measures
they proposed were triggered not by external shareholder pressure but were
internally generated from within the discourses of senior management, as a
response to what they saw as the crisis then facing the Japanese model.

The year 1994 was also the one in which the JCGF was established. As
Inagami explains, the Forum argued that the key questions for corporate
governance were: for whom is the firm to be run; and who should make
managers accountable? The principles of corporate governance published
by the Forum in 1998 argued clearly for the "Americanization" of Japanese
corporate governance with shareholders described as residual claimants
and the true owners of the enterprise. By contrast, the Keizai Doyukai, at
the same time, was stressing the importance of "good corporate
citizenship" and the Nikkeiren (the Japan Association of Employers' Fed-
erations) was arguing against "one size fits all." By 2006,[1] the Nippon
Keidanren's *Interim Statement on Corporate Governance* was referring to the
importance of increasing the long-term value of the corporation, arguing
against the relevance of universal models of governance, and describing
the listed company as a "public institution." Inagami argues that there has
been considerable continuity in the views of senior executives from the
first documents of the 1990s up to the more recent *Interim Statement* of the
Keidanren. There has been no conversion to American-style corporate
governance, not simply because of the fallout from the Enron and Worldcom scandals in the early 2000s or because of the reaction to the Livedoor
case but because, more fundamentally, Japan's community firms have not
collapsed, contradicting predictions of their demise. Employees and senior
managers have moved to more formal and institutionalized cooperation,
he suggests, recognizing that the underlying objective of the community
firm is to maintain a viable business.

George Olcott reports the results of interviews with senior managers of
large Japanese companies that he and Ronald Dore carried out in 2007 and
2008. Those interviewed include ten current presidents, ten chairmen who
are former presidents of companies, and four former chairmen; three generations of corporate leaders are included in the sample, ranging from
former executives now in their 80s who were executives in the late 1970s
to current executives who are now in their 40s. The interviews focused on
five topics: the role of the CEO, the impact of share price movements on

---

[1] The Keidanren and Nikkeiren merged in 2002.

corporate decision making, board structure, executive pay, and the question of to whom the company belongs. Olcott argues, on the basis of these interviews, that communitarianism, as a guiding ethic for executives, is far from having been delegitimized. There is still a "managerialist paradigm" in place. Recent changes include a greater role for the CEO, and less of a collegial approach to management. There is more direct communication with shareholders than there used to be. However, the interviewees played down the significance of the Bull-Dog Sauce case, with the company and its reaction to Steel Partners being seen as atypical of the wider corporate sector. There is, the interviews reveal, greater sensitivity to share price, but railway and utility companies, for example, continue to stress regularity of supply to customers as the main priority; and currently such companies are relatively immune to takeover. It is accepted that dividend payouts are not going to be as stable as in the past. There is a growing role for outside directors but they tend to be seen as advisers, not the representatives of the shareholders. On executive pay, there is a perception that the gap between the pay of senior managers and the rest had not become excessive. Finally, the idea that shareholders "own" the company has very little support among the senior executives interviewed by Olcott and Dore.

Takashi Araki provides a comprehensive overview of recent developments in the labor law and employment relations areas as they relate to corporate governance. He charts the rise that has taken place in the number of atypical or flexible employees, and demonstrates the link between this trend and corporate governance changes including the decline in cross-shareholdings and the growing role for external directors on boards. However, he argues that the job security of lifetime employees in the "core" has not been much affected by these changes. Notwithstanding some deregulation, including laws loosening controls on agency labor, the legal standards governing dismissal are tight and were clarified in the 2000s; the 2003 changes to the Labour Standards Act put the idea of the nullification of "abusive dismissal" into statutory form. Yet, Araki shows how labor law doctrine also supports the idea of internal consensus and flexibility in the performance of the employment relationship. Thus while the place and type of work must be set out in the employment contract, these do not form contract terms that cannot be altered without the individual employee's consent or, where relevant, through collective bargaining (as they do, for example, in UK labor law). The employer can change the place of work and the tasks to be performed, with minimal review by the courts. The Supreme Court had held in the 1960s that "unfavorable" modifications to terms and conditions can be made binding on all employees as long as they are "reasonable." Thus the employer can make unilateral changes. In 2007, this principle received statutory backing. Although union membership has declined, voluntary joint consultation, which goes back to the productivity movement of the 1950s, remains strong, and valued by both managers and employees. Araki charts recent statutory initiatives which provide institutional support for more formal labor-management joint committees. Referring to the concept of "countervailing power" he concludes that the changes to labor law have acted as a brake on the move toward shareholder value in company law and corporate governance.

Finally, Hisayoshi Fuwa, the CEO of a company in the Toshiba group and a former corporate vice president at the Toshiba parent company with responsibilities including strategic planning and corporate governance structures, describes the process which accompanied Toshiba's adoption of the company with committees option, and its implications for organizational structures at the company. He shows how Toshiba's corporate governance changes were linked to innovation in management structures. The shift to a managing officer system began in the late 1990s, but the 2002 legislation was important to the company, as it brought about a clearer demarcation between the board and the senior tiers of managers; previously, senior managing officers would have been expected to reach the board, and execution and monitoring were combined at board level. After the shift to the company with committees structure, there was a clearer demarcation between these two functions. This allowed for a clearer focus on the part of senior executives, and more streamlined decision making. The board, in turn, assumed a more explicit supervisory role in relation to strategic decision making in both the short and long run. In addition to taking a long-term view of strategic matters, it was able to act quickly when short-run strategic decisions were necessary such as those involving mergers and acquisitions. Internal controls were also strengthened along with risk-compliance systems below board level. Thus, corporate governance in Toshiba has evolved in response to the modernization of the company's managerial structures; the adoption of the company with committees system was just one part of this. Fuwa's account is a striking illustration of a particularly Japanese conception of corporate governance, which is nevertheless one that may have a wider resonance; as he puts it:

What Toshiba's experience shows is that corporate governance is about much more than just the behaviour of the board of directors. If it is to be effective, it needs to have a comprehensive approach that covers all considerations of board structure, the supervisory role of the board, management systems and execution, internal controls, attention to stakeholders, and CSR. Moreover, it must penetrate the thinking of the entire company, at all levels. It is often said that good corporate governance does not translate automatically into good performance. Toshiba feels that it should, and is trying to ensure that it does, by combining its principles of governance with management systems innovation, leading to improved quality of execution by empowered managers under the supervision of the board.

A Different Path?

The chapters in this book have provided new evidence on the trajectory of Japanese corporate governance which reflects the distinctiveness of the Japanese case, but also illustrates that the system has been changing. Japan's response to globalizing pressures has been highly path-dependent in the sense of being shaped not simply by historical forces in general, but more specifically by the particular configuration of complementary institutions and practices which grew up in the postwar period. But while the system's reaction could be described as one of resistance to external change, we think that it is better characterized as one of adjustment and adaptation to a changing institutional environment, with legal reforms acting as a trigger or stimulus. Another stimulus is the changing competitive environment. The path of Japanese corporate governance has been altered, if not necessarily in the direction expected by the reformers. What lessons can we draw from this process?

One relates to the nature of the so-called global template of corporate governance. The recent Japanese experience has highlighted the considerable extent to which this supposed universal model is a product of the particular context and background of the American and British systems from which it has been distilled. These systems, notwithstanding their differences (see Armour and Skeel 2007), nevertheless share certain core features including dispersed share ownership, liquid capital markets, a prominent role for institutional investors (in particular in Britain), and a relatively weak role for employee voice in the firm (in particular in the United States). Very few other countries in the world, even in systems with a common law origin, possess all these features. The considerable degree of formal convergence of corporate governance systems over the past decade represents alignment on institutional features which are specific to the British and American systems, with laws and self-regulatory codes on board structure and hostile takeover bids leading the way (Armour et al. 2008). However, it is becoming clear that the functional alignment of systems is much more limited than convergence

21

of form. Corporate governance and comparative law scholars have tended to stress the sense in which formal differences between the laws of national systems masked a deeper, underlying functional continuity across market-based systems (Gilson 2001). The evidence reported in this book shows that the formal convergence of the past decade has coexisted with significant functional discontinuities (see, to the same effect, Shishido 2007). Institutional mechanisms, in the form of independent boards and bid-friendly takeover regulations, which originated in systems where dispersed shareholder ownership and liquid capital markets were the norm, have not worked as expected or intended in a context where those conditions are, still, largely absent. Above all, they have not brought about the fundamental change in managerial practice and behavior toward the shareholder value norm that the proponents of reform were hoping for.

But there is, as we have suggested, a further lesson from the recent Japanese experience, which is that transplants are rarely without effects of any kind. The metaphor of the "irritant" or "catalyst" may be a more appropriate one than the image of the system rejecting the transplant in its entirety (Teubner 2001). In the Japanese case, there have been three broad consequences of the institutional reforms of the 2000s.

Firstly, there has been a strengthening of the community firm in terms of the effectiveness of its managerial procedures (see Chapters 2, 7, and 9). The slimming down of boards and the introduction of corporate officer systems were the catalyst for a shift from the collegiate style of management which had come to prevail in the postwar period, to one in which there was a clearer demarcation between oversight and execution, and an enhanced role for internal audit and formal risk management. In the firms interviewed for the studies reported here, this was seen as a positive development which was likely to enhance the effectiveness of longer-term strategic decision making, although the risks in moving away from peer-based monitoring among senior executives were also recognized. A more formal role for employee voice within the firm (as described by Araki) is being put forward as a counterweight to the concentration of power in the hands of an ever smaller number of very senior executives, although it is not clear how far this movement will go.

The predominant theme running through these developments, notably, has been the role of managers in shaping corporate governance reform. The values and interests of the senior managers who are at the apex of the community firm system were a decisive influence during the process of reform itself. The Keizai Doyukai and other representative bodies articulated a conception of corporate governance which, despite some vacillation, remained faithful to the organizational goals of the community firm. The Keidanren's intervention, in turn, was important in ensuring that the company with committees law was only optional. In the period following the Livedoor bid, the publicly expressed views of senior managers helped bring about a situation in which hostile takeovers, although no longer seen as impractical, were nevertheless still viewed as exceptional, thereby helping to create the context in which the legal and regulatory system continued to allow listed companies considerable leeway in putting in place defenses to hostile bids. Our case studies show that the managerial shaping of corporate governance continued at the implementation stage, as the governance reforms were used to put into effect a wider strategy for the renewal and modernization of decision-making processes in large firms.

The second change has been, notwithstanding the continuing influence of managerial interests and values, the enhancement of shareholder power. Despite setbacks for shareholder activism, on the part of both pension funds (see Chapter 4) and hedge funds (see Chapter 2), it seems unlikely that, in the aftermath of the takeover battles of the past three years, shareholders will be as passive in the future as they have been in the past. A greater degree of influence for shareholders over managerial decision making, and a growing assertiveness on the part of domestic pension funds and insurance companies, can be expected. This trend may well be encouraged in the immediate term by the deliberations of the Corporate Value Study Group, as Hayakawa and Whittaker make clear.

Can these two tendencies – continuing managerial control, but coupled with growing shareholder influence – be reconciled? A third major change which emerges from our findings is the appearance of new forms of corporate governance which are hybrids in the sense of combining institutional mechanisms with different origins and/or functions. These emergent forms combine elements of relational governance and an internal orientation to management, with a growing role for external monitoring by capital markets. When judged against the practices which grew up around the postwar mode, such a combination appears inherently unstable: will growing shareholder pressure not inevitably undermine the compromises on which the community firm has been constructed? A governance structure which allows the board to mediate between the different stakeholder groups, rather than seeing itself as the representative of shareholder interests, is arguably not just functional but essential for organizations which depend on the long-term value created by firm-specific physical and human assets. This would be threatened, in the longer run at any rate, by growing reliance on independent directors. Similarly, takeover bids, insofar as they lead to restructurings, asset disposals, and greenmail-type payments as a way of hostile third parties, would disproportionately benefit the present shareholders at the expense of the longer-term interests of employees and other stakeholders in maintaining the organizational unity of the firm. How can a growing role for shareholder voice within corporate governance, together with the use of the capital market as a mechanism of resource allocation, be rendered compatible with the organizational practice of the community firm?

One way in which this might be done is through the "countervailing power" of labor law regulations in placing a limit on the pursuit of shareholder value (see Chapter 8). In this respect, there are similarities between the Japanese developments that we report here, and the practice of "negotiated shareholder value" in Germany, France, and, in certain more regulated sectors of the economy, Britain, involving rent-sharing between long-term shareholders and core employees (Vitols 2004; Jackson et al. 2005; Conway et al. 2008).

The same trend may be furthered by developments in corporate governance which assist the processes by which the capital market monitors and evaluates the "internal linkages" between labor and management which are, potentially, the source of long-term value for the firm (Aoki 2007; Aoki and Jackson 2008), although some observers see them as giving rise, less positively, to "stakeholder tunnelling," or the diversion of rents away from investors (Gilson and Milhaupt 2005). Such developments include the emergence of accounting standards aimed at enhancing the disclosure by firms of the details of how they manage relations with stakeholders, and of how they deal with long-term risks of a reputational and competitive kind. The corporate social responsibility movement is part of this process, and this is arguably playing a role in shifting attitudes of both investors and managers in Japan (see Inagami in this volume), as it has in the European context, although less so in the United States (Deakin and Whittaker 2007). But while, in this context, stock markets may be well placed "to predict future outcomes by aggregating dispersed information, expectations and values prevailing in the economy if they can filter noises to a reasonable degree," it remains the case that "the last condition . . . is a long way from yet being taken for granted" (Aoki 2007: 444).

The emergence of hybrid forms in a number of different national contexts suggests the possibility of a paradigm shift in the theory and practice of corporate governance, as the pursuit of shareholder value along Anglo-American lines ceases to be seen as synonymous with the modernization of governance mechanisms. Yet it remains to be seen how viable such hybrid forms prove to be in charting a new pathway for corporate governance, both in Japan and elsewhere. As Japanese corporations enter a new period of uncertainty, in the aftermath of the global financial crisis of September 2008, the effectiveness of the changes made against the backgrounds of the governance reforms of the mid-2000s will be tested in a new and unexpectedly demanding environment. We return to this theme, and some implications of the global financial crisis for corporate governance and varieties of capitalism, in Chapter 10.

Bibliography

Ahmadjian, C. (2003). "Changing Japanese Corporate Governance," in U. Schaede and W.W. Grimes (eds.), *Japan's Managed Globalization: Adapting to the Twenty-First Century*. New York: M.E. Sharpe.

—— (2007). "Foreign Investors and Corporate Governance in Japan," in M. Aoki, G. Jackson, and H. Miyajima (eds.), *Corporate Governance in Japan: Institutional Change and Organizational Diversity*. New York: Oxford University Press.

Aoki, M. (1994). "The Japanese Firm as a System of Attributes: A Survey and Research Agenda," in M. Aoki and R. Dore (eds.), *The Japanese Firm: Sources of Competitive Strength*. Oxford: Oxford University Press.

—— (2007). "Conclusion: Whither Japan's Corporate Governance?" in M. Aoki, G. Jackson, and H. Miyajima (eds.), *Corporate Governance in Japan: Institutional Change and Organizational Diversity*. New York: Oxford University Press.

—— and Jackson, G. (2008). "Understanding an Emergent Diversity of Corporate Governance: An Essentiality-Based Analysis." *Industrial and Corporate Change*, 17: 1–27.

—— and Patrick, H. (1994). *The Japanese Main Bank System: Its Relevance for Developing and Transforming Economies*. Oxford: Oxford University Press.

Arikawa, Y. and Miyajima, H. (2007). "Relationship Banking in Post-Bubble Japan: Coexistence of Soft- and Hard-Budget Constraints," in M. Aoki, G. Jackson, and H. Miyajima (eds.), *Corporate Governance in Japan: Institutional Change and Organizational Diversity*. New York: Oxford University Press.

Armour, J. and Skeel, D. (2007). "Who Writes the Rules for Hostile Takeovers, and Why? – The Peculiar Divergence of US and UK Takeover Regulation." *Georgetown Law Journal*, 95: 1727–94.

—— Deakin, S., and Konzelmann, S. (2003). "Shareholder Primacy and the Trajectory of UK Corporate Governance." *British Journal of Industrial Relations*, 41: 531–55.

—— —— Sarkar, P., Siems, M., and Singh, A. (2008). "Shareholder Protection and Stock Market Development: An Empirical Test of the Legal Origins Hypothesis," CBR Working Paper No. 358 (http://www.cbr.cam.ac.uk).

Conway, N., Deakin, S., Konzelmann, S., Petit, H., Rebérioux, A., and Wilkinson, F. (2008). "The Influence of Stock Exchange Listing on Human Resource Management: Evidence from France and Britain." *British Journal of Industrial Relations*, 46: 631–73.

Cosh, A. and Hughes, A. (2008). "Takeovers after 'Takeovers'," in P. Arestis and J. Eatwell (eds.), *Issues in Finance and Industry*. Basingstoke: Palgrave Macmillan.

Deakin, S. and Whittaker, D.H. (2007). "Re-embedding the Corporation? Comparative Perspectives on Corporate Governance, Employment Relations and Corporate Social Responsibility." *Corporate Governance: An International Review*, 15: 1–4.

——Hobbs, R., Nash, D., and Slinger, G. (2003). "Implicit Contracts, Takeovers and Corporate Governance: In the Shadow of the City Code," in D. Campbell, H. Collins, and J. Wightman (eds.), *Implicit Dimensions of Contract*. Oxford: Hart.

Dore, R. (1973). *British Factory, Japanese Factory: The Origins of National Diversity in Industrial Relations*. London: Allen and Unwin.

Gilson, R. (2001). "Globalising Corporate Governance: Convergence of Form or Function." *American Journal of Comparative Law*, 49: 329–57.

——and Milhaupt, C. (2005). "Choice as Regulatory Reform: The Case of Japanese Corporate Governance." *American Journal of Comparative Law*, 53: 343–77.

Gordon, J. (2007). "Independent Directors and Stock Market Prices: The New Corporate Governance Paradigm." *Stanford Law Review*, 59: 1465–568.

——(2008). "The Rise of Corporate Directors in Italy: A Comparative Perspective," mimeo, Columbia Law School.

Inagami, T. and Whittaker, D.H. (2005). *The New Community Firm: Employment, Governance and Management Reform in Japan*. Cambridge: Cambridge University Press.

Jackson, G. (2007). "Employment Adjustment and Distributional Conflict in Japanese Firms," in M. Aoki, G. Jackson, and H. Miyajima (eds.), *Corporate Governance in Japan: Institutional Change and Organizational Diversity*. New York: Oxford University Press.

——Höpner, M., and Kurdelbush, A. (2005). "Corporate Governance and Employees in Germany: Changing Linkages, Complementarities, and Tensions," in H. Gospel and A. Pendleton (eds.), *Corporate Governance and Labour Management: An International Comparison*. Oxford: Oxford University Press.

Jacoby, S. (2005). *The Embedded Corporation: Corporate Governance and Employment Relations in Japan and the United States*. Princeton, NJ: Princeton University Press.

Miyajima, H. (2007). "The Performance Effects and Determinants of Corporate Governance Reform," in M. Aoki, G. Jackson, and H. Miyajima (eds.), *Corporate Governance in Japan: Institutional Change and Organizational Diversity*. New York: Oxford University Press.

——and Kuroki, F. (2007). "The Unwinding of Cross-Shareholdings in Japan: Causes, Effects, and Implications," in M. Aoki, G. Jackson, and H. Miyajima (eds.), *Corporate Governance in Japan: Institutional Change and Organizational Diversity*. New York: Oxford University Press.

Okazaki, T. (1999). "Corporate Governance," in T. Okazaki and T. Okuno-Fujiwara (eds.), *The Japanese Economic System and Its Historical Origins*. Oxford: Oxford University Press.

—— and Okuno-Fujiwara, T. (1999). "Japan's Present-Day Economic System and Its Historical Origins," in T. Okazaki and T. Okuno-Fujiwara (eds.), *The Japanese Economic System and Its Historical Origins*. Oxford: Oxford University Press.

O'Sullivan, M. (2001). *Contests for Corporate Control: Corporate Governance and Economic Performance in the United States and Germany*. Oxford: Oxford University Press.

Sako, M. (2006). *Shifting Boundaries of the Firm: Japanese Company–Japanese Labour*. Oxford: Oxford University Press.

Sheard, P. (1994). "Interlocking Shareholdings and Corporate Governance in Japan," in M. Aoki and R. Dore (eds.), *The Japanese Firm: Sources of Competitive Strength*. Oxford: Oxford University Press.

Shishido, Z. (2007). "The Turnaround of 1997: Changes in Japanese Corporate Law and Governance," in M. Aoki, G. Jackson, and H. Miyajima (eds.), *Corporate Governance in Japan: Institutional Change and Organizational Diversity*. New York: Oxford University Press.

Teubner, G. (2001). "Legal Irritants: How Unifying Law Ends Up in New Divergences," in P. Hall and D. Soskice (eds.), *Varieties of Capitalism*. Oxford: Oxford University Press.

Vitols S. (2004). "Negotiated Shareholder Value: the German Variant of an Anglo-American Practice." *Competition and Change*, 8: 357–74.

West, M. (2001). "The Puzzling Divergence of Corporate Law: Evidence and Explanations from Japan and the United States." *University of Pennsylvania Law Review*, 150: 527–601.

2

In the Shadow of Corporate Governance Reform: Change and Continuity in Managerial Practice at Listed Companies in Japan

John Buchanan and Simon Deakin

Introduction

During the latter half of the twentieth century listed Japanese companies developed a style of corporate governance which was unusual in the degree to which it was focused on the internal needs of the organization. Almost all large firms offered stable employment for core employees, with progression through the managerial ranks being based on internal promotion, up to the most senior levels. The attention of managers was focused on the firm as an organizational entity and hence on its employees, customers, and suppliers, with relatively little concern for shareholders unless they were concurrently customers or suppliers who held their shares as tokens of good faith. This model, which came to be described as the "community firm," owed much to the particular circumstances of the immediate postwar years, but its relevance extended well beyond that point. It came to be considered "traditional," and was seen as

We are grateful to Curtis Milhaupt and Hugh Whittaker for comments on an earlier draft, and to the MEXT Twenty-First Century COE Program at ITEC, Doshisha University, and the ESRC World Economy and Finance Programme for financial support.

a major factor in sustaining Japan's economic growth. It was more or less unquestioned until a suspicion grew in the 1990s, in the aftermath to the "bubble," that Japan's economic difficulties at this time were the result of inefficient corporate governance. There then followed a period of enthusiasm for largely US-inspired "global" standards of corporate governance and many Japanese companies adopted new structures after 1997, either as part of informal arrangements or by way of opting into new legal frameworks. However, "traditional" practices proved robust: although there were far-ranging legal reforms and a significant degree of structural change at company level, the essence of corporate governance practice in Japan appears to have changed relatively little. In particular, it can plausibly be argued, as we shall see below, that the community firm has survived, and may even have been strengthened as changes in corporate governance structures are used to streamline managerial procedures. In Japan, "corporate governance is changing slowly, sometimes more in form than in substance" (Jacoby 2005: 77).

But this is not to say that the present situation is stable. The changes to board structure triggered by the reforms, both informal and legislated, are still unraveling. In addition, hostile takeover bids and growing hedge fund activism are accelerating a reevaluation of the position of shareholders in the Japanese model – a development whose beginnings can be traced to the capital markets finance model increasingly favored by larger Japanese companies from the late 1970s. The acquiescence of shareholders in internal managerial control, which underpinned the "traditional" system, was the product of conditions which no longer prevail. The view is taking hold that if the community firm and its distinctive governance practices are to survive, management will need to address the needs of portfolio shareholders. Some striking instances of what can happen when conflicts between management and shareholders come into the open are provided by recent experiences of tender offer situations and interventions by activist hedge funds. These high-profile cases have highlighted the extent to which managerial attitudes are still shaped by a very different conception of the firm to that of the global corporate governance "standard." At the same time, the intensity of the debate over the proper response of management at listed companies to external shareholder pressure of this kind suggests that there is potential for further change within the system.

To explore these issues in more detail we first of all review, in the next section, the main features of the "traditional" system as it emerged in the decades following the end of the Second World War, and its period of crisis in the late 1990s. The section after that looks at the emergence of structural changes in response to this crisis, both informal arrangements developing within the scope of existing laws after 1997 and the optional "company with committees" system, implemented from 2003. The following section presents evidence to support our view that practice of corporate governance at widely held listed Japanese companies has not changed radically from its "traditional" style; we consider first the degree to which introduction of the company with committees system has affected actual practice at companies which have adopted it, and then the widespread concept of corporate governance as a management tool, which appears further to blur the distinction between adopters of the new system and others. In the next section, the focus shifts to shareholders. We suggest that their position in Japanese corporate governance is an anomaly that has been overlooked for many years and consider the motivations of the main shareholder categories and how their nature may be changing. The following section looks at some recent cases of hostile takeover bids and hedge fund interventions in listed companies and considers how these contribute to understanding management attitudes, and their implications. We then offer some concluding remarks.

In building up a picture of corporate governance practice at a time of change, we have drawn on ninety-five in-depth interviews with directors and senior executives of listed companies of various sizes, institutional investors, legal and financial advisers, policy-makers, civil servants, and other interested parties. The interviews were carried out in four main exercises, essentially beginning in 2004 (additionally two meetings were held in late 2003), with the most recent completed in early 2008. Within this research, fifty-three interviews were held with management at twenty companies. Most of the interviews were electronically recorded and transcribed and the others were noted by hand. We therefore have an informationally rich and detailed account of perceptions toward corporate governance on the part of management and other practitioners, and case-studies of a significant number of organizations, some of them based on repeat visits. A list of interviews, which, because of the confidential nature of the material discussed, were conducted on a nonattributable basis and are defined here only by sector and general indicators of size and other characteristics are provided in Appendices 1 and 2. In addition, we have drawn on press reports and other contemporary written sources to produce detailed accounts of certain hostile bids and hedge fund interventions.

The Emergence of Japan's Postwar "Traditional" Corporate Governance and its Crisis in the 1990s

In the years following the Second World War, a distinctive style of corporate governance evolved at large Japanese companies. This is often described in Japan as the "traditional" system, even though it appears to be a phenomenon that has developed since 1945, and there is often vagueness about its precise nature. Its main components in the early years included the following:

> ...the characteristic features of labour-management relations in Japan, such as long-term fixed employment, pay by seniority, and internal promotion; the features of the financial markets such as the preference for indirect funding and the main bank system; the characteristics of relations among firms, such as subcontracting and *keiretsu*[1] alignments; the weakness of small shareholders, their power undermined by the practice of crossholdings of shares as well as boards comprised almost exclusively of internally promoted directors; government-enterprise relations, such as the liberal use of administrative guidance and the unique status of industrial associations run by ex-Ministry officials.
>
> (Okuno-Fujiwara 1999: 266)

The situation described above did not appear spontaneously after 1945; some of its elements were already in existence and others manifested themselves as products of Japan's economic troubles in the immediate postwar period. The employment practices, in particular, were mainly a considered response to contemporary problems. Serious labor unrest in the late 1940s and early 1950s, as workers demanded more say in the running of firms, was gradually resolved by a general understanding between managers and employees that the survival of the business was in their mutual interest. This created what Gordon calls the "corporate hegemony," whereby the benefit of the firm took precedence over individual needs or those of any single corporate constituency (Gordon 1998: 201). The end-product of these and other forces was the community firm as the standard format for large, widely held listed companies. Here, a network of shared interests among employees at all levels held the organization together (Inagami and Whittaker 2005: 15–16). Employment in such firms, at least among the full-time workforce, was generally

[1] The word *keiretsu* is often used loosely to refer to corporate groups in Japan, but *keiretsu* sometimes means a series of subcontractors organized under a principal manufacturer (vertical *keiretsu*), and at other times a group of large firms in diverse industries (horizontal *keiretsu*) (Hoshi 1994: 287).

stable and promotion to all levels of seniority was overwhelmingly internal. This, in turn, fostered an internally focused style of governance in which management was dominated by internal candidates and generally hostile to outside influence. Close relationships between firms that supplied goods and services to one another were often formalized through shareholdings and this reinforced the concept of the internally focused community firm by creating friendly shareholder blocs whose main interest was in preserving the continuity of their trading partners' businesses rather than in extracting investment income.

Ordinary shareholders were in a weak position for a variety of reasons. They had effectively been disfranchised during the war years to the point that they had no say in the running of listed companies, dividends were controlled, and shares had become tantamount to fixed income securities (Okazaki 1996: 373). Since finance for the postwar industrial recovery was provided mostly by banks rather than by the capital markets, ordinary shareholders remained on the fringe of a corporate environment shaped by official pressure, management initiative, and bank lending.

The picture of Japanese corporate governance given by Okuno-Fujiwara's summary above reflects most accurately the situation in the 1950s and 1960s, when all the players in the Japanese economy were focusing on the need to rebuild industry and to survive. By the 1970s and 1980s, the community firm was still strong but its environment had changed. The influence of the main bank system had declined as successful companies became less dependent on indirect finance from the 1970s, and banks were no longer in a position to dictate to their stronger corporate customers (Aoki 1994: 135). Official guidance to industry and industrial associations run by ex-Ministry officials – what Aoki calls *bureaupluralism* – had ceased to be a driving force as stronger elements of the economy no longer wanted such help and wished to avoid its costs, while declining sectors were becoming increasingly dependent on it (Aoki 1988: 258–97). Throughout these changes, the community firm and its internally focused management style continued to prosper. Internal monitoring, based on informal peer review and other internal social pressures, usually made up for the absence of external controls of the kind being proposed by agency theorists in the US system (Dore 2005: 441), but by the 1980s this situation had intensified to the point where there was no credible source of external supervision at most large, listed Japanese companies. The early postwar corporate monitoring system has been described as having had three constituent elements, "government control over banks, the main bank system, and management autonomy" (Teranishi 1999: 81). By the 1980s, autonomous management was increasingly in sole possession of governance processes at most widely held listed companies.

Corporate governance tends to attract most attention when things go wrong and Japan's evident economic success from the early 1950s until the end of the 1980s ensured that few questions were posed regarding the way that Japanese companies were being run. Dore observed in the early 1970s that there was an assumption that Japanese practices in the years before the oil crisis of 1973 were basically inefficient – they were oddities that would eventually be eroded by market pressures (Dore 1973: 421–2) – but, by the end of that decade, both foreign and Japanese commentators had begun to emphasize the strengths of Japanese corporate governance systems and frequently recommended them to western companies (Vogel 1979; Pascale and Athos 1982; Matsumoto 1983). However, the collapse of the stock market and real estate "bubble" that had developed in Japan during the latter half of the 1980s, which is usually traced from the beginning of the stock market decline at the end of 1989, revealed widespread overexposure to poorly evaluated risk among many Japanese industrial and commercial companies and at virtually all of its financial institutions. Scandals emerged soon after, as managements found themselves unable to cope with the new environment, beginning with the discovery in 1991 of Nomura Securities' illegal compensation of equity investors and gaining momentum thereafter until the period from 1997 to 2004 saw evidence of multiple corporate misdemeanors and bankruptcies in every single year. The 1990s have been described as a "lost decade" of economic stagnation in Japan (Hayashi and Prescott 2002: 206) and the contrast with the confidence of the "bubble years" is very marked; one result was a new focus on poor corporate governance as the likely cause of it all.

Japan's "traditional" corporate governance system, which had been praised as one of the economy's greatest assets, had suddenly become suspect as a source of weakness and was increasingly contrasted with "global" standards. The Japan Corporate Governance Forum, then a new association that seemed likely to become influential in the Japanese corporate governance debate, began its interim report on corporate governance principles in October 1997 by saying:

The globalization of the marketplace has ushered in an era in which the quality of corporate governance is a crucial component of corporate survival. The compatibility of corporate governance practices with global standards has also become an important part of corporate success. (JCGF 1997)

It is questionable whether "global standards" of corporate governance even exist, but most Japanese commentators in the late 1990s appeared to associate such a notion with US practice. A public debate soon developed in the press and elsewhere which presented the situation as a clearly defined clash between the two extremes of "traditional" and "global" corporate governance (Ahmadjian 2003: 216, 222). At the end of the 1990s, it even seemed possible that existing patterns of Japanese corporate governance might be discredited entirely, and replaced with concepts inspired by Japanese understanding of US practice. This did not happen, partly because scandals at companies such as Enron and WorldCom in 2001–2 showed that the US system also had its weaknesses, and partly because the Japanese industrial establishment, led by the principal business association, the Keidanren, ensured that changes subsequently proposed to corporate governance systems through legal amendments were severely curtailed (Jackson and Miyajima 2007: 16).

Structural Change in Japanese Corporate Governance Since 1997

Despite these setbacks to the "global standards" movement in Japan, extensive structural changes to corporate governance systems – both within the parameters of existing regulations and through newly legislated structures – were implemented at many Japanese companies from the late 1990s onward. The radical nature of these changes, at least at a formal level, is unusual and contrasts with the approach adopted in the United Kingdom in the early 1980s or in the USA in the early 2000s, when the reaction to corporate scandals was to remedy loopholes in existing systems rather than to introduce a totally new approach.

In May 1997 Sony, which was then considered to be one of Japan's most successful and innovative companies, announced that it would reform its board of directors and create a new position of "corporate executive officer." In its 1997 annual report Sony stated, "this new system provides a clear division between individuals responsible for policy-making and oversight and those responsible for operational management" (Sony 1997: 2). The new system was duly implemented following approval at the AGM on June 27 that year. The immediate result was that Sony moved from a board of thirty-eight directors, of whom two were external, to a board of ten directors, of whom three were external. Apart from the normal effect of retirements and promotions, the remaining former directors were all now styled "corporate executive officers" (*shikkoyakuin*). In its 1998 annual report, Sony gave a further explanation of the change, "this move was made to reinforce corporate governance by speeding up decision-making, making management more efficient and clarifying the responsibilities of managers" (Sony 1998: 4). Sony described these changes as part of a continuing process of reforming its group structures in order to make them more efficient and responsive. In May 1998, it established committees for compensation and nomination to advise the board, although because of the requirements of the Commercial Code at that time, decisions on these matters had to remain with the board itself.

Sony's reforms attracted a great deal of attention in Japan. Board numbers had increased at many companies as an indirect result of their internal focus, since a board appointment was an important element of executive progression: it had become the final stage of reward in a series of incentives for the company's executives and the board tended to be large in order to make those incentives plausible (Dore 2000: 87). Real authority had long since migrated to committees of senior directors, and many chief executives felt stifled by the need to hold essentially meaningless meetings with the full board (Learmount 2002: 128). Sony's ideas therefore addressed a widely held concern about the efficiency of prevailing practices, and were also in keeping with general dissatisfaction about the way that governance was being conducted at large firms. Many companies followed Sony in introducing corporate executive officer systems and reducing their board numbers. Others merely cut their board numbers. A survey by the Tokyo Stock Exchange (TSE) in September 2000, to which 1,310 companies replied, found that 279 companies had already instituted corporate executive officer systems (Koyama and Shinozaki 2001: 64).

Sony's reforms operated within the scope of existing laws and regulations; its new concept of "*shikkoyakuin*" had no legal standing and there was no formal mechanism to allow delegation of powers from the board of directors to these officers. The title was therefore purely an internal managerial rank and although these officers could wield considerable power, they had no distinctive legal status as such (Matsui 1999: 75; Egashira 2005: 354–5; Kanda 2005: 130). This was thought to create an untidy situation, which the amendments to the Commercial Code of 2002 (implemented in 2003) sought to address through the creation of the "company with committees" system. However, before that happened, the powers and duties of the internal body traditionally given the task of monitoring management – the board of corporate auditors – were strengthened by an amendment in 2001 (implemented in 2002). There is an element of contradiction in that the "traditional" system should have been amended in this way, thereby implying that it had future value, when the company with committees system, which was seen as the introduction of "global standards" and which dispensed with the role of corporate auditors, was just about to be announced. One of the reasons for these reforms occurring in parallel appears to be that the initiative to strengthen the position of the corporate auditors was taken by the Administrative Reform Task Force of the governing party (the LDP), whereas the preparations for the company with committees system followed the more usual route of consultation with expert committees and compilation by ministries; it is likely that the enthusiasm for "global standards" did not extend to the politicians, or to the industrialists whom they consulted (Gilson and Milhaupt 2005: 354).

In April 2003, the company with committees (*iinkaitosetchikaisha*) system was introduced as an optional governance structure for "large companies."[2] Qualifying companies could change to the new system by amending their articles of association appropriately. The main features of the new optional system are that there are no corporate auditors; three committees with full discretionary powers are selected from the board of directors to handle audit, nomination, and remuneration, all of which must comprise at least three directors, of whom a majority must be external directors (defined as persons who are nonexecutive directors, who have not been executive directors or employees of any kind of the company or of its subsidiaries, and who currently hold no executive appointments in the company or its subsidiaries); the board of directors concerns itself with strategy and with supervision of the executive members of the company; a new class of executive officers (*shikkoyaku*), appointed and dismissed by the board, is created to handle executive operations whose functions are virtually the same as those of Sony's corporate executive officers (*shikkoyakuin*)[3] but whose status is now

---

[2] Defined as those with capital of more than ¥500 million or total liabilities of more than ¥20,000 million.

[3] The English translations "corporate executive officer" (for *shikkoyakuin*) and "executive officer" (for *shikkoyaku*) are used here to preserve the distinction between the two Japanese terms, which have basically the same meaning but have been preserved unchanged in Japanese usage to distinguish between the informal *shikkoyakuin* system and the legally recognized rank of *shikkoyaku*.

recognized at law; and dividend payments are determined by the board and not the AGM. Certain dispensations – apart from the main element of optionality – were also incorporated into the new system: directors (excepting external directors and members of the audit committee) are permitted to be simultaneously executive officers, the same external directors may serve on any or all of the committees, external directors may be directors or officers of parent companies, and there is no requirement for a majority of external directors on the board (Horiuchi 2002; Tanaka 2003).

The fundamental elements of the new system are the splitting of supervision and strategic planning from execution and day-to-day running of the business, together with the concept of externality to ensure that executive activity is objectively assessed and controlled. Parts of this system are similar to Sony's reforms of 1997 and it is possible that these acted to some extent as an inspiration; at the same time, it is possible to see both the developments as the result of the same enthusiasm for more formal, externally orientated governance, looking to the USA for inspiration. In its explanation of the new system in June 2003, *Nihon Keizai Shimbun* implied both that it was inspired by US experience in the 1980s and 1990s of seeking to control corporate managements through independent directors, and that it was driven by a desire to find an improvement on the existing corporate auditor system (Nikkei 2003). Following enactment of a new consolidated Company Law in 2006, this system became known in Japanese as *iinkaisetchikaisha* rather than as *iinkaitosetchikaisha* and was made available to smaller companies. At about this time, the expression *kansayakusetchikaisha* (company with corporate auditors) came into general use to describe the majority of companies which had maintained the old corporate structure.

As of July 8 2008, the Japan Corporate Auditors' Association counted 110 companies that had become and remained companies with committees, although this total includes various Hitachi and Nomura group companies and others which are not truly independent. Nevertheless, this list includes many well-known companies – although there are some notable exceptions. In 2003, some commentators saw the new corporate structure as a decisive moment in Japanese corporate governance and Yoshihiko Miyauchi, chairman of ORIX – which was one of the first companies to adopt the new system – said in a newspaper interview in June 2003, "the opportunity created by the Commercial Code amendment has for the moment divided up those firms that take governance seriously and those that do not" (Nikkei Sangyo 2003).

The Resilience of Japanese Corporate Governance Practice

Those companies that have adopted the company with committees system now have a structural appearance that is very different from the "traditional" style of Japanese corporate governance. However, 110 companies represent only 4.6 percent of the TSE's first and second sections and Mothers market, and the rate of adoption is decreasing, having slowed to only a few companies every year, as shown in Figure 2.1 (JCAA 2008).

The informal structure of corporate executive officers has had a much wider impact and the TSE's 2007 *White Paper of Corporate Governance* (using data as at October 2006) reported that the average number of executive officers, at companies of all kinds listed on its markets, was 12.85 per company (TSE 2007). Both Toyota and Canon, popularly regarded as bastions of traditional Japanese corporate governance, have introduced such systems. This may suggest that there is a core of companies in Japan which have a completely new style of governance, while those that have not adopted the new system are nevertheless introducing important changes to their structures by segregating the supervisory duties of their boards from executive management. In fact actual practice at both groups of companies is less radical. Our interview materials and corporate

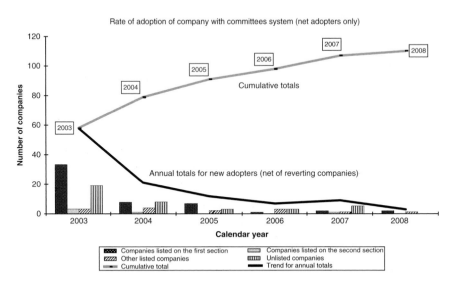

Figure 2.1. Rate of adoption of company with committees system
Source: JCAA: Companies with Committees List as at 8 July 2008.

case-studies (see Buchanan and Deakin 2008) suggest that Japanese corporate governance has indeed changed, but that practices have changed much less than the legal and structural framework; the overall impression is one of evolutionary development rather than a concerted move away from the forms of Japan's postwar governance legacy.

Continuity of Practice at Companies with Committees

Several interviews were conducted with senior management at companies with committees in the course of the research exercises mentioned above. Three companies in particular are considered here. They comprise one relatively small manufacturing company, one large financial company (which had announced its intention to move over to the new system but had not yet done so at the time of our first meeting), and one very large manufacturing company. The interviews at these companies were conducted in 2004 and 2006.

The smallest company, which is family dominated, had adopted the new system early and had changed its outward governance structures extensively. Seven of its ten directors were now external. Apart from all being acquainted with the president, they appeared to be independent, and five seemed to be well qualified by their experience to supervise a business of this kind. There were only three executive officers: the president, the COO, and the CFO, the first two of whom were concurrently directors. In the process of becoming a company with committees, the company had eliminated members of the controlling family, aside from the president, from senior positions. As a director explained, "with the move to become a company with committees, what you might call the big shareholders concentrated on supervision and the executive officers actually ran the business." The three executive officers appeared to enjoy a high degree of freedom. At the time of our interview they had recently committed the company to a hostile takeover attempt without board consultation, although there had apparently been some subsequent objections from the external directors. There was an impression here that the head of a family firm was continuing to run his business in consultation with two close associates much as before; he had incorporated trusted advisers into his board but they did not appear to be determining strategy.

At the large financial company, there were fourteen directors, of whom nine were executives, including both the chairman and the CEO. One of the nonexecutives was an internal appointee and the other four were external. All the three committees had majorities of external directors, as the law requires, but the committee chairman in each case was an internal director. The chairman conceded that in principle he should have become a nonexecutive, but he justified his continuing executive role by the need to keep himself informed about executive matters in order to supervise management effectively. However, he did not explain how this could be reconciled with the presence on the board of the four nonexecutive, external directors who lacked this facility. Three of these were specialists rather than businessmen and they seemed to be viewed as adjuncts to the executive board rather than as integral parts of it. The chairman told us, "my feeling is that we need specialists and then we need business professionals – people like management consultants – and we should introduce these sorts of persons in a well-balanced way as external directors." Although the board and the executive committee were formally separate bodies, only half of the fourteen executive officers were not concurrently directors. This was not greatly different from the situation at many companies in the 1980s and 1990s whereby a large executive board governed the firm, with the more senior members participating in committees that wielded real power and the junior members acting as executive divisional heads, approving board resolutions already decided at the committees without debate.

The very large company had four external directors; they appeared to be independent but were more specialists than industrialists. Together with three nonexecutive internal directors they formed half of the fourteen-person board. The president saw the even split between executives and nonexecutives as an important element of his company's new governance structure but admitted that the presence of so many executive directors was not strictly in keeping with the concept of segregating supervision from execution. In 2004, not long after implementation of the new structure, he commented:

It's essential to bring people together who have operational experience. On the other hand, these people are directors at the same time so basically they are in the position of supervising themselves.

However, there was no desire to eliminate the executives from the board. The same person, speaking as chairman in 2006, emphasized that there were natural limits to what external directors could do: "I think it is not possible to reach decisions on things like the company's ideology and matters of importance through discussions just among external directors." It was also considered important that four of the executive directors represented the company's four main operating divisions.

All three companies were fulfilling the legal requirements of the company with committees system but none appeared to have a complete segregation of supervision by predominantly nonexecutives from execution by internal management. The first company was continuing to operate as a family business, though with a formalized advisory body in the form of the external directors to assist the president. The other two companies seemed to be aware of the theoretical contradiction in having such strong executive boards but saw no alternative; they simply did not consider that their companies could be run well by boards that were isolated from executive matters. The identity of the external directors chosen by these two companies – they were mostly specialists in particular areas relevant to each company's operations, not managers with general business experience – also made it unlikely that they would have either the desire or the ability to compete with their internal colleagues for strategic control. Despite the new formal structures, the location of power at these companies did not appear to have shifted appreciably as a result of the changes made, and there seemed to be a basic belief that long-term strategy, planning, and implementation were integral and could not be separated without endangering the firm's stability.

Corporate Governance as a Management Tool

One factor that unites both companies with committees and "traditional" companies with corporate auditors in Japan is the concept of corporate governance as a management tool. In the USA or the United Kingdom, in particular, the most pressing aspect of corporate governance is often assumed to be the treatment of shareholders. This attitude was reflected in the Japan Corporate Governance Forum's Revised Corporate Governance Principles of 2001 which stated:

A company is the economic property of its shareholders. Even where the shareholders have a governance system in place, management practices that ignore economical or efficiency issues with respect to the use of precious economic resources of the company will not be tolerated.   (JCGF 2001: 5)

These Principles also recommend splitting supervision from execution. However, as demonstrated by the attitudes at the companies with committees reported above, in Japan, supervision and management are usually seen as parts of an integrated process and most Japanese managers tend to understand corporate governance instinctively in the purer sense of "how the firm is run." This has colored the way that corporate governance reforms are implemented internally, with shareholders playing a minimal monitoring role. Examples of this attitude were found both at companies with committees and at companies with corporate auditors.

When AEON decided to become a company with committees, it announced in its 2003 annual report that "this will establish a strategically integrated management system for the Group and greatly strengthen management oversight of Group companies" (AEON 2003: 6–7). The large financial company we first interviewed in 2004, then about to adopt the new system, described the chain of logic behind its move in this way:

... we have already introduced external directors, we are improving transparency of the business management. Next is transfer of authority, that is, from the AGM to the board, from the board to the executive committee or executive officers – further strengthening of transfer and acceptance of authority – and improving the efficiency of the business management: that is what I think it is all about.

The smallest of the companies with committees interviewed, looking back in 2006 on its decision, saw the greatest attraction of the new system as improved efficiency in decision-making:

The first objective in becoming a company with committees like this was to speed up the decision-making and to be able to transfer all the authority to the executive officers. That was the big thing.

The chairman of the very large company with committees that we visited expressed the view in 2006 that the effectiveness of corporate structures rather than the formal names given to them was what mattered, and that there was less of a difference than popularly imagined between the attitudes of companies that either had or had not adopted the new company with committees system:

... for example, companies like Toyota and Canon, from our point of view, are some of the first movers among Japanese companies and began to change their business structures early on: probably in the beginning of the 1990s, they responded very quickly to a sort of globalization and spread of networking, with the result that they came to have very sound structures. Now although the top people at these various companies talk a lot about their Japanese-style management, in fact from that time they were already building a management style and structure suited to the environment of the 21st century. That's why the companies that are not making efforts to reform their corporate governance further are the companies that currently have good results and began to reform their structures ten years back.

As mentioned earlier, many companies with corporate auditors have introduced corporate executive officer systems for the same motives of efficiency that led others to become companies with committees. A member of middle management at one very large company with corporate auditors explained his company's reasons for introducing a corporate executive officer system: "We introduced this management system and actually the purpose of this new reorganization is the speed-up of our business operations – that means a quick business machine."

As noted above, Canon, often seen as a very traditionally minded company, introduced its own corporate executive officer system in January 2008. In its press release it stated, "By promoting capable human resources with wide knowledge of business as Executive Officers and entrusting them with operations responsibilities for specific business areas, the Company intends to enhance its corporate value through more flexible and more efficient management operations" (Canon 2008).

Because the company with committees system has not been applied uniformly or even particularly rigorously in many cases, there is remarkably little difference in the internal workings of many companies with committees and many companies with corporate auditors. Mr Miyauchi appears to have been mistaken when he greeted the new system as a dividing line which would separate companies that took governance seriously from those that did not. If the new system had genuinely entailed giving power to external directors and eliminating most executive management from boards, there would have been a much greater chance of real differences developing.[4] An academic commentator to whom we spoke in 2006 – who also holds business positions – saw this flexible style of implementation negatively, as a proof that Japanese managements did not understand corporate governance, "So they just introduce a system, but the Japanese don't obey the new system." However it can also be seen as a demonstration that the institutionalized attitudes and practices of Japanese corporate governance are robust, forcing new structures to serve their purposes rather than the other way around.

---

[4] To similar effect see Gilson and Milhaupt (2005: 361), who point out that if the intention of the 2002 law had been to enable firms which wanted to move away from what we have referred to as the community firm model (which they associate, more negatively, with the notion of "stakeholder tunnelling" or the diversion of rents to employees and other insiders) to signal this intention, it was ill-equipped to do so, because, among other things, it did not require external directors to be truly independent. They also suggest (at 364–5) that the loose definition of external director in the 2002 law enabled some firms to use it to strengthen the cohesion of group structures, through the appointment of "outside" directors from other companies within the group.

Moreover, the widespread streamlining of procedures that has taken place alongside the introduction of corporate executive officers and the slimming down of boards has encouraged many companies to implement long-awaited improvements in internal management which previously were hindered by the need to maintain incentives for middle managers, without abandoning their focus as community firms. Whether the reduction in board size and the separation of the corporate executive officer class from board-level directors will, in the long run, erode the expectation of internal progression on which the system has traditionally depended remains to be seen. It is also possible that the widening of the gap, in terms of position and prestige, between the most senior executives and those immediately below them, could result in a weakening of the implicit monitoring which went on in the past, at a stage when formal internal control systems of the kind found in large American or British companies are still in the process of development at some companies. But on balance, the impression is that the community firm, far from being weakened, has been reinvigorated by the wave of new thinking and structural reform symbolized by the company with committees system.

In its survey of corporate governance at companies listed on its exchange, carried out in 2006–7 and published as the *White Paper of Corporate Governance 2007*, the TSE began by asking companies to describe their basic governance priorities. The results are shown in Figure 2.2, distinguishing between respondents which were companies with committees and those which were companies with corporate auditors. Predictably, companies with committees tended to stress "surveillance and supervision" and "execution" more than companies with corporate auditors, these being fundamental pillars of their new system. However, these aspects were also considered to be important by many companies with corporate auditors. There was generally agreement between both groups on the importance of "corporate value" (which has emerged as a major topic of discussion, as discussed below in the section entitled "High profile situations revealing managerial attitudes in Japan"), "stakeholders," and "transparency." "Shareholders' value" is surprisingly lowly rated and, although the companies with committees attached more importance to it, it does not seem to have been a major priority for them. Apart from "surveillance and supervision" and "execution" (and "soundness" where the result suggests that some companies with corporate auditors were stressing their adherence to well tried systems), there is a great deal of similarity.

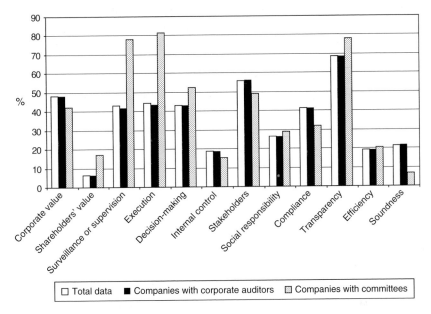

Figure 2.2. Underlying concepts of corporate governance
Source: TSE White Paper of Corporate Governance 2007.

Shareholders: the Dormant Contradiction in the Japanese System

Our review of what has happened to board structure thus suggests that Japan's "traditional" style of corporate governance has emerged relatively unscathed from its contact with "global standards." The community firm is so firmly entrenched that new ideas have mostly been accepted on its terms, and even apparently radical structural change has not transformed the practice of corporate governance or its perceived purpose as a management tool. Meanwhile, throughout these upheavals, the future role of shareholders in governance matters has not received great attention. Japan's often heated corporate governance debate in the late 1990s and early 2000s tended to focus on structural matters and, although the subject was not totally ignored, few explicit reforms seem to have been attempted regarding the status of shareholders.

Although most listed companies in Japan are community firms, with all that this implies with regard to internalism of attitudes and internally promoted management, they are also joint stock companies whose shareholders have the right to sell their shares freely to whomsoever they choose, and to control the company's board composition and strategy through properly constituted majority votes at shareholders' meetings. This situation was regularly exploited in the past by speculators such as *shite* ("stock cornerers") who cornered shareholdings in companies in expectation of being bought out by concerned stable shareholders, and extortioners such as *sokaiya* ("AGM-operators") who in effect demanded blackmail not to cause disruption at AGMs. This tradition of corporate extortion, which has its roots in the beginnings of Japanese stock market capitalism in the late nineteenth century, generally remained a bearable cost and attracted official pressure only when it grew too burdensome (Kester 1991; Szymkowiak 2002). The broader issue of shareholder rights was not a problem for many years because normal shareholders did not exercise most of their powers. The reasons why they did not do so varied with each type of shareholder, and as there has been a gradual shift in recent years in the composition of Japanese companies' shareholders and the particular circumstances of each of these groups, so their long-standing position of acquiescence has come into question.

According to share ownership data on the five largest Japanese stock exchanges (Tokyo, Osaka, Nagoya, Fukuoka, and Sapporo) for fiscal 2007 (year to March 31 2008), published in June 2008 (National Stock Exchanges 2008), the principal groups of shareholders in Japan's listed companies were public bodies (4.7%), financial institutions (30.9%), corporates (21.3%), securities companies (1.6%), individuals (18.2%), and nonresidents (27.6%).[5] Thus the four largest groups are financial institutions, corporates, individuals, and nonresidents (most of whom are believed to be institutions). As investors, they might all be expected to show interest in improving their yields. In practice, for perfectly good reasons, this is often not the case with either financial institutions or corporates.

The "financial institutions" category comprises principally banks, insurance companies, and pension funds, all of which have slightly different motivations. Banks are interested in banking business and they tend to hold shares to reinforce banking relationships, not to obtain portfolio profits. Insurance companies are interested in underwriting business but they need to make investment profits on the premiums that they receive, as well as managing some pension assets, putting them in a more tenuous

---

[5] These data are derived from rounded figures received from the various exchanges: their total exceeds 100 percent.

position. Moreover they are also lenders on the wholesale markets and have traditionally relied on relationship goodwill to sell often undifferentiated products to corporate customers, tilting them away from the position of pure portfolio investors. Pension funds have a much clearer motive to maximize investment returns and one major fund, the Pension Fund Association (*Kigyo Nenkin Rengokai* – "PFA"), has for several years now systematically demanded improved performance and higher standards of corporate governance from companies in which it invests. This initiative has attracted a great deal of attention but has not been emulated by other funds. The Government Pension Investment Fund (*Nenkin Tsumitatekin Kanri Unyo Dokuritsu Gyosei Hojin* – "GPIF"), which is the largest pension fund in Japan (and in the world), with total investment assets estimated to be worth approximately ¥119,886,800 million as at March 31 2008, appears to have exerted little or no pressure on its investment targets to raise performance or payout. There has been discussion about diverting some of its funds to a new sovereign wealth fund, to be managed independently by professional managers, but no action had been taken on this at the time of writing (Financial Times 2008*a*). Smaller pension funds seldom manage actively and lack the mass to exert real pressure. One pension fund head described the situation in 2004, contrasting the smaller funds to the PFA:

You see, most of the pension funds don't do in-house management, so generally their position is different. Then there's the aspect of the amount of money involved: as I said, the PFA has ¥8,000,000 million, while the ordinary small pension funds might have ¥10,000 or ¥20,000 million – that accounts for three quarters of them. These sorts of funds just don't have it in them to do this.

The urgency for insurers and pension funds to raise yields on their domestic share portfolios has lessened because they have reduced their weightings of equities since the disaster of the post-"bubble" years in the 1990s. The GPIF, which has reduced further than most, had only 11.5 percent in domestic shares as of March 31 2008, down from 16.7 percent at the previous year end (GPIF 2008: 9).

Corporate shareholders in Japan tend to hold their shares for commercial reasons, usually to sustain a continuing business relationship. In this sense, they are similar to the banks and insurance companies, although they tend to have a narrower spread of deeper relationships. These shareholdings at companies, banks, and insurers may be unilateral or held as part of a mutual exchange of holdings, but in either case they constitute an illiquid and stable element in the shareholder base. Such shares are normally booked separately from portfolio investments and are seen as "important symbolic tokens, that being exchanged with another company served to embody a relationship or affiliation" (Learmount 2002: 56–7). Holders of such shareholdings are more likely to be interested in the performance of the companies in which they participate as trading partners, lenders or underwriters than in the returns they obtain as pure investors; dividend yields and capital appreciation are not key issues. These shareholdings have declined from their peak in 1974, when they were estimated to have accounted for 62.2 percent of the entire stock market (Miyajima and Kuroki 2007: 85), and by 2003 stable shareholdings were thought to have fallen to around 24.3 percent and cross-held shareholdings, included within the stable shareholding figure, to 7.6 percent of the market (NLI Research 2004). This decline has continued until it was marginally reversed in recent years, as companies have once again begun to feel a need for reliable shareholders (NLI Research 2008: 12).

Individual shareholders logically want returns on their investments and, unless they are major shareholders in family-dominated firms, are not concerned with business relationships. However they have the same problems in Japan that they face elsewhere in communicating with each other and taking concerted action. Historically they have tended to be fringe investors, without power to influence management, although the internet and the appearance of activists who solicit support from individual shareholders may be changing this situation. In February 2007, Ichigo Asset Management was able to prevent the merger of Tokyo Kohtetsu and Osaka Steel, partly with institutional support but also helped by many individuals to whom the fund had written to solicit their votes (Nikkei 2007b). A Japanese private equity investor observed in 2008 that private shareholders who considered that MBOs and other deals arranged by management had diluted their shareholdings were increasingly prepared to take legal action in support of their position: "awareness is growing of these minority shareholders being treated in a cavalier fashion – of their being caused loss – so they sue, you see."

The greatest single change to the Japanese investment scene has come from the rise of nonresident shareholders. In fiscal 1994, foreigners held 8.1 percent of shares listed on the five major Japanese stock exchanges but in 2007 they held 27.6 percent, slightly down on the previous year (National Stock Exchanges 2005, 2008). Mostly they are internationally active institutional investors who are not restrained by business relationships with Japanese companies and whose main interest is to obtain the best possible return on their investments. Their importance in the Japanese market is magnified because stable shareholdings have effectively removed liquidity from circulation and foreign shareholders tend to trade more actively, accounting for a disproportionate level of market movement. In 2002 and 2003, when their aggregate holdings were still below 22 percent, they were estimated to have accounted for more than 30 percent of all trading in Japanese shares (Ahmadjian 2007: 131–3). Investments by foreigners tend to be concentrated among larger and financially stronger companies, and the TSE noted 196 companies listed on its markets in October 2006 which had a foreign shareholding of 30 percent or more (TSE 2007). These companies have responded to the increased importance of foreign shareholders by strengthening their investor relations ("IR") and creating specialized IR departments to provide the kind of detailed information that foreign institutional investors expect. Speaking in 2004, the head of IR at one such company described how this trend had developed there:

The reason it began as it did is because in the 1980s our finance was centred on the issue of convertible bonds to foreign investors. So there was a period when we were raising funds in that fashion and we have developed from overseas fundraising to the need to have foreign investors buy our shares. Then, after they buy, there has to be a follow-up, so we started IR.

The head of IR at another large company specifically linked the growth of IR to the fall in stable shareholdings and the rise of holdings by foreigners who tended to be more demanding, "... stable shareholdings in Japan have been decreasing steadily and shareholders who speak out have been increasing, so the question arose of shareholder strategy, as you might call it: of how to create stable shareholders henceforth." Awareness of the delicacy of this situation has been growing in Japan and there are now many companies like the one quoted above which are looking for "stable shareholders." This process has been accelerated by the emergence of activist funds, as we shall see in more detail below in the next section.

Many Japanese managements therefore find themselves now in a potentially difficult position. They administer companies which are organized largely around the interests of stakeholders other than shareholders, in a system that assumes considerable management autonomy, supervised mainly by pressures from the firm's own internal society and from external agencies linked to the firm by business interests. It has been possible to subordinate shareholders' interests for most of the period since 1945 not because they lacked legal rights but because they chose not to exercise them. The most obvious source of shareholder pressure is the foreign activist hedge funds that have started to operate in Japan, but foreign shareholders in general are much more likely to make demands than the stable domestic shareholders whom they have partially replaced. At the same time, Japanese institutional shareholders such as pension funds have need of higher yields for their investments and private shareholders are increasingly likely to express dissatisfaction with corporate performance and to coordinate their efforts to raise returns.

The general trend of shareholding patterns over approximately the past two decades is shown in Figure 2.3. Corporate and financial shareholders, which have traditionally supported management but may not always do so henceforth, have been in general decline, while the ratio of nonresident investors has steadily increased. In combination with private shareholders, these foreign investors constitute a now significant shareholder class which normally values returns more than business

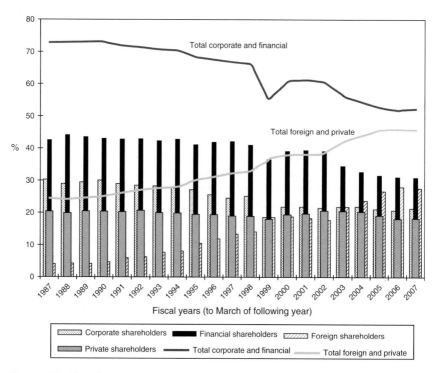

Figure 2.3. Trends in Japanese shareholding patterns
Source: National Stock Exchanges Fiscal 2007 Shareholder Distribution Survey.

relationships. As the chart shows, the aggregate market weightings of the two groups are moving closer, leaving managements much less certainty that their traditional sources of support will suffice if plausible criticisms are raised.

High Profile Situations Revealing Managerial Attitudes in Japan: Hostile Takeover Bids and Hedge Fund Interventions

There is still a great deal of inertia in the Japanese shareholding environment and managements certainly do not face concerted pressure from all of their shareholders. As discussed above, many Japanese institutional shareholders are effectively compromised in their roles as portfolio investors. Moreover there has existed a tacit understanding that "managers should be left to manage," which inhibits all except the most determined shareholders. However, two exceptional situations where stress on the management-shareholder relationship is particularly severe are those in which tender offers are made by hostile acquirers and in which foreign activist hedge funds take shareholdings with a view to extracting unusually high yields from their investments. Such situations were rare in Japan until the past five years or so, and the reactions of management when they occur are highly revealing of attitudes toward corporate governance.

Tender Offers by Hostile Acquirers

In February 2005 Livedoor, an internet services provider, tried to take control of Nippon Broadcasting System ("NBS"), part of the Fuji Sankei media group, through a hostile bid. The attraction of NBS was that the cross shareholdings in which it participated could give its owner control of the whole Fuji Sankei group. The bid ended in compromise but not before two courts had declared illegal the attempt by NBS's board to dilute Livedoor's shareholding in time-honored manner by issuing new share rights to friendly parties, on the grounds that there was no economic justification for such a fund-raising exercise, implying that it was purely a means to sustain the position of existing management. A snap survey by Nihon Keizai Shimbun of thirty-four company presidents and twenty-nine investors and market commentators found that a majority of the presidents and all the investors and commentators considered the courts' decisions to be correct (Nikkei 2005). This affair has been described as a watershed in the recent history of mergers and acquisitions in Japan whose "net result was not a return to business as before" (Whittaker and Hayakawa 2007: 16). It showed that incumbent management could no longer rely on the courts to approve dilution exercises as the raising of working capital, as they had often done in the past, and also that many industrialists and investors were not prepared to support management autonomy unreservedly. Most importantly, it stimulated a debate on management's right to hinder acquisitions which inevitably came to focus on the relationship between management and the shareholders, who could theoretically deliver the company to acquirers by selling their shares in sufficient numbers, and the degree to which management might justifiably prevent them from doing so.

In May 2005, apparently stimulated by the Livedoor-NBS affair, the Ministry of Justice and the Ministry of Economy, Trade and Industry jointly published guidelines based on the findings of a committee they had assembled which later came to be called the Corporate Value Study Group (*Kigyo Kachi Kenkyukai*). As the introduction to these Guidelines, which are not legally binding but were intended to influence the development of the related debate, explained:

The Ministry of Economy, Trade and Industry (METI) and the Ministry of Justice (MOJ) have formulated "Guidelines Regarding Takeover Defence for the Purposes of Protection and Enhancement of Corporate Value and Shareholders' Common Interests" (hereinafter referred to as the "Guidelines") which set forth principles that must be satisfied for defensive measures adopted in anticipation of takeovers which are detrimental to corporate value and shareholders' common interests to be considered reasonable, with the goal of preventing excessive defensive measures, enhancing the reasonableness of takeover defence measures and thereby promoting the establishment of fair rules governing corporate takeovers in the business community.

(METI and MOJ 2005)

These Guidelines focused on antitakeover measures put in place before acquirers emerged, although reactive blocking measures were also an issue (a point noted subsequently in the same study group's June 2008 report) and stated that it was legally permissible for either the shareholders in general meeting or the board as their representative to establish defensive measures, provided only that, if the board took such action, the shareholders should have the opportunity to review matters subsequently. Most of the Guidelines' content is uncontroversial; they note the danger of managers erecting defenses to preserve their own position and recommend independent surveillance of the implementation of defensive measures. The most revealing aspect of the Guidelines is not the recommendations which they put forward, but the assumptions that appear to underlie them. "Corporate value" (defined by the Guidelines as "those attributes of the company or the level of such attributes that contribute to shareholder value, such as the company's assets, its profitability, its stability, its efficiency and its growth") and the joint benefit of all shareholders (defined as "the aggregate benefit to the whole shareholder body in common") are placed together as the core concepts to be defended. The right of shareholders to buy and sell their shares in their own self-interest, without concern for the fate of the company as an organizational entity, is potentially modified by the importance attached to the idea of the "company's interests." Since the Guidelines are aimed at managers rather than shareholders, they effectively encourage management to focus on the good of the company as something inextricably linked to the benefit of shareholders over time, even though some shareholders might consider themselves better rewarded in the short term by a high exit price. Moreover, the motives of the acquirer are considered relevant: defensive measures are justified against harmful buyers such as "greenmailers," "asset strippers," and anyone else considered unlikely to preserve the company in the long term. In such cases, it is implied that the right of shareholders to sell their shares may be subordinated to the needs of the company and legitimately hindered by defensive measures (see Chapters 3 and 5 for further analysis of the work of the Corporate Value Study Group).

In July 2006, Oji Paper launched a hostile bid for Hokuetsu Paper at ¥800 per share, representing a premium of around 34 percent over the past monthly average share price (later conditionally increased to ¥860 in an effort to prevent Hokuetsu's subsequent share allocation to its allies). Hokuetsu's management responded by appealing to its local financial and political relationships, and ultimately allocated sufficient new shares at a discount to market value to Mitsubishi Corporation, with further purchases by Nippon Paper, that by the end of August 2006 Oji had no hope of acquiring a majority and withdrew its offer. Hokuetsu took the precaution of obtaining a favorable opinion on its share allocations from an ostensibly independent committee that included two of its external corporate auditors, presumably in order to protect itself from accusations that its board had acted purely to protect its own interests (Miyake 2007: 172–81). During the very public debate concerning Oji's proposed acquisition, Hokuetsu's management stressed its concern for the company's stakeholders. Nevertheless, because of the means it used to evade Oji, its shareholders were prevented from realizing a substantial gain on the recent market price and their holdings were diluted; throughout all this, their opinion was not formally sought. The concern of management seemed entirely focused on what it saw as corporate survival and there was no room for other considerations. One major Japanese investor, whose fund held shares in several of the companies involved, explained why he had not bothered to demand an explanation:

Well, even if they explained, the general lines of what they would answer are already clear. They would only say something specious. We know what they would say, so at present we are not demanding an explanation.

The impact of this affair was possibly even greater than that of Livedoor's offer for NBS, because both Oji and Hokuetsu are mainstream industrial companies; if such things could happen between companies such as this, others could find themselves similarly exposed. By June 2007, *Nihon Keizai Shimbun* reported that 210 companies had put antitakeover defenses in place and by June 2008 this had risen to over 500 companies. In a commentary published on June 7 2008 on whether the Guidelines issued by MOJ and METI might have affected this situation, *Nihon Keizai Shimbun* quoted Professor Osugi of Chuo University: "they are being used in the fashion that happens to suit management" (Nikkei 2007c, 2008).

Perhaps the most striking comment with regard to referring matters to shareholders came from the chairman of a company, speaking to us in 2006, who named a major Japanese company with an aggregate majority of foreign shareholders as an example of why it was not feasible just to leave reaction to bids and defensive measures to the shareholders' vote:

So if it became a question of someone trying to acquire [the company], if a shareholders' meeting were held – if they asked everyone to gather together... 51% would raise their hands and that would be the end of it, wouldn't it? There's a huge risk of that, you see.

The next report of the Corporate Value Study Group was issued in June 2008 (CVSG 2008). *Nihon Keizai Shimbun* reported the comment of an anonymous member of the committee made, apparently, when it had reconvened some months earlier:

It never gets beyond technical discussions. It's a complete disappointment.

The same article stated that METI had sought to rebalance the committee in March 2008 by introducing more members from the investment sector (Nikkei 2008). The 2008 report adds relatively little to the original in terms of new concepts but it does deal reactively with some issues that had arisen in the interval. With reference to the Bull-Dog Sauce affair (discussed below), it stresses that paying off acquirers is not good and reduces shareholders' wealth; it identifies antitakeover measures adopted after approaches have been made as an area for study; and it notes that independent committees advise the board rather than the shareholders, so that when the board justifies its actions purely on this basis, it may not necessarily be acting in the shareholders' interests. It quotes a number of legal precedents (although judges are often neither inclined nor well equipped to venture into areas of business judgment), but makes no conceptual suggestions to establish clearer protocols for managers to observe. In particular, it does not discuss in any detail the extent to which management has a duty of care to shareholders in takeover situations – as opposed to the responsibility to realize both corporate and shareholder value – and where the parameters of this duty might lie.

Activist Hedge Fund Interventions

Activist hedge funds entered the Japanese market from 1999, with M&A Consulting (the "Murakami Fund"), followed by foreign funds such as Steel Partners from 2002. After the winding-up of the Murakami Fund in 2006, foreign activist hedge funds have predominated, bringing with them methods that have served them well in the USA or Europe to unlock perceived dormant value. They differ from Japan's traditional "extortionists" in that they are conventional fund managers who are guided, among other things, by theories of shareholder value and who make use of sophisticated background research to aid them in their choice of target and in the strategy they pursue; however, the public is sometimes unsure of the difference. The fact that a tender offer is part of their usual arsenal, albeit as a last resort when managements refuse to cooperate, encourages confusion with old-style corporate raiders. This is not a uniquely Japanese predicament and managers in the USA and Europe have experienced similar confrontations. However, particularly in the case of Japan, the tensions created tend to highlight the gulf between management's view of the firm as a continuing community and the activist hedge funds' view of joint stock companies as opportunities to maximize investment returns. Larger Japanese companies are generally more familiar with IR and better at justifying their policies, but the managements of certain smaller companies have not always responded to activist hedge funds with such equanimity. Four such cases, all involving the activist hedge fund Steel Partners, which initially adopted an aggressive approach to the Japanese market, are considered below.

In December 2003, Steel Partners announced tender offers for two relatively small companies: Yushiro, a first section listed manufacturer of cutting oils, and Sotoh, a second section listed fabric dyer. The Yushiro investment had begun over one year before and the tender offer appears to have been the fund's reaction to a lack of cooperation from management. The management's response was to raise the annual dividend from ¥14 to ¥200, bringing the share price above the level of Steel Partners' offer. In order to pay this dividend, Yushiro utilized reserves and paid out the equivalent of 230 percent of its net profit for the financial year in question. In the case of Sotoh, Steel Partners seem to have launched their bid with little preamble. Sotoh's management expressed concern that Steel Partners might not adhere to Sotoh's business principles and first attempted to arrange an MBO; finally they raised the annual dividend from ¥13 to ¥200 per share, bringing the share price above the offer level. The president commented that although reserves had been exhausted, this did not matter as there were no major investment plans for the next two years (Nikkei 2004*a*, 2004*b*).

Both these situations show managements fighting to preserve the independence of their companies as community firms, whose established principles and practices were now under threat from outsiders. The likelihood that Steel Partners were using tender offers as a tool to extract returns and had no interest in becoming involved in the running of either business in the long run seems to have been widely overlooked. Although the targets evaded the bids by raising dividends, they effectively gave Steel Partners what they wanted, in a manner suggesting that managers valued independence above all else. Neither management seems to have included shareholders in their calculations prior to the appearance of Steel Partners and their lack of engagement with their shareholders made them especially vulnerable to Steel Partners' style of approach. The comment by Sotoh's president in justification of paying out accumulated reserves is perhaps indicative of the low priority accorded to financial matters by the incumbent management; it is easy to see why Steel Partners considered the company an attractive target.

In October 2006 Steel Partners made a tender offer for Myojo Foods, a second section listed manufacturer of instant noodles. This situation was closer to the classic style of activist hedge fund intervention because Steel Partners had begun investing in November 2003, pressuring management over nearly three years and persuading them to accept an external director from Steel Partners in December 2004. The tender offer appears to have been the final push to achieve the desired return and it was noted that the premium to the previous closing price was surprisingly low, leading commentators to wonder whether the fund really wanted to succeed. In November 2006 Nissin Foods, Myojo's competitor, made a higher counteroffer with the support of Myojo's management. Steel Partners sold their shares to Nissin and are believed to have doubled the value of their investment (Nikkei Sangyo 2004; Nikkei 2006*a*, 2006*b*).

In this case, again, the management of a relatively small Japanese company was shown to be poorly equipped to deal with an activist shareholder, largely because it was not engaging with its existing shareholders and appeared to have difficulty in justifying the way it ran the firm in a manner that would convince them to support it. Rather than face acquisition by a fund, which was felt unlikely to respect the internal conventions that defined Myojo as a community firm, its management preferred to become part of Nissin, in return for assurances – which seem to have been honored – that Myojo would retain operating independence within the new group. Perhaps not coincidentally, Steel Partners, which held Nissin shares already and acquired more after the merger, subsequently began to complain to Nissin's management in April 2008 about failure to achieve synergies from the Myojo acquisition (Nikkei Sangyo 2008). Throughout this situation, the position of ordinary shareholders does not seem to have been a consideration. The issues at stake were managerial independence, which was effectively identified by Myojo's management with the firm's survival, and the need to preserve the firm from what was seen to be an uncaring acquirer. Merger with a competitor was considered preferable to being controlled by a shareholder.

The intervention that attracted most publicity was Steel Partners' investment in Bull-Dog Sauce ("Bull-Dog"), a second section listed manufacturer of Worcester sauces and a household name in Japan, mainly because it involved three court judgments as Steel Partners sought to prevent Bull-Dog from diluting their shareholding. Steel Partners applied pressure to management by launching a tender offer in May 2007, perhaps encouraged by their success with this method in earlier cases. Bull-Dog's management chose to view Steel Partners as an acquirer rather than as a fund seeking to expedite managerial acquiescence to its demands for higher distributions; it expressed concern regarding Steel Partners' degree of understanding of the food industry and wondered publicly what their motives might be. Finally, with the support of over 80 percent of its shareholders, many of whom are believed to have had long-term business relationships with the company, Bull-Dog proposed to introduce a defensive structure whereby rights for new shares would be issued to all shareholders, but Steel Partners alone would not be able to convert its rights into shares, being offered cash instead. Steel Partners appealed to the courts to have the plan overturned, but their action failed. The defense plan was implemented and Steel Partners subsequently received a sum variously reported as ¥2,100 million and ¥2,300 million for its unconvertible rights (Miyake 2007: 184–210; Nikkei 2007*a*, 2007*d*). This affair attracted widespread criticism to all involved, especially Bull-Dog's management. As a civil servant observed to us, reflecting what seems to have been a widely held view:

Paying money to someone seeking to buy them in that sort of instance is green-mail. A dividend goes evenly to all the shareholders, doesn't it? That's why the most distasteful aspect of the Bull-Dog affair was that when someone tried to buy them they paid ¥2,100 million, but that company's operating profit is only ¥500 million, you know. They paid out four year's worth of money. And when you consider Steel Partners' net return there, I estimate that they took perhaps around ¥600 or ¥700 million profit. Where did that return come from? They took it away from the money that other shareholders would normally have had the company pay as dividends or else from the money that would have been invested and might have generated future profits.

A senior member of management at an industrial company focused on what he saw as the unnecessary nature of it all:

The question is why they did things that way when it was a takeover attempt that had no chance of succeeding . . . I think the important things are basically not so much what sort of lawsuits should be brought or what sort of defensive measures should be made but how the style of management can win the trust of shareholders.

With hindsight, 2007 appears to have been the high point for foreign activist hedge funds in Japan. As economic problems intensified during 2008, the funds' own investors withdrew cash and arguments for increasing payouts and financial debt became increasingly difficult to justify. But even before this, their progress in Japan seemed to be faltering. Partly this may be the result of Japanese managers responding more confidently to activist pressure but it may also be linked to the fact that foreign activist hedge funds had begun to target larger companies where management was more accustomed to presenting its ideas to institutional investors. The intervention by the UK-based activist hedge fund The Children's Investment Fund ("TCI") in J-Power, a large electrical utility company, is interesting because it shows an activist with a strong record of achieving its objectives at big organizations in continental Europe confronting managers who saw their first obligation as being to the firm itself but were sufficiently engaged with both foreign and domestic shareholders to present their arguments effectively. The situation was complicated by TCI's attempt to exceed the 10% limit on shareholdings by individual non-residents in utilities and other industries designated of strategic importance, for which ministerial permission was refused in May 2008. During the approximately two years of this intervention, from late 2006 until October 2008, TCI submitted proposals for an increased dividend at both the 2007 and 2008 AGMs, further proposing share buy-backs, restriction on stock investments, and the appointment of external directors at the 2008 AGM, and mounted a very public campaign in the interim criticising J-Power's business strategy, financial structure, tariff policy, cross-shareholdings, and general quality of its corporate governance. After the 2007 AGM, where TCI's proposals are reported to have attracted support from 30% of the votes, J-Power's president stated that he would bear shareholders' wishes in mind and consider future dividend increases should the company's financial performance so permit. After the 2008 AGM, when support for TCI's proposals had fallen generally to the 20% range, though exceeding 30% in some cases, the president stressed that management had made considerable efforts to explain its position to shareholders. Shortly before that, in May 2008, J-Power's management had carried out its annual visits to international investors and stated its intention to study appointment of external directors in 2009. TCI ultimately sold its 9.9% shareholding to J-Power in October 2008, taking advantage of the ability of minority shareholders to require purchase of their shares at a 'fair price' if they objected to any major reorganization of corporate assets, which J-Power was proposing with regard to an Australian subsidiary. The agreed price exceeded the then market price of J-Power's shares but was estimated by the Financial Times to represent a loss of some ¥12,500 million for TCI (Financial Times 2008*b*).

TCI's ability to secure votes in support of at least some of its proposals at the 2008 AGM in excess of 30% demonstrates the degree to which it could convince shareholders with its arguments. Foreign shareholders in J-Power were reported to hold 36.87% of the total as at 31st March 2008, suggesting that many voted with TCI. Equally important is that some of TCI's proposals in 2008 attracted only in the region of 20% support, suggesting that management had persuaded some foreign shareholders to back its position on these issues. It will never be known what might have occurred if TCI had been able to increase its shareholding or if the economic climate had not soured but the J-Power intervention seems to show how a confident management, in touch with the company's shareholder base, can face down a concerted campaign by a strong foreign activist fund while generally maintaining the tenets of the community firm. Nevertheless, the spread of antitakeover measures at so many companies and the recent resurgence in cross-shareholdings suggest that many managers still believe instinctively that defenses to protect the community firm from shareholders' caprice are preferable to engagement.

Conclusions

On the basis of in-depth interviews with managers and corporate governance practitioners spanning a four-year period and longitudinal studies of several significant listed companies, our assessment in this chapter has been that Japanese corporate governance has survived its crisis of confidence in the 1990s and that most of its "traditional" practices persist: notably, the power of internally appointed executives, the exclusion of external influence, the association of corporate governance with managing the business (and hence a blurring of the line between supervision and execution), and a belief in the need to preserve the community firm. New structures have been introduced and the system is evolving, but it has not diverged far from the direction it took in the middle of the twentieth century.

The roots of this resilience lie in the community firm, where employee loyalty is tightly focused and managers see themselves as accredited representatives of an entity that deserves to be preserved. The community firm, in turn, rests on various supports, such as security of employment for at least full-time employees and the willingness of most managers to pursue their careers within the same company. Changing circumstances, such as inability to honor the commitment to stable employment or the development of an intercompany market for managers, could seriously weaken the community firm, but such a scenario has yet to emerge. There have clearly been social changes in Japan over the past half century or more, both in the wider context of national attitudes and in the narrower context of corporate employment conditions, but, as Inagami and Whittaker observed, despite marginal adjustments, most of the features of the traditional community firm such as long-term employment, lack of remuneration divergence, and labor-management communication appear to be surviving. They could not identify "another type of community which might take the place of the community firm" (Inagami and Whittaker 2005: 109–10).

Japanese corporate governance has developed from the community firm and its robustness depends on the stability of this organizational model. However, one supporting factor for the community firm and hence its style of governance that has tended to be ignored is the acquiescence of shareholders throughout most of the postwar period. As long as institutional shareholders had economic reasons not to demand increasing returns on their investments and as long as individual shareholders accepted their lack of influence, this was not a problem. But the rights of shareholders to appoint or dismiss boards and to vote on matters of strategy have existed since the first Japanese Commercial Code in the nineteenth century. In other markets, such as those of the United States or the United Kingdom, managements at widely held listed companies have been forced to accommodate their styles of governance to the portfolio investment needs of at least their most powerful shareholder groups. In Japan this has generally not happened, but the legal mechanisms for shareholders to assert their rights already exist. The decline in stable shareholdings and the entry of foreign portfolio investors have begun to change the environment. In addition, some Japanese institutional investors, who have tended to support management positions in the past, may be tempted to seek higher investment returns in the future.

Larger listed companies in Japan have begun to adapt their approaches to these changing circumstances. They have invested heavily in IR resources and are increasingly geared to providing information to institutional shareholders in particular and all shareholders in general. Some of their senior managers, at least, seem prepared to coexist with portfolio shareholders who seek to maximize returns within limits that do not threaten the company's viability. However, it is less clear whether management even at these companies is ready to accept an environment where shareholders are permitted to influence corporate strategy directly. The response of management at several relatively small listed companies to activist pressure from Steel Partners has demonstrated that the senior management of the community firm is often ill-prepared to deal with assertive shareholders. Foreign activist hedge funds are not typical investors: they are specialists who have expended great effort in perfecting ways of extracting rents from unwilling managers. However, the reaction to their interventions by senior managers at some of these smaller Japanese companies suggests that they continue to be insensitive to the task of managing shareholder expectations and have a lack of understanding about how shareholders might be accepted constructively by the community firm. The community firm requires loyalty and focus on the firm's interest from its managers but has hitherto not required them to be adept at handling relations with portfolio shareholders.

The rise of antitakeover measures is a predictable response to these developments but it may not be a sustainable one. In principle, it is an accepted feature of the community firm that Japanese managers should be subject to monitoring from social pressures within their firms, however much they are protected from outside interference. In this sense, the erection of antitakeover defenses seems to be an attempt to return to the situation that prevailed in the latter part of the twentieth century, when shareholders chose not to interfere. However, the erection of such defenses at this point is unlikely to encourage communication between management and shareholders, and there are likely to be more conflicts which will have to be adjudicated by the courts.

The efforts of the Corporate Value Study Group to date appear to have done little to remedy this situation, possibly because the committee's remit has not extended to suggesting anything other than minor and incremental changes to practice. The work of the committee nevertheless continues, and in its 2008 report it appeared to lean in favor of a clearer articulation of the principle of shareholder value (as opposed to "corporate value") than hitherto (see Chapter 3). Moreover, in December 2008, an additional Corporate Governance Study Group was set up under the auspices of METI with the aim of developing "a discussion about the introduction of independent board members for the purpose of protecting the interests of dispersed shareholders" (METI 2008: 1). This Group is to consider "whether to impose on all the corporations or listed companies the duty to introduce one or more outside board members" and how to define independence "in the corporations which have one or more parent corporations," as well as "other issues related to corporate governance" (METI 2008: 1). In a sign of its potential significance, its membership is broadly based, including senior managers from several large industrial companies as well as representatives of finance, the accounting and legal professions, and corporate governance scholars. The Group is expected to produce a first report by the middle of 2009. Clearly, the debate over the future of corporate governance in Japan is far from settled, and a revision of the corporate law or a "soft law" approach are two possible outcomes of the current deliberations.

The establishment of the Corporate Governance Study Group can be seen as a recognition of the growing importance of the shareholder interest in Japan. It seems unlikely that foreign institutional shareholders will leave the Japanese market in the near future or that Japanese institutional shareholders will not become increasingly more interested in their investment returns. Japanese managements appear to be faced with several options if they wish to protect their autonomy: they can erect defensive barriers to shareholder action, ostensibly against takeovers but effectively against any shareholders who seek to amass sufficient shares to influence the way that the company is run; they can recreate the pattern of majority stable shareholdings that existed in the early 1970s; or they can press government for legislated restrictions to shareholder powers which would remove the present contradiction between the autonomy of management and shareholders' rights. All of these approaches have a defensive orientation and suggest that the community firm can only survive by shutting out the external world; this might be more feasible if shareholder pressure came only from outside Japan, but it is likely to become increasingly a Japanese phenomenon too. As one senior director at a large company observed, "After all, there's no such thing as an investor that says he does not want an increased dividend." A less defensive and more positive reaction seems to be needed.

One alternative is to adapt more gradually to an environment where shareholders receive attention and to establish a consensus with regard to what rents they can reasonably expect to receive, which some companies do seem to be attempting. This is much more than just a policy of "appeasement." Unless growing shareholder pressure can be accommodated in some form that is compatible with the community firm and its style of corporate governance, the community firm itself may not survive. While such an outcome might reassure agency theorists that their view of the world was fundamentally correct, turning the focus of Japanese capitalism from the cultivation of the firm as an organizational entity to the promotion of shareholder returns as an end in itself would not necessarily result in economic or social advantage. The community firm is still seen as having brought Japan many economic and social benefits and Japan currently lacks the institutional infrastructure for companies to switch suddenly to a perspective dominated by shareholders' rights, without running the risk of severe disruption. So far, the community firm and its governance system have successfully survived extensive structural changes, more through adaptation than confrontation. Rather than attempting to shut out shareholders and to defend the system of managerial autonomy at all costs – a process which is likely to be difficult because it runs counter to the interests of so many shareholders who are increasingly prepared to assert their interests – a more pragmatic and, indeed, characteristic reaction would be to seek some way to coexist with shareholders' rights, absorbing and co-opting them into the structures of the community firm.

Appendix 1

Table 2.1A. Summary by sector of entities visited and meetings conducted during four research exercises (April and July 2004[a], September 2006, September 2007 and January 2008)

Sectors	Subsectors	Entities	Meetings
Manufacturing	Electrical	3	11
Twelve entities; thirty-one meetings	Chemicals	3	10
	Machinery	5	9
	Construction	1	1
Services	Trading	2	5
Six entities; twelve meetings	Transport	2	3
	Utility	2	4
Financial	Financial	2	10
Two entities; ten meetings			
Subtotal for companies		20	53
Investors	Insurers	2	2
Ten entities; twelve meetings	Pure investors	8	10
Others	Associations	6	10
Seventeen entities; thirty meetings	Ministries	3	5
	Other entities	8	15
Subtotal for investors and others		27	42
Total		47	95

[a] Includes two meetings in late 2003.

Appendix 2

Table 2.2A. List of the twenty companies, described by sector, consolidated sales size, and other factors, visited during the four research exercises summarized in Appendix 1

	Sector	Consolidated Sales	Company with Committees	Executive Officers	External Directors	IR Effort	Foreign Exposure	Foreign Ownership (%)
1	Construction	Small		✓					<10
2	Machinery	Small	✓	✓	✓	✓	✓	>10
3	Machinery	Small			✓	✓	✓	>10
4	Trading	Medium						<10
5	Transport	Medium		✓				<10
6	Chemical	Medium		✓	✓	✓		>10
7	Machinery	Medium		✓	✓	✓	✓	>10
8	Financial	Medium	✓	✓	✓	✓	✓	>20
9	Trading	Medium		✓	✓	✓	✓	>10
10	Utility	Medium				✓	✓	>20
11	Chemical	Large				✓	✓	>10
12	Chemical	Large		✓			✓	>20
13	Machinery	Large			✓		✓	>20
14	Transport	Large		✓	✓	✓	✓	<10
15	Utility	Large		✓	✓	✓		>10
16	Electrical	Very large				✓	✓	>20
17	Financial	Very large		✓	✓	✓	✓	>20
18	Electrical	Very large	✓	✓	✓	✓	✓	>10
19	Electrical	Very large	✓	✓	✓	✓	✓	>20
20	Machinery	Very large		✓		✓	✓	>10

Notes

1. Consolidated sales at the time of the first meeting have been used to give a rough indication of each company's size. This indicator can be misleading for some sorts of businesses but it was chosen because it is the single indicator that best shows the size and complexity of most companies. Four subcategories of small, medium-sized, large, and very large were determined as follows (using a single exchange rate of US$1 = ¥110, irrespective of the actual rates current at the time).

Description		Consolidated Sales (millions)	
Small	Up to	¥110,000	US$1,000
Medium-sized	Over	¥110,000	US$1,000
Large	Over	¥570,000	US$5,182
Very large	Over	¥3,300,000	US$30,000

2. Foreign ownership is given as at the time of the first meeting and is indicated in approximate terms in order to maintain the anonymity of the companies concerned.

3. Companies were selected to a certain extent by size, because larger companies were considered to be more likely to be influential in shaping opinion regarding corporate governance, but also by access to the most senior management, because it was felt that corporate governance in Japan is driven internally and from the top— Ahmadjian's comment that, "the principal players in corporate governance reform in the 1990s and early 2000s were corporations themselves" still holds true (Ahmadjian 2003: 232). In terms of industrial sectors, our sample is biased toward manufacturers but we believe that these are precisely the companies that have most prestige in Japan and tend to influence corporate governance attitudes most.

Bibliography

AEON (2003). *Annual Report (Year to 20 February 2003)*. Tokyo: AEON Co., Ltd.

Ahmadjian, C. (2003). "Changing Japanese Corporate Governance," in U. Schaede and W. Grimes (eds.), *Japan's Managed Globalization: Adapting to the Twenty-First Century*. New York: M.E. Sharpe.

Ahmadjian, C. (2007). "Foreign Investors and Corporate Governance in Japan," in M. Aoki, G. Jackson and H. Miyajima (eds.), *Corporate Governance in Japan: Institutional Change and Organizational Diversity*. Oxford: Oxford University Press.

Aoki, M. (1988). *Information, Incentives, and Bargaining in the Japanese Economy*. Cambridge: Cambridge University Press.

——(1994). "Monitoring Characteristics of the Main Bank System: An Analytical and Developmental View," in M. Aoki and H. Patrick (eds.), *The Japanese Main Bank System*. Oxford: Oxford University Press.

Buchanan, J. and Deakin, S. (2008). "Japan's Paradoxical Response to the New 'Global Standard' in Corporate Governance." *Zeitschrift für Japanisches Recht*, 13(26) 59–84.

Canon (2008). *Notice Regarding Introduction of Executive Officer System*. Tokyo: Canon Inc. (http://canon.jp/).

CVSG (2008). *Kinji no shokankyo no henka o fumaeta baishu boeisaku no arikata (Report of Takeover Defence Measures in View of Recent Environmental Changes)*. Tokyo: Corporate Value Study Group.

Dore, R. (1973). *British Factory – Japanese Factory*. Berkeley and Los Angeles: University of California Press.

——(2000). *Stock Market Capitalism: Welfare Capitalism – Japan and Germany versus the Anglo-Saxons*. Oxford: Oxford University Press.

——(2005). "Deviant or Different? Corporate Governance in Japan and Germany." *Corporate Governance: An International Review*, 13: 437–46.

Egashira, K. (2005). *Kabushiki-kaisha/yugen-kaisha ho (daiyon-ban) (Laws of Stock Corporations and Limited Liability Companies – 4th edition)*. Tokyo: Yuhikaku.

Financial Times (2008a). "Sovereign Fund Idea to Boost Japan's Pensions." *Financial Times*, 4 July.

——(2008b). "TCI Sells Out of J-Power at a Loss." *Financial Times*, 31 October.

Gilson, R. and Milhaupt, C. (2005). "Choice as Regulatory Reform: The Case of Japanese Corporate Governance." *American Journal of Comparative Law*, 53: 343–77.

Gordon, A. (1998). *The Wages of Affluence: Labor and Management in Postwar Japan*. Cambridge, MA: Harvard University Press.

GPIF (2008). *Summary of Operations in Fiscal 2007*. Tokyo: Government Pension Investment Fund (GPIF).

Hayashi, F. and Prescott, E. (2002). "The 1990s in Japan: A Lost Decade." *Review of Economic Dynamics*, 5: 206–35.

Horiuchi, Y. (2002). *Heisei 14-nen shoho kaisei an no gaiyo (Outline of the 2002 Revision of the Commercial Code)*. Tokyo: Daiwa Institute of Research.

Hoshi, T. (1994). "The Economic Role of Corporate Grouping and the Main Bank System," in M. Aoki and R. Dore (eds.), *The Japanese Firm: Sources of Competitive Strength*. Oxford: Oxford University Press.

Inagami, T. and Whittaker, D.H. (2005). *The New Community Firm: Employment, Governance and Management Reform in Japan*. Cambridge: Cambridge University Press.

Jackson, G. and Miyajima, H. (2007). "Introduction: the Diversity and Change of Corporate Governance in Japan," in M. Aoki, G. Jackson and H. Miyajima (eds.), *Corporate Governance in Japan: Institutional Change and Corporate Diversity*. Oxford: Oxford University Press.

Jacoby, S. (2005). *The Embedded Corporation: Corporate Governance and Employment Relations in Japan and the United States*. Princeton: Princeton University Press.

JCAA (2008). *Iinkaisetchigaisha risuto/iinkaisetchigaisha ni iko shita kaisha* (*Companies with Committees List: Companies That Have Transferred to Become Companies with Committees*). Tokyo: Japan Corporate Auditors' Association (www.kansa.or.jp).

JCGF (1997). *Corporate Governance Principles – A Japanese View* (*Interim Report*). Tokyo: Japan Corporate Governance Forum (www.jcgf.org).

—— (2001). *Revised Corporate Governance Principles*. Tokyo: Japan Corporate Governance Forum (www.jcgf.org).

Kanda, H. (2005). *Kaisha ho* (*dairoku-ban*) (*Company Law – 6th edition*). Tokyo: Kobundo.

Kester, W. (1991). *Japanese Takeovers: the Global Contest for Corporate Control*. Boston, MA: Harvard Business School.

Koyama, A. and Shinozaki, T. (2001). "Ishi kettei kozo to kigyo pafomansu" ("Decision Making Structures and Corporate Performance"), in Japan Corporate Governance Forum (ed.), *Koporeto gabanansu to kigyo pafomansu* ("*Corporate Governance and Corporate Performance*"). Tokyo: Hakuto Shobo.

Learmount, S. (2002). *Corporate Governance: What Can Be Learned from Japan?* Oxford: Oxford University Press.

Matsui, S. (1999). "Shikkoyakuin seido o meguru riron to jitsumu" ("Theory and Actual Practice Surrounding the Corporate Executive Officer System"). *Shoji homu*, 1539/5, October.

Matsumoto, K. (1983). *The Rise of the Japanese Corporate System*. London: Kegan Paul International.

METI (2008). *Establishment of "Corporate Governance Study Group."* Tokyo: Ministry of Economy, Trade and Industry, Corporate System Division.

METI and MOJ (2005). *Kigyo kachi/kabunushi no kyodo rieki no kakuho mata wa kojo no tame no baishu boeisaku ni kansuru shishin* (*Guidelines Regarding Takeover Defence for the Purposes of Protection and Enhancement of Corporate Value and Shareholders' Common Interests*). Tokyo: Ministry of Economy, Trade and Industry, and Ministry of Justice.

Miyajima, H. and Kuroki, F. (2007). "The Unwinding of Cross-Shareholding in Japan: Causes, Effects, and Implications," in M. Aoki, G. Jackson and H. Miyajima (eds.), *Corporate Governance in Japan: Institutional Change and Organizational Diversity*. Oxford: Oxford University Press.

Miyake, S. (2007). *Shijo to ho – ima nani ga okotte iru no ka (The Market and the Law: What Is Happening Now?)*. Tokyo: Nikkei BP-sha.

National Stock Exchanges (2005). *Heisei 16-nendo kabushiki bunpu jokyo chosa kekka ni tsuite (Results of Shareholding Distribution Survey for 2004)*. Tokyo: National Stock Exchanges.

National Stock Exchanges (2008). *Heisei 19-nendo kabushiki bunpu jokyo chosa kekka ni tsuite (Results of Shareholding Distribution Survey for 2007)*. Tokyo: National Stock Exchanges.

Nikkei (2003). "Beikoku-kei tochi mazu 36 sha" ("American Style Governance: Initially 36 Companies"). *Nihon Keizai Shimbun*, 15 June.

——(2004a). "Yushiro kagaku kabu – TOB shutoku nashi – fando 'hoyu o keizoku' – haito seisaku no henko 'kangei' " ("Yushiro Chemical Shares – No Take-Up for TOB; Fund Says It Will Continue to Hold and Welcomes Change in Dividend Policy"). *Nihon Keizai Shimbun*, 28 January.

——(2004b). "Chukaku jigyo e no eikyo kaihi, sotoh, taiko TOB e no sando tekkai – haito wa naibu ryuho de taio" ("Avoiding Effects on Core Businesses: Sotoh Withdraws Support for Competing Takeover – Dividend to Be Met from Internal Reserves"). *Nihon Keizai Shimbun*, 17 February.

——(2005). " 'Dato' keieisha no 7-wari" ("70% of Managers Concur"). *Nihon Keizai Shimbun*, 13 March.

——(2006a). "Nissin TOB seiritsu – myojo kabu 86% shutoku – sogaku 320 oku en – beikei fando zenkabu baikyaku" ("Nissin Succeeds in Takeover: Obtains 86% of Myojo Shares – Total Cost ¥32,000m – US Fund Sells Out Completely"). *Nihon Keizai Shimbun*, 15 December.

——(2006b). "Bei steiru – doko made honki ka" ("Steel of the USA: How Serious Are They?"). *Nihon Keizai Shimbun*, 14 November.

——(2007a). "Burudokku boeisaku shonin – 'kabunushi rieki' meguri oshu (07 kabunushi sokai")") ("Bull-Dog's Defence Strategy Approved: Response That This Concerns Shareholders' Value – 2007 AGM"). *Nihon Keizai Shimbun*, 25 June.

——(2007b). "Kigyo kachi o saguru – hikaiji nara kabunushi keishi" ("In Search of Corporate Value; Lack of Transparency Means Contempt for Shareholders"). *Nihon Keizai Shimbun*, 24 March.

——(2007c). "Baishu boeisaku no donyu teian – 6-gatsu sokai de 1-wari jaku no 210 sha" ("Proposals for Introduction of Anti-Takeover Strategies: Just Under 10% – 210 Companies – at the June AGMs"). *Nihon Keizai Shimbun*, 20 June.

——(2007d). "Bei steiru – burudokku ni TOB teian – tekitaiteki baishu ni hatten mo" ("Steel of the USA Plans Tender Offer for Bull-Dog – Possibility That This Will Develop into Hostile Takeover"). *Nihon Keizai Shimbun*, 17 May.

——(2008). "Hirogaru baishu boeisaku (chu) shijo – minaoshi atsuryoku tsuyomeru" ("Spreading Anti-Takeover Strategies (no. 2 of 3): Pressure for Revision Strengthens in the Market"). *Nihon Keizai Shimbun*, 7 June.

Nikkei Sangyo (2003). "Beikoku-kei tochi: ze ka hi ka" ("Yes or No to American-Style Governance?"). *Nikkei Sangyo Shimbun*, 24 June.

——(2004). "Myojo shokuhin – shagai-torishimariyaku ni kuroda-shi – bei-kei fando daihyo – nihon de hatsu no haken" ("Myojo Foods: Mr. Kuroda as External Director Representing a US Fund – the First Nomination of this Sort in Japan"). *Nikkei Sangyo Shimbun*, 22 November.

——(2008). "Nissin shokuhin ni teigen bunsho – bei steiru: myojo to no gyomu togo nado" ("Steel of the USA Sends Written Proposal to Nissin re Business Amalgamation with Myojo etc."). *Nikkei Sangyo Shimbun*, 3 April.

NLI Research (2004). *Kabushiki mochiai jokyo chosa 2003-nendoban* (*Cross-Shareholding Survey 2003*). Tokyo: NLI Research.

——(2008). *Kabunushi kosei no henyo to sono eikyo* (*Changes in the Appearance of Corporate Ownership Structure and Their Impact*). Tokyo: NLI Research.

Okazaki, T. (1996). "The Japanese Firm under the Wartime Planned Economy," in M. Aoki and R. Dore (eds.), *The Japanese Firm – Sources of Competitive Strength*. Oxford: Oxford University Press.

Okuno-Fujiwara, M. (1999). "Japan's Present-Day Economic System: Its Structure and Potential for Reform," in T. Okazaki and M. Okuno-Fujiwara (eds.), *The Japanese Economic System and Its Historical Origins*. Oxford: Oxford University Press.

Pascale, R. and Athos, A. (1982). *The Art of Japanese Management – Applications for American Executives*. Harmondsworth: Penguin.

Sony (1997). *Annual Report (Year to 31 March 1997)*. Tokyo: Sony Corporation.

——(1998). *Annual Report (Year to 31 March 1998)*. Tokyo: Sony Corporation.

Szymkowiak, K. (2002). *Sokaiya: Extortion, Protection, and the Japanese Corporation*. Armonk. New York: M.E. Sharpe.

Tanaka, M. (2003). "Japanese Corporate Governance." *International Financial Law Review* 9 October.

Teranishi, J. (1999). "The Main Bank System," in T. Okazaki and M. Okuno-Fujiwara (eds.), *The Japanese Economic System and Its Historical Origins*. Oxford: Oxford University Press.

TSE (2007). *TSE-Listed Companies White Paper of Corporate Governance 2007*. Tokyo: Tokyo Stock Exchange Inc.

Vogel, E. (1979). *Japan as No. 1*. Cambridge, MA: Harvard University Press.

Whittaker, D.H. and Hayakawa, M. (2007). "Contesting 'Corporate Value' through Takeover Bids in Japan." *Corporate Governance: An International Review*, 15: 16–26.

3

Takeovers and Corporate Governance: Three Years of Tensions

Masaru Hayakawa and D. Hugh Whittaker

What a difference three years makes. In early 2005, the "T-shirt president" of Livedoor, Takafumi Horie, sent shock waves through corporate Japan when he launched an audacious hostile takeover bid (TOB) for Nippon Broadcasting System Inc. (NBS). Shock followed shock when the Tokyo District Court granted an injunction preventing NBS from using a warrant issue to fend off Livedoor's attack, and when the Tokyo High Court upheld the injunction in the following weeks. A new era appeared to be dawning, in which corporate executives were no longer free to defend their "castles" from would-be invaders, just as a new breed of aggressive invader was appearing on the scene, unencumbered by regard for Japan's cherished business traditions, and armed with the ideological certainty that the pursuit of self interest was a virtue and that castle walls needed to come tumbling down. The invaders' own castle was the dazzling Roppongi Hills, a tower of opulence in the center of a growing financial, IT, and luxury brand shopping district, a beacon for the new Japan. Horie's symbolic value was seized upon by the reformist Prime Minister Koizumi, who urged Horie to stand in the House of Representatives election in September, against a symbol of the "old guard" whom he had expelled from his own party.

Horie stood as an independent and was beaten. Within months, in January 2006, he was under investigation by public prosecutors and officials of the Securities and Exchange Commission for falsifying financial

Parts of this chapter draw on Whittaker and Hayakawa (2007). We gratefully acknowledge helpful comments from Simon Deakin, with the usual disclaimers, and support from the MEXT Twenty-First Century COE Program through ITEC, Doshisha University.

reports of a subsidiary, and of his own company. A month later he and other Livedoor executives were arrested, and by April Livedoor had been delisted from the Mothers stock exchange. From beacon, moreover, Roppongi Hills was soon recast as a symbol of greed and the growing wealth gap blighting the new Japan. In March 2007, Horie was sentenced by the Tokyo District Court to two years and six months in prison. Investors who had joined his bandwagon or had been flattened by it sought financial compensation in the courts, and to complete the ignominious fall, in 2008 Horie's own former company turned on him and his close associates, seeking ¥3.5 billion in damages for losses they had caused the company.

In the meantime, in mid-2007, another hostile TOB gripped the attention of corporate Japan. This time Bull-Dog Sauce actually issued stock warrants to fend off the unsolicited offer of its largest shareholder, Steel Partners Strategic Fund. Steel Partners' request for an injunction was rebuffed, first by the same Tokyo District Court that had upheld Livedoor's request, then by the Tokyo High Court, which labeled Steel Partners an "abusive acquirer," and finally by the Supreme Court.

On the surface, the contrast could not be starker, and it could be seen, as the UK's *Financial Times* predicted in its editorial of January 18 2006 following the launch of the Livedoor investigation, as a triumph of Japan's "old guard" whose "over-riding aim in preserving the status quo is to cling to a quiet life, untroubled by shareholders' interests in better returns." A closer look, however, reveals far-reaching changes in Japan over this period of three years which have influenced not just the practice of takeovers, but which have cast a shadow over corporate governance practices as well. To appreciate these changes, we need to look at legal developments, judicial rulings, administrative initiatives – specifically the reports and influence of METI's (Ministry of Economy, Trade and Industry) Corporate Value Study Group (CVSG) – and the activities and reactions of investors and corporate executives, and how these have interacted in real time. These interactions are significant not just for understanding corporate control and corporate governance in Japan, but more broadly as a case study in the evolution of institutions as well.

The chapter is structured as follows. The first section looks at legal changes affecting the "market" for corporate control, focusing on changes to the Securities and Exchange Act in 2005 and again in 2006 which regulate TOBs, as well as revisions to company law in 2006 which allowed, among other things, the introduction of new classes of shares and potentially created new means of defending against hostile takeovers. Section 2 looks at a series of judicial rulings, involving Livedoor–NBS and Steel

Partners–Bull-Dog Sauce, focusing on the principles implicit in the rulings, as well as their impact. Section 3 examines the activities of the CVSG, the changing nuances of its reports, their significance, and the vexing question of how "corporate value" should be defined and who may be fit to define it. We then look at how investor and executive behavior has changed from 2005 through 2008, before concluding with some observations about how all of these institutional changes and forces have interacted, and what this tells us about institutional change and the role of law in general. The story is one of institutional borrowing, adaptation, and indigenization through a series of complex interactions. This process is still unfolding, and we will speculate briefly on directions it might take in the future.

The Legal Framework for Takeover Bids

Whatever else may be said about him, Takafumi Horie can be credited with prompting a spate of reforms to the regulation of mergers and acquisitions (M&As) and TOBs in Japan which have begun to create a more comprehensive framework based on domestic circumstances and case rulings rather than adapted importation. Before we look at this framework, let us review briefly the background prior to 2005.

Background

Japan's original Securities and Exchange Law (SEL) dates from 1971, when a Japanese version of the (US) Williams Act was introduced. Unlike the latter, however, which was essentially neutral on whether to prioritize the interests of bidders or targets involved in M&As, seeking instead to safeguard minority shareholder rights and to enhance transparency in capital markets, Japan's SEL was introduced in the context of financial liberalization, and fears that US giants would move in and buy up Japan's financially weaker corporations. Consequently, it favored the interests of targets of takeovers.[1] For the next two decades the provisions for public tenders were virtually unused, partly because of the strength of "stable" and reciprocal shareholdings (Tatsuta 1994: 231). When hostile TOBs were

---

[1] For example, public tenders could only be initiated ten days after notification of the Minister of Finance. The notification was copied and sent to the target company, giving it time to prepare its response in advance.

launched, targets typically responded through "capital procurement" from third parties, diluting the bidders' share ratio.

The SEL was revised in 1990, as a result of pressure from US trade negotiators in the so-called Structural Impediments Initiative of the late 1980s, which sought to create a "level playing field" for trade and investment. The revision changed the notification system to public (newspaper) announcement, and introduced compulsory public tender offers for acquisitions in excess of one third of shares from a small number of shareholders – the so-called "one third rule" – and disclosure of holdings over 5 percent. The one third rule was intended to ensure all shareholders were given equal access to a "control premium," and drew (selectively) on the UK City Code on takeovers and mergers, as distinct from the original (US) emphasis on disclosure (cf. Naito 1990; also Kuronuma 2007).

In the 1990s, Japan's Commercial Code was revised to facilitate corporate restructuring. Holding companies were legalized; procedures for M&A and corporate restructuring were simplified; the prohibition on share buybacks was lifted; and stock swaps were introduced. Japan began to see a sharp rise in M&A, from several hundred a year to several thousand by the early 2000s, as executives pursued first restructuring, and then expansion in a context of limited domestic organic growth opportunities. In the 1990s, too, there was a decline in reciprocal shareholding, led by banks struggling with bad loans and needing to improve their balance sheets and capital adequacy ratios. The grounds were thus created for emergence of unsolicited TOBs. From close to zero in 1995, they had climbed to over forty by 2005, and their exponents were becoming more audacious and devious.

ToSTNeT-1, the after-hours network system for block and basket trading introduced by the Tokyo Stock Exchange (TSE) in 1998, drew little attention outside the professional investment community prior to 2005. On February 8, 2005, however, in just half an hour, Livedoor was able to acquire almost 30 percent of NBS shares from this network, bringing its total to almost 35 percent. The Fuji Sankei group, to which NBS belonged, cried foul, complaining that Livedoor should have made a tender offer, as stipulated by the one third rule. Livedoor claimed that it had made the purchases on a stock exchange-operated market, and hence was not obliged to make a public offer. Opinion was divided as to who was technically right, but clearly the purchase subverted the intent of the regulations, which was that such purchases be open and fair, giving all shareholders the opportunity to benefit from a "control premium." This was one of the gray zones which were being exposed, and which the Financial Services Agency sought to close.

Changes to Securities Law

The Agency began (later in the year) by declaring that if shares bought through off-floor trading brought the total held to more than one third, a public tender offer had to be made. And it began to prepare a more comprehensive overhaul of the SEL, which was introduced in June 2006 as the Financial Instruments and Exchange Law (FIEL).[2] This law stipulated the procedures involved in a public tender, from the announcement of the tender to the day after the offer closes, when the results are notified publicly in a report to the Minister of Finance and letters to shareholders who have responded to the offer. It expanded the scope of the "one third rule" to include purchases of 10 percent or more shares over a three month period, and it introduced speed of purchase restrictions similar to those of the United Kingdom, which prevent purchases of more than 10 percent in a seven-day period. It required a would-be acquirer competing against a party with a public offer in progress also to make a public offer. It thus introduced exceptions to the principle that public offering rules are not applied to purchases made through stock exchanges. The FIEL also introduced new regulations for management buyouts to prevent managers from manipulating information to their advantage, requiring third party evaluation and evidence of measures to prevent conflicts of interest.[3]

Tender offers may last from twenty to sixty working days. Under the FIEL, if an offer is less than thirty days, the target company may request an extension of up to thirty days. If a rival bidder appears, the offer period may be extended until the end of the rival's offer period. During the offer term, the bidder may only purchase shares from those receiving the tender offer (and not from third parties or the stock exchange). The bidder may place various conditions on the number of shares purchased, including forgoing any purchase if the number secured falls short of the target, or some or all of those which exceed it, unless the share exceeds two thirds. This two third threshold is very high according to some commentators (see below), but it marks the first time a requirement to purchase all shares – meaning delisting – has been specified.

There are various other stipulations. The tender price must be clearly stated and uniform, and in principle the offer price cannot be lowered, with certain specific exceptions, such as when the target company issues

[2] This section draws on Kuronuma (2007).

[3] According to a report by the Corporate Value Study Group (2007), the number of MBOs of listed companies was zero in 2004, four in 2005, ten in 2006, and six by May 2007 (cf. Umezu 2007). The number subsequently declined, however, although it continued to rise in nonlisted SMEs: *Nikkei shimbun*, January 7 2008.

warrants or stock splits which dilute the share price. The bidder may also withdraw the offer if there is a significant change in the asset base of the target company (or its subsidiaries) during the bid period. In fact, in recognition of the spread of defensive measures, the FIEL expands the scope for offer withdrawal, such as if a new share issue would lower its holding by 10 percent or more, when new shares with veto rights are issued, or "similar" actions are taken. The target company is now required to send a written response to the Prime Minister as well as the offerer and the stock exchange within ten working days, giving an opinion, the reasons for arriving at that opinion, and whether defensive measures will be employed or not. The target may also reserve an opinion, however, as well as pose questions (once), which the offerer must respond to within five working days, or state why it is not responding.

Although the legal revisions of 2005 and 2006 went some way toward creating a regulatory framework rooted in Japanese experience, a number of issues remain. First, the original motive for introducing TOB regulations was information disclosure which shareholders could base a decision upon. In practice, however, the success or failure of an unsolicited tender offer is strongly influenced by the reaction of the workers – especially the union – in the target company. In Japan, unlike the EU, there are no requirements for disclosure of plans regarding changes to employment or employment conditions, and hence it is unclear what information the frequently observed employee opposition is based on. The result is typically favorable for the management of the target company. Given the nature of long-term employment in Japan, even if somewhat more limited and conditional than in the past, there is a strong case for legal provisions requiring disclosure to the union, employee representative body, shareholder association, or similar of the target company.

Second, as mentioned, there is now a requirement to extend an offer to all shares if the acquisition exceeds two thirds, but there is no obligation to purchase the shares of those who do not respond to the offer in time, and no requirement to buy the remainder in a contested bid. This raises a number of issues (cf. Kuronuma 2007). The logic of the two third threshold is that, if exceeded, it becomes impossible for the minority to block special resolutions at a shareholders meeting, thus it was thought appropriate to give shareholders the right to cash out their holdings in anticipation of this threshold being reached. The reluctance to introduce a more formal sell-out requirement of the sort that exists in some other countries (see Davies and Hopt 2009), and which would give postbid protection to minority shareholders, was derived from concern that this would have unduly added to the costs of TOBs. However, introducing such a require-ment would lower the likelihood of coerced selling, reducing the necessity for the deployment of takeover defenses.

The requirement to extend the offer to all remaining shareholders was introduced to make the premium available to all shareholders fairly. Other provisions also suggest the heightened importance of fairness, rather than the goal of information disclosure which first informed the law. From the point of view of fairness, however, the threshold at which the offer must become unconditional could have been set at 51 percent, or even lower, since on average only 70 percent of voting rights are actually exercised at shareholders' meetings (Fujinawa 2007: 18). And the right to sell out should probably be recognized (Nakahigashi 2006: 66). Minority shareholder rights are dealt with under company law, but it is now widely recognized that relief of shareholders shut out should be addressed in securities law as well.

Third, and related to this, the 2006 changes aimed at regulating the interests of the bidder and the target company in unsolicited TOBs. They aimed at bringing hitherto gray zones within the scope of tender offer regulation, maintaining fairness in changing the conditions of the tender offer or withdrawing it, and ensuring sufficient information disclosure (cf. Kawachi 2007: 17). By introducing regulations with different purposes, however, and seeking to regulate the interests of the different parties, the issue of balance and mutual compatibility arises, as well as the intercon-nectedness of securities and company law. Resolving these is a work in progress, and may well require the construction of a unified law addressing tender offers and TOBs.

Company Law, Classes of Shares, and Takeover Defenses

Along with a number of other countries, Japan has recently introduced substantial changes to its company law, with a view not just to modern-ization, but to strengthening competitiveness of companies facing rapid technological change, increased global competition, and expansion of capital markets (Kanda 2006). The 2005 Companies Act, which came into effect in 2006, represented a major change to Japan's commercial code, first introduced in 1899.

Although not debated in the outline stages, included in the actual draft-ing of the Act were provisions for classes of shares which could be used in defense against hostile takeovers. If allowed in a company's articles, these can include common shares with veto rights, or golden shares, whereby the appointment or removal of directors, issue of new shares or transfer of major assets requires the approval of shareholders possessing the shares. Originally intended for joint ventures and entrepreneurial ventures, such shares can also be placed with friendly parties with limited transfer rights, potentially creating a powerful defense against hostile takeovers.

In the debates leading up to the new law, moreover, business interests had argued for allowing distressed companies to reduce their capital to zero and issue new shares as a means of restructuring. The new Companies Act allowed for any company with relevant provisions in its articles, through a special shareholders resolution, to acquire a class of shares in its entirety. This could be used as a defense measure, for instance allowing a company to buy back the shares of a shareholder acquiring more than 10 percent of its outstanding shares, while giving opposing shareholders a sell-out right.[4] Further, the new law recognized a class of shares with restricted transfer rights, which can be placed with friendly parties as an antitakeover measure.[5]

It also became possible to issue new warrants which can be exercised with certain exceptions, or can be exercised by all shareholders with less than a certain ratio of shares. (Since this is not restricted by law, it is presumably deemed not to violate the principle of equitable treatment of shareholders.) A similar defensive result can be achieved by shares stipulating compulsory conversion to shares with restricted voting rights.

If used as a defense against hostile takeovers, such classes of shares offer an advantage to the target company. On the other hand, the new law also requires greater information disclosure, which is advantageous to a would-be acquirer. This includes the requirement for disclosure in its annual report of the basic stance of a company regarding corporate control (if it has one), as well as defenses against control by an inappropriate party, and reasons why such measures would not harm overall shareholder interests or be used for management entrenchment (Egashira 2008; Kanda 2008). In practice, companies have hesitated about introducing classes of shares while it is unclear how they will be received in financial markets. And the Tokyo Stock Exchange has revised its listing requirements, making it very difficult to issue special share classes like golden shares.[6]

---

[4] Cf. Egashira (2008) and Iwahara (2005). If this were applied to all common shares already issued, the influence of shareholder resolutions at shareholder meetings could be undermined.

[5] In addition, new provisions were introduced for companies to solicit all shareholders to buy back shares – a so-called "mini tender offer." If the number solicited is exceeded, the shares are purchased proportionately.

[6] METI's Corporate Value Study Group (see below) favored recognizing golden shares under certain conditions such as limited duration, while the Tokyo Stock Exchange banned their issue in guidelines it published on antitakeover mechanisms in November 2005. The Financial Services Agency director declared they were legal under company law and, pointing out that Nasdaq recognized them under certain circumstances, argued that refusing to newly list

Judicial Rulings – Livedoor and Bull-Dog Sauce

Livedoor's Unsolicited Bid for NBS

Legislative changes over the past few years will strongly influence how TOBs are handled, and to some extent the means available to defend against hostile bids, but they do not stipulate how defenses can actually be deployed. Here, too, thinking and practice are evolving, with powerful signals coming from judicial rulings on the one hand, and administrative guidelines on the other. Let us begin with judicial rulings.

For many years prior to the NBS ruling, Japanese courts ruled that it was legal for companies to dilute a would-be acquirer's shares through a new share issue if a need for capital raising could be demonstrated. According to the primary (or "proper") purpose rule, companies could legitimately issue new shares alleged to be necessary for raising funds, but which also maintained management control.[7] The courts did this because in most cases they were not ruling on hostile TOBs, but on cases strongly suggestive of greenmail, in which an investor acquires large amounts of shares not for control, but to force the target company or its allies to buy back the shares at an inflated price. In such cases they had little alternative but to adopt the primary purpose rule.

From the 1990s, however, shareholder composition changed. "Stable" – often reciprocal – shareholding declined, and the proportion held by institutional investors, notably foreign institutional investors, rose. The practice of using new share issues to ward off unwanted investor interest came under closer scrutiny, although it was basically supported until 2005. In the NBS case, however, the Tokyo District Court deemed that the primary purpose of NBS's defense measures was to ensure that the company remained under the control of the Fuji Sankei Group and preferably under its current management. It therefore prevented the company from issuing warrants to Fuji Television Network Inc., which would have reduced Livedoor's stake from 42 to 17 percent, while raising Fuji Television's stake to 59 percent. In this case, the court granted the injunction not

companies that issued them was problematic. The peak business organization Nippon Keidanren also argued that a blanket ban was excessive. The Tokyo Stock Exchange yielded to such pressure and recognized them conditionally in its revised guidelines of March 2006, but exceptionally only one company had such shares in 2008.

[7] Niigata District Court ruling, February 1967; Osaka District Court Sakai Branch November 1973; Osaka District Court, November 1987 (Takuma case); Tokyo District Court September 1989 (second Miyairi Valve case); Tokyo District Court, July 2004 (Bell System 24 case). In August 1992, the Kyoto District Court made a ruling based on the distribution of authority principle, similar to the second Tokyo District Court ruling in the NBS case below.

for a new share issue, but for a warrant issue to its parent company, and Livedoor was not in the process of making a tender offer, but had acquired its shares in off-floor trading. The March 11 2005 ruling noted that:

It is inappropriate for the board of directors of a publicly listed company, during a contest for control of the company, to take such measures as the issue of equity warrants with the primary purpose of reducing the stake held by a particular party involved in the dispute, and hence maintain their own control. In principle the board, which is merely the executive organ of the company, should not decide who controls the company, and the issuing of equity warrants, etc., should only be recognized in special circumstances in which they preserve the interests of the company, or the common interests of shareholders.

In the ensuing legal battle, the Tokyo District Court and then the Tokyo High Court offered various reasons for upholding the injunction, but the principle underlying these appeared to shift from the primary purpose principle to the "distribution of authority" (*kengen bunpai*) principle. On March 11, the District Court stated:

The issuing of equity warrants to third parties during a contest for control, resulting in a dilution of the share ratio of one party in the dispute, and maintenance of control by the incumbent management, is in principle an extremely unfair use of a new share issue ... The reason new equity warrants cannot be issued for the primary purpose of maintenance or securing of incumbent control is that the legitimacy of the board's authority is grounded in the wishes of the shareholders who are the company's owners; they may only be issued in special circumstances from the perspective of protecting the common interests of shareholders.

And on March 23 the High Court stated:

The issue of equity warrants, etc., by the directors, who are appointed by the shareholders, for the primary purpose of changing the composition of those who appoint them clearly contravenes the intent of the Commercial Code and in principle should not be allowed. The issue of equity warrants for the entrenchment of management control cannot be countenanced because the authority of the directors derives from trust placed in them by the owners of the company, the shareholders. The only circumstances in which a new rights issue aimed primarily at protecting management control would not be unfair is when, under special circumstances, it aims to protect the common interests of shareholders.

Simply put, the board of directors is an organ of the company appointed by the shareholders, whose business does not include issuing new warrants or shares in order to change the composition of the shareholders for its own benefit. Such issues are deemed unlawful under this principle, except in special circumstances. Significantly, the High Court outlined those circumstances: (*a*) when the unsolicited bidder is a greenmailer; (*b*) when the bidder plans a "scorched earth" approach or crown jewel asset stripping; (*c*) a leveraged buyout to repay existing debt; and (*d*) share price manipulation through disposal of assets. When one or more of these circumstances can be demonstrated, the directors may not be deemed to be acting inappropriately by making a new rights issue which preserves their control. The influence of the Delaware Supreme Court can be seen in this ruling, but it did not go as far as, for instance, the latter's *Unocal* ruling (cf. Milhaupt 2005).

The distribution of authority principle was applied against NBS. As we shall see, one subsequent interpretation is that if a shareholders' meeting rather than the board of directors authorizes such an issue, it can legitimately be used to prevent takeovers. On the other hand, in a case in April 2006, when the Tokyo District Court ordered Nireco Corp. to abandon its poison pill based on the distribution of authority principle, it is not clear whether the ruling would have changed even if a shareholders' meeting had approved the warrant plan.

The Livedoor–NBS drama was ultimately resolved out of court. Unable to issue share warrants, NBS loaned its Fuji Television shares, minus voting rights, to Softbank Investment Corp. and Daiwa Securities SMBC Co. Eventually NBS and Fuji Television agreed to business and capital ties with Livedoor in return for Livedoor selling its NBS shares to Fuji Television, and in September 2005 NBS became a wholly owned subsidiary of Fuji Television.

As a footnote to this case, we note in passing a very similar scenario later in 2005 involving the internet company Rakuten's attempted takeover of Tokyo Broadcasting System (TBS). Rakuten had acquired a large volume of TBS shares and boldly announced that it intended to create a new media company with TBS. Between March and November 2005, however, many companies including TBS had deduced from the NBS case that they had to have takeover defenses in place before being attacked. As well as boosting its stable shareholding, it had issued warrants to an investment company to exercise if a hostile bidder should acquire 20 percent or more of its shares. Rakuten stopped after acquiring 19.09 percent of TBS's shares, thus avoiding exercise of the rights, as well as possible litigation. Rakuten and TBS entered negotiations mediated by Mizuho Corporate Bank, aimed at an alliance and pursuing joint business opportunities, but these eventually went nowhere. Ultimately, TBS's defenses were not subject to judicial scrutiny.

Steel Partners' Unsolicited Offer for Bull-Dog Sauce

Of almost 2000 companies surveyed by *Shoji homu* in 2005, 118 (6.0%) had adopted takeover defenses in 2005 and 860 (44.4%) were not considering them. In 2006, the proportions were 8.8 and 44.3 percent respectively, and in 2007 they were 14.5 and 43.3 percent (*Shoji homu* ed., respective years). In 2008, 213 companies intended to introduce them in June shareholder meetings, one third of which required changes to articles through special resolution.[8] While the number of companies with takeover defenses has surged, the number of times these have actually been used, and tested in court, is tiny. (And, it might be added, of thirteen recorded cases of hostile TOBs since 2000, none has resulted in a change of management control.) Bull-Dog Sauce's deployment of stock warrants to block an unsolicited tender offer by the US investment fund Steel Partners is therefore particularly significant, in that it was tested in the courts, and for the first time the Supreme Court gave a ruling on such a case. Moreover, it involved the new Companies Act. Let us review the background of this case and the rulings.

Steel Partners first gained notoriety in Japan by buying up shares of mainly second tier companies with large cash reserves, forcing them to raise their dividend payouts, and exiting with substantial gains (see Chapter 2). Sotoh Co. and Yushiro Chemical Co. were its first targets, in 2003. In May 2007, having acquired a 10.3 percent stake in second tier Worcester sauce maker Bull-Dog Sauce, Steel Partners launched an unsolicited tender offer for 100 percent of Bull-Dog's shares. The next month, at its annual shareholders meeting, a special resolution proposed by the management was passed by 83 percent of those present. The resolution proposed the issue of warrants at a ratio of three per share, which could be exercised by all except Steel Partners, who would receive an equivalent amount in cash compensation, but would see its stake diluted to under 3 percent.

Steel Partners filed an injunction with the Tokyo District Court, and then the Tokyo High Court, which both rejected Steel Partner's complaint that the warrant issue was unfair and discriminatory, and hence prohibited by Companies Act. The case then went to the Supreme Court, which upheld the rulings of the District and High Courts. The grounds for the rejections are informative and controversial. The Tokyo District Court ruled that:

Even if a particular shareholder suffers a decline in its shareholder ratio owing to discriminatory terms placed on the exercise or acquisition of stock warrants

---

[8] *Nikkei shimbun*, June 11 2008. Special resolutions require approval by two thirds of shareholders present.

distributed to shareholders, when the decision to issue said stock warrants is made by special resolution at the general shareholders' meeting, and shareholders are properly and equally compensated in proportion to the number of shares they own, said stock warrants do not violate the principle of equal treatment of shareholders.[9]

The Court decided, moreover, that even if the intent of the action was to prevent Steel Partners from gaining management control, as the shareholders themselves had authorized the action, the Court should not intervene unless it was clearly irrational or there were procedural irregularities, which in this case there were not. The shareholders themselves were in a position to judge whether Steel Partners' unsolicited offer represented a threat to corporate value, and given the lack of any clear business plan offered by Steel Partners, their decision could not be seen as irrational. The warrant issue was discriminatory in terms of exercise rights, but Steel Partners' economic interests had been preserved.

The Tokyo High Court went further and labeled Steel Partners an "abusive acquirer," a term which did not fit neatly into one of the four categories identified by the Court in the earlier NBS case:

An "abusive" acquirer, with the intention of buying up shares for its own benefit as a majority shareholder, engages in abusive company management or control, without due regard to the sound management of the company. This leads to a damaging of said company's enterprise value or a harming of the common interests of shareholders. That such an abusive acquirer would be subject to discriminatory treatment as a shareholder is unavoidable.   (cited in Ozaki 2007: 7)

As the above quotes suggest, the grounds for the judgments differed between the two courts. The Tokyo District Court argued that the principle of equal treatment was not violated because Steel Partners was compensated fairly, and its economic interests had been preserved, while the Tokyo High Court argued that the principle was not violated because of the unavoidability of discriminatory treatment of an "abusive" acquirer. Ultimately, by pointing to the source of the decision as the annual shareholders meeting, the former appeared to emphasize shareholders' rights, while the latter, in drawing attention to corporate value and the sound management of the company, appeared to be recognizing the importance of other stakeholders as well (Ozaki 2007: 10).

In August 2007 the Supreme Court rejected Steel Partners' appeal(s). Again, we note that this was the first ever ruling by the Supreme Court on takeover defenses. It ruled that:

[9] Translated quotation from Ozaki (2007: 4).

To protect the interests of individual shareholders, the company is obligated to treat shareholders fairly based on the type and number of shares they hold, but since individual shareholders' interests are normally inconceivable without an ongoing and thriving company, if there is a risk that the acquisition of management control by a particular shareholder would damage the company's enterprise value, such as interfering with the company's survival or growth, or would harm the company's interests or the common interests of shareholders, discriminatory treatment of said shareholder aimed at preventing such acquisition cannot be immediately construed as a violation of the intent of said principle unless said treatment is unreasonable and contrary to the equal treatment principle.   (cited in Ozaki 2007: 13)

It argued that the shareholders themselves should decide whether corporate value would be damaged, and that as long as their decision was not patently unreasonable, it should be respected. In this case, Steel Partners had received compensation approximating the value of the warrants, and hence the action should not be considered unreasonable. Moreover, the procedures followed had been fair and reasonable and were not aimed at entrenching management control.

Thus the Supreme Court ruled that defense measures aimed at preventing damage to corporate value were just and proper even if they were discriminatory. Judgments about damage to corporate value should be made by the residual owners of the income stream generated by the company, the shareholders, and not by the courts, although the latter could make a judgment as to whether the process used in arriving at that decision was flawed or not. Clearly this judgment was not based on the primary purpose principle. And by stating that the decision of whether to introduce and deploy defenses should be made by the shareholders, not because of the structure of authority in a stock company but because the profits ultimately accrue to them, it does not appear to be based on the distribution of authority principle, either. Thus there appears to be some movement in the basis of judicial rulings.

There were special circumstances in this case. The annual shareholder meeting happened to be held while Steel Partners' tender offer was in progress. The measures were adopted after the bid. Steel Partners had not produced a convincing management plan. Such circumstances make it difficult to know how widely this ruling will influence future rulings. A number of observers have pointed out that the Supreme Court did not indicate clear criteria for shareholder resolutions (special or ordinary), or the level of economic compensation for the bidder or even its necessity, and that criteria for these might be very strict (Egashira 2008: 710). The issue of financial compensation to the acquirer – Steel Partners received ¥2.1 billion – not breaching the principle of shareholder equality is also controversial.

Various consequences have been envisaged as a result of the case. On the one hand, it may further stimulate the resurgence of "stable" shareholdings – shareholders who might be likely to endorse a resolution supporting defense measures proposed by managers. On the other hand, there are fears that it might encourage greenmailers or create moral hazard for would-be raiders. Indeed this was one of the issues METI's CVSG considered when it reconvened after the ruling. As the courts clearly considered corporate value in their rulings, and as the concept has been influential in the broader debates about TOBs in Japan, let us now look at the evolving "soft law" emanating from this Group.

The Corporate Value Study Group

The CVSG was set up by the METI in September 2004, under the chairmanship of Tokyo University Professor Hideki Kanda. While the establishment of the CVSG preceded the NBS–Livedoor drama, its work took on an added significance as a result of the events of early 2005. In the absence of clear criteria and standards for adopting takeover defenses, many corporate managers began to look to the Group for guidance. On May 27 2005, the Group issued its "Corporate Value Report," (CV Report) and additionally METI and the Ministry of Justice jointly issued their even more influential "Guidelines Regarding Takeover Defense for the Purposes of Protection and Enhancement of Corporate Value and Shareholders' Common Interests" (Guidelines).[10]

According to the Guidelines: (a) the purpose of takeover defenses is "to maintain and enhance corporate value ... as well as the interests of shareholders as a whole"; (b) their introduction should be accompanied by a clear indication of their purpose and contents (prior disclosure), and should reflect the reasonable will of the shareholders; and (c) the defenses should not be excessive (principles of threat and proportionality).[11] They give concrete examples of measures or provisions which might be adopted by approval from a shareholders meeting, and those which might be adopted by the board of directors. The former include provisions for

---

[10] There were different nuances in the conception of antitakeover defence measures between the two. The former sees takeover defences as setting the field for negotiation and competition between the acquirer and incumbent management, while the latter sees them as a means of repelling an attack, and focuses on grounds for their deployment (Osugi 2008).

[11] Cf. www.meti.go.jp/policy/economic_organization/pdf/shishin|youyaku.pdf. The implication is that measures which meet these conditions might be considered legitimate; in this the Guidelines have been influential, though they do not have the force of law.

nonadoption if the acquirer's proposal improves shareholders' common interests, regular approval from shareholders meetings to reflect current shareholder thinking and extreme care regarding shares with differential voting rights. The latter are more likely to be valid if there are provisions allowing shareholders to rescind them, if they do not discriminate against shareholders other than the acquirer without rational grounds, and if there are safeguards against abuse of management discretion. (The last of these can include securing the views of an independent committee, and establishing objective criteria for not adopting the measures.) The Guidelines encapsulated the essence of case rulings and practitioner thinking from the United States, but following them would be no guarantee of legality, since they had not been tested in Japanese courts.

Notably, the Guidelines did not set out clearly what was meant by "corporate value." It was obviously not considered to be the same as "shareholder value," but the definition offered – the attributes of a corporation, such as earnings power, financial soundness, effectiveness and growth potential, and so on, that contribute to shareholder interests – was decidedly vague. The CV Report was less reticent. It defined corporate value as "the company's assets, its ability to generate profits, stability, efficiency, growth ability etc. which contribute to profits for shareholders. In other words, it is the total future profits created by the company, which are distributed as shareholder value belonging to the shareholders, and value of the stakeholders." Here stakeholder interests appear to be recognized, and this raises thorny questions about prioritization, scope, and measurement.

Given the ambiguities of the term "corporate value," the reluctance of the courts to use it is understandable. It is worth noting, however, that even before the publication of the CV Report and the Guidelines, the Tokyo District Court judge responsible for the NBS case commented: "It is a mistake to think only of the interests of shareholders. Raising benefits to stakeholders such as employees, suppliers, customers and the local community accords with the overall interests of shareholders" (see Whittaker and Hayakawa 2007: 25). And as we have seen, moreover, the concept was used by the judges in the Bull-Dog Sauce rulings, pointing to its continued legal importance as well as to its wider significance in policy debates.

The CVSG issued its third report in June 2008, following the Bull-Dog Sauce rulings, and some would say, implicitly (and problematically) critical of them (e.g., H. Ota in *Nikkei shimbun* July 29 2008). As Dore notes in Chapter 5, the composition of the Group had changed by this time: in

85

response to the criticism that its composition was too "corporate manager-orientated," METI had replaced three of its industry members with three from the financial sector (*Nikkei shimbun* June 5 2008). No doubt reflecting this different composition, and the evolving dynamics of TOBs, there were some differences in nuance between the Group's 2008 report, and its earlier ones.

It began by reminding the reader that the purpose of takeover defenses is to protect shareholder interests, and then went on to state that hostile takeovers can play a positive role; the threat of them keeps managers on their toes, and sometimes they can benefit the common interests of shareholders (Kigyo kachi kenkyukai 2008). A lot of attention was paid to the behavior of the board of the target company. The Report criticized the view that it should be up to the shareholders to decide whether the potential damage to corporate value justifies the deployment of antitake-over measures, and that financial compensation to the acquirer is accept-able if the majority of other shareholders approve it. It argued that directors should make a preliminary assessment of whether corporate value would be damaged instead of passing the buck to shareholders. Directors should be wary of invoking the interests of parties other than the shareholders, should not prolong the period for studying a buyout proposal longer than necessary, should resolve promptly not to imple-ment defense measures where an offer would raise corporate value, and should take responsibility for carrying out the recommendations of an independent body.

The 2008 Report viewed unsolicited bids as potentially improving corporate value and indeed corporate governance. It argued for a tight definition of corporate value based on cash flow, and above all, it argued against practices which might, even indirectly, be used as an excuse to entrench management control. There is undoubtedly a gap between these views and those of corporate executives (cf. Chapters 2 and 6). If so, are they best expressed through administrative "guidelines" or through legis-lation? What is clear is that these views also do not represent a final destination, but a work in progress. The establishment of the new Corpor-ate Governance Study Group in December 2008 (METI 2008; see Chapter 2) may be seen in the same light. Although this Study Group will not address the specific question of takeover defenses (this remains within the remit of the CVSG), it has been given the task of considering which "hard law" or "soft law" mechanisms are most appropriate for the regulation of corporate governance issues, and, in this context, is taking a close look at the workings of the UK's Takeover Panel.

Management Responses

Since 2005, Japanese executives have found themselves in a flurry of legal, judicial, and investor relations developments, as well as the possibility of becoming the target of an unsolicited TOB. In response to the changing environment, a substantial minority of firms have adopted takeover defenses, as noted in the beginning of our Bull-Dog Sauce discussion. Probably the most common response, however, has been to look to the traditional method of reciprocal shareholdings. These decreased from over 30 percent of outstanding shares in the early 1990s to just 11 percent by 2005. The figure rose to 12 percent in 2006, and 12.3 percent in 2007, and was expected to rise further in the wake of the Bull-Dog Sauce rulings.[12] Also noticeable is the rise of share buybacks. In 2007 some 35 percent of listed companies counted themselves among the top ten shareholders.[13]

In 2005–6, Japan's three leading steelmakers – Nippon Steel, Sumitomo Metal Industries, and Kobe Steel – created an alliance which included cross-shareholdings and a mutual defense pact, clearly wary of Mittal's hostile bid for Arcelor SA. They were prevented by the Antimonopoly Law from merging, but subsequently used the pact for increasing collaboration in operations and R&D.[14] Other cases, too, reflect growing interfirm and inter-industry collaboration, such as Matsushita Electric's cross-shareholdings with Daikin, and with Toyota, and Toshiba's cross-shareholdings with Sharp.[15] In other cases, however, the increase in cross- or "stable-" shareholdings has been less strategic (in a business sense), and increases the risk for individual companies, and systemically, when share prices decline. More than this, however, according to the CVSG and many investors, their resurgence is a retrograde step which encourages management complacency if not entrenchment.

Another popular measure has been gaining shareholder permission to increase authorized capital, which can be used defensively. In the shareholder meeting round of June 2005, however, Fanuc, Tokyo Electron, and

[12] These Nomura Securities figures exclude shares cross-held by Group companies: *Nikkei shimbun*, July 19 2008.
[13] Again, Nomura Securities figures: *Nikkei shimbun*, September 5 2008. Repurchased shares can be used for cross-shareholdings, or for equity swaps, or they can be retired to boost per share earnings.
[14] *Nikkei shimbun*, July 18 2008. Some of the increased level of M&A activity in Japan, both within enterprise groups and between them, is undoubtedly defensive.
[15] *Nikkei shimbun*, September 7 and 18 2008. Toyota has also increased cross-shareholding within its Group, beginning in early 2006 with increased shareholding of Toyota Industries, a key company somewhat analogous to NBS in the Fuji Sankei Group.

Yokogawa Electric Corp. had proposals to increase authorized stock voted down by shareholders, who took the view that there was no need for an increase. Similarly, some early warning measures have encountered resistance, with the length of the specified period, independence of the evaluation committees, etc., coming under close scrutiny.

In April 2006, the Tokyo District Court ordered Nireco Corp. to abandon its poison pill, arguing that it was unclear that the company's management would respect the recommendations of its independent committee, and that the criteria for triggering an equity warrant – undermining the interests of customers and employees – were too broad and lacked clarity.[16] In brief, the increase in takeover defenses has not been uncontested, either by investors or the courts. The Tokyo Stock Exchange, moreover, announced in August 2008 that it would further strengthen its code on takeover defenses, most probably making its reporting requirements more frequent and more detailed.

Even in the relative (compared with 2007) quiet of the 2008 shareholder meeting round, an increasing proportion of investors exercised their "voice." A survey of eighty asset management firms by the Japan Securities Investment Advisors Association found that 60 percent had disapproved of resolutions, with 90 percent of these casting dissenting or abstention votes in director elections (*Nikkei shimbun*, August 8 2008). This is significant because directors are on an average coming up for reelection more frequently than in the past. The company with committees system requires directors to be reelected annually, while under the new Companies Act companies which have transferred dividend decisions from the annual shareholder meeting to the Board of Directors are required to have shorter director tenures. And dismissing directors now requires a simple rather than a two thirds majority of voting shareholders.

Indeed, many firms which have introduced antitakeover measures introduced shorter director tenures at the same time, a combination which worked to the strong disadvantage of Aderans Holdings' senior management. In late 2005, Steel Partners became Aderans' largest shareholder and in 2006, Aderans introduced early-warning defense measures. A shareholder resolution put forward by Steel Partners aimed at forcing Aderans to drop the plan narrowly failed in 2007, but in 2008 seven top Aderans executives, who were up for reelection because of the one year

---

[16] *Nikkei shimbun* (June 2 2006) commented: "This ruling effectively means that companies are not allowed to take the interests of customers and employees into consideration when deciding whether an unsolicited takeover would damage their corporate value...(T)his severely limits the conditions under which defensive measures can be adopted, experts say."

tenures introduced with the defense measures, were ousted. Some 85 percent of voting rights were exercised (*Nikkei shimbun*, May 30 2008). Evidently Aderans' top management had miscalculated the "softer" approach of Steel Partners following the Bull-Dog Sauce drama.

In sum, the interface of investor relations has become more tense in recent years. This tension holds an uneasy balance, in which legal changes, judicial rulings, and quasi-official guidelines appear to increase executives' defense options, while also making them more accountable to shareholders. At the very least, top executives have had to gain a better grasp of investor relations, relevant law, and judicial rulings. They have done this with the help of a rapidly growing IR service industry. A lot has changed in the past three years.

Concluding Comments

Moves toward creating a "market" for corporate control in Japan have been fiercely resisted. Although there have been few if any successful hostile TOBs to date, however, the environment which corporate executives confronted in 2008 was very different from the one they confronted just three years earlier. Would-be norm and institution changers like Yoshiaki Murakami, Takafumi Horie, and the fund managers of Steel Partners have been thwarted at one level, but their actions have brought about fierce debate and far-reaching changes at another. The prerogative of executives to manage their companies on their own terms as "elders" of the community firm has been challenged, and as a result this prerogative has become more conditional. In the past continued poor performance or improper behavior constituted grounds for removal in exceptional circumstances; now a principle has been established that appointment is contingent on improving corporate value, and that different versions of corporate value may be contested. In defending the community firm, moreover, executives have had to give ground to their challengers – in the form of enhancing transparency, improving dividend payout rates, and indeed courting shareholders, thereby acknowledging in practice their legal ownership rights.

Instead of speculating as to where this will lead, in our concluding comments we would like to step back and reflect on how these changes have occurred, as they can shed light on how institutions and norms change. For many years, there was a rather obvious gap between the ownership rights of shareholders as expressed in law, and the normative behavior of senior managers as community firm "elders." Shareholders were not ignored, but neither were their interests prioritized. The status quo has been challenged in recent years, enabled in part by US pressure to create a "level playing field" for investment, by the effects of prolonged deflationary recession, and by a series of legal changes beginning in the 1990s aimed at facilitating corporate restructuring.

Livedoor's audacious bid for control of NBS introduced an immediate and highly visible set of issues which were framed in various ways. Initially the media – and politicians and other opinion leaders – flirted with the idea of framing it as a contest between old and new, and with backing Horie as a Trojan horse for accelerating change. This line was abandoned with Horie's arrest and subsequent fall from grace. The Pandora's box that Horie had opened, however, had to be dealt with. Lacking an adequate legal framework or accumulation of judicial rulings, the courts first looked abroad, especially to Delaware. In his analysis, Milhaupt notes the emergence of "a judicial standard for takeover defenses that might be called a *Unocal* rule with Japanese characteristics" and how the Guidelines were "heavily influenced by the familiar 'threat' and 'proportionality' tests under Delaware law, along with many of the doctrinal nuances following *Unocal*" (Milhaupt 2005: 2171). He interprets this not so much as a case of institutional convergence, but as a "highly unpredictable telescoping and stacking of two decades of Delaware takeover jurisprudence on Japanese institutions" (ibid).

He is undoubtedly right. Delaware might be the starting point of the response, but only the starting point which triggered a process of friction, negotiation, and realignment toward a different destination. The Tokyo High Court NBS ruling appeared to restrict the use of poison pills to specific circumstances. The METI/Justice Ministry Guidelines appeared to endorse the use of defense measures, including poison pills, under certain circumstances. The legislative response addressed off-floor trading and other gray areas which Livedoor's activities (and those of the Murakami Fund) had exposed, drawing in part on European and UK law. Additionally, in addressing the issue of classes of shares, especially for emerging companies and corporate restructurings, the Companies Act added new mechanisms of takeover defense (which the Tokyo Stock Exchange immediately sought to limit). Many companies rushed to introduce defenses, creating a response from investors, and sometimes the courts. These interactions are beginning to shape a new trajectory of evolution with distinctively "Japanese characteristics."

Looking forward, there are growing voices for new legislation specifically on takeovers, for a variety of reasons, not least of which are spiraling legal costs and uncertainties for businesses involved in takeovers. Such legislation would be expected to address newly emerging issues, and help to resolve current tensions between the FIEL and Companies Act. It is quite likely that European law would provide at least some of the inspiration for such a law, although poison pills and Delaware-based concepts are unlikely to be abandoned. It is not inconceivable – though perhaps increasingly unlikely – that out of the mound of the "corporate value" debates will emerge a Takeover Panel comprised of industry, investor, and academic members, but it is unlikely that such a panel would gain the autonomous status of the UK's Panel on Takeovers and Mergers. Out of this melee, in other words, a distinctively Japanese response to takeovers is likely to emerge which has both US/Delaware characteristics – the initial input – and European and UK characteristics – potentially in subsequent law, and possibly a Panel – but which also has Japanese characteristics both in terms of the resolution of these inputs, and the resolution of tensions and domestic dynamics.

This response, in turn, will have an impact on corporate governance. Whether this points to corporate governance as a focus of the "new community firm" (Inagami and Whittaker 2005) or "Japanese-style shareholder capitalism" is open to debate, but the former is more likely on current evidence.

Bibliography

Davies, P. and Hopt, P. (forthcoming). "Control Transactions," in R. Kraakman, P. Davies, H. Hansmann, G. Hertig, K. Hopt, H. Kanda and E. Rock (eds.), *The Anatomy of Corporate Law: A Comparative and Functional Approach*. Oxford: Oxford University Press.

Egashira, K. (2008). *Kabushiki kaishaho, dainihan* (*Stock Company Law, 2nd edition*). Tokyo: Yuhikaku.

Fujinawa, K. (2007). "Kensho – Nihon no kigyo baishu ruru: Raitsu puran gata boeisaku no donyu wa tadashikattaka" ("Investigation of Japan's Corporate Acquisition Rules: Was It Right to Introduce Rights Plan Defences?"). *Shoji homu*, 1818: 17–24.

Hamada, M. (2006). "Ogon kabu" ("Golden Shares"). *Hogaku kyoshitsu*, 306: 2–3.

Hayakawa, M. (2005). "M&A ni okeru torishimariyaku no gimu to sekinin" ("Obligations and Responsibilities of Directors in M&A"). *Shoji homu*, 1740: 25–32.

Inagami, T. and Whittaker, D.H. (2005). *The New Community Firm: Governance, Employment and Management Reform in Japan*. Cambridge: Cambridge University Press.

Iwahara, S. (2005). "Jiko kabushiki shutoku, kabushiki no heigo, tangen kabu, boshu shinkabuto" ("Share Buy-backs, Share Amalgamations, Unitary Stock, etc."). *Juristo*, 1295: 36–45.

Kanda, H. (2006). *Kaishaho nyumon (Introduction to Company Law)*. Tokyo: Iwanami shoten.

—— (2008). *Kaishaho daijuhan (Company Law, 10th edition)*. Tokyo: Kobundo.

Kawachi, T. (2007). "Kigyo baishu, soshiki saihen to kin'yu shohin torihikiho – kokai kaitsuki to tairyo torihiki hokoku seido no kaisei" ("Corporate Acquisition, Restructuring and the FIEL: Revisions to Public Tender and Reporting of Large Volume Trades"). *Horitsu jiho*, 79/5: 4–6.

Kawamoto, I. and Otake, T. (2005). *Shoken torihikiho dokuhon dainanahan (SEA Reader, 7th edition)*. Tokyo: Yuhikaku.

Kigyo kachi kenkyukai (2008). "Kinji no shokankyo no henka o fumaeta baishu boeisaku no arikata" ("Takeover Defences in the Light of Recent Environmental Changes"). Reproduced in *Shoji homu*, 1838: 53–9.

Kuronuma, E. (2007). "Kigyo baishu ruru toshite no kokai kaitsuki kisei" ("Public Tender Regulations as Corporate Acquisition Rules"). *Juristo*, 1346: 26–34.

Milhaupt, C. (2005). "In the Shadow of Delaware? The Rise of Hostile Takeovers in Japan." *Columbia Law Review*, 105: 2171–216.

Naito, J. (1990). "Kokai kaitsuki seido no kaisei" ("Revision of the Public Tender System"). *Shoji homu*, 1208: 2–11.

Nakahigashi, M. (2006). "Kaiseiho to tekitaiteki kigyo baishu boeisaku" ("Revised Law and Defence Measures Against Hostile Takeovers"). *Hogaku kyoshitsu*, 304: 64–74.

Osugi, K. (2008). "Baishu boeisaku no genzai,kako, mirai – Bull-Dog jiken o keiki ni" ("Takeover Defences Present, Past and Future: Prompted by the Bull-Dog Case"). *Horitsu jiho*, 80/3: 41–45.

Ozaki, S. (2007). "The Bull-Dog Takeover Defence." *Nomura Capital Market Review*, 10: 2–20.

Shoji homu (2005, 2006, 2007). *Kabunushi sokai hakusho (White Paper on Annual Shareholder Meetings)*. Tokyo: Shoji homu.

Tatsuta, M. (1994). *Shoken torihikiho I (SEA I)*. Tokyo: Yuyusha.

Umezu, H. (2007). "Kigyo kachi no kojo oyobi kosei na tetsuzuki kakuho no tame no keieisha ni yoru kigyo baishu (MBO) ni kansuru shishin no gaiyo" (Outline of "Guidelines Concerning Procedures for Ensuring Corporate Value-Raising and Fair MBOs"). *Shoji homu*, 1811: 4–11.

4

Foreign Investors and Corporate Governance in Japan

Sanford M. Jacoby

Japan's distinctive corporate governance system developed during and after the Second World War. The features of that system – insider boards, cross-holding, enterprise unions, and main banks – rested on two assumptions. One was that the company comprised a community of stakeholders rather than being the shareholders' property. The responsibility of senior executives was to maximize the enterprise's long-term value by balancing the interests of shareholders as well as creditors, employees, suppliers, and business group (*keiretsu*) members. The second assumption had to do with trust in the selection and incentive systems for corporate executives. Those who rose to the top were assumed to be competent, honest, and hardworking. They were closely monitored only when there was a marked decline in earnings, sales, or share price. In these instances, the CEO might be ousted and sometimes an independent director was placed on the board (Kaplan 1994; Kaplan and Minton 1994; Inagami and Whittaker 2005).

Today the traditional system is under pressure to become more like the US governance model that took hold in the 1980s and 1990s. The US

This is an updated, abridged version of an earlier paper "Convergence by Design: The Case of CalPERS in Japan," *American Journal of Comparative Law*, 55: 239–94 (2007). The author is grateful to the publishers and editors of the American Journal of Comparative Law for permission to draw on the earlier paper here. For financial support the author thanks the Institute for Technology, Enterprise, and Competitiveness (ITEC) at Doshisha University, and UCLA's Institute for Research on Labor & Employment and its Price Center for Entrepreneurial Studies. The opinions expressed here, as well as any errors or omissions, are entirely the author's.

model treats share price as the chief criterion for judging management performance. Adherence to that standard is insured through boards comprised of independent directors, through stock-based executive compensation, and through acquisitions – the market for corporate control – when performance is poor (Dore 2000; Jacoby 2005a).

The pressure for change stems from Japan's slow economic growth between the early 1990s and 2002. The weak economy frayed ties between banks and corporate borrowers and between members of the *keiretsu*, causing sales of cross-held equity (Lincoln and Gerlach 2004). A second vector for change is the Japanese government, which repeatedly has revised Japan's commercial law to facilitate implementation of the US model (Ahmadjian 2000; Katz 2003; Gilson and Milhaupt 2005; Hall 2005).

Foreign investment, especially from the United States, is a third source of change. Whereas foreign investors owned only 1 percent of Tokyo Stock Exchange (TSE) shares in 1960 and 6 percent in 1992, the figure rose to 18 percent in 2000 and to 27 percent in 2007. Foreign owners are more likely to trade their shares than domestic owners, thereby magnifying their impact on share prices (Tokyo Stock Exchange 2005: 7–8, 60).

Some foreign investors in Japan merely buy and sell shares. Others are activists seeking to repeat the governance transformations they wrought in Europe and the United States. The activists include individuals, private equity funds, and institutional investors. In Japan, the dominant institutional investors are US pension funds, the largest of which is the California Public Employees' Retirement System or CalPERS. CalPERS, with pre-crisis assets of around $240 billion, provides pensions to nearly 1.5 million active and retired state, school, and public-agency employees in California. Many beneficiaries are current or retired union members.[1]

CalPERS is often cited as the paradigmatic activist foreign investor in Japan. It was among the first overseas pension funds to make major investments in Japanese equities and remains one of Japan's largest foreign investors. As early as 1992, when foreigners were beginning to ramp up their Japan investments, CalPERS owned $3.7 billion in Japanese equities, a stake that constituted approximately 3 percent of the total value of TSE shares owned by foreign investors. By 2000, many more foreign investors had flocked to Japan so that CalPERS now constituted slightly less than 1 percent of the total value of shares owned by foreign investors.

---

[1] CalPERS is not, however, a "union" pension fund. See Schwab and Thomas (1998). On the other hand, California's public sector is heavily unionized, with a coverage rate of 58 percent in 2005 versus 40 percent nationally. See data at http://www.trinity.edu/bhirsch/unionstats/.

These figures are impressive but even with its vast holdings, CalPERS remained a flea on the elephant.[2] So how could it have had an effect on Japanese corporate governance?

One answer is that CalPERS was an aggressive advocate of change. During its first phase of activism, it acted on its own. The second phase came when CalPERS leveraged its stake by teaming with other foreign investors and with domestic groups seeking to change Japanese corporate governance. In the end, however, the fruits of CalPERS' activities were modest. It had more of an effect on changes related to transparency than on those related to board structure, executive compensation, and control (takeover barriers). Perhaps this is because disclosure is an add-on that can be adapted to the existing Japanese system with minimal disruption; reconfiguring boards or permitting hostile acquisitions requires more radical change of the sort that many Japanese companies are still unwilling to initiate. CalPERS blamed this resistance on self-serving, entrenched management. But many Japanese corporate executives felt that the existing system per-formed reasonably well and that the solution to Japan's economic prob-lems lay outside the corporate sector – in monetary and banking policies.

By 2002, CalPERS began to lose interest in leading the push for share-holder-oriented governance in Japan. There were free-rider costs that it was less willing to bear as more foreigners entered the Japanese market. Also, CalPERS discovered that it could achieve better results by pressing for change behind the scenes in companies where it held large stakes – the relational investing approach – than by pursuing the same activities on a marketwide basis. The combination of relational investing and lower levels of activism marks the third phase of CalPERS' involvement in Japan.

Last but not least, the economic environment changed. Flaws in the US model became evident in the myriad scandals that followed the Enron implosion in 2001. And in 2002, Japanese firms finally began to pull out of their prolonged stagnation and, consequently, were less motivated to appease foreign investors.

The following article presents the history of CalPERS in Japan. It shows how institutional investors promote change in overseas corporate govern-ance as well as the limits of foreign influence. Previous studies of Japan have statistically confirmed an association between foreign ownership and outcomes such as asset restructuring and downsizing. But the studies are unable to determine whether causal links exist between foreign ownership

---

[2] Calculations based on Tokyo Stock Exchange (2005: 60, 74), and CalPERS data supplied by Susan Kane in letter to author (March 10 2005).

and observed outcomes. The present case study unpacks those causal ambiguities by examining the actual processes by which CalPERS and other institutional investors tried to change corporate governance and strategy in Japan. It also provides data for the debate on the global convergence of governance systems, emphasizing that there are political and distributional, and not only economic and efficiency, forces driving convergence.

CalPERS in the United States

To appreciate CalPERS in Japan, one must understand how the fund evolved in the United States, not just for reasons of perspective but because many of the policies CalPERS pursued in Japan had their origins in its home country. CalPERS' transformation from a sleepy public pension fund to active institutional investor began in 1984, when California lifted a requirement limiting CalPERS' stock investments to 25 percent of its portfolio. 1984 also was the year that the Bass brothers of Texas made a hostile bid for oil giant Texaco. To stave them off, Texaco paid a premium of $138 million for their shares – an instance of "greenmail." Infuriated by the deal was California State Treasurer, Jesse Unruh, who was a trustee of the CalPERS board. Unruh tried but could not block the payoff. But he drew from the episode two lessons: that executives cared more about their jobs than about shareholder value, and that public pension funds needed to coordinate their common interests (Stevenson 1991*b*; Castaneda 2004: chapters 1, 7. For a legally-informed overview of the "shareholder value" concept, see Deakin 2005).

In 1985, Unruh founded the Council of Institutional Investors (CII), an association of public pension funds. Representing $132 billion in assets, CII was a force to be reckoned with. Among its first acts was adoption of a "shareholder bill of rights" calling for equal treatment of shareholders, shareholder approval of key corporate decisions, and independent vetting of executive compensation and corporate auditors (Castaneda 2004). The CII was put to the test by another Texan, T. Boone Pickens, who was trying to take over Phillips Petroleum. Although the bid failed, CII – because of its collective clout – participated in meetings with company representatives. CalPERS supported raiders like Pickens, even if it did not align itself with them in every bid, because it believed that takeovers could raise shareholder value. CalPERS professed to be interested in long-term value and used the term "shareowner" instead of "shareholder" to transmit this message. But according to disgruntled corporate executives, CalPERS was quick to abandon its philosophy if a raider offered a sufficiently juicy premium for its shares (Stevenson 1991*b*; Castaneda 2004: chapter 7).

At the time around 80 percent of CalPERS' US equities were in index funds, a cheap way to track the market. Also, any above-average losses incurred by CalPERS were sure to attract public criticism, so indexing kept it free from blame. Because CalPERS could not sell its indexed shares when a company performed poorly, it thought that the best way to raise returns was to propose marketwide changes in corporate governance (Castaneda 2004).

The thesis that corporate governance was responsible for poor performance was advanced with increasing regularity in the 1980s. The investing community asserted that US companies had failed to respond effectively to globalization because they subscribed to a managerialist system in which executives and boards sought to balance the interests of corporate stakeholders. This caused them to defer excessively to incumbent employees through takeover barriers, overly high wage and staffing levels, and wasteful spending on unrelated acquisitions.

During the late 1980s, CalPERS began to openly criticize companies with what it considered to be shareholder-unfriendly policies. It introduced shareholder resolutions opposing poison pills and insufficiently independent boards. CalPERS felt that the deck was stacked against shareholder activism. So it sought broader shareholder rights: greater disclosure, fewer barriers to dissident proposals, and advisory committees for large shareholders (Wayne 1991; Stevenson 1991*a*; Smith 1996).

Around this time, CalPERS adopted a new approach. Instead of going after companies with faulty corporate governance, regardless of performance, it took aim at companies with governance defects *and* that had poor performance. Only companies in the bottom performance quartile (measured over five years) were targeted, because these companies could not argue, as better performers sometimes did, that "if it ain't broke, don't fix it" (Guercio and Hawkins 1999; Sailer 2000).

In the first year of targeting, CalPERS had a much higher "win" rate than under its previous strategy. The names of targeted companies were shared with the media, putting an unwelcome spotlight on their internal affairs. Some members of the corporate community were furious about these tactics and California Governor Pete Wilson, a Republican, responded with a plan to pack the CalPERS board entirely with his appointees (Stevenson 1991*a*; Gillan 1997). Although the plan was not implemented, it chilled CalPERS' aggressive tactics. Now, rather than publicly identifying a targeted company, it first sent a confidential letter asking to meet with the CEO to discuss governance. At the same time it discreetly put into motion the machinery for a shareholder proposal. If management agreed to go along with CalPERS, even part way, CalPERS promised to halt the machinery (Clowes 2000).

Research on Activism

As shareholders flexed their muscles, researchers began studying whether activism had an effect on corporate performance. CalPERS touted a study by Wilshire Associates showing an improvement in stock price at companies targeted by CalPERS, a phenomenon dubbed "the CalPERS effect." The study, however, was marred by various methodological problems. Wilshire Associates was also an investment advisor to CalPERS and may have felt compelled to tell CalPERS what it wanted to hear (CalPERS 1995, 2005; also Nesbitt 1994; for a critique of Wilshire Associates' methodology, see Romano 2001).

Other studies are more ambiguous. Romano distinguishes between activism based on shareholder votes and proposals, and that based on nonproxy activity such as targeting and negotiations. The effect of shareholder proposals on corporate performance is insignificant in all studies she reviewed, including a study of CalPERS. Gillan and Starks find a negative effect of institutional proposals on share price. The evidence on nonproxy activity is inconclusive. Of nine studies reviewed by Romano, five show positive performance effects and four find insignificant or mixed effects. Of these studies, two were based on CalPERS: one finds significant performance effects; the other does not. A more recent study examines the stock–price effect of CalPERS' targeting and finds that it occurs immediately after targeting and dissipates within six months. Another recent study finds that public disclosure by CalPERS of poor-performing companies leads to a greater likelihood of CEO dismissal. The latest study – by Nelson – claims that all previous studies were deficient because they failed to control for contaminating events (e.g., positive news stories released shortly before announcement of the CalPERS list) and for biases caused by estimation during periods of known underperformance. Controlling for these biases, he finds that, while there are positive effects of CalPERS targeting during the 1990–3 period, there is no evidence of effects since then (Smith 1996; Crutchley et al. 1998; Gillan and Starks 2000; Romano 2001; English et al. 2004; Wu 2004; Nelson 2006).

Given these ambiguous effects and the costs of targeting, CalPERS tried a new approach. As part of its equity portfolio it acquired large stakes

(5–10% or more) in a few underperforming companies and used those holdings as leverage to effect changes such as divestitures and higher payouts. This was "relational investing." Like other types of block holding, it allowed investors to focus directly on business decisions rather than, as with governance reform, the methods used to reach those decisions (Gordon and Pound 1993; Berry 2004: 1; CalPERS 2004*a*; Business Week 2004*b*).

Another change was an effort to codify principles of corporate governance. In 1997, CalPERS issued its preliminary governance code, which distinguished between "fundamental" and "ideal" principles. CalPERS planned to grade companies on these principles, publicize the results, and prod recalcitrants to change. But the code was met with a barrage of criticism. A *New York Times* analysis of Fortune 1,000 companies found only one, Texas Instruments, meeting the full range of CalPERS' fundamental tests. In a statistical analysis, *The New York Times* did not detect any pattern linking the principles to performance.[3]

Research on Corporate Governance

Since then, there has been a plethora of academic research on the governance–performance relationship. One widely cited study by Gompers et al. finds a strong, positive relation between an index of twenty-four governance rules and stock returns during the 1990s. Well more than half the rules pertain to the absence of antitakeover defenses such as staggered board terms and supermajority voting on mergers. The others concern shareholder rights in proxy voting, shareholder meetings, and bylaw amendment. While Gompers et al. did not identify the rules most strongly associated with performance, a subsequent study finds that most of the performance effect derives from rules facilitating takeovers. However, recent studies do not find a casual relationship between takeover rules and performance.[4]

Although elimination of takeover defenses is mentioned in the CalPERS principles, the core is concerned with other issues such as monitoring (board structure) and incentives (executive compensation). Here performance effects are difficult to find. In fact, the preponderance of evidence

---

[3] "A Conversation with Richard Koppes," 1995, www.corpgov.net/forums/conversation/koppes.html; Bryant (1997).
[4] Gompers et al. (2003); Bebchuk et al. (2004). Not only do studies fail to find causality between governance features and performance, some actually find *positive* share-price effects associated with takeover defenses such as golden parachutes. The inference is that entrenchment

shows that board independence and small board size, which CalPERS repeatedly emphasized, are not associated with performance. There is also no conclusive evidence that splitting the chairman and CEO positions is associated with performance. However, board independence is associated with higher CEO dismissal rates during periods of poor performance (Dalton et al. 1998, 1999; Romano 2001; Bhagat and Black 2002).

As for executive pay, CalPERS sought greater use of stock-based compensation for boards and executives. There is no consensus regarding the effect of board stockholding on performance; studies find positive and null effects. Whether executive stock compensation improves performance is a vexed issue. Although some studies find a positive relationship between performance and stock-based pay, other studies reveal a slew of problems. Options create incentives to manipulate earnings and to extract gains that benefit executives at the expense of shareholders. To its credit, CalPERS criticized some of the more egregious practices related to options, such as reloading in the face of a firm-specific decline, but remained an enthusiastic proponent of equity-based pay (Mehran 1995; CalPERS 1999; Dalton and Daily 2001; Romano 2001; Bebchuk and Fried 2004; Economist 2005; regarding option backdating, a potential source of fraud, see Heron and Lie 2006). Part of the problem here is defining performance. If one discards the efficient markets hypothesis, there can be a wedge between share price and a company's long-term prospects, so share price may not be the best performance metric. Alternate measures of performance, such as economic value-added (EVA), present problems of their own (Rehfeld 1997; Kennedy 2001).

---

has not only costs but benefits: it prevents boards from being overly sensitive to uninformed shareholders and permits boards to negotiate a better price with bidders. Also, the existence of a stock premium associated with takeover-friendly governance does not mean that takeovers or the threat of them improve efficiency. We know that takeovers are not associated with preexisting governance or performance defects and that they do not lead to improved performance in the long term. One study can find no evidence of greater profitability nine years after a takeover; in fact profitability declined. We do know, however, that hostile bids generate a spike in stock prices immediately after the bid is announced. The spike reflects the tendency of bidders to overpay for acquisitions (the hubris effect). It also reflects the expectation that the takeover will lead to asset sales (asset sales command price premia because bidders are seeking market power) and to tax benefits associated with the deal. Hence it is possible for takeovers to boost share price but not efficiency. Takeovers cause a flow of resources to shareholders – from customers, creditors, employees, and taxpayers – and lead to underspending on R&D and human capital. This is what currently worries some investors, who think that US public companies are endangering their long-term health by paying out too much cash. However, we do not know precisely the extent to which stockholder gains are offset by losses of acquirers and of stakeholders. See Jacoby (2007: note 31).

Early Days in Japan

Until the 1980s, US public-employee pension funds had strict rules limiting their overseas investments. But the limits were relaxed after the stock market crash of 1987. CalPERS was one of the first to invest heavily overseas. It made an initial purchase of foreign equities in 1988 and quickly ramped up after that. By 1991, 12 percent of its equity portfolio was in foreign stock and this doubled to 24 percent in 2000. Japan was an important investment target for CalPERS (CalPERS, various years).

CalPERS' early days in Japan were rocky. It relied heavily on services provided by Nomura and other local agents but was shocked when, in 1991, Nomura was swept up in a trading scandal. In response, CalPERS suspended relationships with Nomura Securities in Japan and wrote to the Minister of Finance, the late Ryutaro Hashimoto, asking for an investigation of trading practices. In 1993, CalPERS demanded that Nomura and Daiwa Securities appoint outside directors to their boards and warned that it might seek the same from other Japanese companies (Jiji Press 1991; Stern 1991: 16; Wall Street Journal 1991; Business Week 1993).

Proxies

Proxy issues in Japan typically include approval of the income allocation proposal (which includes dividends, directors' bonuses, and allocations to reserve accounts and retained earnings); director elections and statutory auditor elections; directors' retirement bonuses; and amendments to the articles of incorporation (which can include everything from entering a new business to adoption of a holding company structure). As in the United States, an issue of concern to CalPERS in Japan had to do with corporate boards: the paucity of independent directors and the large number of directors, such that a Japanese board with thirty or more members was not unusual. CalPERS routinely would vote its proxies against internal directors and against proposals to expand board size. Another concern was executive entrenchment. CalPERS opposed the issuance of new equity if it thought this was being done to defend against takeovers. In 1993, Japan amended the commercial code to require companies to have at least one independent statutory auditor. After this, CalPERS made it a policy of voting against auditors who were judged to lack independence, such as former company executives. CalPERS also opposed the re-appointment of directors at companies whose corporate governance it deemed unsatisfactory (Sterngold 1993; Business Wire 1994; IRRC 2001b: 1).

Dividend levels were another matter of concern. Japanese companies held more of their assets in cash than their US counterparts partly to accommodate relatively larger bank loans. In spite of these cash hoards, dividends were meager and based on par value rather than earnings. CalPERS wanted Japanese companies to return more cash to shareholders either through dividends or stock repurchases. But it knew that this was a sensitive issue that could make CalPERS look greedy or indifferent to Japanese financial norms. Therefore, CalPERS was careful to appear even-handed. It publicized the fact that, although it had voted proxies against inadequate dividends and was concerned about their generally low levels, it had also voted against *excessive* dividends being paid by some unprofitable companies such as Nissan (Kester 1991; Financial Times 1992; Sterngold 1994; Milhaupt and West 2004).

CalPERS announced in 1993 that it had selected Britain and Japan as targets for a campaign to improve overseas corporate governance. The following year it issued global proxy voting guidelines that emphasized director accountability to shareholders; transparency of corporate information; shareholder-friendly distribution of proxy materials; and publication of final proxy tallies. The concern about proxy distribution reflected a problem that occurred in Japan during the previous proxy season, when CalPERS' "no" votes against more than 200 Japanese companies went unrecorded. Sumitomo Trust said that CalPERS' completed proxies were received after the deadline, although the same glitch seems to have affected other US institutional investors, a fact that CalPERS deemed "very disturbing" (Economist 1993; Nikkei 1993; Sterngold 1993; on CalPERS' guidelines governing proxy voting, see CalPERS 2001).

Proxy voting is a noisy signal. A vote against the income allocation proposal is subject to multiple interpretations that are based on knowing the identities of voters and their specific concerns. Yet CalPERS did not publicize its individual proxy votes nor did it publish a "target list" and mount its own shareholder resolutions, as in the United States. Moreover, because Japan has no legal provisions for ownership disclosure, companies could not always identify the beneficial owners casting negative votes. However, CalPERS sometimes sent letters to company management before or after a vote to explain its actions.[5]

Proxy voting was not an effectual way of inducing change. Rarely did antimanagement votes exceed 30 percent of the total and, even then,

[5] Interviews in Tokyo with Marc Goldstein, March 19 2005; Ariyoshi Okumura, March 15 2005; Kuny Kobayaschi, March 17 2005; and Raita Sakai, President, Multilateral Investment Dev. Corp., March 18 2005. Interview with Dr. William D. Crist, Former President of CalPERS and Chairman of the Board, 1992–2003, in Turlock, Cal., February 2005.

companies rarely announced the outcome, despite CalPERS' requests that they do so. Although CalPERS sought larger payouts to shareholders, payouts actually declined during the 1990s. In addition, although CalPERS voted against insiders who were nominated to be independent auditors, the percentage of firms listing auditors whose outsider status was questionable rose between 1994 and 1996, from 11 to 20 percent (IRRC 2001*a*: 1; Ryder 2005).

Black Ships

During the 1980s the Keidanren, the peak business association for Japanese corporations, monitored US economic, legal, and social issues through its Council for Better Corporate Citizenship (CBCC). In 1989, the CBCC expanded its ambit to include monitoring of corporate governance issues in the United States, such as "the influence of public pension funds and other institutional investors." CBCC wanted to know how the funds made investment decisions, how they viewed the role of directors, and what were their expectations for Japanese companies, especially with regard to conflict between shareholders and other stakeholders. It led a study mission to the United States in 1993 seeking answers to these questions.[6]

That same year, CBCC invited Bill Crist to visit Tokyo and address the Keidanren. This was an historic event, widely reported in the Japanese media. Some likened Crist's visit to Admiral Perry's "black ships." In the ensuing years, the Keidanren would prove to be an agile and ardent opponent of changes promoted by CalPERS. Nevertheless, the group was interested in hearing what Crist had to say, although, says Crist, "they were interested in a very defensive way."[7]

Crist reminded his audience that CalPERS was not a speculative investor but instead was interested in long-term returns. He reassured the Keidanren that CalPERS' leaders "are not crusaders – we do not want to make over countries' corporate structure." Then, however, Crist laid out a detailed proposal for changing Japanese corporate governance that was based on the CalPERS program in the United States. Crist's "wish list" for Japan covered five areas:

1. Boards: More independent directors and smaller boards.
2. Payouts: Companies with limited growth prospects should return excess cash to shareholders.

---

[6] Council for Better Corporate Citizenship (1993); Crist interview.   [7] Ibid.

3. Financial disclosure: Adoption of consolidated accounting and independent auditors.
4. Investor relations: Create investor relations (IR) departments to relay financial information to investors.
5. Proxy voting: Spread out shareholder meetings and give investors more time to vote.

Crist cited no evidence that any of these changes would improve shareholder value, although he did mention the Wilshire Associates study showing a relationship between share price and CalPERS activism. With respect to Japan, he criticized the fact that stable domestic shareholders received deference from senior management while foreigners and other minority shareholders were given "only cursory consideration" (Crist 1993). After the speech, Crist and others visited companies in the Tokyo and Osaka regions. These and subsequent visits would be preceded by letters and phone calls requesting to see the company's president (*shacho*). But except in a few rare instances, the requests were declined. CalPERS would be told that the company only recognized registered shareholders and that it had no record of CalPERS' shareholder status. At best, the CalPERS officials met with a relatively insignificant managing director for overseas issues. Over time, however, Japanese corporations grew more receptive to these visits. By the late 1990s, IR departments were becoming ubiquitous. Companies even began to send their own delegations to Sacramento to meet with CalPERS officials, some on a regular basis.[8]

The meetings were uncomfortable because they included touchy topics such as board structure and return of cash to shareholders. Starting in the mid-1990s, CalPERS intentionally shifted its discussions to general principles of corporate governance rather than a company's performance, what one participant described as "policy-oriented" as opposed to "financial-oriented" issues. Crist would explain that CalPERS was a long-term shareholder and that companies which produced long-term returns for their shareholders would end up rewarding other stakeholders. Layoffs, says Crist, were never on the table: "I hate to see that sort of Wall Street psychology that layoffs are a good thing. And especially in Japan, where the labor market is not liquid and it is hard for people to find new jobs."[9]

CalPERS was trying to build a different image – less adversarial and more discreet – than it had in the United States or Europe. Its company visits were never publicized nor did it publish target lists or sponsor shareholder

---

[8] Learmount (2002); Sakai, Crist and Kobayaschi interviews.
[9] Viner in Sterngold (1993); Sakai and Crist interviews.

proposals. CalPERS selected companies to visit based on stock performance and calculations of EVA. But EVA can rise merely as a result of deferring profitable investments or shedding assets. Evidence shows that companies using EVA as a performance metric are more likely to sell assets, delay investments, and buy back shares. By encouraging companies to target EVA, CalPERS gave a subtle nudge in favor of "shareholder value." (Fernandez 2002; Ahmadjian and Robbins 2005).

Local Partners

As CalPERS boosted its allocation for overseas equities, it redoubled efforts to internationalize its governance programs. It conducted an in-house study of how it could best bring the shareholder-primacy approach to overseas markets. The study saw substantial benefits to adopting shareholder activism overseas (this based again on the Wilshire Associates study) but predicted that an uphill battle would occur in Japan. In 1996, the CalPERS board voted to develop a new governance program focusing on Britain, France, Germany, and Japan. The program had four parts: specifying principles for each market; participation in local governance debates; outreach to local media, governments, and academics; and finding local partners. Local partners would give CalPERS legitimacy in markets hostile to foreign interference while helping to adapt its message to diverse national cultures (CalPERS 1996; Daily Yomiuri 1996).

Corporate Governance Forum

The entity that CalPERS initially partnered with in Japan was a small organization called the Corporate Governance Forum of Japan (JCGF). The JCGF was created in October 1994, one year after Crist's speech to the Keidanren. A key figure behind the JCGF was Ariyoshi Okumura, who ran the asset management division of the Industrial Bank of Japan. Okumura was familiar to CalPERS because he periodically made trips to Sacramento to solicit CalPERS' business in Japan. Another key figure was Takaaki Wakasugi, then a finance professor at the University of Tokyo. The JCGF's board was made up of academics and business leaders committed to reforming corporate governance in Japan, such as Yoshihiko Miyauchi, president of ORIX.

Wakasugi drafted the JCGF's corporate governance statement, a process that started in 1996 and ended in October 1997 with the publication of an interim set of principles. The 1997 document is a marvel of diplomacy. It consists of three parts: a philosophical introduction, principles to be implemented in the short term (next five years) and principles for the medium term (next ten years). The introduction acknowledges a stakeholder approach but puts shareholders in a special category above other stakeholders. It says that the board of directors' job is to maximize shareholder value and to represent the immediate interests of shareholders. On the other hand, the board is also supposed to coordinate stakeholder interests, provide information to stakeholders, and be accountable for its actions to all stakeholders but particularly to shareholders.

Beyond that, the principles say nothing more about stakeholders. The focus is on disclosure to shareholders and on monitoring. Regarding disclosure, the report urges that information be provided to shareholders in a timely fashion and on a quarterly basis, adjusted to global accounting rules, and facilitated by an upgrading of the investor relations function. It also calls for more dialogue at shareholders' meetings and separate meetings for major shareholders. Regarding monitoring, it urges the inclusion of independent directors (short term) until boards are comprised of a majority of independents (medium term). The principles call for a reduction in board size and separation of the CEO and chairman positions. Boards should include more than one independent auditor (short term) and an auditing committee comprised entirely of independent directors (medium term). The principles strongly resemble the ideas promulgated by CalPERS in Japan, and, as one scholar said, are "close in tone to that of an assertive-type classical model" of corporate governance (Inagami 2001).

Four months after publication of the JCGF document, CalPERS issued its own governance principles for Japan. The advantages of following on the JCGF's heels are obvious. Instead of being seen as an insensitive interloper, CalPERS could – and did – give the impression that it was merely endorsing indigenous ideas promulgated by Japan's own leaders. As the CalPERS principles stated, "The Corporate Governance Forum of Japan, a body consisting of representatives from Japanese corporations, institutional investors, and academia, has developed an interim report that promotes a sensible two-step approach to changing Japanese corporate governance." The CalPERS principles listed all of the short- and medium-term proposals contained in the JCGF report and noted, "CalPERS believes that Japanese corporations that adopt the JCGF's proposals sooner rather than later will best be able to attract investor capital and contend with global competitors." However, the CalPERS principles did not include any of the JCGF language concerning stakeholders. Included, however, were two provisions not mentioned by the JCGF: an endorsement of stock option plans for directors and executives, and reduction of "unproductive" cross-shareholding. CalPERS sent Japanese translations of its principles to all major interest groups in Japan, including the Liberal Democratic Party (LDP), the Keidanren, and the Nikkeiren, the employers' federation. Coming at a time when Japan was being rocked by bankruptcies of major banks and brokerages, the principles received wide press coverage (Jiji Press 1998; CalPERS 1998*a*, 1998*b*).

Crist introduced JCGF to other institutional investors through the International Corporate Governance Network (ICGN). The ICGN's origins go back to the early 1990s, when Crist, Robert Monks, and other shareholder activists discussed the creation of an international analogue to the CII, one that would coordinate and legitimate activities of institutional investors around the world. Crist and other institutional heavyweights met at the CII in 1994 to form an international association. The ICGN officially was established in 1995 at a conference attended by delegates from the AFL-CIO, the Association of British Insurers, the CII, the National Association of Pension Funds (United Kingdom), and various state and local public pension funds. CalPERS envisioned the ICGN as a "clearinghouse for local market standards of conduct and governance procedures. It could also be a conduit for cross-border shareholder initiatives." Concerned about the ICGN's lack of Asian involvement, Crist recommended that the JCGF be permitted to affiliate, which occurred around 1996. Later, Ariyoshi Okumura of the JCGF was elected to the ICGN's board, the first board member from Asia.[10]

The ICGN's membership was broad, including not only pension funds but also union representatives and financial companies. When it issued its own governance principles in 1999, they endorsed shareholder value as the corporation's "overriding objective," but followed the OECD's principles in calling for cooperation between corporations and stakeholders. ICGN recommended employee participation to "align shareholder and stakeholder interests." This was more pluralistic than anything previously published by CalPERS. While CalPERS incorporated the ICGN language in its own Global Principles, it omitted any mention of stakeholders in any of its country-specific guidelines (ICGN 1999).

The JCGF, the TSE, and the Pension Fund Association of Japan hosted the annual ICGN conference in Tokyo in July 2001. It was a major media event and, according to Okumura, was a "timely kick to deliver a positive

[10] ICGN (1999); Koppes memo to CalPERS Board, August 1995, quoted in Kissane (1997); Okumura and Crist interviews.

message to the Japanese corporate executives who were still somewhat suspicious of corporate governance concepts imported from abroad." Over 400 attendees listened to ORIX's Yoshihiko Miyauchi call for a corporate rating system to improve governance in Japan. Awards were handed out to Sir Adrian Cadbury and Ira Millstein.

In charge of the ICGN Tokyo conference was Nobuo Tateishi, CEO of Omron. Although Tateishi had become a board member of the JCGF, he was also active in the Nikkeiren and Keidanren. His views on corporate governance were more traditional than those of the JCGF or CalPERS, as reflected in the 1998 report issued by a Nikkeiren special committee that he chaired. The report presented the mainstream managerial view in Japan that, while transparency in reporting to shareholders was desirable, "it would be rather imprudent to think that British or American style corporate governance is the global standard." The goal of governance change in Japan should be "not to negate everything Japanese but to preserve those basic features of Japanese management which are laudable," presumably including insider boards and a stakeholder orientation.[11]

Perhaps Tateishi was the person responsible for inviting Hiroshi Okuda to give the keynote address at the ICGN conference. Okuda was then chairman of Toyota and of the Nikkeiren. His speech was a polite rebuke of the assertive shareholder-primacy model that CalPERS was promoting in Japan. Okuda stressed the social dimension of corporate activity in Japan. Any approach to corporate governance that failed to take this into account, he said, "could cause major problems." The commitment of Japanese companies to stakeholders, he said, "is in our DNA." While acknowledging the importance of holding managers accountable, Okuda said that this had to come from "different perspectives," including banks and enterprise unions, and not only from shareholders. As for shareholders, who were then urging Toyota to hand over more of its cash, Okuda said, "We prefer to aggressively promote R&D. We aren't ignoring ROE but we must balance it with R&D."[12]

Bill Crist was dumbfounded to hear Okuda express "almost identical" words to those expressed by the Keidanren in 1993. The speech marked the beginning of the end of CalPERS' hopes that the JCGF would be a vehicle for governance change in Japan. Crist believes that the Keidanren had decided to use the Tokyo conference to publicize its views through

---

[11] Nikkeiren International Special Committee report (1998), quoted in Inagami (2001: 229); see also IRRC (2001*b*).

[12] *The $10 Trillion Question*, http://www.irmag.com/newsarticle.asp?articleID = 1461; Benes (2001*b*); Gourevitch and Shinn (2005).

Tateishi, who Crist calls "Mr. Inside/Mr. Outside" and a likely "mole [who] keeps an eye on things" for the Keidanren. At the time of the conference, the Keidanren was backing a Diet bill to limit director liability and to quash rules facilitating appointment of independent directors.[13]

Another theory of Crist's is that the Keidanren backed the JCGF in its early years as a foil against foreign pressure but that the JCGF fell out of favor because it had failed to stop "this new bunch of crazy Japanese guys at the Pension Fund Association." Whatever the explanation, the fact is that CalPERS' alliance with the JCGF was yielding little fruit. The JCGF, said Crist, was "very big on having meetings and putting out publications" but it was "useless" as an instrument of transformation. Who, then, would help CalPERS bring change to Japan? Perhaps it would be those "crazy guys" at the Pension Fund Association.[14]

Pension Fund Association

The Japanese pension fund system includes a first tier of old-age insurance and a second tier of employer-provided pension plans (defined-benefit, as well as some defined-contribution plans since 2001). One large quasi-public fund is the Japan Pension Fund Association (PFA), which was established by the Ministry of Health and Welfare in 1967 to pay benefits to employees who had left corporate plans prior to vesting or whose corporate plans had been terminated. The PFA is an umbrella for over a thousand corporate plans and has assets of around $100 billion.

The PFA was lost in obscurity for most of its history. Its investments were in the hands of asset managers who rarely challenged company managements. But the PFA began to change in the late 1990s as its unfunded liabilities rose and new leaders took over. It published a white paper on proxy voting in 1999 that called for an end to the taboo of voting against management at shareholder meetings. The following year a Health and Welfare advisory commission headed by Takaaki Wakasugi recommended that public pension funds like the PFA hold their asset managers to fiduciary standards including active proxy voting and promotion of shareholder value.[15]

---

[13] Crist interview; Benes (2001*b*); Gourevitch and Shinn (2005); Suzuki (2005). On the Keidanren's position on independent directors and the "company with committees" law which came into effect in 2003, see Chapter 2.

[14] Crist interview.

[15] IRRC (2002); Wakasugi (2003). Wakasugi further recommended that the Government Pension Investment Fund (GPIF) be required to follow similar principles when investing its

The person in charge of pensions at the Health and Welfare ministry, Tomomi Yano, became managing director of the PFA around the time of Wakasugi's report. Yano well knew the dire situation faced by Japan's pension funds. Due to slow population growth, the funds were projected to show widening deficits as the ratio of retired to active citizens steadily crept up. Japan's stock-market woes also contributed to the problem. The PFA, for example, had a minus 10 percent return in 2001, its first loss ever. Since then it has posted negative returns in several other years (Amyx 2004; Katsumata 2004; McClellan 2004).

Knowing that he would be running the PFA for only a few years, Yano quickly created an aggressive program to raise the PFA's portfolio returns through shareholder activism. Yano's model for transforming the PFA was CalPERS. The two funds have cooperated in various ways over the years. PFA representatives have visited Sacramento repeatedly and there have also been meetings in Japan. When asked in 2003 if the PFA would become like CalPERS, Yano responded, "We may turn out to be a Don Quixote, but as a representative of pension funds in Japan we have no choice but to be an active shareholder [like CalPERS]."[16]

Yano's first step was to introduce proxy voting guidelines for the PFA's asset managers in 2001. In keeping with Wakasugi's report, the guidelines required the PFA's asset managers to designate staff responsible for proxy voting, vote according to principles – favoring shareholders over management if need be – and to report results back to the PFA. In 2002, Yano started to internally manage some of the PFA's domestic investments and he initiated proxy voting on its passively-invested portfolio.[17]

The most dramatic change came in 2003, when the PFA published its proxy principles. Receiving the most attention was the PFA's plan to vote

$1.4 trillion in assets. However, to avoid charges of political interference in business, the decision was made to leave proxy voting in the hands of the GPIF's asset managers with the proviso that the managers were to "maximize long-term shareholder value." Wakasugi's enthusiasm for shareholder primacy as a remedy for pension problems resurfaced in a May 2008 report of a panel of academic economists appointed by the Prime Minister. It recommended that GPIF be split up into smaller funds several of which should be assigned to foreign investment managers; urged removal of takeover defenses so as to attract foreign capital; and asked that the TSE take the lead on this, an idea that Tomomi Yano of the PFA had been pushing for several years (see main text, infra). The proposal was supported by the powerful Ministry of Economy, Trade, and Industry (METI), which hoped that the GPIF would serve as a battering ram, just as the Health and Welfare Ministry wanted the same from the PFA. However, some in government were concerned about excessive risk-taking by public pension funds and skeptical that takeovers would uncover hidden inefficiencies. *Japan Times*, May 24 2008; *Nikkei Weekly*, June 16 2008. Yano retired from the PFA later in 2008.

[16] Crist interview; interview with Tomomi Yano in Tokyo, March 16 2005; Nikkei (2003c).
[17] IRRC (2002): Benes (2001a); Tomomi Yano, "Corporate Governance Activities of Pension Fund Association," at http://www.usajapan.org/pdf/tyano_1104.ppt; Yano interview.

against renomination of, and retirement payments for, directors of companies that had not paid dividends for three years or that had losses for the previous five years.[18] The PFA developed its principles after culling ideas from Anglo-American pension funds such as CalPERS, TIAA-CREF, and Hermes (CalPERS' partner in the United Kingdom) The PFA said that it would vote proxies against companies whose boards had more than twenty people; who failed to separate the CEO and chairman positions; and who failed to hire independent statutory auditors and to nominate independents for at least one-third of the board seats. The PFA met with asset managers and told them to follow its principles (Pensions & Investments 2003; Nikkei 2003c, 2003d).

In light of proxy voting's ambiguous effects in the United States, the PFA's emphasis seems a bit surprising. But proxy voting is partly a means to the larger end of promoting a shareholder-primacy ethos. Yano envisioned the creation of a broad coalition of institutional investors in Japan. In the meantime, the PFA was setting an example by voting against over 40 percent of all management proposals, including votes against nonindependent directors and paying them bonuses. While this was a high rate of antimanagement voting as compared to other Japanese pension funds, it was relatively modest as compared to US funds like CalPERS and TIAA-CREF. In 2004, US pension funds in Japan voted against director appointments at a 93 percent rate versus 49 percent for the PFA, leading one to suspect that the PFA's bite might be milder than its bark.[19]

After 2003, Yano took a page out of CalPERS' book and held a greater number of private discussions with under-performing and under-paying firms. Yano said that this kind of pressure got better results than proxies, yet Yano lamented the fact that CalPERS had better access to CEOs of Japanese companies than did the PFA.[20]

Yano relished confrontation with complacent managers and the ensuing publicity. When the proxy battle between corporate raider Yoshiaki Murakami and Tokyo Style heated up, Yano supported Murakami's unsuccessful bid to have Tokyo Style distribute to shareholders its hoard of nearly $1 billion in cash and securities. Yano publicly excoriated one of PFA's asset management companies for opposing Murakami.[21]

---

[18] The PFA's current criterion is to oppose director renomination at firms with return on equity of less than 8 percent for three years.

[19] Yano interview; Pensions & Investments (2003); IRRC, unpublished voting data, June 2004, courtesy of Kuny Kobayaschi.

[20] Reuters Asia (2002); Yano interview.

[21] Nikkei (2002b). In 2007 Murakami was given a two-year prison sentence for insider trading (New York Times, July 20 2007: 20).

It made sense that the PFA became CalPERS' favorite partner in Japan. Both were public pension funds; both were aggressive with a flair for publicity. Crist called Yano "a good friend" and said that Yano was willing to shake things up in a way that the JCGF never could because the PFA was outside the business system. After leaving CalPERS, Crist founded an organization called the Pacific Pension Institute, which held conferences for institutional investors from Asia and the United States. At one such conference, Ted White, then in charge of CalPERS' corporate governance program, explained the fund's relationship with the PFA. CalPERS was best suited to a "macro" approach to governance change in Japan, one that involved "exerting pressure on regulatory or legislative bodies. This included guidelines for best practice." But the "micro" approach, which was company by company, was better carried out by local entities like the PFA. In the micro area, CalPERS preferred to be "a facilitator where it can assist and mobilize Japanese investors to take the lead role in enacting change." Whereas CalPERS had a focus list in the United States, it was difficult for CalPERS to be publicly critical of individual Japanese companies. But, said White, "this type of tool can readily be mimicked by foreign players such as the PFA." While CalPERS did not publicize its proxy votes for Japanese companies, the PFA was not shy to do so. Even the kind of "macro" change that CalPERS sought, such as urging more dispersed shareholder meetings, might better come from a group like the PFA in the form of a domestic-led initiative, said White.[22]

CalPERS has also established a relationship with *Chikyoren*, the giant pension fund for local government employees. *Chikyoren* is part of the Council of Public Institutional Investors that was launched in 2002 as a way for public pension funds to discuss issues of mutual interest, including governance change. Members include the PFA, the Government Pension Investment Fund, and several others. Thus far, however, the Council has resisted requests that members coordinate their proxy votes, as CalPERS does with CII. CalPERS has also reached out to Japan's corporate pension funds. Heretofore, most corporate pension plans have ceded authority to asset managers with little direct involvement. The asset managers often were complacent because of their dual role of managing pension fund assets and selling products to the companies in which they invest, as in the United States. Recently, however, some asset managers have become more assertive.[23]

[22] Crist and Okumura interviews; White (2003).
[23] Pensions & Investments (2002); Nikkei (2003c, 2004a); Crist interview; Borrell (2003: 14); Taylor (2006); Yano interview.

Thus it may turn out that the most effective proponents of governance change in Japan will be, as in the United States, domestic institutional investors, especially public pension funds. How present trends unfold will depend on how many funds imitate Yano's aggressive stance and whether his successor at the PFA will be cut from the same cloth. One must be careful, however, not to exaggerate Yano's influence. For example, the TSE had a corporate governance advisory committee that included Yano, academics, consultants, and Keidanren representatives. Yano wanted the TSE to create a code of best governance practice, including independent boards and reduced takeover barriers, that would be attached to listing requirements. But due to resistance from the corporate community, the idea went nowhere. At the microlevel, the PFA has not had many notable successes, perhaps because the balance of power at many Japanese companies remains in the hands of management-friendly investors. Also, the PFA is hamstrung by social norms regarding appropriate behavior. Noting that CalPERS has on numerous occasions proposed a CEO dismissal, Yano said, "PFA cannot do such a thing yet, though we want to. If we do, we will be criticized in the Japanese society. We cannot be such an activist as CalPERS."[24]

Withdrawal

CalPERS' visibility in Japan has declined markedly since 2002: no new governance initiatives, few visits by CalPERS officials, and, until recently, near-invisibility in the Japanese media and business forums. The reasons for the withdrawal are complex, having to do with internal changes at CalPERS, diminishing returns on activism, and new investment strategies.

One internal factor is the diversification of CalPERS' overseas portfolio. Japan holdings fell from 45 percent of the portfolio in 1993 to 20 percent in 2005. Also, Bill Crist's retirement from the board was significant in that Crist had a stronger commitment to Japan than his successor, Sean Harrigan, a former official of the retail workers' union. Harrigan was interested in domestic policy issues, especially those in which shareholder activism and labor-movement interests coincide. His successor, Rob Fechner, has as yet shown little interest in overseas investments.[25]

[24] Kobayaschi interview; Whitten (2003).

[25] Pensions & Investments (2000); Sakai and Crist interviews; CalPERS, "Written Testimony of Sean Harrigan to the U.S. Senate Commerce Committee," May 20 2003; *Los Angeles Times* (2004); CalPERS data as of October 31 2005, courtesy of Mary Cottrill.

By 2003, CalPERS faced diminishing returns to its "macro" approach of promoting the shareholder-primacy model. Ten years after Crist made his speech to the Keidanren, the governance principles he espoused had become widely known in Japan. Several had been adopted into the Commercial Code, such as rules facilitating share buybacks (1994, 1997, 1998), issuance of stock options (2001), and the "company with committees" system (2003). The latter, known in Japan as the "American system," gives companies the choice of doing away with statutory auditors if they appoint a majority of outside directors on three key board committees and if the board eschews operational responsibilities (see Chapter 2). At the "micro" level of firm-by-firm monitoring, CalPERS experienced some of the same problems that had cropped up in the United States. It rarely held more than one percent of a company's stock and, even when it did, it faced a free-rider problem in that other investors were happy to have CalPERS incur the cost of active shareholding while they reaped any benefit. As the head of international corporate governance for TIAA-CREF said, "Why bother to expend any effort on behalf of monitoring portfolio companies, when someone else will do it for you without cost to yourself?" (Hashimoto 2002; Clearfield 2005).

Robert Monks (2003) and Michael Porter (1994) had foreseen this problem years earlier. Monks understood that public pension funds were political entities whose boards could not or would not maintain pressure on individual companies for the long term. Both Monks and Porter proposed as a solution that institutional investors increase the size of their stakes and pool their enlarged holdings in "relational" or "turnaround" funds that target underperforming companies. Since 2000, CalPERS has invested $12 billion with Relational Investors and similar funds in the United States and Europe. Relational investing mitigates the free-rider problem and its usually substantial returns help CalPERS to "beat the index." This, in turn, reduces the incentive to pursue macrogovernance change, which may explain why CalPERS' public activism has declined as its stake in these funds has grown. It has increasingly been the hedge funds, rather than CalPERS itself, which have applied direct pressure to companies.

The first relational investments in Japan came in 2002, when CalPERS invested $200 million (a 20% stake) in Sparx Value Creation Fund. Since then it has invested several hundred million more with Sparx.[26] Sparx was started by Shuhei Abe, a former Nomura analyst and admirer of

[26] CalPERS Press Release, "CalPERS Turns Up Corporate Governance Heat," November 15 2001; *Financial Times* (2002); Nikkei (2002).

Warren Buffett. Abe and his analysts take large stakes in undervalued mid-sized companies and then "influence" their managements to restructure operations and raise shareholder returns. According to Abe, "Many Japanese CEOs don't know why they have to improve their return on equity because they have no sense of ownership and no sense of being part of the market."[27]

Before CalPERS invested with Abe it vetted him to make sure that he wasn't "a raider like Murakami." As compared to Murakami, who was insensitive to social norms and prone to making outrageous public statements, Abe is relatively low key, although he is consistently contemptuous of Japanese CEOs. While the Sparx fund has not pursued hostile takeovers, its approach of pressuring companies to return cash to shareholders is not very different from what Murakami attempted at Tokyo Style. Abe's time horizon is shaped by the fact that the fund will exist for ten years. Of $365 million invested in one of his funds, $200 million was distributed to the partners in the first two years. In at least one case, Sparx bought shares in a small company, Miyairi Valve, and sold all of them six months later. One observer says that Sparx is "using the corporate governance idea but not following it. . . . it's rather hard to call them long-term investors." Crist defends the Sparx approach, saying that "nothing is pure" and that the bulk of CalPERS' investments in Japan remain long-term, passive holdings.[28]

Another relational outfit in which CalPERS invests is Taiyo Pacific Partners, which is managed by two *gaijin* (non-Japanese). One is Wilbur L. Ross, a New York-based billionaire who helped reorganize Continental Airlines in the 1980s and more recently has been a private equity investor in mature, unionized US industries such as coal, steel, textiles, and auto parts. The other is Brian Heywood, a onetime missionary who later worked for Citibank in Japan. CalPERS signed a deal with Taiyo in 2003 and invested $200 million, a 20 percent stake. Taiyo's approach is similar to Sparx's. It wants to avoid Murakami-like controversy, while invoking the possibility of takeovers to induce managers to raise shareholder payouts. The fear of hostile takeovers is genuine. A recent survey found that executives at 70 percent of Japanese companies were concerned about them. Taiyo tries to persuade companies that it can help them avoid the clutches of raiders like Steel Partners by working cooperatively to boost payouts. Agreeing to partner with Taiyo doesn't mean that a company has accepted

---

[27] Nikkei (2003*a*); CalPERS (2004); "SPARX Founder Shuhei Abe on 'Why He's Bullish On Corporate Japan'' October 1 2003, Japan Society, New York at http://www.japansociety.org/corporate/event_corp_note.cfm?id_note = 191080341; DiBasio (2004).
[28] Interviews with Crist, Sakai and Kobayaschi.

shareholder-primacy principles, however. Says Heywood, "In general the mindset is not so much, 'I've been converted to governance,' but 'I'm afraid of being taken over so I've got religion.' "[29]

Once Taiyo takes a stake in a company, it trims "bloated" balance sheets by selling unrelated assets and returning cash to shareholders. The fund's major success story is an auto-parts firm called Nifco. Nifco had diversified into a variety of unrelated businesses such as ballpoint pens, Australian real estate, and media properties (including *The Japan Times*). Taiyo is helping Nifco get ride of noncore assets that do not meet a hurdle rate of return. At Maezawa Kasei, maker of plumbing fixtures, Taiyo zeroed in on the firm's cash hoard. Said Heywood, "They had a lot of cash sitting there doing nothing. We said, 'Lots of cash makes you a target.' "[30] The firm has since raised its dividends. At Nifco, Taiyo recommended that the company send out press releases in English to explain that the divestments were not made willy-nilly but were driven by a focus strategy. Taiyo told Maezawa Kasei to establish ties to investment analysts and make sure that they covered the relatively obscure company. Many of these moves were intended to attract foreign investors, the one group that has consistently been buying Japanese equities in recent years. While Taiyo says it is not seeking a quick buck, its time horizon is far from the long term touted by CalPERS. Ross' biggest deal in Japan came in 2003, right before Taiyo was formed. Ross sold his shares in Kansai Sawayaka Bank for double his initial investment, having held the shares for a little over two years. Ross bristles at the "vulture fund" label and prefers to describe Taiyo as a "phoenix" (JETRO 2002; New York Times 2003*b*; Financial Times 2004; Nikkei 2004*b*).

While the majority of CalPERS' Japanese investments are passive, its interest in securing good returns on alternative investments has inevitably skewed CalPERS' focus more to the short-term horizons of hedge and private equity funds. Over 10 percent of its Japan assets are in these vehicles. Ironically, the funds do not require firms in which they invest to adhere to the CalPERS governance principles. Neither are they seeking to affect economywide governance practice. This is of little concern to Heywood, who says, "We don't need to change the whole market."[31]

[29] Nikkei (2004*b*); *Financial Times* (2004); see also Milhaupt (2005).
[30] Heywood quoted in Wiseman (2004).
[31] *New York Times* (2003*a*); *Financial Times* (2004); Joncarlo Mark to author, December 27 2005. Other public pension funds followed CalPERS' lead and boosted their target allocations for alternative investments such as private equity, hedge funds, and real estate: *Business Week* (2006).

The Consequences of CalPERS

CalPERS sedulously sought to change Japanese law and public opinion. It regularly appeared in the media while working closely with domestic norm entrepreneurs such as the JCGF and the PFA and indirectly with government ministries such as METI and MHLW. The results of its labors were – at least in part – the various commercial code revisions consistent with positions originally espoused by CalPERS. However, it is difficult to assess the extent to which CalPERS was a catalyst for legal reforms or whether government officials used pressure from CalPERS as a justification to adopt them, an old tactic in Japan known as *gaiatsu*. Some officials saw governance change as a fiscally neutral way to jump-start the Japanese economy; others, such as the economists working at METI, were – and are – keen to achieve the efficiency gains they attribute to shareholder primacy. The Ministry of Foreign Affairs hopes that commercial code changes will reduce economic friction between the United States and Japan. The US government has repeatedly pressured Japan to Americanize its governance system, starting in 1989 with the Structural Impediments Initiative (SII) talks, which have continued since then. The SII's most recent incarnation was the Bush administration's "Investment Initiative," whose objective is to facilitate foreign direct investment in Japan, including foreign acquisitions (State Department 2006).

However, CalPERS' influence at the macrolevel was curtailed by business groups like the Keidanren, by skeptics in government, and by organized labor. The Keidanren tried to preserve internal boards, to maintain crossholdings as barriers to hostile acquisitions, and to keep TSE listing standards free of mandatory criteria. It worked to ensure that most of the commercial code revisions were permissive rather than mandatory. Also, the revisions lacked enforcement mechanisms, leaving companies free to stick with the status quo or to adopt changes that met the letter but not the spirit of the law by, for example, claiming quasi-insiders as independent directors and statutory auditors (Gilson and Milhaupt 2005; Buchanan and Deakin 2008 and Chapter 2). The Nippon Keidanren (as it has now become) hasn't been opposed to all changes. In recent years, it has urged Japanese companies to improve auditing, control, and disclosure practices. As noted, these changes are relatively easy to graft onto existing governance structures.[32]

---

[32] Dore (2000); Crist interview; Patrick (2004); Nippon Keidanren (2001). The Keidanren has accepted proposals that benefit incumbent managers, however, such as stock options.

CalPERS has more sway in the United States, where it need not worry about an "ugly American" image and so is able to use a panoply of influence tactics. It also has more power in emerging nations that depend heavily on foreign capital. CalPERS carefully rates emerging nations on factors such as corporate governance, political stability, and openness. It consistently reminds countries – and their leaders – that adherence to international governance standards will make them more attractive to international investors. CalPERS repeatedly advanced this argument in Japan. The difference, however, is that while Japan welcomes foreign investors, it hardly suffers from capital scarcity.[33]

At the microlevel CalPERS has greater leeway to exert pressure in Japan, although its concerns here have more to do with boosting shareholder returns than with specific governance practices. In fact, studies show an association between foreign ownership of Japanese companies and subsequent restructuring via asset divestments, as is true of US companies targeted by CalPERS. Foreign ownership of Japanese companies also is associated with a propensity to downsize.[34]

To what extent have Japanese companies adopted the CalPERS governance model? It helps to break the model down into four parts: disclosure and transparency; boards and directors; shareholder rights and minority protection; and control (absence of takeover barriers). Of the four, by far the most prevalent part is disclosure, which includes accounting standards, publishing reports and disseminating information, meeting with analysts, creating IR departments, and so forth. This is also the area where statutory reforms – such as consolidated accounting, fair-value accounting, and disclosure of takeover defenses and internal controls – have become mandatory instead of permissive. The 2006 law known as J-SOX, passed in the wake of the Horie and Murakami scandals, requires public companies to strengthen internal controls and disclosure (Nakata and Takehiro 2001; Miyajima 2007).

Less prevalent have been changes in boards and directors. In 2003, the average number of outside board members in the Nikkei 225 companies

---

[33] Hebb and Wojcik (2003). In 1993, Crist had predicted that Japanese corporations would pay more attention to shareholder value as their need for capital "forces them to woo foreign sources of capital" (Crist 1993). CalPERS made a similar argument when it released its 1998 Japan principles: CalPERS (1998b).

[34] Miyajima (2007); Ahmadjian and Robbins (2005: 451); Coffee (2002). A recent study finds that domestic financial ownership is positively associated with Japanese downsizing, which is consistent with the main-bank monitoring hypothesis, but that foreign ownership has no significant effect on layoffs, hiring, or pay cuts, contrary to the aforementioned studies: Abe and Shimizutani (2005).

was one; it was less than one for the 1,500 companies on the TSE's first section. These numbers reflected the fact that nearly two-thirds of publicly-traded companies had no independent directors. An investor group in 2008 lamented the fact that most Japanese firms still lack independent directors. Board size has declined since 1990, from an average of seventeen to fifteen, although some of this reflects a cosmetic change associated with adoption of the executive officer system, which formalizes the preexisting division of the board between a core group that makes strategic decisions (the *Jomukai*) and a larger group that discusses (and often rubber stamps) them. The company with committees system is not catching on, with successively fewer companies adopting it each year (see Chapter 2). However, since 2000, stock options have become more popular, with 35 percent of large Japanese companies reporting their use, especially in large firms with high foreign ownership. As a proportion of CEO pay, however, options and related types of equity compensation are far less important than in the United States (Seki 2003; Hayakawa 2004, and communication to author; Nikkei 2004*d*; Abe and Shimizutani 2007; Towers Perrin 2005: 6; 2006: 24; Miyajima 2007: Appendix 1; AGCA 2008).

Shareholder rights have strengthened since the late 1980s. Change *de jure* has been modest partly because Japanese law regarding shareholder rights has always been protective and in conformance with global standards. The big change has come in practice. There are more votes against management at shareholder meetings than in the past. Executives now are peppered with difficult and sometimes embarrassing questions. There are more share-holder derivative suits than before 1990, when there were hardly any. The number of companies holding shareholder meetings on the same day has fallen. In other respects, however, the pace has been glacial. Minority share-holders filing derivative lawsuits still find it difficult to obtain information and usually can win only if there are criminal charges involved. Shareholder meetings remain concentrated in the same period during June, if not on the same day. Few companies use electronic mail for meeting notifications or voting, although both are permissible. There are more foreign shareholders in attendance at meetings but less than 1 percent of large companies provide simultaneous English translation. In 2007, foreign shareholder activists failed to win majority support from other shareholders for a single one of several resolutions calling on firms to raise dividends. The press announced vote results with headlines such as "Foreigners Shut Out."[35]

[35] Kester (1991); West (2001); Utsumi (2001); Miyajima (2007); Givens (2007); Goldstein interview.

The fourth element in the CalPERS model was removing barriers to managerial entrenchment so that higher payout rates and a market for corporate control could flourish. Without doubt, dramatic and unprecedented hostile actions have occurred recently, including highly publicized bids to raise dividends in 2008 by Steel Partners at Bull-Dog Sauce and a shareholder fight by TCI to double dividends at J-Power. However, both efforts were thwarted by domestic shareholders and by the courts, as was the case with several other foreign activist interventions (Higashino 2004; Business Week 2004a; Tokyo Stock Exchange 2005; Jacoby 2005a: 73; Miyajima and Kuroki 2007; Chapters 2 and 3).

Just as cross-shareholding accelerated in the 1950s to stave off foreign takeovers, so today a new set of barriers is being erected. The government revised the commercial code to permit foreign firms to use their own stock (or a local subsidiary's) to acquire Japanese firms, effective May 2007. Concerned that Japanese companies are undervalued and lack adequate takeover defenses, the government included provisions for firms to issue special class shares, golden shares, and related poison pills, all of which are being used more heavily. Japanese companies are erecting defenses such as expanded cross-holding and issuance of new shares (Nikkei 2004c, 2005, 2006; Whittaker and Hayakawa 2007; Economist 2008; Chapters 2 and 3 in this volume).

It is also worth asking what the implications are of the CalPERS model for corporate performance in Japan. Miyajima recently examined the relationship between performance and different types of governance change in Japan. He found that disclosure was the only type significantly associated with stock-market returns (Tobin's q, the ratio of a company's market value to its asset value) and with accounting measures of performance (ROA, return on assets). Neither board structure nor shareholder rights show an association with performance.[36]

Miyajima also considers antitakeover practices in Japan, such as block holding by a parent corporation and cross-shareholding by banks and other corporations. He finds that the sole antitakeover measure that is negatively associated with performance is shareholding by banks, which has declined sharply in recent years. Similarly, in the United States and the United Kingdom, antitakeover measures do not have a consistent association with performance, contrary to the entrenchment thesis. Speaking

---

[36] Miyajima (2007: Table 4–10); Miwa and Ramseyer (2005). On another matter of concern to CalPERS – cross shareholding – the evidence shows a positive effect of concentrated ownership on profitability of Japanese companies: Gedajlovic and Shapiro (2002).

conservatively, we can say that efficiency gains from takeovers and from low barriers to their occurrence are unproven (Shleifer and Vishny 2003; Miyajima 2007: Table 4; Miyajima and Kuroki 2007).

In short, the most widely adopted governance reforms in Japan – concerning information and disclosure – are positively related to performance. Changes whose link to performance are weak or unproven – in board structure, shareholder rights, and takeover barriers – have been less extensive. Hence the Keidanren was not far off the mark when it insisted that the CalPERS principles were a poor fit to Japanese business practices.

Why, then, have foreign investors so doggedly pursued governance change in Japan? One explanation is *hubris*: investors watched what happened in the United States, where efforts to change corporate governance were followed by an equity boom, and thought that they could repeat these events in Japan and elsewhere. Believing that governance change had *caused* share prices to rise and economic growth to accelerate (and, by extension, that the absence of shareholder primacy had depressed stock prices and hindered economic growth in Japan) is an instance of *post hoc ergo propter hoc* reasoning.[37] Another answer is that investors suffered from *economic ethnocentrism*: to the extent that the CalPERS principles were valid in the United States, the assumption was made that they were equally valid in other economies. The problem, however, is that the average Japanese company is unlike its US counterpart with respect to factors that determine governance effectiveness, such as incentives (executives are lifers who are motivated by duty, reputation, and trust) and business strategy (in Japan strategy is relatively resource-based and relational) (Jacoby 2005a: chapter 2). The third explanation is that investors are *myopic*. Even professional managers at the helm of pension portfolios have short-term biases. What matters is not how to maximize the corporate pie tomorrow, an uncertain recipe at best, but how it is sliced today: more for current shareholders; less for bondholders, creditors, employees, customers, taxpayers, and future shareholders. That is, shareholder primacy is not about creating value but extracting it (Kaplan 1989; Benartzi and Thaler 1995; Jensen 2005; Jacoby 2005a; Jacoby 2008).

In short, governance change has been modest. Foreign investors remain critical of Japanese companies for resisting takeovers and for

---

[37] An alternative interpretation is that US economic growth was caused by fiscal policies, which stimulated markets and set off a speculative boom resulting in spiraling share prices. Corporate governance was orthogonal to growth, although it played a role in spurring the stock bubble. For evidence refuting the notion that Japan's stagnation was related to corporate governance, see Jacoby (2000) and Ramseyer and Miwa (2001).

"hoarding" cash. In May 2008, a White Paper was issued by the Asian Corporate Governance Association, a consortium of nearly seventy foreign institutional investors, including giants such as CalPERS, CalSTRS, Hermes, and Fidelity. Harking back to the 1990s, the White Paper blasted Japanese companies for mistreating foreign owners, erecting takeover defenses, and for hoarding cash instead of paying it to shareholders (AGCA 2008). *Tout ça change, tout c'est la même chose.*

However, although the structure of Japanese corporate governance is inertial, its distributional outcomes are changing. From 1999 to 2006, dividends and other shareholders payouts rose much more rapidly than labor payments (211% versus 11%), although shareholder payments started from a lower base. In other words, firms are cutting their labor costs by substituting part-time for regular employees and using a portion of the savings to raise shareholder payouts. Even so, foreign shareholders remain enormously dissatisfied and continue to demand more.[38]

The fact that CalPERS and its allies in Japan have not made more headway usually is explained as the result of resistance from entrenched and pampered executives, in particular those represented by Nippon Keidanren. This is the argument made by Yano and Crist as well as by foreign investors. The entrenchment argument is overstated in light of the relatively modest salary and perquisites associated with executive status in Japan, where CEO compensation is one-fourth of US levels (Mishel et al. 2005: Table 2.49). If anything, Japanese executives would, based on US experience, make out better under a shareholder-primacy approach, although there would be a risk that some might lose their positions after a takeover.[39] The other – and more important – explanation of modest change is the Demsetz–Lehn thesis that corporate governance is endogenous and that there is no one-best way of structuring it (Demsetz and Lehn 1985). Japanese corporations have adopted only those changes that are a good fit with their existing incentives and institutions, which is to say, those that have an unambiguous relationship to performance (Dore 2000; Fisman et al. 2005).

[38] *Nikkei Weekly,* June 16 2008.
[39] Recall that US executives opposed shareholder primacy until the early 1990s, when stock options and a bull market caused a shift in their orientation (see Jacoby 2005b). What makes such a shift less likely in Japan are two factors: first, Japanese shares remain concentrated in the hands of domestic investors who are reluctant to rock the boat; second, the options scandals in the United States have made domestic owners wary of claims from foreign investors that options are a panacea. If and when domestic institutional investors follow the lead taken by the PFA in the 2000s, the system might quickly change.

Conclusions

Institutional investors are an important mechanism for transmitting US governance principles to overseas markets. In Japan, CalPERS worked with other institutional investors and domestic norm entrepreneurs to promote shareholder primacy in corporate governance. CalPERS was most successful in affecting aspects of corporate governance with a clear relationship to performance, such as disclosure. It was less successful, but not without influence, in other areas.

CalPERS officials well understood, as should we, that corporate governance is grounded not only in efficiency considerations but also distributional politics. The manifest objective of the CalPERS program was to redesign governance institutions to improve performance; the latent intent was to reallocate corporate resources to current shareholders. When CalPERS' own power was insufficient, it sought alliances to bring about change. CalPERS chose to ignore evidence that its principles could not be verified according to its stated objective of bolstering long-term performance. One can surmise various reasons for this, including strong ideological support for the CalPERS principles from the wider investment community.

The CalPERS principles were not fixed in a vacuum but instead reflected the prevailing wisdom among US investors and financial economists. Agency theory views managers (agents) as prone to self-serving or irrational behavior at the expense of shareholders (principals). While any single shareholder may not be rational, dispersed ownership creates financial markets whose collective wisdom promotes efficiency when managers are incentivized to pursue shareholder interests. Reinforcing agency theory is a law-and-economics movement that seeks to reorient legal thinking to agency theory and related doctrines. The merger wave of the 1980s and the US bull market of the 1990s provided vindication for practices derived from agency theory; so too did the mediocre performance of shareholder-wary economies in continental Europe and Japan (Jensen and Meckling 1976; Jacoby 2000).

Economic ideas come and go; agency theory today is under assault by the new behavioral approach to economics and finance. The behavioral approach is grounded in empirical anomalies: between rational-choice predictions and actual behavior, and between theoretical explanations of how institutions operate and their actual performance. The presumption that financial markets are efficient and that shareholders are more rational than managers has been replaced by the hypothesis, consistent with empirical evidence, that financial markets are prone to mispricing and that shareholders often are less rational than managers. Hence behavioral finance offers justification for institutions held suspect by agency theory, ranging from insider boards and takeover defenses to government regulation. Another assault has come from team-production theory, which is based on the idea that the corporation is a cooperative endeavor whose members all have made firm-specific investments, not only shareholders. A few law-and-economics doyens recognize the challenges and have responded defensively.[40]

What is missing from contemporary discussions of corporate governance is the recognition that the shareholder–executive relationship is not the sole interdependency that organizations must balance. Also critical are relations between headquarters and subunits, and between the corporation and its employees, creditors, customers, suppliers, and regulators. The variety of relationships suggests the infeasibility of a single best way to structure corporate governance (Fligstein and Freeland 1995).

Agency theory, which treats shareholders as residual claimants, favors a distribution of rents that privileges shareholders; behavioral theory, while agnostic on distributional issues, is compatible with the notion that shareholders do not consistently promote the firm's best interests or even their own. Team-production theory suggests that the board's role is to allocate rents; no stakeholder has primacy in receiving them (Blair and Stout 1999). Mark Roe has a view closer to my own that emphasizes how politics – normative and distributional – drives corporate governance and law.[41]

The recent economic crisis has put a dent in claims that the Anglo-American financial system, which includes mechanisms for corporate governance, is superior to different systems, such as those found in Japan. Japanese banks, with lots of cash on hand (ironically cash that Western shareholders previously had demanded be paid to them) have swooped in and purchased various pieces of the Wall Street wreckage. At this time, nonfinancial companies like Toyota are weathering the crisis more successfully than their counterparts in the United States and the United Kingdom. Hence the future of national governance systems is unlikely to be the result of market forces selecting an optimal model.

[40] On this, see Korobkin and Ulen (2000); Shleifer (2000); Baker et al. (2007); Bebchuk and Fried (2004); and for a law and economics approach which is critical of the mainstream position, Blair and Stout (1999).

[41] Roe (2003); see also Fligstein (1990); Roy (1997); Gourevitch and Shinn (2005); Okazaki and Okuno-Fujiwara (1999). There is also an emerging neoclassical approach to governance and politics but it tends to see politics as an anti-market activity rather than a means by which markets are constituted. See Rajan and Zingales (2003).

Instead, the CalPERS story suggests that the evolution of corporate governance will be shaped by historical actors committed to contending definitions of the corporation's legal, social, and economic responsibilities. There is no one best way; there never was and never will be.

Bibliography

Abe, N. and Shimizutani, S. (2007). "Employment Policy and Corporate Governance: An Empirical Comparison of the Stakeholder and the Profit–Maximization Model." *Journal of Comparative Economics*, 35: 346–68.

AGCA (2008). *AGCA White Paper on Corporate Governance in Japan.* Hong Kong: Asian Corporate Governance Association.

Ahmadjian, C. (2000). "Changing Japanese Corporate Governance." In U. Schaede and W. Grimes (eds.) *Japan's Managed Globalization: Adapting to the 21st Century.* New York: M.E. Sharpe.

——and Robbins, G. (2005). "A Clash of Capitalisms: Foreign Ownership and Restructuring in 1990s Japan." *American Sociological Review*, 70: 451–71.

Amyx, J. (2004). *Japan's Financial Crisis: Institutional Rigidity and Reluctant Change.* Princeton: Princeton University Press.

Baker, M., Ruback, R. and Wurgler, J. (2007). "Behavioral Corporate Finance." In E. Eckbo (ed.), *Handbook of Corporate Finance: Empirical Corporate Finance*, Vol. 1. Amsterdam: Elsevier.

Bebchuk, L. and Fried, J. (2004). *Pay without Performance: The Unfulfilled Promise of Executive Compensation.* Cambridge, MA: Harvard University Press.

——Cohen, A. and Ferrell, A. (2004). "What Matters in Corporate Governance?" Harvard Law School John M. Olin Discussion Paper No. 491.

Benartzi, S. and Thaler, R. (1995). "Myopic Loss Aversion and the Equity Premium Puzzle." *Quarterly Journal of Economics*, 110: 73–92.

Benes, N. (2001a). "Japan's Coming Shareholder Revolution." *Asia Wall Street Journal*, February 14.

——(2001b). "The Keidanren Circles the Wagons." *Asian Wall Street Journal*, July 20–22.

Berry, K. (2004). "Battle for Better Corporate Governance Earns Cheers for Fund." *Los Angeles Business Journal*, May 10: 1.

Bhagat, S. and Black, B. (2002.) "The Non-Correlation between Board Independence and Long-Term Firm Performance." *Journal of Corporation Law*, 27: 231–73.

Blair, M. and Stout, L. (1999). "A Team Production Theory of Corporate Law." *Virginia Law Review*, 85: 247–328.

Borrell, J. (2003). "How to Play Chikoren." *Venture Capital Journal*, June 1.

Bryant, A. (1997). "The Search for the Perfect Corporate Board." *New York Times*, August 3: 1.

Buchanan, J. and Deakin, S. (2008). "Japan's Paradoxical Response to the New 'Global Standard' in Corporate Governance." *Zeitschrift für Japanisches Recht*, 13(26): 59–84.

Business Week (1993). "International Outlook: Japan." *Business Week*, January 18.

—— (2004*a*). "So 'Takeover' Does Translate." *Business Week*, February 9.

—— (2004*b*). "Meet the Friendly Corporate Raiders." *Business Week*, September 20.

—— (2006). "Hopped Up on Hedge Funds." *Business Week*, September 25.

Business Wire (1994). "CalPERS Announces Votes Regarding Japanese Companies." *Business Wire*, June 24.

CalPERS (1995). *Why Corporate Governance Today? A Policy Statement*. August.

—— (1996). "CalPERS Adopts International Corporate Governance Program." Press Release, March 18.

—— (1998*a*). *Japan Market Principles*. Sacramento, CA: CalPERS.

—— (1998*b*). "CalPERS Adopts Corporate Governance Practices for Japan." Press Release, March 18.

—— (1999). *Domestic Voting Principles*. Sacramento, CA: CalPERS.

—— (2001). *Global Proxy Voting Principles*. Sacramento, CA: CalPERS.

—— (2004*a*). *Hybrid Investments Monitoring Report. Relational Investors, Fourth Quarter, 2004*, at http://www.CalPERS.ca.gov/eip-docs/about/board-cal-agenda/agendas/invest/200503/item05-02.pdf.

—— (2004*b*). *CalPERS, Hybrid Investments Monitoring Report: Sparx Asset Management, Fourth Quarter 2004*, at http://www.CalPERS.ca.gov/eip-docs/about/board-cal-agenda/agendas/invest/200503/item05-02.pdf.

—— (2005). *Facts at a Glance*. CalPERS: Sacramento, CA.

—— (various years). *Annual Investment Report*. Sacramento, CA: CalPERS.

Castaneda, C. (2004). "To Retire in Dignity and Comfort: A Decade-by-Decade History of CalPERS, 1920–1990." Unpublished manuscript on file with the CalPERS Library, Sacramento, CA.

Clearfield, A. (2005). " 'With Friends Like These, Who Needs Enemies?' The Structure of the Investment Industry and Its Reluctance to Exercise Governance Oversight." *Corporate Governance: An International Review*, 13: 114–21.

Clowes, M. (2000). *The Money Flood: How Pension Funds Revolutionized Investing*. New York: John Wiley & Sons.

Coffee, J. (2002). "Racing towards the Top? The Impact of Cross-Listings and Stock Market Competition on International Corporate Governance." *Columbia Law Review*, 102: 1757–851.

Council for Better Corporate Citizenship (1993). *Purpose of the CBCC Study Mission*. Tokyo: Keidanren.

Crist, W. (1993). "CalPERS' Experiences in Corporate Governance and Suggestions for Improvement." *Japanese Corporate Governance and Investor Relations*. Tokyo, May 10 1993, typescript.

Crutchley, C, Hudson, C and Jensen, M. (1998). "Shareholder Wealth Effects of CalPERS' Activism." *Financial Services Review*, 7: 1–10.

Daily Yomiuri (1996). "CalPERS Adopts International Governance Program." *Daily Yomiuri*, March 20: 9–86.

Dalton, D. and Daily, C. (2001). "Director Stock Compensation: An Invitation to a Conspicuous Conflict of Interests?" *Business Ethics Quarterly*, 11: 89–108.

————Ellstrand, A. and Johnson, J. (1998). "Meta-Analytic Reviews of Board Composition, Leadership Structure and Financial Performance." *Strategic Management Journal*, 19: 269–90.

————Johnson, J. and Ellstrand, A. (1999). "Number of Directors and Financial Performance: A Meta-Analysis." *Academy of Management Journal*, 42: 674–86

Deakin, S. (2005). "The Coming Transformation of Shareholder Value." *Corporate Governance: An International Review*, 13: 11–18.

Demsetz, H. and Lehn, K. (1985). "The Structure of Corporate Ownership: Causes and Consequences." *Journal of Political Economy*, 93: 1155–77.

DiBiasio, J. (2004). "Japan Fund Weighs Aggressive Governance." *FinanceAsia.Com*, January 8.

Dore, R. (2000). *Stock Market Capitalism – Welfare Capitalism: Japan and Germany versus the Anglo-Saxons*. Oxford: Oxford University Press.

Economist (1993). "Japanese Corporate Governance: Dawning." *The Economist*, May 22.

——(2005). "Fat Cats Turn to Low Fat." *The Economist*, March 5.

——(2008). "Japanese Businesses and Bureaucrats Block Outsiders." *The Economist*, May 29.

English, P., Smythe, T. and McNeil, C. (2004). "The 'CalPERS Effect' Revisited." *Journal of Corporate Finance*, 10: 157–74.

Fernandez, P. (2002). "EVA, Economic Profit, and Cash Value Added Do Not Measure Shareholder Value Creation." IESE Research Paper No. 453, Barcelona.

Financial Times (1992). "Japanese Oil Refiner Surprises with Large Increases in Dividends." *Financial Times*, February 2.

——(2002). "Biggest Pension Fund Spies an Opportunity in Japan's Ailing Economy." *Financial Times*, September 24.

——(2004). "Japan Fund Drives at Governance Change." *Financial Times*, July 19.

Fisman, R., Khurana, R. and Rhodes-Kropf, M. (2005). "Governance and CEO Turnover: Do Something Right or Do the Right Thing?" Columbia University mimeo.

Fligstein, N. (1990). *The Transformation of Corporate Control*, Harvard: Harvard University Press.

——and Freeland, E. (1995). "Theoretical and Comparative Perspective on Corporate Organization." *Annual Review of Sociology*, 21:21–43.

Gedajlovic, E. and Shapiro, D. (2002). "Ownership Structure and Firm Profitability in Japan." *Academy of Management Journal*, 45: 575–85.

Gillan, K. (1997). "California 'RAID' History." Unpublished Speech, February 1997, at http://www.CalPERS.governance.org/viewpoint/speeches/gillan.asp.

127

Gillan, K. and Starks, L. (2000). "A Survey of Shareholder Activism: Motivation and Empirical Evidence." *Contemporary Finance Digest*, 2: 10–34.

Gilson, R. and Milhaupt, C. (2005). "Choice as a Regulatory Reform: The Case of Japanese Corporate Governance." *American Journal of Comparative Law*, 53: 343–78.

Givens, S. (2007). *Indecent Proposals*. Hong Kong: CLSA Asia-Pacific Markets.

Gompers, P., Ishii, J. and Metrick, A. (2003). "Corporate Governance and Equity Prices." *Quarterly Journal of Economics*, 118: 107–55.

Gordon, L. and Pound, J. (1993). "Information, Ownership Structure, and Shareholder Voting: Evidence from Shareholder-Sponsored Corporate Governance Proposals." *Journal of Finance*, 68: 697–718.

Gourevitch, P. and Shinn, J. (2005). *Political Power and Corporate Control: The New Global Politics of Corporate Governance*. Princeton: Princeton University Press.

Guercio, D. and Hawkins, J. (1999). "The Motivation and Impact of Pension Fund Activism." *Journal of Financial Economics*, 52: 293–340.

Hall, D. (2005). "Japanese Spirit, Western Economics: The Continuing Salience of Economic Nationalism in Japan." In E. Helleiner and A. Pickel (eds.), *Economic Nationalism in a Globalizing World*. Ithaca: Cornell University Press.

Hashimoto, M. (2002). "Commercial Code Revisions: Promoting the Evolution of Japanese Companies." Nomura Research Institute Working Paper 48.

Hayakawa, M. (2004). "Business of Commercial Law and Change of Corporate Governance." Doshisha University Law School Occasional Paper.

Hebb, T. and Wojcik, D. (2003). "Global Standards and Emerging Markets: The Institutional Investment Value Chain and CalPERS' Investment Strategy." University of Oxford School of Geography and the Environment Working Paper.

Heron, R. and Lie, E. (2006). "What Fraction of Stock Option Grants to Top Executives Have Been Backdated or Manipulated?" Indiana University Kelly School of Business Working Paper.

Higashino, D. (2004). "Corporate Restructuring Picks Up Steam." *JETRO Japan Economic Monthly*: 9.

ICGN (International Corporate Governance Network) (1999). *Statement on Global Corporate Governance Principles*. Tokyo: ICGN.

Inagami, T. (2001). "From Industrial Relations to Investor Relations? Persistence and Change in Japanese Corporate Governance." *Social Science Japan Journal*, 4: 225–41.

—— and Whittaker, D.H. (2005). *The New Community Firm: Employment, Governance and Management Reform in Japan*. Cambridge: Cambridge University Press.

IRRC (Investor Responsibility Research Centre) (2001a). "Less Japanese Companies Use Governance Loophole." *IRRC Corporate Governance Bulletin*, October.

—— (2001b). "ICGN Conference Highlights Growing Awareness of Need to Improve Governance in Japan." *IRRC Corporate Governance Bulletin*, October.

—— (2002). "Japan's Pension Fund Association Urges Funds to Vote Their Proxies." *IRRC Corporate Governance Bulletin*, January.

Jacoby, S. (2000). "Corporate Governance in Comparative Perspective: Prospects for Convergence." *Comparative Labor Law and Policy Journal*, 22: 5–32.

——(2005a). *The Embedded Corporation: Corporate Governance and Employment Relations in Japan and the United States*. Princeton: Princeton University Press.

——(2005b). "Corporate Governance and Society." *Challenge*, 48: 69–87.

——(2007). "Convergence by Design: The Case of CalPERS in Japan." *American Journal of Comparative Law*, 55: 239–94.

——(2008). "Finance and Labor: Perspectives on Risk, Inequality, and Democracy." *Comparative Labor Law and Policy Journal*, 30: 17–66.

Jensen, M. (2005). "The Puzzling State of Low-Integrity Relations between Managers and Capital Markets." SSRN Working Paper.

——and Meckling, W. (1976)."Theory of the Firm: Managerial Behaviour, Agency Costs and Ownership Structure." *Journal of Financial Economics*, 3: 305–60.

JETRO (2002). "W.L. Ross Introduces Change through Private Equity Investments." *JETRO: Investing in Japan*, April.

Jiji Press (1991). "California Pension Fund Suspends Nomura Trading." *Jiji Press*, August 21.

——(1998). "CalPERS Proposes Corporate Governance Principles for Japan." *Jiji Press*, March 17.

Kaplan, S. (1989). "Management Buyouts: Evidence on Taxes as a Source of Value." *Journal of Finance*, 44: 611–32.

——(1994). "Top Executive Rewards and Firm Performance: A Comparison of Japan and the US." *Journal of Political Economy*, 102: 510–46.

——and Minton, B. (1994). "Appointments of Outsiders to Japanese Boards: Determinants and Implications for Managers." *Journal of Financial Economics*, 36: 225–58.

Katsumata, Y. (2004). "The Relationship between the Role of the Public Pension and the Public Pension Plan in Japan." In M. Rhein and W. Schmal (eds.), *Rethinking the Welfare State: The Political Economy of Pension Change*. Cheltenham: Edward Elgar.

Katz, R. (2003). *The Japanese Phoenix: The Long Road to Economic Revival*. New York: M.E. Sharpe.

Kennedy, A. (2001). *The End of Shareholder Value: Corporations at the Crossroads*. New York: Basic Books.

Kester, W.C. (1991). *Japanese Takeovers: The Global Contest for Corporate Control*. Washington DC: Beard Books.

Kissane, M. (1997). "Global Gadflies: Applications and Implications of US-Style Corporate Governance Abroad." *New York Law School Journal of International and Comparative Law*, 17: 621–75.

Korobkin, R. and Ulen, T. (2000). "Law and Behavioral Science: Removing the Rationality Assumption from Law and Economics." *California Law Review*, 88: 1051–144.

Learmount, S. (2002). *Corporate Governance: What Can Be Learned from Japan?* Oxford: Oxford University Press.

Lincoln, J. and Gerlach, M. (2004). *Japan's Network Economy: Structure, Persistence and Change*. Cambridge: Cambridge University Press.

Los Angeles Times (2004). "Activist Chief at CalPERS is Voted Out." *Los Angeles Times*, December 2.

McClellan, S. (2004). "Corporate Pension Change in Japan: Big Bang or Big Bust?" Pension Research Council. University of Pennsylvania Working Paper.

Mehran, H. (1995). "Executive Compensation Structure, Ownership and Firm Performance." *Journal of Financial Economics*, 38: 163–84.

Milhaupt, C. (2005). "In the Shadow of Delaware? The Rise of Hostile Takeovers in Japan." *Columbia Law Review*, 105: 2171–216.

—— and West, M. (2004), *Economic Organizations and Corporate Governance in Japan*. New York: Oxford University Press.

Mishel, L., Bernstein, J. and Allegretto, S. (2005). *The State of Working America 2004/ 2005*. Ithaca: Cornell University Press.

Miwa, Y. and Ramseyer, M. (2005). "Who Appoints Them? What Do They Do? Evidence on Outside directors From Japan." *Journal of Economics and Management Strategy*, 14: 299–337.

Miyajima, H. (2007). "The Performance Effects and Determinants of Corporate Governance Reform." In M. Aoki, G. Jackson and H. Miyajima (eds.), *Corporate Governance in Japan: Institutional Change and Organizational Diversity*. Oxford: Oxford University Press.

—— and Kuroki, F. (2007). "The Unwinding of Cross-Shareholding in Japan: Causes, Effects and Implications." In M. Aoki, G. Jackson and H. Miyajima (eds.), *Corporate Governance in Japan: Institutional Change and Organizational Diversity*. Oxford: Oxford University Press.

Monks, R. (2003). "Relationship Investing," at http://www.lens-library.com/info/ column.html.

Nakata, Y. and Takehiro, R. (2001). "Joint Accounting System and Human Resource Management by Company Group." *Japan Labour Bulletin*, 40/10.

Nelson, J. (2006). "The CalPERS Effect Revisited Again." *Journal of Corporate Finance*, 12: 187–213.

Nesbitt, S. (1994). "Long-Term Rewards from Shareholder Activism: A Study of the CalPERS Effect." *Journal of Applied Corporate Finance*, 6: 75–80.

New York Times (2003a). "CalPERS to Invest $200 Million in Japan Turnaround Fund." *New York Times*, April 14.

—— (2003b) "Turnarounds Are Drawing Foreign Prospectors to Japan." *New York Times*, June 4.

Nikkei (1993). "California Pension System Misses Deadline to Vote No." *Nikkei Weekly*, July 5.

—— (2002a) "Institutions Threaten Corporate Governance." *Nikkei Weekly*, July 22.

—— (2002*b*). "External Forces Take Aim at Governance." *Nikkei Weekly*, November 25.

—— (2003*a*) "Sparx to Bolster Ties with CalPERS, Offer Stock Options." *Nikkei Weekly*, January 23.

—— (2003*b*) "Disclosure: Firms Called on to Satisfy Activist Shareholders." *Nikkei Weekly*, June 13.

—— (2003*c*). "Hidden Giants: Past Bureaucrat Takes Pension Issues to Heart." *Nikkei Weekly*, August 5.

—— (2003*d*). "Can Japanese Fund Managers Emulate CalPERS?" *Nikkei Weekly*, September 18.

—— (2004*a*). "Global M&A Wave Heading for Japan." *Nikkei Weekly*, March 22.

—— (2004*b*) "U.S. Players Get Involved." *Nikkei Weekly*, August 1.

—— (2004*c*) "Trade Ministry Mulls Giving Companies More Options for Fending off Takeover Bids." *Nikkei Weekly*, September 13.

—— (2004*d*) "More Firms Tap Outside Directors." *Nikkei Weekly*, September 13.

—— (2005) "Shareholders' Meetings Reflect Huge Changes in Japan." *Nikkei Weekly*, June 27.

—— (2006) "Buyout Funds Targeting Japan To Be Tested by Rate Hike." *Nikkei Weekly*, July 17.

Nippon Keidanren (2001). *A Proposal for Better Corporate Accounting*. Tokyo: Nippon Keidanren.

Okazaki, T. and Okuno-Fujiwara, M. (1999). *The Japanese Economic System and Its Historical Origins*. Oxford: Oxford University Press.

Patrick, H. (2004). "Evolving Corporate Governance in Japan." Columbia Business School Center on Japanese Economy and Business Working Paper 220.

Pensions & Investments (2000). "Staff Slammed: CalPERS Blasts International Equity Search." *Pensions & Investments*, October 30.

—— (2002). "Big Players: Top Japanese Public Funds Discuss Future with Tokyo Stock Exchange." *Pensions & Investments*, October 14.

—— (2003) "Japan Pension Fund Puts Muscle into Guidelines." *Pensions & Investments*, March 31.

Porter, M. (1994). *Capital Choices: Changing the Way America Invests in Industry*. Boston: Harvard Business School Press.

Rajan, R. and Zingales, L. (2003). "The Great Reversals: The Politics of Financial Development in the Twentieth Century." *Journal of Financial Economics*, 69: 5–50.

Ramseyer, M. and Miwa, Y. (2001). "Financial Malaise and the Myth of the Misgoverned Firm." SSRN Working Paper.

Rehfeld, B. (1997). "Low-cal CalPERS." *Institutional Investor* (International edition), 22: 107–16.

Reuters Asia (2002). "Japanese Pension Fund Manager Pushes Accountability." *Reuters Asia*, March 17.

Roe, M. (2003). *Political Determinants of Corporate Governance: Political Context, Corporate Impact*. New York: Oxford University Press.

Romano, R. (2001). "Less is More: Making Institutional Investor Activism a Valuable Mechanism of Corporate Governance." *Yale Journal on Regulation*, 18: 174–252.

Roy, W. (1997). *Socializing Capital: The Rise of the Large Industrial Corporation in America*. Princeton: Princeton University Press.

Ryder, C. (2005) "The Japan Turnaround Is Real." Capital Guardian Trust Company mimeo.

Sailer, J. (2000). "California PERS (A)." Harvard Business School Case.

Schwab, S. and Thomas, R. (1998). "Realigning Corporate Governance: Shareholder Activism by Labour Unions." *Michigan Law Review*, 96: 1018–94.

Seki, T. (2003). "Towards the Establishment of a New Shareholder–Corporate Relationship in Japan." RIETI Working Paper, Tokyo.

Shleifer, A. (2000). *Inefficient Markets: An Introduction to Behavioral Finance*. Oxford: Oxford University Press.

——and Vishny, R. (2003). "Stock Market Driven Acquisitions." *Journal of Financial Economics*, 70: 295–311.

Smith, M. (1996). "Shareholder Activism by Institutional Investors: Evidence from CalPERS." *Journal of Finance*, 51: 227–52.

State Department (2006). *U.S.–Japan Economic Partnership for Growth: U.S.–Japan Investment Initiative Report 2006*, at http://www.state.gov/p/eap/rls/rpt/68428.htm. Washington DC: US Department of State.

Stern, W. (1991). "Do As I Say." *Forbes*, December 23.

Sterngold, J. (1993). "Japanese Companies Rebuff Mighty U.S. Pension Funds." *New York Times*, June 30.

——(1994). "Lessons in Shareholder Power for Japanese Refiner." *New York Times*, January 17.

Stevenson, R. (1991*a*). "Large Foot in Board-Room Door." *New York Times*, June 6.

——(1991*b*). "California Battle Over State Fund." *New York Times*, June 18.

Suzuki, F. (2005). "Corporate Governance Reform and Industrial Democracy in Japan." *Japan Labour Review*, 2: 81–104.

Taylor, J. (2006). "Japanese Investors Step Up Activism." *ISS*, July 6.

Tokyo Stock Exchange (2005). *Fact Book*. Tokyo: Tokyo Stock Exchange Inc.

Towers Perrin (2005). *Equity Incentives Around the World*. Stamford, CT: Towers Perrin.

——(2006). *Worldwide Total Remuneration*. Stamford, CT: Towers Perrin.

Utsumi, K. (2001). "The Business Judgment Rule and Shareholder Derivative Suits in Japan: A Comparison with Those in the United States." *New York International Law Review*, 14: 129–66.

Wakasugi, T. (2003). "Government Pension Fund and Shareholder's Right." Corporate Governance in the New Japan (Conference sponsored by the Pacific Pension Institute, San Francisco State University, the Japan Society, and JETRO, San Francisco, November).

Wall Street Journal (1991) "California Pension Fund Urges Inquiry by Japan." *Wall Street Journal*, August 12 1991: C9.

Wayne, L. (1991). "Seeking to Stay Out of Proxy Battles." *New York Times*, August 8.

White, T. (2003). "A Foreign Perspective." Corporate Governance in the New Japan (Conference sponsored by the Pacific Pension Institute, San Francisco State University, the Japan Society, and JETRO, San Francisco, November).

Whittaker, D.H. and Hayakawa, M. (2007). "Contesting 'Corporate Value' through Takeover Bids in Japan." *Corporate Governance: An International Review*, 15: 16–26.

Whitten D. (2003). "Comply or Explain: Japan's Shareholders Speak Up." *Money-watch: Weekly Financial Commentary from Tokyo*, 1: 34.

Wiseman, P. (2004). "Funds Bring American Ideas to Japanese Business." *USA Today*, August 10: D1.

Wu, Y. (2004). "The Impact of Public Opinion on Board Structure Changes, Director Career Progression, and CEO Turnover: Evidence from CalPERS' Corporate Governance Program." *Journal of Corporate Finance*, 10: 199–227.

5

Japan's Conversion to Investor Capitalism

Ronald Dore

The then vice-minister, that is, civil servant head, of the Ministry of Economy, Trade, and Industry (METI), Takao Kitabata, made an interesting speech in January 2008 to what he had assumed was a private audience. It attracted no attention until a newspaper which had got hold of a tape recording quoted some forcefully but clearly injudiciously disparaging remarks about day traders. After he had duly apologized, his vetted speech was subsequently published as a pamphlet (Kitabata 2008). Apparently, but not surprisingly, the only place where the substance of his speech got substantial press attention was in the newspaper of the manufacturing sector, the *Nihon kogyo shimbun* (February 29 2008). But it is a fascinating document, clearly revealing the ambivalent assumptions and the constraining taboos surrounding the discussion of corporate governance issues in Japan today. It is worth an extensive summary since it bears directly on the subject of this paper, the contrast between frequent rhetoric about the corporation's duties to its multiple stakeholders, and the absence of any proposals to modify the extent to which the law makes shareholders the sole sovereign controller of the fate of companies.

Many thanks to friends who have provided advice, comments, and materials: Takashi Hatchoji, Takeshi Inagami, Junichiro Mori, George Olcott, Fujikazu Suzuki, and the editors.

The Background

First, a word about the context, the most relevant element of which, and the element which has had the strongest effect on the objectives that managers set themselves, is the recent history of hostile takeovers.

In the 1980s, hostile takeovers did not happen. There were agreed mergers aplenty, but a managerial culture which involved a code of mutual restraint, reinforced by the acknowledged difficulties of absorbing organizations with strongly particularistic loyalties, was one reason which prevented attempts at mergers for business strategy reasons from resulting in hostile tender offers. The other major inhibitor was the system of cross-holdings. A takeover bidder would face a defensive barrier of friends of the firm. As for takeovers for purely financial rather than business reasons, the only recorded – or at least well-remembered – attempt to squeeze assets out of undervalued companies, namely the Boone Pickens 1989 attempt to take over Koito Manufacturing, was thwarted when the whole of corporate Japan rallied round to defend the firm, and the incident prompted a 1990 amendment of the Securities Exchange Law to make a repetition of the event more difficult.

By January 2008, the situation was very different. First, the code of restraint inhibiting business strategy takeovers was breaking down, although the most spectacular demonstration of this, the attempted take-over of one paper company, Hokuetsu Paper by another, Oji Paper, remains very much a one-off, unless one counts the Livedoor assault on Nippon Broadcasting System as having been originally motivated by business strat-egy reasons. But much more important are two other things. First, the final approval of a much-debated provision allowing for the acquisition of Japanese firms paid for in the shares of an acquiring foreign company (provided it is done via a subsidiary of that foreign firm incorporated in Japan). This, coming at a time when Mittal is buying up the world's steel firms, has caused considerable alarm to Japan's flagship steel firms: NHK made a documentary highlighting Nippon Steel's preparations for self-defense.

The second big change is the appearance of investment funds which seek to acquire a controlling stake in medium-sized companies which are rich in relatively liquid assets but have a low market capitalization (see Chapters 2 and 3). The chief aim is to force higher returns to shareholders, the raider's chief profit being derived from selling the shares whose value it thus causes to increase. The first major exercise was by a Japanese fund, the Murakami Fund in its assault on a clothing firm, Tokyo Style, in 2002 and 2003, but of much greater impact, because they arouse nationalist as well as other sentiments, are the activities of foreign funds. Of these, the most well-known is Steel Partners which has succeeded in using tender offers, or the threat of such, to extract considerable sums from a number of companies, and which, in 2007, was the centre of a notable court case. It had applied for an injunction to stop its dislodgement from Bull-Dog Sauce, fought the case to the Supreme Court, and lost. (Bull-Dog had used a share-diluting rights issue to other shareholders and an equal-value cash payment to Steel Partners, an arrangement for which it got its shareholders' overwhelming approval). The other newsworthy issue at the time of Kitabata's speech was the application by the British fund TCI for permission to raise to 20 percent its stake in J-Power, the owner of the electricity grid and prospective builder of Japan's first fast-breeder reactor. (In certain designated industries foreigners are required to get approval to raise an ownership stake above 10 percent. It was widely expected – and subsequently proved to be the case – that TCI's application would be the first of some 700 such applications to be refused – on national security grounds.)

Two Cheers for Stakeholders

Kitabata's first point reflected the arrival of these cash-rich investment funds on the Japanese scene. Japan's competitive strength, he says, depends particularly on the organizational strength of Japanese corporations (it is not, he says, that Japan has a lot of Nobel prizewinners, nor that its R&D is outstandingly innovative) and that organizational strength is threatened by the financialization (his word is *maneeka*, monetization) of the world economy. As evidence of financialization, he cites the growth of world household savings between 1995 and 2005 at a rate three times as fast as the growth of world GNP, with an even faster rate of growth in the proportion going into speculation – as evidenced by the growth of funds invested in the oil futures market, a 20-fold increase from $6.5 billion to $120 billion in ten years. "We are shifting from a real world economy to a world in which finance dominates the economy, which cannot but have implications for the corporation. If the firm belongs to the shareholder and if you can buy anything for money, then Japanese firms are bound to be influenced by the way the world's surplus cash flows. We need to think how to deal with that."[1]

---

[1] Later on in the lecture, a propos of the proposition – which he endorses – that the best way to defend yourself against takeovers is to treat shareholders so generously that you raise your

He then goes on to declare that he belongs to the small minority in Japan who disagree with the dominant "omnipotent-shareholder" view that the firm does, indeed, belong exclusively to the shareholders – the view espoused, he says, by all those executives and opinion-leaders in the media who have been trained in American business schools over the last twenty or thirty years, and who seem to think that all Japan has to do to become efficient and successful is to import American practices.

But Kitabata explicitly disassociates himself from any patriotic attachment to a unique Japanese culture. "The world wouldn't buy that" (*Sekai ni tsuyo shinai.*) He refers several times in his speech to a METI study mission to study the actual nature of American "excellent companies," specifically, IBM, Johnson & Johnson, Dupont, and General Electric. The mission discovered that these companies were much more like Japanese companies than like what those who espouse "omnipotent-shareholder" beliefs speak of as an "American-style company." They are all more than 100 years old, they believe themselves to be working for all their stakeholders – employees, customers, and the society at large, as well as their shareholders – and they put great stress on building up reserves and investing in R&D, and their investor relations department concentrates on such things when explaining what the firm is about.

Much of the speech is devoted to takeovers. He claims credit for METI for various measures over the years (making the holding company legal, for instance) to facilitate M&A. Much of the recent restructuring of Japanese companies was carried out through M&A and it had many advantages. "However, it was all based on the somewhat crude (*ranbo na*) notion of buying and selling companies. What you are in fact selling is a lot of employees, invisible organizational strength, and customer goodwill, and that gives pause for thought: one needs to consider whether it is right to simply buy and sell companies as if they were just some material object."

Kitabata describes at length one of the earliest exploits of Steel Partners; its threat to acquire a controlling interest (one third of the shares) in the textile dye firm, Sotoh, and to take it private (see Chapter 2). It dropped the threat when Sotoh promised a large increase in dividends over the next two years, which raised its share price well above Steel's tender offer and gave Steel a

share price, he effectively negates the value of that prescription by talking of Mittal and its ability to mobilize vast sums of capital which could defeat anything a Japanese firm could do to raise its market capitalization. The total capitalization on Japanese markets, he notes, is less than ¥500 trillion. Some of the oil sovereign funds have several tens of trillions of yen, and private equity funds can mobilize several trillion. No attempts to raise your share price can be proof against that.

handsome profit for its large existing holding. This cost Sotoh one-fifth of its original ¥15 billion liquid assets (the size of which Kitabata described as justified by the need to meet retirement bonuses for its employees and the need for diversification investment in a declining industry).

His comments on the affair are interesting. He asks why a firm like Sotoh, which has no need to raise money from the stock market, should get itself quoted at all, and suggests that the answer is partly pure prestige, and partly the practically useful prestige that allows a firm to recruit good employees from good universities. He hears, he says, that the jolt did Sotoh good and improved its investment strategy,[2] but that is an incidental effect, unrelated to the evaluation of the affair which, he suggests, came as a surprise and a lesson to METI. He knew in theory that such investor behavior was possible, but it was the first time it happened. There had indeed appeared in recent years people (he refers, presumably, to the activist funds such as Murakami's) who argued that shareholders had a right to demand anything of the companies they owned – even forcing firms to cut back on investment in order to pay higher dividends – if only they could scrape together enough shareholder votes to enforce it, but it was the Sotoh affair that brought home to him "to what an extraordinary degree shareholders' rights are respected."

This leads him to another anecdote. Heavy industry firm with a market cap of around a trillion yen. Wants to raise share price and asks advice of analyst – an MBA from top US university. Advice: get out of low-profit activities. First candidate: ship-building, "Can't do that: it's where the firm started; it's the core and essence of the firm." Second candidate: equipment for rolling heavy steel boiler plate, "Can't do that: we're the only Japanese firm in the business: the steel industry relies on us and we can't let it down." "So if you've got a monopoly why don't you put the price up?" "Well, we have a lot of dealings with the steel industry and we can't really hold them up to ransom." In this dialogue of the deaf, contrasting the logic of profit-maximization and what Kitabata calls the practical realities of management, his audience could have had no problem guessing where his sympathies lie.

He then gets down to the legal practical realities of takeovers and defenses against them. Britain requires a compulsory offer for the whole

---

[2] In a subsequent visit to the firm – as far as one could judge a firm efficiently run by thoroughly decent, hard-working, serious people – it transpired that the chief effect of the Steel experience had been the adoption of an ROE target and the decision to put as much spare cash as possible into share buybacks in order to boost the proportion of their shares held by their stable shareholders as well as raise their market value.

company if anyone acquires thirty percent of the shares, and requires showing that you can finance the purchase of the whole company before you can make a bid. America has rights plans which 40 percent of companies have formally established. This enables boards of directors, with or without a shareholder vote, to defend the firm against immediate takeover by issuing shares to shareholders other than the would-be acquirer, thereby diluting the latter's shareholding. This then leads to a proxy fight to oust the directors which is a substitute for, and has the same effect as, a tender offer, but is much superior in that it gives time for both sides to bombard the shareholders with information, thus enabling them to make a reasoned choice. Such reasoned choice is often difficult in the short period in which a tender offer requires a response. METI's Study Group on Corporate Value has issued Guidelines which more or less recommend the American system. About 400 firms have adopted such measures. Rather than "defense" it should be called "imposition of a pause" to make sure that shareholders have the best information on which to base their judgment. It is not – and this is a key word in contemporary Japanese debate – *heisateki*, or clannishly exclusive.

One thing that seems to be feared by all Japanese participants in the corporate governance debate, including those of stakeholder theory persuasion, is that anything they say will be seized on by foreigners as reinforcement of their "reacting to Commodore Perry" image of Japan: Japanese, set in their feudal ways, getting together, jabbering away in their own language, and devising some formula for seeming to accept the principles of openness, universalism, and justice which the enlightened foreigners are insisting on, while managing in substance to avoid having to put them in practice. In a later passage in his speech he defends the system of vetting foreign takeovers in particular industries (presumably already having decided to deny TCI the right to increase its stake in J-Power – see above). and goes on to a general defense of Japan against the charge of being *heisateki*. Japan is far less so than America or France when it comes to vetoing foreign takeovers on national security grounds. As for defensive rights plans, only 10 percent of Japanese firms have them, compared with 40 percent of American firms, and the Americans allow directors to get away with things which would not be allowed in Japan. And, moreover, Japan has an active Invest in Japan Campaign designed to invite foreign firms to bring their innovations and their innovativeness to Japan. (Japan is not at the moment starved of capital, but, he says, might be one day as a result of demographic change, if they cannot persuade Japanese households to put their savings into equities.)

And so he moves toward his peroration which takes the form of a quotation from the recent Tokyo High Court judgment in the Bull-Dog Sauce case.

The joint-stock company is in theory a profit-making organization which seeks to maximize corporate value and distribute it to the shareholders, but at the same time a corporation cannot perform its profit-making activities by itself. It is a social entity; internally it carries its employees, externally it gains its profits from its economic relations with its suppliers and customers. That being clear, in pursuing its efforts to increase corporate value, it must recognize its indispensable relations with employees and customers and other diverse interested parties (stakeholders). There is a limit to the extent to which one can think of corporate value solely in terms to profit to the shareholders.

And yet, says, Kitabata, company law says that the corporation belongs to shareholders. "The main framework of company law is based on an international standard and cannot be changed. With firms operating all over the world in our global economic system, it would not be appropriate to try to change it." So Japan has to find devices to maintain the reality as expressed by that judge within the framework of that "omnipotent shareholder" law.

The actual devices he mentions make a thin list: managers should make clear their devotion to the long-term build-up of organizational capacity and thus appeal to long-term shareholders; the stock exchange should consider changing its listing rules to allow shares with differential voting rights – something which Japanese company law permits, but not the Tokyo Stock Exchange; the exchange should also change its rules to make it easier to delist and take companies private; the definition of external directors' duties in the law might be amended to make clear that they are expected to provide long-term vision, not detailed monitoring; employee share ownership should be facilitated and a law governing ESOPs should be prepared; the tax on share transactions might be graduated to the length of time shares have been held.

Significant Omission: The Orthodoxy

But of the standard device by which, until a decade ago, managers who wanted to concentrate on building excellent companies made themselves secure against takeovers – namely cross-shareholdings with financial institutions, joint venture partners, suppliers, trading companies, etc. – there is

no mention. In the past, these cross-shareholdings were of crucial importance in effectively neutralizing the shareholder sovereignty which was
mandated by Japan's Anglo-Saxon type company law, in order to allow
companies to have the characteristics of which Kitabata approves – by and
large the characteristics for which they were praised in courses on Japanese
management in American business schools in the 1980s. The omission
must surely be a case of deliberate avoidance.

The avoidance is presumably in order not to challenge the prevailing
orthodoxy. Kitabata accepts as a fact of life that Japan has to have a
shareholder-sovereignty company law even though, as the whole thrust
of his speech demonstrates, it causes a lot of problems for well-motivated
managers. The prevailing orthodoxy goes further; it denies that there are
any problems.

It holds that (*a*) shareholder sovereignty is in accord with natural justice
concerning fundamental principles of private property, (*b*) that it has the
most beneficial effects in promoting the efficient use of resources (and
hence maximizing Japan's international competitiveness) through the
way it subjects managers to the discipline of the market, (*c*) that poison
pills and other antitakeover defenses that, if abused, might serve to
weaken the discipline of the market, must be used under strict conditions
and only to maximize the profit of shareholders, and (*d*) in particular, the
attempt to weaken the discipline of the market by cross-shareholdings or
the cultivation of stable friendly shareholders who can be relied on to
reject all takeover bids are a form of cheating.

A propos of point (*c*), a committee was created in METI in 2004 to define
the nature of acceptable poison pills. The press release at its formation,
citing some examples of relative financial strength (Pfizer with a market
cap of ¥30 trillion, Takeda Seiyaku 4 trillion; Microsoft with ¥35 trillion
versus Canon's 5 trillion, etc.), made it quite clear that a major motivation
was protection of Japanese firms against more powerful foreign competitors, but it would have been hard to guess those origins from the guidelines that the committee issued, with Ministry of Justice endorsement, in
2005. The model, as stated in Kitabata's description quoted earlier, was the
American rights plan, under which new shares, or warrants, can be issued
to all existing shareholders except a would-be acquirer, but under greater
restrictions than in Delaware. The tactic may only be used if such share
issuance has been already approved in principle by a shareholder resolution, and the directors are strongly advised to delegate the decision
whether or not a threatened takeover should be so countered to an independent committee which will judge whether or not the collective

interests of shareholders would be served. We will return to that, and the 2008 controversies surrounding it, later.

There was a fifth proposition about the discipline of a thriving market in corporate control, to which the purists who dominate the legal discussions subscribe, but about which many of the otherwise orthodox have some qualms. It is that even when that discipline is exercised as in the Steel Partners versus Sotoh case described earlier, purely for distributional rather than productive purposes – that is, in order to force managers to disgorge more cash – it is beneficial. No-one perhaps has put this point of view more forcefully than an editorial writer of the *Financial Times*. A propos the convictions of the two pioneer operators of such activist funds, Horie and Murakami, the writer argued that they had "performed a public service in a country where companies' performance has often been handicapped by supine boards, sleepy managers and stubborn disdain for shareholders' rights."[3]

Reactions to the Bull-Dog Judgment: Abusive Acquirers

Quite widespread discussion of that fifth proposition was triggered by the judgments given by the courts against Steel Partners in its suit against Bull-Dog Sauce. The reader may recall Kitabata's quotation from the Tokyo High Court judgment, subsequently upheld by the Supreme Court.

First, a further word of elaboration on that judgment: The newspapers generally reported that the judge had described Steel as an "abusive acquirer," and gave the impression that he had thrown out its suit accordingly. In fact the grounds for the judgment were different – the affirming vote of the assembled shareholders and the fact that Steel was given handsome compensation – but the judge did recount the Steel–Sotoh episode by way of examining Bull-Dog's charge that Steel clearly came into the category which has come to be called "abusive acquirer." It is a category, defined in an earlier (March 23 2005) Tokyo High Court judgment on the Livedoor case, as examples of situations in which, because of the "predatory and abusive intentions" of the would-be acquirer[4] it would be "necessary and appropriate" for a board of directors to issue share warrants to defend itself against takeover. Four examples were given,

---

[3] *Financial Times*, June 6 2006, quoted in Whittaker and Hayakawa (2007: 19).
[4] "Kaisha wo kuimono ni shiyou to shite iru baai ni wa, ranyo mokuteki wo motte kabushiki wo shutoku shita baishusha."

but followed by an "etcetera" which suggests that the list may not be exhaustive.

1. Greenmailers – defined as people who buy up a company's shares, ramp up their price, and then get the company or its associates to buy the shares back.

2. Those intending scorched-earth management – gaining control of a company in order to transfer the intellectual property, know-how, commercial secrets or customers, which are essential to that company's business operations, to the acquirer or the acquirer's group.

3. Indebted acquirers who seek control of the company in order to use its assets to provide collateral for, or to liquidate, their indebtedness.

4. Those seeking to gain temporary control of a company, sell off assets such as real estate and securities of no immediate importance for the company's business, to use the proceeds to pay a high level of dividends or to take the opportunity of high dividends, and an enhanced share price to sell its holding at a profit.

The Bull-Dog case judge had quite clearly believed Bull-Dog's charge that Steel Partners belonged to category 4, and disbelieved Steel Partner's claim that it simply admired Bull-Dog and wanted a long-term association with it. This aroused the ire of, for example, the Liberal Democrat member of the Diet, Kotaro Tamura. He wrote in his blog:

Reading the judgment my first thought was "My God! does he want to kill our efforts to globalize the Tokyo stock market?"

If Steel Partners are "abusive acquirers" then there's no scope for any fund to be active in Japan . . .

It's not clear which of the four kinds of "abusive acquirers" set out in that 2005 judgment Steel Partners are supposed to be (and I have grave doubts about that judgment itself anyway.)

"As for enterprise value", the judge says, "there is a limit to the extent to which one can interpret it entirely in terms of profit for the shareholder". Ho! Ho! The man's talking like a mindless TV presenter. Where in the company law does it say any such thing? I can't believe that this judge is anybody with a legal training. It's the mere emotional judgement of somebody with absolutely no business experience.

"Investment funds", he says, "by their very nature, are organizations which are dedicated to making the maximum profit for their investors in the short and medium term, through the buying and selling of shares". So what's wrong with that? The man doesn't understand the first thing about why the Tokyo Stock Exchange exists. It's frightening to think that important business matters are entrusted to such ignorant characters.

A more trenchant, and indeed influential, critic of that judgment was Tomomi Yano, the former head of the Ministry of Welfare's Pension Bureau, who at that point was director of Japan's largest pension fund association, the PFA (Yano 2008). The Guidelines he refers to are those mentioned above, issued by METI's Corporate Value Study Group and the Ministry of Justice.

In the case of Bull-Dog Sauce, the managers and directors went all-out to repel the would-be acquirer. They not only resorted to a defensive [issue of shares] – and did so after the battle had begun, something which was not envisioned in the Guidelines, but are said to have paid out 2.1 billion yen to Steel and 0.7 billion to the lawyers. As a result Bull-Dog Sauce went into the red; its share price collapsed, and its shareholders have been denied the right to respond to a high-premium tender offer, their rights trampled in the dirt. But the astonishing thing is that 80 percent of the shareholders voted to support the company's policy. Behaviour completely inexplicable in terms of economic rationality. Many of them were stable cross-shareholders and since they have chosen to disadvantage themselves they have only themselves to blame, but minority shareholders have suffered a terrible loss. And now the Supreme Court has given its approval to this kind of company behaviour. It is tantamount to sending the message that Japan is a country where capitalism and the rules of the market are not understood, which is not unrelated to the large fall in Japanese share prices.

According to Yano, this is a typical consequence of the unreconstructed character of Japanese corporations, as a result of which the intentions of the Guidelines are thwarted by widespread evasion:

In America boards of directors have a majority of independent external directors who have absolutely no personal interest stake in the company, and whose fiduciary duty towards shareholders is guaranteed both by law and in practice. If directors oppose a takeover offer and shareholders thereby lose the chance to sell their shares at a high price, they run a high risk of being sued by disgruntled shareholders. In Japan, by contrast, there are hardly any independent external directors; nearly all the directors come from inside the firm and while they may have a sense of fiduciary duty towards the CEO or Chairman who appointed them, their sense of duty towards the shareholders is weak in the extreme. The background to this is the strength of the sense that the firm does not belong to the shareholders, but to the employees and the customers and the other stakeholders. Bringing in an American-style rights plan to a Japan where the cultural soil is so different is like trying to graft bamboo on a tree. There were many misgivings as to whether the Guidelines would work, and, sure enough, things are moving in a direction they did not intend to endorse.

Such reactions to the Bull-Dog case were sufficiently strong and wide-spread to prompt pressure on METI to get the Corporate Value Study Group working on the case. The strongest pressure to do so (the *Nikkei shimbun* June 8 2008 reported that it had succumbed to "pressures from the market") probably came from Yano's Pension Fund Association which on March 23 2008 revised its own "Guidelines for the exercise of voting rights with respect to anti-takeover defences."[5] These, the PFA's representative on the Study Group expounded to the Group at the beginning of its April meeting.[6] The main points of the PFA's guidelines revision were, first, to condemn the payment of cash to would-be acquirers in lieu of the share warrant purchase rights given to other shareholders, and second, to spell out in concrete detail the features which should prompt its members to vote down rights plan proposals.

Those features now are

- When the firm has no external directors;
- When the so-called "independent committee" charged with the decision whether or not to put a rights plan into operation contains people with connections to the firm;
- When the period the proposal stipulates for such a committee, or the board of directors, to come to such a decision is excessively long, or multiply renewable;
- When the specified criteria for reaching such a decision can be interpreted too broadly: for example "Whether or not there is a danger that the proposed takeover would militate against the consolidation or increase of enterprise value, including in that concept the profit [sic] of employees, customers, suppliers, the local community or other stakeholders" or, "When it is deemed that the conditions of the offer, including the treatment of employees, customers, suppliers and other stakeholders, are, in the light of the company's basic value [or 'underlying value' ? *hongenteki kachi*], inadequate or inappropriate."

The last is clearly the crucial point, the point of collision between the fundamentalist supporters of a "firm = shareholder's property" legal system, and managers who cling to the orthodoxy of a decade and a half ago, and think it morally enjoined on them to make sure that all decisions about corporate control are taken with full consideration, above all, of the welfare

---

[5] "Kigyo baishu-boeisaku ni okeru kabunushi-giketsukenkoshi kijun": www.pfa.or.jp/top/jigyou/pdf/gov_20080324-point.pdf.
[6] http://www.meti.go.jp/committee/summary/eic0004/index27.html.

of their current employees, but also of other stakeholders. It is a collision between the investment community and the mainstream nonfinancial managerial community. (Mainstream, because there is an increasing number of younger managers, particularly of nonmanufacturing start-ups, who share the values of the investment community). The attempt to straddle that collision is what led to all the ambiguities and ambivalences of the Kitabata speech with which this paper began.

Clarification from the Corporate Value Study Group

To return to the Corporate Value Study Group: problems posed by the Bull-Dog case had been raised in the committee in the autumn of 2007, but its main concern at the end of that year had been the matter of differential voting rights (see the reference in Kitabata's speech, above). After producing a paper on that question in December (primarily for action by the Tokyo Stock Exchange and its listing requirements, rather than for any change in the law), it had gone into hibernation, but was reconvened at the end of March 2008 to consider, "what action should be deemed appropriate, for target firms and tender-offering firms, when a bid has been or is about to be made." After four monthly sessions, it published on June 11 2008 – in time for the shareholder AGMs generally held in June – what was still, for some reason, called a "draft" entitled *Appropriate forms of defence against takeovers, taking into account recent changes in various aspects of the environment.*

At whose behest it is unclear, but at the April meeting a significant change in the composition of the committee was announced. Three of the six manufacturing representatives – from Toyota, Asteras, and Rohm – resigned (according to *Nikkei shimbun* June 8 2008 had been asked to resign) and two new members, both from the financial community, were appointed. This left the composition of the committee as follows: Professorial experts on corporate governance: seven (including the chairman), lawyers: four, manufacturing company managers: three, (Sony, Hitachi, Nippon Steel) financial firm representatives (including an M&A consultant): thirteen, plus a representative of the Nippon Keidanren who does not fit any of the other categories.

Not surprisingly, given the weighting of the committee, the report was wholly directed at narrowing the options for defense against takeovers, repeating several times that the whole point of them should be to interpose a pause so that shareholders would have more time and better information to decide the merits of the bid, never to seek to deprive shareholders of the chance of selling their shares at a premium in order to preserve the incumbent management's skins. Its seven prescriptions for correct managerial behavior in the face of a hostile bid call for a saintly selflessness going well beyond due diligence, a level of disinterested concern exclusively for the interests of the "shareholders as a whole," such as is more likely to be found in the fantasies of lawyers than in the real world. The main points of substance were

1. Declaring the pay-off to Steel Partners by Bull-Dog to be a deplorable precedent, not to be repeated.

2. The second lesson from Steel-Bull-Dog: it is a dereliction of duty on the part of managers not to make an objective reasoned assessment of how far a bidder's bid might be in the interests of shareholders, but instead to rely on getting a favorable vote from the shareholders for defensive measures. "This can send out the message that if you get a shareholder structure which allows you to be sure of a favourable vote, you have a cast-iron defence system." In other words, it encourages the build-up of cross-shareholdings and friendly stable shareholdings which damages the discipline of the market.

3. Endorsing the position of the PFA about rejecting any consideration of other stakeholders besides the shareholder. Twisting the clarity of the PFA's formulation into a tortuous and barely intelligible form, it says, "The board of directors must not adopt liberal interpretations of the circumstances which might trigger defensive measures in order to save their own skins, for example by referring to the interests of other stakeholders in spite of their not being compatible with advancing the common interests of shareholders, and thereby blurring the definition of the interests to be protected."

4. And fourthly a clear declaration in favor of what I called the fifth proposition above, denying that corporate raiders out to squeeze cash for shareholders out of reluctant firms can be considered "abusive would-be acquirers." "Boards of directors must not judge that a defence is necessary simply because it is expected that the acquirer intends to use the assets of the company as collateral for loans, or to sell off the company's assets in order temporarily to pay out high dividends: such a likelihood does not mean that the bid cannot be in the interests of the shareholders as a whole."

The most forthright attack on the report that I have come across, and the only one that interested bloggers seem to have noticed, appeared in the

Nikkei shimbun on July 29 (Ota 2008). It was written by a lawyer who takes issue with the report, not for its "shareholder value" philosophy, but chiefly on the grounds that in condemning the practice of paying compensation to buy off hostile bidders, the Study Group was also condemning the Supreme Court, which had endorsed such payment in the Bull-Dog case and treated it as one reason for awarding judgment to Bull-Dog. What did this Study Group think it was about? If it wanted a change in the law it should have issued a legislative proposal. Guidelines? "I thought the days when Japan was ruled by administrative discretion and rules formulated by bureaucrats on a dubious legal basis were supposed to be over." He insists that the takeover scene is constantly changing, with funds hunting in "wolf packs," and the clever use of derivatives and share-lending to evade disclosure requirements. "Only if the rules for takeovers emerge from the accumulation of the judgements in particular concrete cases will they acquire the rationality which gains them authority among shareholders, investors, employees, local communities and other stakeholders."

The Chairman of the Corporate Value Study Group, Hideki Kanda, a professor of law at Tokyo University, offered a defensive reply the next day (Kanda 2008). He explained the intentions of the report as being chiefly to get across the two main points of policy (the first two of the four points listed above). As for the charge of contradicting the Supreme Court he says, "We say that payments should not be made, but as for the legality of such payments, we simply point out that it is perfectly within the law not to pay [i.e. to discriminate against a hostile bidder in the issue of warrants without compensation] and consequently we are not contradicting the judgment of the Supreme Court."

The bulk of his article is devoted to the claim that the Study Group was only spelling out universally accepted principles. The limited liability joint-stock company is universally seen as the best agent for economic activity and "the legal code of every country takes as its starting point the will of the shareholders who provide the capital." The only acknowledgement of the existence of philosophies of stakeholder accountability as opposed to exclusive shareholder accountability is the admission that there is a "contradiction" (*mujun*) in the fact that "in practice the value that a corporation has in society is not just the sum of the value it has for all of its shareholders, but adds other values." But that does not prevent him from drawing comparisons of what bidders and boards of directors can and cannot do in the matter of takeovers in the United States, Britain, and Germany, without any reference to the way different approaches to that "contradiction" produce crucial differences among those countries in the composition of the boards of directors – with employee representatives sharing power with shareholder representatives in Germany.

But the criticism he most eagerly seeks to rebut is that the Corporate Study Group has changed its stance, from the time when it issued its first guidelines. Whereas it had seemed to be encouraging the adoption of antitakeover defense preparations, albeit within strict shareholder-respecting limits, it was now, in its latest report, actively seeking to discourage them. Not at all, he says, we have had a consistent line of thought and the new report simply spells out its implications in the light of recent cases.

Nobody who has followed the Study Group will believe that. There clearly has been an evolution. As mentioned earlier, the METI press release announcing the formation of the group in 2004 suggested that a major motive for convening the group was the perception that Japanese firms were vulnerable in a world of global capital and needed to think about defending themselves, and to underline the point quoted comparative figures for the market capitalization of leading firms in the United States and Japan. The secretariat reproduced those figures to concentrate the Study Group's minds in a paper for its seventh meeting. But by the time the 2005 guidelines were issued, the insistence on priority to shareholder interests and the promotion of M&A as a means of strengthening the discipline of the market had more or less taken over. The latest report strengthens that insistence.

Why Insist?

As to why anybody felt it needed to do so, and to do so in time to influence the summer round of shareholder meetings, the answer probably lies in the increasingly articulate pressure on, and complaints about the closed (*heisateki*) nature of, Japanese firms coming from the investor community, particularly the foreign investor community. The *Nikkei shimbun* (April 7 2008) reported that the Bull-Dog judgment was having a big effect on the defense plans being prepared for the summer's shareholder meetings; whereas most existing plans allowed for the directors to trigger a warrant issue on the advice of an independent committee, most were being revised to make the trigger a positive vote at a shareholders' meeting – which the Supreme Court judgment had made a legally unassailable procedure. As a result, it was said, foreign investors were leaving Japan, resulting in a bigger drop in Tokyo than in other parts of the world's markets. (Foreign investors make 60 percent of the trades on the Tokyo Stock Exchange and are effectively the price-makers for major corporations.)

The Council on Economic and Fiscal Policy, the high-powered committee chaired by the prime minister, also weighed in on the *heisateki* issue two weeks before the Corporate Value Study Group reported,[7] by taking up the Invest in Japan Campaign which Kitabata mentioned in his speech. The Koizumi government had declared as a national objective the doubling of the volume of inward foreign direct investment by 2010 – as a means of "revitalizing" (*kasseika*) the economy. The lack of much progress had prompted the creation of an Inward Investment Wise Men's Group in January 2008. The invitation to the chairman of that group to report to the Council in May seems to have been prompted by all the *heisateki* charges following the refusal of permission to TCI to raise its stake in J-Power, and rumbles about antitakeover defense measures. Both figured in his report. There was a need for total transparency and predictability in the national security issue and careful restriction of antitakeover defenses. This was necessary to improve the investment climate in Japan, and thereby raising the volume of inward investment which, in relation to GDP, was still abysmally low – "by an order of magnitude compared with other countries both developed and developing."

The salience of this issue is enhanced by government-to-government pressure from the United States. Ever since the Structural Impediments Initiative of 1990, in some guise or other, the United States has sent an "Annual Reform Recommendations from the Government of the United States to the Government of Japan." The financial section of the most recent one[8] deals with regulatory transparency, credit bureaus, and firewalls, but like many earlier ones, it carries the implicit "don't come *heisateki* on us" message.

The United States believes that competitive financial and capital markets are a key element contributing to sustained economic growth, efficient capital allocation, job creation and innovation. The United States encourages Japan to adopt measures necessary to assure global financial center status.

It is probable that American pressure carries somewhat less weight under Fukuda than under the Abe government. An official close to the battle in

[7] Twelfth session, May 20 2008. www.keizai-shimon.go.jp/minutes/2008/0520/shimon-s.pdf.
[8] www.ustr.gov/assets/Document_Library/Reports_Publications/2007/asset_upload_file751_13383.pdf – October 18 2007. I believe the recommendation process is in principle reciprocal, but I have been unable to find Japan's recommendations on how America should reform itself.

the summer of 2006 between the government and the Nippon Keidanren, which wanted restrictive limits on share-swap foreign acquisitions, predicted that Keidanren would have a better chance of winning against the open-everything reformers if Fukuda won the nomination than if (as in the event happened) the winner was Abe.

Foreign investors themselves weighed in. In addition to frequent memoranda from the American Chamber of Commerce in Japan and its annual publication of a Financial White Paper (ACCJ 2008) – the latest offering "a strategic road map" for enhancing the international competitiveness of Japan's financial and capital markets – private groups of investors have also been active. The Asian Corporate Governance Association, a Hong Kong-based consortium of 6 foreign funds, including Hermes and CalPERS, who claim to be "long-term shareowners who seek to invest in well-managed companies that are both profitable and good corporate citizens," issued in May 2008 a White Paper (ACGA 2008) on the defects of Japanese firms with recommendations as to how they should improve.

There is, they say, a "still widely held view" in Japan that managers "can safely be entrusted not only with control of operations, but also with guardianship of the interests of the key stakeholders (employees, suppliers, customers, creditors and shareholders)." That may have been viable twenty years ago, but "the importance and function of share ownership has changed" and now that Japan is part of a global financial system, "the portrayal of the Japanese system as stakeholder capitalism is, therefore, outdated and fundamentally inaccurate." It deals in detail with such practices as holding excessive reserves of liquid assets on balance sheets, improper poison pill arrangements (its recommendations are similar to those of the Corporate Study Group, but endorse the detailed requirements for acceptable plans set out by Riskmetrics, the former Institutional Shareholders Services), not having external directors, or having external directors who are not independent, arrangements for shareholder meetings that are not accessible, fair or transparent, and building up cross-shareholdings which mean that outcomes desired by independent shareholders are thwarted by "cross-shareholders who vote their own self-protective and conflicting interests." Members of the group told reporters that if firms did not take these recommendations seriously they would risk votes against the reappointment of directors (*Nikkei shimbun* May 11 2008).

Several Japanese funds also made it clear that they intended to be more actively demanding. Nomura Asset Management, for example, decided that it would vote against the reappointment of directors in any firm whose return on equity had been below 5 percent for three years running, and against any antitakeover defense which allowed directors more than 150 days to issue an evaluation of a takeover proposal (*Nikkei shimbun* May 9 2008). The PFA also announced similar criteria for voting down management proposals. The press gave some prominence to the news that Shiseido had declared its intention of dropping its poison pill rights plan, and experienced a 5 percent increase in its share price as a result (*Nikkei shimbun* June 4 2008).

In the Event: The 2008 AGM Round

The last few years have seen a slow but steady trend away from the so-called *shanshan sokai* – the ritualized and choreographed, twenty-minute shareholder AGM – held on one of the last legally possible days when several hundred other firms are also holding theirs, thereby spreading thin the supply of articulately disgruntled shareholders. More companies are holding their meetings earlier, some on Saturdays and Sundays, and if they do not welcome, are at least resigned to entertaining and taking seriously the motions proposed by increasingly articulate shareholders. The meetings in the summer of 2008 continued that trend, though without any dramatic developments, save the success of Steel Partners in mobilizing enough votes to oust the management at Aderans, a struggling wig-maker, and to replace it with a new board containing two Steel nominees as external directors (neither of them noted experts on the wig market or wig production, though doubtless very clever at reading balance sheets). TCI (the firm referred to above as the first to be denied permission to increase its holding in J-Power), whose very public criticism of that firm's failure to give shareholders their proper due had been widely reported, got the support of some third of the votes for its motions to increase dividends and to oppose the reappointment of directors. Whereas in previous years proposals for antitakeover defenses had been voted down at a number of firms, this year, though frequently opposed, none received a majority of negative votes, presumably because they were more cautiously drafted. The announcement of a September lecture by a lawyer on "Lessons from the 2008 round of Shareholder AGMs" summarizes, "with the support of cross-shareholdings and with attempts to improve management, apart from a small number of exceptions this year's AGMs passed off peacefully."

And What do Managers Think?

The notable thing about all this debate is how few managers of nonfinancial corporations are actually taking part in it. They, very sensibly, are busy getting on with the business of building up friendly shareholdings – getting the long-term shareholders who will be sympathetic to their desire to keep substantial sums back for investment and contingency reserves even if it does mean a less than spectacular share price. In companies which see themselves in line for very specific attacks, this activity can consume considerable managerial resources, though far less than the Investor Relations activities of firms which rely only on creating a favorable image in the minds of uncommitted independent shareholders.

One such firm is Nippon Steel which, since Mittal's acquisition of Arcelor, has seen itself as very much the next potential Mittal target. As noted above, an NHK documentary was devoted to its attempts to prepare for such a battle (NHK 2007). The story as told emphasized that Nippon Steel's analysis revealed that Arcelor's failure to defend itself stemmed from the defection of its individual shareholders, many of whom sold their shares to hedge funds banking on a rise in the tender price. Long sequences of the documentary were devoted to the efforts of Nippon Steel to win the affection of the 400,000 individuals who own a quarter of its stock – offering them all-day outings to see factories, hear pep talks, and receive modest entertainment. Four thousand were given such attention, apparently occupying a good deal of the time of the Chief Financial Officer. But the enthusiasm for targeting individual shareholders dropped off when it was realized that the visitors represented only one percent of the shareholders, when an attempt at a questionnaire to individual shareholders produced only a 10 percent response, and most definitively when the share price soared in December 2006 and many individual shareholders took the chance of a considerable profit – particularly as it was suspected that hedge fund buying might be behind the surge in the firm's share price.

Nippon Steel's more serious attempts at defense have involved acquiring committed large shareholders, often through cross-shareholdings. The three major Japanese steel companies announced a pact to help each other's defense should any one of them come under attack (*Nikkei shimbun* March 29 2006). Nippon Steel made a 5 percent exchange of shares with Posco in Korea and negotiated some sort of capital tie-up confirming its long-term association with Baoshan Steel in Shanghai. It also issued, through a Cayman Islands subsidiary, ¥30 billion worth of bonds bought by Japan's three major banks, which are convertible to equity under certain conditions, and if converted would amount to nearly 6 percent of Nippon Steel's stock.[9]

Other firms are cautiously doing likewise. *Nikkei shimbun* reported in October 2007, "publicly traded companies snapped up shares of other companies in fiscal 2006, lifting their long-term securities holdings by 7% to 28.9 trillion yen as of March 31, 2007." The Tokyo Stock Exchange figures for new share issues show that from the beginning of 1998 to June 2008, there had been 1,382 offerings of new ordinary shares. Of these, only 433 had been public offerings, accounting for ¥6.4 trillion, less than the 949 private placements yielding 7.9 trillion. Even so, the level of real cross-shareholdings – that is, A holding B's shares and B holding A's – was put at only 5.9 percent of all shares issued in a survey by Daiwa Shoken in late 2007.[10]

There are other signs that managers are seeking to get their shares into friendly hands, and that there is still some fiduciary value in the "trust" implied by the word "friendly" – the ability to count on solidarity against a would-be takeover bidder, even one who is offering a large premium over current share price. The *Nikkei shimbun* (June 6 2008) quoted an IR consultant who severely criticized the life insurance companies. "I have seen not one case in which they have voted against a poison pill plan proposed by management. What is more they buy shares of companies, hoping to get more business from them, when although they claim purely to be making investments, they know in fact that they are being sold the shares as potential defenders against takeover." The contrast with other investors – the foreign institutions or the Japanese PFA – is said to be marked.

It is unlikely that the level of cross-shareholders and stable friendly shareholders will ever regain 1990 levels. The banks have had their holdings of equities capped by legislation. Mark-to-market accounting means that other companies' shares cannot just sleep on the balance sheet at their original purchase price; they now introduce volatility into the balance sheet as prices rise and fall, and the 1980s general expectation that they would continuously rise has evaporated. The collapse of share prices in October 2008 has caused such serious problems at the banks which still have sizeable equity holdings that their capital adequacy is in question and, as this is written, serious consideration is being given to a suspension of the mark-to-market rules.

[9] These highly complex financial instruments, described as Euro-yen Convertible Bonds, were issued to Mitsui-Sumitomo, Mitsubishi-TokyoUFJ, and Mizuho Corporate.
[10] News release, November 27 2007.

Equally, trust and a sense of obligation, particularly the obligations implicit in membership in the former *keiretsu* enterprise groups, are slowly eroding. But with all these factors stacked against them, managers are at least trying to enlarge that segment of their shareholders who are committed to the firm and concerned about its long-term prospects rather than about its current share price. They are trying to recruit the sort of shareholder whom Kitabata extolled in the speech with which this paper began.

But they do so furtively, frequently denying any such intention, for the near-universal opinion is that building up cross-holdings is an unworthy and cowardly way of cheating by escaping the discipline of the market.

One manager[11] contrasted the days when Japanese banks were willing to earn a reasonable rate of return on loans to industrial corporations with today when miserably low interest rates saw the banks putting their spare cash into high-yielding hedge funds. Those hedge funds, moreover, seeking quick returns, were providing an ever-increasing proportion of the speculative capital on the Tokyo exchange, often directed at shakedowns of companies like Sotoh and Bull-Dog Sauce. The dominance of such investors with an extreme short term perspective:

is not good, in my view. All the press comment has it that this is all being done for shareholders so it's great. The press glorifies it. We feel a strong reaction against this, but there is a feeling that if you went against the tide, you would be penalised by having your share price go down. Industrial capital has been pitted against financial capital and unfortunately the outlook for industrial capital is not good. So what can we do to change things? I think it's up to us to stand up and say the things that we are thinking. We need to say out loud: "This is a negative aspect of capitalism. The papers may admire it and say it's great for shareholders but that's not the way it is." We should say this more clearly.

The Inhibitions

But they do not say it clearly. One much-respected manager, the President of Nippon Steel, in a speech to the Statutory Auditors Association (Mimura 2008) made the point that any firm that was worth its salt had to prepare antitakeover defenses. He surveyed the various ways of doing so. When he came to cross-holdings he had this to say: "Of course there is no absolutely

---

[11] One of a series of interviews of top managers conducted with George Olcott (see Chapter 7), to whom I am indebted for the transcription.

certain defence against takeovers: the basic defence is to increase profits, thereby increasing enterprise value and your market capitalization. But also, although old-fashioned kinds of cross-shareholding are ruled out on efficiency-of-use-of-capital grounds, it is also important to move toward an axis of stability by furthering business tie-ups and capital tie-ups with firms with whom one shares common values, and firms with whom one can have cooperative projects from which both sides can draw benefit."

It may be that Nippon Steel is in fact confining its cross-shareholdings to those which have a primary production-project purpose. But can investment for the explicit purpose of achieving a 50 percent majority of friendly shareholders really be ruled out on capital-efficiency grounds? Would it be deemed unprofitable even if one counts into the equation the potential savings in the very substantial amount of cash and managerial resources now devoted to investor relations, rather than to increasing the revenues in which employees and shareholders can share?

The answer is most probably no. Their dominant consideration in ostensibly ruling out the building up of cross-holdings is not at all capital efficiency, but fear – the fear (a) of being considered the sort of wimp that is too cowardly to face the challenge of market discipline and (b) the fear of being accused of despising shareholders and thereby suffering a fall in their share price. And that is a perfectly rational fear even for managers whose worry about takeovers is not at all what harm it might bring to them personally (the "saving their own skins" – *hoshin* – that the committee declarations and scholarly literature harp on so constantly) but what harm it might do to the company they have lived and breathed in for forty years and the colleagues they have worked with over that time.

So even managers who feel they ought to speak out and speak out loud to counter the prevailing extreme version of shareholder value hegemony are unlikely to do so. Are there not journalists, publicists, pundits, academics who will speak out for them?

The Opinion-Formers

Here is a country which flourished under a corporate regime in which shareholder control was effectively and deliberately neutralized by a system of cross-shareholdings. It was a system that worked because, despite the absence of external monitoring – a firm's bank creditors would interfere only if its failure was abject – managers' consciences, their sense of responsibility to "the company" in the abstract, and their fellow-employees in particular, gave them strong motives for being diligent and efficient.[12] And even if on occasion those motives were not strong enough to produce optimal performance, they rarely produced the sort of outrageous pursuit of self-interest as shocked the world at Enron or is currently a favorite explanation for the recent financial cataclysm. Those of their shareholders with whom they did not have reciprocal arrangements were untroubled by the low level of dividends, because they expected substantial long-run capital gains – and bought shares for that reason with such enthusiasm that the disastrous bubble resulted.

That last aspect of the 1980s system is not going to be restored. The expectation of certain long-run capital gains has evaporated. New funds may still come predominantly from retained earnings, but access to capital clearly depends on providing shareholders with income streams, in dividends and share buybacks, on a scale much greater than in the 1980s. But that is an entirely different question from the question of how managers are to be kept honest and firms are to be efficiently run. It constitutes no reason at all for adding to existing sources of discipline – above all the discipline of product markets and the discipline involved in the need to retain the respect of colleagues and subordinates – by turning what used to be a stock market solely for the buying and selling of the right to income streams into a market for corporate control.

Nevertheless, the belief that making it so is a triumph of institutional reform, that the pressure it thereby puts on managers is wholly desirable, has become an unshakeable orthodoxy. As one of the leading proponents of shareholder value institutions puts it in a private communication, "the idea that managers will behave with proper discipline in the absence of external pressure rests on the [Confucian] Original Virtue delusion." Business leaders and permanent secretaries of METI may make pretty speeches about stakeholders and the desirability of firms being run with due regard to all stakeholder interests, but the real guardians of Japan's business institutions are united in thinking otherwise.

One would expect that, only twenty years since all but a small minority of shareholder rights advocates were intent on trumpeting the virtues of Japanese employee-sovereign management, there would be some dissidents who would advocate changes in the regulations that served to restrict the scope for hostile takeovers and introduce rules that tried to ensure that changes in management control should take into account the interests of other stakeholders besides managers.

---

[12] On the importance of "capillary controls" from subordinates and peers see Dore (2003).

But it is hard to find them. One would expect, for instance, to find someone bringing into the debate the recent concession made to stakeholder prescriptions for corporate governance in the birthplace of Anglo-Saxon capitalism. But after intensive googling, I have come across only one reference (by an octogenarian Keynesian economist, Ito 2007) to section 172 (1) of the British 2006 Companies Act, which defines the duties of a director as follows:

> A director of a company must act in the way he considers, in good faith, would be most likely to promote the success of the company for the benefit of its members as a whole, and in doing so have regard (among other matters) to:
>
> (a) The likely consequence of any decision in the long term,
> (b) The interests of the company's employees,
> (c) The need to foster the company's business relationships with suppliers, customers, and others,
> (d) The impact of the company's operations on the community and the environment, the desirability of the company maintaining a reputation for high standards of business conduct, and
> (e) The need to act fairly as between members of the company.

A brief sampling[13] of the writings of academic lawyers which relate to the shareholder value versus stakeholder value issue suggests that the most common theme is an analysis of the concept of *kigyo kachi* translated as "corporate value" in the title of the Corporate Value Study Group, though "enterprise value" (EV) would be more accurate. The term was practically unknown until that study group was created in 2004. It seems to have been introduced to give the impression that, while the point of view of the "shareholder value" theorists was being adopted, it was not adopted enthusiastically and was given a Japanese slant. The technical use of the term enterprise value by investment banks to mean simply "net debt plus market cap," that is, how much an acquisition would cost ex any premium bait to shareholders, seems not to be widely used, though one manager who had recently made a large and highly leveraged acquisition did use it in that sense – congratulating himself that the size of his huge debt meant that he no longer had to worry about takeover threats.

The Study Group itself, though the agenda for its first meeting spoke of the need to define the term, failed to do so, though Nomura's economic

---

[13] The sampling was under the guidance of Professor Junichiro Mori to whom I am deeply grateful.

dictionary (Nomura 2008) says that in some document it offered the definition:

A company's assets, its earning power, its stability, its efficiency, its ability to grow etc. those characteristics, and the degree of those characteristics which contribute to shareholder profit.

It appears, however, that the Study Group has lived to regret its name. It has a footnote at the beginning of its latest June 2008 report, which recalls that it did entitle its 2005 guidelines, "Guidelines concerning takeovers designed to maintain and improve corporate value/the common interest of share-holders." However, it goes on, while the slash in that title meant "corporate value, *viz.* common interest of shareholders" it now proposes exclusively to use the latter term, while affirming that, "conceptually," "corporate value" should be taken to mean "the discounted present value of future cash flows." The inwardness of this is explained, in a magazine roundtable discussion on the report, by Hiromoto Kimura, the Corporate Governance Director of the Pension Fund Association, and probably the most influential member of the committee. They had dropped the term, he said, because the abstraction "corporate value" was being defined so broadly so as to justify taking into consideration, a propos takeover defenses, all sorts of other factors other than pure shareholder interest, such factors – such irrelevancies, he seemed to imply – as "providing society with fine products, having high R&D capacity, providing stable employment for employees, etc."(Kanda et al. 2008: 7)

A typical and clear statement of the dominant position is that of a professor of Tokyo University (Ochiai 2005). There are, he says, two ver-sions of EV: the value the enterprise has for the shareholders and the value it has for all the stakeholders including the shareholders, the former being the orthodox view, but the latter view being held by a sizeable number of managers who criticize "shareholder value as an American principle of corporate governance or claim that management should give greatest priority to employees." So which should one take as the EV which all takeover and takeover defense rules should seek to preserve and increase? There is a lot to be said for the importance of stakeholders, but the fact is that the interests of employees or the interest of creditors often conflict with the interests of shareholders. There is no way of adding up all these interests; where they conflict one is bound in the end to favor one or the other. Thus, making the relevant EV the sum of the value to all stake-holders, "is to enforce something which is impossible as a practical norm or a legal rule, and something which can act as a cloak to justify arbitrary decisions by managers."

Other scholars try to square that circle with metaphysics, including one who is a member of the Corporate Value Study Group (Osugi 2005). He takes the meaning of EV to be equivalent to "shareholders' long-term interest" and argues, "this is not just the simple sum of the interests of the existing shareholders at the present moment (what one might call the 'raw' shareholder interest); it is something which is, as it were, an ideal concept derived by abstraction from individual shareholders' interest... [and] can be measured in such a way as to include the interests of other stakeholders besides shareholders, and as such can be compared, at least in scalar terms with the price a takeover bidder is offering." The automatic "inclusion" of other stakeholders rests on the fact that the long-term income stream to shareholders depends on treating employees, suppliers etc. well – the so-called "enlightened" version of the shareholder value doctrine. He does not tackle the small problem of how to persuade "raw" shareholders like hedge funds to be interested in long-run returns.

A more concrete treatment of the issue is by a younger associate professor at Seikei University (Tanaka 2008) who is also the only one to refer to German codetermination as a possibly relevant model. He deploys economists' arguments about incomplete and implicit contracts as grounds for urging that stakeholders,' particularly employees,' interests justify giving them partial control over the decisions of managers. That would be fine if the sum total of control was not reduced, but "one may doubt whether employees who are in a subordinate position, subject to the orders of management, will exercise that control effectively and so the result would probably be simply a reduction in shareholder control and in the discipline to which managers are subjected."

But his main point is that the case for giving to the providers of human capital a share in the control of the firm along with the providers of monetary capital differs from firm to firm, and is greatest when the enterprise uses a lot of enterprise specific skills. Therefore there should be flexibility, allowing firms to choose to give potential control partly to their employees, by means, for instance, of a rights plan under which they could issue warrants to their employees for shares with voting rights but no dividend rights, at ¥1 a share – which, he claims, would be perfectly legal under existing law. Provided the shareholders voted in favor of such a system – committed themselves to it in full knowledge that it might prevent takeovers of which they might otherwise approve – managers could not be sued for breach of fiduciary duty.

He concludes with the small matter of feasibility. "Whether in practice such schemes would be accepted and such commitment given depends on whether capital markets would recognise their efficiency."

In the minds of such scholars, it never, ever, of course, depends on whether the society's political choice should be to allow capital markets to have such a dominant last word. "Efficiency" is the ultimate value of Japan's twenty-first century intellectual community, and, in spite of the evidence our newspapers provide us with every day in the autumn of 2008, the belief still holds that capital markets produce it.

Conclusion

No-one, in short, challenges either the supremacy of shareholder interests nor the thesis that vulnerability to takeover is an essential instrument for the discipline of managers, nor the corollary that the stock market should be designed to facilitate its role as a market for corporate control. A few managers may mutter their dissatisfaction, but after less than two decades of missionary activity, the conversion of Japan to the theology of shareholder sovereignty seems complete.

Bibliography

ACCJ (2008). *White Paper 2008.* Tokyo: American Chamber of Commerce in Japan.

ACGA (2008). *White Paper on Corporate Governance in Japan.* Hong Kong: Asian Corporate Governance Association.

Dore, R. (2003). "The Globalization of Corporate Governance: External and Internal Mechanisms of Control." *Journal of Japanese Trade and Industry,* April/March 2003 and *Journal of Interdisciplinary Economics* 14.

Ito, M. (2007). "Nijuisseiki, nihon no kigyo no bihebia ga kawatta no ka." ("Has the Behaviour of Japanese Enterprises Changed in the 21st Century.") *Sekai,* August.

Kanda, H. (2008). "Kihonteki kangaekata to kihan teiji." ("Part 2 on the Study Group Report, 'Basic Principles and an Indication of Norms.' ") *Nihon Keizai Shimbun,* 30 July.

Kanda, H., Niihara H., Kimura H., and Takei K. (2008). "Kigyo kachi kenkyukai hokokusho to kongo no baishu boei no arikata Jo." ("The Report of the Corporate Value Study Group and the Future Shape of Corporate Takeovers, Part 1.") *Shoji homu* No. 1843, 15 September. Parts 2 and 3 appeared in subsequent numbers.

Kitabata, T. (2008). "Kaisha wa kabunushi dake no mono ka?" ("Does the Corporation Belong Only to the Shareholders?") *Keizai sangyo chosakai,* 15 February.

Mimura, A. (2008). "Sekai tekko kogyo ni okeru gyokaisaihen no doko to Shin Nittetsu ni okeru corporate governance." ("Trends in the Restructuring of the World Steel Industry and Corporate Governance at Nippon Steel.") Lecture at the 64th annual Meeting of the Nihon Kansayaku Kyokai (Japan Statutory Auditors Association). *Gekkan Kansayaku*, June 2007.

NHK (2007). "Tekitaiteki baishu wo fusege: Shinnittetsu toppu no ketsudan." ("Defend Yourself Against Hostile Takeovers! The Resolve of Nippon Steel's Top Management.") *NHK Special*, 7 June.

Nomura shoken (2008). *Shoken yogo kaisetsushu, EV (Explanation of Securities Terminology, EV)* www.nomura.co.jp/terms/category/management/ev.html.

Ochiai, S. (2005). "Tekitai baishu ni okeru jakkan no kihoneki mondai." ("Some Basic Problems Concerning Hostile Takeovers.") *Kigyo kaikei*, 57/10.

Osugi, K. (2005). "Kigyo baishu boeisaku no arikata." ("Appropriate Means of Defence Against Takeovers.") *Shoji homu* 1723, February.

Ota, H. (2008). "Baishu boeisaku: kigyo kachi kenkyukai hokokusho wo megutte. Jo: Shiho handan ni teishoku suru naiyo." ("Defence Against Takeovers; Concerning the Report of the Corporate Value Study Group, Part 1: The Contents Clash with Judicial Opinion.") *Nihon Keizai Shimbun*, 29 July.

Tamura, K. (2007). *Blog* (http://kotarotamura.net/index_blog.php?itemiid = 448).

Tanaka, W. (2008). "Sutekuhoruda to gabanansu." ("Stakeholders and Corporate Governance.") *Kigyo kaikei* 2005, 57/7.

Whittaker, D.H. and M. Hayakawa (2007). "Contesting 'Corporate Value' through Takeover Bids in Japan." *Corporate Governance: An International Review*, 15: 16–26.

Yano, T. (2008). "Baishu-boeisaku no mae ni torishimariyaku no chujitsu-gimu no kakuho Wo." ("Let Us Get the Fiduciary Duty of Directors Straight Before Talking of Takeover Defences.") *Nikkei Net, Keizai Rashinban*, 2 June.

6

Managers and Corporate Governance Reform in Japan: Restoring Self-Confidence or Shareholder Revolution?

Takeshi Inagami

Debates about reforming corporate governance in Japan began in 1992, soon after the bursting of the bubble economy. "Corporate governance" was a novel term, and not popular among executives.[1] Kaneo Nakamura, a counselor of the Industrial Bank of Japan who took the initiative in discussions in business circles, later reminisced: "I first became aware of the term 'corporate governance' when I was asked in June 1992 to be the chair of Enterprise Trend Study Group of Keizai Doyukai (KD – Japan Committee for Economic Development) and also to write about the future of Japanese management in the KD *11th Enterprise White Paper*."[2] To do so, in September 1992, he got together fifteen prominent presidents of representative firms to debate a new Japanese economic and managerial system, or a new Japanese-style of capitalism.[3]

---

[1] Tadao Suzuki, a member of Enterprise Trends Study Group and chair of the Working Committee for the Principles of Corporate Governance commented: "At that time (in the early 1990s), most executives did not know the term 'corporate governance.' Moreover, none of them argued that the shareholders are more important stakeholders than employees." (Suzuki 2005: 5, 16).

[2] Nakamura (2000). Graduating from the University of Tokyo Faculty of Law in 1947, Kaneo Nakamura entered the Industrial Bank of Japan and became President of the Bank in 1984. He was on friendly terms with GE's Jack Welch and became a member of the International Advisory Board of many large firms such as GE, Westminster Bank and Morgan Stanley Group. Cf. Shinagawa and Ushio eds. (2000: 413–8).

[3] The group included Jiro Ushio (vice-chairman; Ushio Inc.), Josei Itoh (Nippon Life Insurance), Takashi Imai (Nippon Steel), Yotaro Kobayashi (Fuji Electric), Shoji Shinagawa (Nippon

In KD's *10th Enterprise White Paper* (published earlier in 1992), Yotaro Kobayashi opined: "Japanese companies have to set sail with neither a marine chart nor a model to emulate" (Kobayashi 1992). Similarly, in his Introduction to the *11th Enterprise White Paper*, Nakamura declared that Japanese society had reached its third turning point after the Meiji Restoration and the defeat of World War II. In retrospect, claims of a "third turning point" appear exaggerated, but they are indicative of how much leading executives worried about the future of Japanese-style management and the economic system then. Their major anxiety was over Japanese competitiveness vis-à-vis the United States and Europe in an era of globalization. Many of them clearly had a sense of crisis.

Debates over the reform of Japanese corporate governance, which started in the context of a reevaluation of Japanese-style management and the Japanese economic system in the early 1990s, now appear to have subsided – momentarily at least – with Nippon Keidanren's (NK – Japan Business Federation) remarkable publication *On the Ideal Way of Japanese Corporate Governance* in 2006, after a decade and a half of legal and institutional reforms. This NK report might be considered an "Interim Summary" of the controversy surrounding corporate governance in Japan.

This chapter evaluates where Japan has traveled in terms of management, and especially corporate governance, in fifteen years with no chart or model. It analyses changes to Japanese corporate governance in terms of institutions and behavior, noting the changing features of corporate corruption, and examining the "silent shareholder revolution" thesis. It also pays particular attention to the career paths and remuneration of company executives, who play a central role in corporate governance reform and practices in Japan, as elsewhere in the world.

Debates on Corporate Governance Reform

The first issue to be addressed in this chapter is the similarities and differences between the initial ideas of leading executives in the early 1990s and the NK publication in 2006. Have the original ideas of Nakamura and his colleagues on reforming corporate governance practices in Japan been realized, or not?

Fire and Marine Insurance), Tadao Suzuki (Mercian), Seiji Tutumi (Saison Group), Sho Nasu (Tokyo Electric Power), Yoshihiko Miyauchi (Orix), and Ken Moroi (Chichibu Cement).

The KD 11th Enterprise White Paper

Anticipating a new age after Japan's "third turning point," the KD *11th Enterprise White Paper* declared that Japanese-style management must be changed from its focus on market share to profit making, from closed to open *keiretsu*, and from rigid to flexible employment. Nonexecutive directors should be introduced, and the interests of shareholders must be given much greater emphasis, for example, by raising return on equity (ROE). In addition, companies must behave as good corporate citizens, and reform their persistent inclination toward dependency on the government. A basic managerial attitude should be to reconstruct new trustworthy relationships with every stakeholder, while preserving tension or healthy distance in the relationships. The desirable relationship with employees was depicted as one of "cocreating," while maintaining respective independence (Keizai Doyukai 1994).

In February, the same members of the Study Group chaired by Nakamura gathered at Tokyo Bay Hilton Hotel in Maihama, Chiba Prefecture. The so-called Maihama Conference resulted in the publication (in May) of *Establishing a New Japanese Corporate Governance*.[4] The contents overlapped with the *White Paper*, but several points were newly made. One concerned the ratio of nonexecutive directors – 20–30 percent was seen as desirable, so that they could play an effective coordinating role between executives and shareholders, but not overturn the practices of internal promotion. Another was the need to transform the *nenko* (seniority plus merit) wage system, complemented by flexible but stable employment. The need to reform the traditional main bank system and indirect financing, and the intention to vitalize capital markets, was also expressed.

It should be noted that both this document and the *11th Enterprise White Paper* were written with a historical perspective. On the one hand, the authors clearly had in mind the famous report *A Draft on Democratizing the Corporation* (Keizai Doyukai 1947) by Banjo Otsuka and a group of young executives, which set out a vision of "revised capitalism" and had a remarkable influence on the management of Japanese firms in the postwar era.[5] On the other hand, in the post Cold War era of "capitalism versus

---

[4] In the Maihama Conference, Imai of Nippon Steel who stressed employees' interests clashed with Miyauchi of Orix, who emphasized shareholders' interests. Cf. Shinagawa and Ushio (eds.) (2000).

[5] *A Draft on Democratizing the Corporation* asserted that capital, labor, and management are basically equal in terms of ownership, decision making, and profit sharing. Also it declared the importance of maintaining a "minimum security" standard, that is, the going rate of interest for shareholders, and securing living wages for employees as well as managers. Moreover, it

capitalism," they stressed the importance of importing the positive aspects of Western management/capitalism, while retaining a base of Japanese management/capitalism, and excluding neither the logic of capital nor the logic of society.

In brief, their basic idea was to reform corporate governance as part of the reform of Japanese management, while retaining the essence of the latter. The thinking came from executives themselves – specifically their own sense of crisis – and was not imposed on them by shareholders or any other stakeholder. Their key ideas had a historical perspective. One was the concept of "revised capitalism," originating in the aftermath of the defeat of World War II, the second turning point. Another was consciousness of the coming era of "varieties of capitalism" after "the end of history," or the third turning point.

Americanization? Principles of the Japan Corporate Governance Forum

Shortly after these events, in November 1994, the Japan Corporate Governance Forum (JCGF) was established. The inaugural letter by Kaneo Nakamura and Takayasu Okushima of Waseda University held that there were two basic issues to clarify in corporate governance – for whom firms should be managed, and who should supervise and check executives' attitudes and behavior. They added: "In order to restrain arbitrary decisions by executives and short-termism of shareholders, to provide the opportunities for fair competition of employees, and with an interdisciplinary emphasis, an international perspective and cooperation between industry and academia, we will establish a new type of association – the Japan Corporate Governance Forum – and through its activities we will advocate effective policies for corporate governance."

Four years later, in May 1998, their *Principles of Corporate Governance* (*Principles*) was published. Many other reports, guidelines, and principles for dealing with corporate governance were published in rapid succession in the same year, marking the height of controversy about corporate governance. The Hampel Committee in the United Kingdom published its *Final Report* (January 1998), CalPERS released its *Principles of Corporate Governance in Japan* (March), Keizai Doyukai published the *13th Enterprise White Paper* (subtitled "Management Stressing Capital Efficiency," April),

---

declared that labor unions should change their activities from "guaranteeing workers' interests outside firms" to "improving workers' interest through building management efficiency from within" (Keizai Doyukai 1947).

the OECD produced the *Millstein Report* (also in April), and Nikkeiren's International Special Committee issued *The Direction of Corporate Govern-ance Reform for Japanese Firms* (subtitled "Towards Firms Favored by Both Capital Markets and Labour Markets," August).[6]

Significantly, there was a large gap in perceptions of corporate govern-ance between the JCGF on the one hand, and Keizai Doyukai and Nikkeiren on the other. According to the *Principles*, "the shareholders in particular, the providers of equity capital, have a special position. As they constitute the final risk-takers of the company who are entitled to claim the residual profits, they are often considered the owners of the company. In this sense and under the system of private ownership, shareholders are granted the right of governance over the company for the benefit of their own interests in the form of maximum returns on their investment" (JCGF 1998: 11). Based on this textbook-like position, the *Principles* argued that the general public should be informed clearly that stock companies are owned by shareholders, and their main purpose is the pursuit of profit. It did mention the necessity for directors to cooperate with their employees to maximize shareholder value, and therefore the need to avoid easy dis-missal. However, it claimed that with the exception of quality management "the myth of Japanese-style management collapsed feebly with the burst-ing of the bubble economy, and consequently the traditional corporate governance practices of Japan should be reformed in accordance with 'global standards'" (JCGF 1998: 13). In sharp contrast to the *11th Enterprise White Paper* by Nakamura et al. (1994), it is possible to say that the *Principles* advocated the Americanization of Japanese corporate governance.

Pluralist Model of Corporate Governance: Keizai Doyukai and Nikkeiren

Not surprisingly, the views of the KD *13th Enterprise White Paper* of 1998 also differed from the *Principles*. Symbolically, the full text of the Hampel Committee's "Final Report" published two months earlier was appended, with the first chapter translated into Japanese. In fact, Akira Kosai and the other members of KD's Enterprise Management Committee met with Sir Ronald Hampel at the ICI head office in October 1997.

On the one hand, the 1998 *White Paper* emphasized the importance of achieving capital-efficient management, and for the directors to pay close attention to the movement of their company's share price. It also claimed

---

[6] Nikkeiren – the Japan Federation of Employers' Associations – was merged with Keidanren – the Federation of Economic Organizations – in 2002 to create the Nippon Keidanren.

that the dysfunctional board of directors and auditors system needed to be reformed. Employment practices should also change. The perception of labor as a fixed cost was already changing, but there needed to be greater fluidity of employment, flexible patterns of work, limited contracts of employment, the introduction of stock option schemes as a sort of performance-related payment, and portability of enterprise pensions.

On the other hand, the *White Paper* declared that it is impossible to legitimate capital-efficient management without good corporate citizenship. Good corporate citizenship meant addressing environmental issues, stressing the interests of customers, and maintaining cooperative relationships with employees and unions (Keizai Doyukai 1998: 7). There was no shareholder sovereignty declaration, and no call for directors to maximize the interests of shareholders. As for the institutional framework of corporate governance, it argued that legal regulations should be minimized and the discretion of individual firms should be stressed. There was no statement calling for the introduction of "global standards" of corporate governance.

This stance is even more apparent in Nikkeiren's International Special Committee (1998), chaired by Nobuo Tateishi, who was a member of the OECD's Millstein Committee. The former declared that there is no possibility of a "one-size-fits-all" approach in corporate governance. While it is necessary to emphasize the interests of shareholders, to make decision-making processes more transparent, to develop an external control system and to stimulate information disclosure, respect for life and dignity and a long-term view of management, which are basic features of Japanese-style management, should be maintained. In fact, it claimed, emphasizing shareholder interests is not incompatible with emphasizing the interests of employees. Thus, although it stressed the discretion of individual firms, it argued that corporations should be managed so as to be favored both by capital markets and labor markets, as suggested by the subtitle of the report.

In brief, there was a large gap between the JCGF and another two representative business/employer bodies in terms of their basic understanding of corporate governance, and the preferred path to be taken.

Interim Summary by the Nippon Keidanren

Eight years after these publications, the NK issued its remarkable "Interim Summary" on corporate governance in Japan (Nippon Keidanren 2006*b*). It declared, first, that the major objective of corporate governance is to increase the long-term value of the corporation, prevent corporate corruption, and improve corporate competitiveness and profitability. Second, there is not an international, universal single model in terms of building the institutional framework of corporate governance. Free choice and diversity should be respected as there is still no clear conclusion as to the relationship between performance and institutional frameworks. What is crucial is not formality but real effectiveness. Third, the joint stock company or public-owned corporation is in a real sense a "public institution." It is disciplined most effectively by customers and society. Fourth, the corporation needs to be managed to create value not only for shareholders but also for employees, consumers, and society. Fifth, fair share trading is a basic foundation for corporate governance and therefore all investors should maintain proper ethics and accountability. Government and stock exchanges are responsible for devising appropriate regulations for the sound operation of stock markets.

Other policies are derived from these basic ideas. Government or stock exchanges should not force blanket procedures such as the introduction of nonexecutive directors or strengthening director independence, given the lack of hard evidence linking this with corporate performance. We should make efforts to clarify the features and merits of the Japanese auditor system, following the 2001 Commercial Code revisions aimed at strengthening the authority and function of auditors. The judgment of independent directors concerning unsolicited takeover bids is not necessarily correct, and other approaches might be considered. Moreover, in order to develop investor relations, companies should attempt to engage "genuine" shareholders. And to improve the base for long-term management and avoid short-termism, consideration should be given to privileging stable shareholders in terms of dividends, voting rights, and tax benefits.

After scrutinizing domestic and foreign corporate governance reforms in the last decade, the *Interim Summary* argued that in order to maintain the beneficial aspects of Japanese-style management, corporations should behave as public or social institutions, and seek to increase corporate value in the long run. Overall, maximizing long-term corporate value would be achieved by maintaining voluntarism and diversity in corporate governance, and securing fair share trading, and privileges for "genuine" shareholders. The style of the Report is self-confident in pointing to the direction to be taken by Japanese firms in reforms of traditional corporate governance practices. More than simply an interim summary, it can be considered an important milestone.

Why the Basic Continuity?

How different is the scenario drawn by Nakamura and colleagues in the early 1990s, and the *Interim Summary*? In a word, there is a basic resonance – *basso ostinato* – between them. Neither considers American-style corporate governance as a global standard. Both refute the idea that the publicly owned corporation is the exclusive property of shareholders, and also that directors are simply the agents of shareholder principals. On the contrary, while conceding the need to strengthen shareholder interests, both are explicit in their commitment to a "pluralist model" of corporate governance.[7] Strengthening shareholder interests does not imply abandoning the notion of the corporation as a socially accountable public institution. Both reports are clearly supportive of the long-termist aspects of Japanese-style management and are very critical of shareholder primacy short-termism.

Many significant developments mark the period between the two reports, such as the financial Big Bang from 1997, the long deflationary recession, the neo-liberal wave of deregulation, declining confidence in Japanese-style management, and the rise of capital-efficient management. Nevertheless, basic continuity can be seen on the part of leading executives as to desirable corporate governance practices. How can we explain this continuity? The following were no doubt contributing factors:

1. Japanese directors became increasingly skeptical of the American model, especially after the Enron and WorldCom scandals.

2. As claimed in the *Interim Summary*, no causal relationship has been demonstrated between the institutional framework of corporate governance and business performance.

3. Based on the evidence of corporate governance reforms in the United States, the United Kingdom, Germany, and France, for example, it was concluded that "every country has their own cultural traditions, commercial and commercial practices, and the management of firms is deeply embedded in its respective society" (Nippon Keidanren 2006*b*).

4. In Japan, criticism of hostile takeover bids such as Nippon Broadcasting System by Livedoor and Bull-Dog Sauce by Steel Partners was very strong, as was condemnation of speculative business symbolized by Takafumi Horie and Yoshiaki Murakami.[8]

---

[7] The terminology follows the UK's DTI (1999) which identifies three models – the classic, enlightened shareholder value, and pluralist models.
[8] According to the Cabinet Office (2008), over two-thirds of those polled responded negatively to hostile takeovers by domestic or foreign firms. From the Meiji Period *jitsugyo* (literally "productive" business) has been contrasted with *kyogyo* (speculative business) by prominent

5. With the surge of dividends and directors' remuneration in the past decade also came a large increase in individual labor disputes.[9] In such circumstances, strong criticism of growing inequality spread, and the implementation of relevant countermeasures became an important political issue.

6. The growing influence of multinationals in developing countries, along with labor problems in developed countries, drew attention to corporate social responsibility (CSR), prompting many declarations and guidelines by business/employer associations, unions, NGOs, and government.

7. Only a limited number of large firms adopted the "company with committees" system (CCS), often regarded as emblematic of American-style corporate governance and legally permitted following amendment of the Commercial Code in 2002. The overwhelming majority of corporations retained the traditional "company with corporate auditors" system.

8. The role of employees in internal control of the firm was clarified through company law reform implemented in May 2006.[10]

9. Most strikingly, Japan's community firms did not collapse, despite predictions of imminent demise.

Renewing Labor–Management Communication within Firms

On May 16 2006, just one month *before* publication of the *Interim Summary*, the NK issued another significant report entitled *Towards Improving Internal Labour–Management Communication in a New Era*. While the former dealt with shareholders, the latter dealt with employees and unions. It argued that Japanese firms had been able to overcome the "three excesses" (excessive debt, capacity and workforces) and other problems through the

---

intellectual and business leaders such as Yukichi Fukuzawa, Eiichi Shibusawa, and Hikojiro Nakagamigawa. Similar support for *jitsugyo* can be found out throughout Mitarai and Niwa (2006), who argue that public-listed companies are "public institutions."

[9] In order to resolve the increasing number of individual labor disputes, the Law on Promoting the Resolution of Individual Labor Disputes was enacted from October 2001, and the Labour Adjudication System was introduced in April 2006. The Ministry of Health, Labour and Welfare (2008) indicated that the total number of consultations concerning individual labor disputes amounted to nearly one million in 2007, an increase of 5.2% over the previous year. Dismissals, harassments, wage cuts, and diminutions of working conditions were major issues. The number of individual labor disputes has increased with the decline of collective labour disputes.

[10] See below. The JCGF issued new Principles in December 2006 in view of this, bringing them closer to the "enlightened shareholder value model."

combined efforts of labor and management, based on mutual trust. Furthermore, "good labour–management communication is the source of competitiveness," and industrial relations is the base of management. Thus a worsening of industrial relations would inevitably have a negative impact on management. Two important elements of Japanese-style management – "respect for people" and "management from a long-term perspective" – were as relevant as ever. In addition, the Three Productivity Principles of employment stabilility, joint (labor–management) consultation and a fair distribution of the fruits of productivity increases, propagated in 1955 by the Japan Productivity Center (JPC), "have universal significance, even now."

Notwithstanding this, there has been a marked increase in atypical workers, union density has continued to decline and individual labor disputes have surged. In these circumstances, efforts must be made to improve workplace human relations, improve the sense of unity between employees and company, and to resolve individual disputes within firms. Additionally, a number of industrial relations issues related to enterprise groups must be addressed, such as responsibilities of holding companies (Nippon Keidanren 2006a).

These two reports from the NK, published almost together in 2006, imply that while a number of issues remain, including defenses against hostile takeovers, Japanese directors have reconstructed their basic stance toward corporate governance and labor–management communication.

Institutions and Behavior of Corporate Governance

We cannot assume that the NK's ideas are widely reflected in the behavior of individual firms. It is necessary to examine the nature of governance behavior itself, meaning who checks and supervises executive behavior, and whose interests are emphasized among the stakeholders. The focus here is primarily on the latter, since corporate governance institutions might be understood as ordering priorities among various stakeholders. In this respect, we shall explore Dore's "silent shareholder revolution" thesis (2006a, 2006b), which sees major changes in the past decade which will eventually bring about a collapse of the (quasi) community firm. We shall explore the extent to which this provocative thesis is empirically supported. First, however, let us look briefly at institutional changes to corporate governance.

Company with Committees and Company with Corporate Auditors

In the past (Inagami 2000), I have defined the Japanese model of corporate governance as (*a*) management for long-term corporate prosperity, (*b*) management by internally-promoted executives, (*c*) supported by silent stable shareholders and cross-shareholdings, main banks, and indirect financing, as well as relational contracting with regular employees and suppliers, and (*d*) a dual control system by the board of directors and board of auditors. As for changes since then, there appear to be no fundamental changes in the aims of the corporation, although some directors now appear to see their mission as the maximization of shareholder interests.[11] The career paths of most directors remains unchanged.

Several institutional elements have changed, however. Cross-shareholdings have declined, although recently they have begun to revive, partially to cope with the rise of hostile takeovers. The main bank system and related indirect financing have also weakened. But the dual control system of corporate governance has basically remained intact, despite the step-by-step introduction of the "company with committees" system ("CCS"). Instead of implementing this system, many firms have tried to revitalize their conventional dual control system by strengthening the function of the board of auditors.

Indeed, in the last quarter of the twentieth century, a series of amendments to the Commercial Code and company law have attempted to strengthen the role of the board of auditors. More recently, in 2001, the independence of auditors was reinforced and their term of office was extended to four years. It was prescribed that more than half the auditors have to be external, and not (ex-)directors or employees of group or related companies. In 2002, large corporations were permitted to move to CCS. In June 2006, Tokyo Stock Exchange (TSE) required all listed companies have to submit a Report on Corporate Governance based on a common format, which is disclosed to the public. And under provisions of the Financial Instruments and Exchange Law – the so-called Japanese version of SOX – from April 2008, in order to prevent corporate malfeasance, all employees are obliged to participate in the internal control of the firm, with the aim of improving business efficiency, reliability of financial reports, compliance, and preservation of resources, including human resources.

---

[11] Inagami and Whittaker (2005: 77–8) estimate the proportion of Japanese directors who see their role as maximizing shareholder value as agents of shareholders at around 10%.

Among these measures, the introduction of CCS undoubtedly represented a major attempt to reform corporate governance in Japan. The number of companies adopting CCS, however, amounted to 110 firms as of December 11 2007, which included fifty-three first section TSE-listed companies (sixteen of them from the Hitachi Group), nineteen from the second section, and thirty-eight nonlisted companies. This represents only 3 percent of first section TSE-listed companies. In fact, some firms have reverted to the "company with corporate auditors" (CCA) system, including Risona Bank, Kanebo Trinity Holdings, and SoftBank Telecom.

How much difference is there actually between the CCS and CCA systems in practice? The TSE (2007) and Japan Association of Corporate Auditors (JACA) (2008) investigated who chairs the board of directors and remuneration and nominating committees of CCS, and how many external directors were appointed to important positions in CCA companies. Despite major differences in the legal frameworks, they found little difference in practice between the two, confirming the findings of Buchanan and Deakin (2008. See also Chapter 2).

Corporate Malfeasance and CSR

What matters, it might be argued, is not institutions per se, but how they function in practice. Two aspects of behavior will be examined here. The first concerns corrupt corporate behavior. If wrongdoings are exposed, all stakeholders to a greater or lesser extent suffer. Naturally, the responsibility of executives becomes an issue. The second is the basic question of whose interests are favored in practice, irrespective of legal provisions. Let us look at corruption first.

JACA (2003) reported that many of the recent cases of corporate wrongdoing have come to light not just as a result of whistle-blowing by employees, but by customers and suppliers as well. The response by consumers and markets has been severe. In many cases, the firms in question have been forced into extensive retrenchment or even dissolution. Companies in which wrongdoing has been discovered have come to own up more quickly, and this often involves the resignation of executives to take responsibility. The government has also begun to respond quickly to corruption stemming from incomplete legislation or institutions. According to a Nippon Keidanren (2005) survey, three out of four company presidents feel very uneasy about the prospect of wrongdoing occurring in their company or group.

As for the types of corruption, JACA selected and analyzed eighteen cases from among nearly 300 covered by newspapers from January 2000 to

January 2003, and classified them into four categories: (*a*) top management, (*b*) "sacred" jobs or sections, (*c*) incubation of bad practices, and (*d*) accidents. The first refers to instances in which the president or top management is insufficiently conscious of contemporary corporate ethics and is too powerful, and the board of directors is incapable of checking him or her, with no overall effective internal monitoring system. In cases of this type, top managers often resign and sometimes the company dissolves. The second type happens when there is a highly specialized but rather inner-directed work ethic, with no effective monitoring system from other sections. In the third, a conservative intra-firm atmosphere with strong customary working practices comes to embody "in-group virtues, out-group vices." The fourth is often the result of a misjudgment at the workplace in responding to an accident or trouble.

Briefly, the 2003 JACA survey showed that many of the examples of corrupt in-group practices were exposed by employees, that long-held practices had become out of step with social norms, and that the number of scandals resulting from orders from top management had increased. In other words, most scandals resulted from (*a*), (*b*), and (*c*). Over half the directors surveyed by JACA thought that deflationary pressures, recession, and deteriorating performance contributed to these scandals. Similar findings were reported by a Keizai Koho Center (2008) survey conducted for the NK.

Looking ahead, it is possible that the legislation like the Whistleblower's Protection Act (2006) and the revised Financial Instruments and Exchange Law (2008) will help to reduce corporate malfeasance. In addition to legislation, however, awareness of keeping the law and preventing wrongdoing has increased as part of the heightened interest in CSR. Prominent among motivations for engaging in CSR in Japan have been "ensuring that corporate corruption is prevented before it happens" (61.9%), "positively carrying out responsibility as corporate citizens" (59.3%) and "improving corporate image" (48.1%). Observing the law and "environmental management" have been important not just as concepts, but in CSR practice as well (Inagami 2007). In this respect, unlike the EU's Green Paper (EU 2001), CSR in Japan has had a "hard law"-related dimension (Keizai Doyukai 2003; Nippon Keidanren 2004).

Whose Company?

More critical as far as corporate governance behavior is concerned is who the company is managed for. In *Who is the Company For?* coauthored with

Fujio Mitarai in 2006, Itochu chairman and member of the Economic and Financial Advisory Council Uichiro Niwa wrote:

It has become fashionable to think that American-style money-capitalism is innova-tive and progressive. But is this really the case? We often hear it asked "Who owns the company?" these days, and of course the shareholders own the company. But this is the legal situation, and not the actual essence. If we want to get to the essence, we shouldn't ask "Who owns the company?" but "Who is the company for?"

He declares: "We must return to the basis that the company is a public institution." Moreover: "From the point of view of economic justice it is unacceptable that companies are bought and sold like toys for money making because share ownership only imparts a share of the rights to control a company's equipment and assets" (Niwa 2006: 180–81).

Niwa is not alone in these views, and the view that the critical issue is not legal ownership, but the function of the company.

In a speech to the JACA Annual Conference in April 2008, his coauthor – Canon CEO and NK chairman Fujio Mitarai – declared:

Any decent executive will think that the company belongs to its employees, to its customers, and to serve the local community and society. At least in Japan they will…They will not entertain the thought of M&A for profit of the moment. Whether it be foreign or domestic capital, we should not tolerate raiders who destroy the public essence of companies and become a nuisance for honest shareholders. They should be shut out of the market. The Nippon Keidanren will not shirk from this task.

He concluded that a major personal task as chairman of the NK was to explain to the world the merits of "Japanese-style management" (as indicated above) as a viable model of corporate governance (Mitarai 2008: 10–2).

The 'Quiet Shareholder Revolution' Thesis

In July 2006, the same month that Mitarai and Niwa's book was published, Ronald Dore published his book titled (in Japanese) *Who is the Company To Be For?* The similarity of the question in the titles is worth noting. Ever since publication of his book *British Factory–Japanese Factory* in 1973, Dore has been a leading analyst and commentator on Japan's (quasi) community firms. In his 2006 book, however, he claims that a "silent revolution" is taking place in Japan, and that Japan's quasi community firms are on the path to demise. Executives have ceased to be "employee elders" and are coming to emphasize shareholder interests. This claim is at odds with the view of Mitarai and the NK just cited. What is the evidence for it?

For evidence he first draws on Ministry of Finance corporate statistics on the changing distribution of profits in firms capitalized at more than ¥1 billion (Dore 2006a: table 4). During the deflationary period of 2001–4, when sales growth and value added were squeezed, directors' pay and bonuses increased by 59 percent and dividends increased by 71 percent while employee remuneration decreased by 5 percent. He notes: "Directors who cut their employees' pay while helping themselves to a 59% increase can no longer be said to be eating out of the same rice bowl – they are no longer elders of the employee group." And "the correct way to interpret these figures is to see large Japanese firms as 'followers' of the path of the 'advanced US' " (Dore 2006a: 153). Indeed, as in many developed countries, directors and shareholders have got "fatter" while employees have got "thinner."

Equally important, however, is how people have perceived this, since how they define the situation will shape their subsequent attitudes and behavior. Before looking at this, some comments on the structure of distribution are in order. Dividing distribution into (a) retained earnings, (b) shareholder dividends, (c) director remuneration, and (d) employee pay (wages and bonuses), let us look at the share for companies capitalized at ¥1 billion or more over a longer time span, from 1960 to 2007. As Figure 6.1 shows, the share of dividends rose over the past decade, but in 2007 it declined.[12] In the early 1960s, it was also relatively high, at 15.8 percent. This was the high growth period, when the community firm was being created. After that, the payout rate declined, and was stable for the last quarter of the century. This suggests there is not a fixed relationship between the payout rate and the rise or fall of the community firm.

The share claimed by directors was slightly higher in the post-bubble period than during the preceding period of economic growth. (The average over the last quarter of the twentieth century was 1.5%.) It was particularly high in 2004–5, at 2.5 and 2.7 percent, but in 2007 it was lower than 2005. After 2001, the share of employee pay declined visibly. This reflects a

---

[12] The payout rate is generally higher in the US than in Japan, but equally notable is the variation by company, and not just the mean. This is much higher in the US than Japan. The highest proportion in the 2007 S&P500 – 19 percent – gave no dividends, and some claim that 80 percent of listed companies gave no dividend that year. Growing companies in particular often do not give dividends. Of TOPIX500 firms in Japan in 2007, roughly 20 percent had a payout rate of 15–20 percent and 60 percent had between 10 and 30 percent. Payout rates tend to cluster around the mean irrespective of growth (*Nikkei shimbun* July 12 2008). It seems that the tradition of stable dividends is still alive in Japan.

reduction in the proportion of regular employees with a reduction in hiring combined with voluntary redundancies, a rise in the share of nonregular employees, a freeze in the starting wage and wage restraint, etc., aimed at restraining total wage costs. But in 2007, conversely, the share had risen again. In the ten years after the bubble burst, the share rose abnormally high, so it may be that the fall from 2001 was a reaction to this.

Finally, retained earnings increased steadily after 2003, after several years of running down reserves.

Taking the same large companies over the same time period, we can also look at the rate of growth of directors' and employees' remuneration (pay

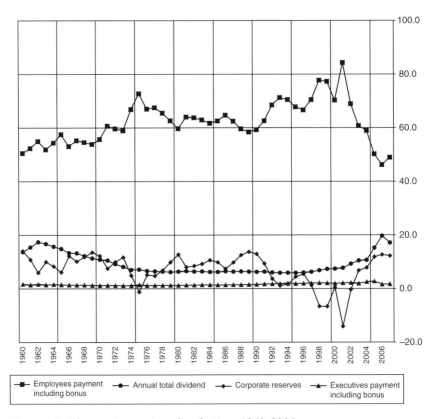

Figure 6.1. Changes in earnings distribution, 1960–2006

Source: Ministry of Finance, *Statistical Survey of Corporations* (respective years).

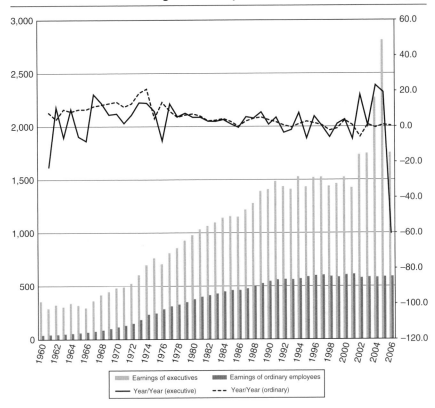

Figure 6.2. Changes in remuneration of executives and employees, 1960–2006

Note: The National Tax Agency's *Survey on Salaries in Private Firms* (respective years) shows that directors' average remuneration (pay and bonus) in firms capitalized at ¥1 billion + was relatively stable from 2000–2007, in sharp contrast to the changes shown in Figures 6.1 and 6.2, which come from MoF's *Statistical Survey of Corporations*.

Source: As for Figure 6.1.

and bonus). Figure 6.2 shows that from 1960 to the first oil shock of 1973 the rate of growth of employee's remuneration was higher than that of executives. Subsequently, until 2001, they grew at roughly the same rate. From 2001, for the next five years, the rate of increase in directors' remuneration grew markedly. But the figure for 2007 was roughly 20 percent below that of 2005.[13] And it is possible that the figures for 2004 and 2005 are abnormal (cf. the Note under Figure 6.2). If so, the silent shareholder

---

[13] Changes to company law in 2006 meant that bonuses moved from distributed profits to expenses, and bonuses showed as zero. In 2007, they were separately recorded, making comparison with 2005 and before possible.

revolution thesis loses an important plank of its evidence. Executive remuneration has risen, but we need to keep watching the figures before concluding that it is being decoupled from that of employees. According to the 2007 *Labour Economy White Paper* (Kosei rodosho 2007), we should note the low rate of average employee remunerations can be mostly explained by the growth of nonregular or "atypical" workers. In other words, the remuneration of *regular* employees has hardly dipped.

Complex Nature of Shareholder Emphasis

Nonetheless, it is undeniable that executives have given more emphasis to shareholder interests, and that the increase in the payout ratio is not a blip. As we have seen, from the early 1990s when they started debating corporate governance reform, top executives were also thinking of shareholders. From the bursting of the bubble, the proportion of shares owned by foreign investors rose steadily, reaching 29.1 percent in 2006, contributing to shareholder activism. Shareholders have loomed larger in executives' consciousness. We should recognize, however, that the growing emphasis on shareholder interests was not a matter of unilateral executive action, but was supported by employees as well. According to one employee survey (JILPT 2006), 90.9 percent of employees in large (3,000 + employees) companies agreed with the statement "If a company is a joint stock company, we should accept that shareholder profits are increased."

One reason for this figure is that employees have become shareholders themselves. As of the end of March 2008, 10,334 companies had introduced 401(k)-type defined contribution pensions (up 19% from the previous year), covering 2.71 million employees (up 24% : by comparison, over 14 million had defined benefit pensions). And not just their pensions; in more than 1900 listed companies – over 50 percent of the total – employee shareholding associations rank in the top ten shareholders, and this is expected to increase (*Nikkei shimbun* July 7 2008).

Equally intriguing, however, are trends in executive and corporate shareholding. Stock options are clearly a factor in the former, but more noteworthy is the recent rise in corporate share buybacks. In 2007, these totaled ¥4.6 trillion, and in the majority of cases these are retained as treasury stock rather than retired. As a result, at the end of March 2008, 156 companies were their own largest shareholder, including Toyota Motor, Matsushita Electric, Nippon Steel, Fanuc, and JR East – a 23 percent increase over the previous year (*Nikkei shimbun* June 20 2008). Treasury stock was permitted in the revised Commercial Code of 2001, and in the 2002 revision company articles could be changed to allow their purchase, within prescribed limits, at the discretion of the board of directors. These changes to the Commercial Code can be seen as favoring executives rather than shareholders. Treasury stock can be bought to raise share prices, increase returns to investors, for stock options, for funds for friendly M&A, or as a defense against hostile takeovers, which most Japanese executives are still opposed to.[14] Share buybacks can be seen as laying up provisions to defend the community firm, as can the recent upturn in reciprocal shareholding. These concerns can be seen in the rise of shareholding by companies, executives, and employees alike.

De-Emphasizing Employees and the Community Firm

It is still possible, however, that greater emphasis on shareholder interests has been at the expense of employees and the community firm. According to Dore, the silent shareholder revolution happened in 2001–4, when Japan's economy was in the trough of deflation and the IT bubble had burst. In this context, raising profits meant cutting down on input costs and reducing total labor costs. The latter involved keeping a tight lid on wage increases for regular employees, while increasing the number of non-regular employees or increasing the use of outsourcing. Relaxation of pro-visions in the Labour Dispatching Law helped employers in this regard. Terms like "recruitment ice age," "NEET" (not in education, employment, or training) and "Freeter" (free arbeiter – casual worker) became popular. Working hours of regular employees increased, and nonpayment of over-time became a social issue. In these regards, profit emphasis, which does not necessarily equate with shareholder emphasis, can be seen as going hand-in-hand with employee de-emphasis.

But does this imply the demise of the community firm?[15] Ironically, it might be argued that in order to save the community firm, of which shareholders and nonregular employees are not full members, shareholders were emphasized and employees de-emphasized. Without a viable busi-ness, there is no community firm. In order to protect the firm, it can be argued that executives as well as (regular) employees and union leaders acted in concert to address the challenges they faced, the latter, for

[14] According to the Cabinet Office (Naikakufu 2008) 68.8 and 71.5 percent were opposed to hostile takeovers by domestic and foreign parties, respectively.
[15] On the community firm, see for example Inagami and Whittaker (2005) and Inagami (2008).

example, accepting voluntary redundancies, pay freezes and other measures. Rather than destroying community firm consciousness, it may have been strengthened.

In the above JILPT (2006) survey, the proportion of regular employees who thought "I personally identify with the reputation and performance of the company" was 72.2 percent. According to a Cabinet Office survey in 2008, "those who will support the company in the long term" were deemed suppliers, customers and group companies (84.0%) and employees (83.7%), in contrast to institutional investors (22.6%) and foreign investors (7.3%). Similarly, a Japan Management Association survey in 2006 found that the proportion of newly appointed executives intending to put more emphasis on employees than shareholders was increasing (Nihon noritsu kyokai 2008), effectively reversing the trend of the past few years. Another survey found that the two are not necessarily opposed, and that community consciousness is still strong (Inagami 2007).

In summary, in the past ten years, Japanese management has experienced changes which suggest a favoring of shareholder interests at the expense of employees. However, community consciousness is still strong, at least among executives and regular employees. This consciousness is especially strong when the company faces serious challenges. Still today, both executives and employees react strongly against attempted hostile takeovers. In fact, there are still no examples of successful hostile takeovers of listed firms. Social norms against outsiders taking over companies from the logic of money only are still strong. The community firm has still not collapsed in Japan.

Executive Pay and Careers

One of the most important influences on corporate governance is career paths of executives. Internally promoted career paths are intrinsically linked with lifetime – or long-term – employment.[16] While directors may be sent

---

[16] The media image of the collapse of lifetime employment is not reflected in reality. In terms of retention rates and average job tenure, the past decade has seen a slight reduction rather than a collapse. In some industries, company size bands and employee age, gender, and education categories, there has been a *deepening* of lifetime employment, and *increased* institutionalization (JILPT 2008). For example, in microbusinesses (1–4 employees, male and female combined) average job tenures have increased over the past two decades, from 7.2 years in 1985 to 11.6 in 2007 (MHLW figures). Attitudes supporting lifetime employment have also strengthened (JILPT 2008) and the proportion of new directors who think that lifetime employment is a thing of the past has declined for several years running (JMA 2008).

from a parent company or main bank, external labor markets for directors are still underdeveloped. There are persistent reports about shortages of external directors. This suggests, conversely, that internal careers are highly developed, with paths reaching top management levels for able employees. But is this pattern changing? As noted, also, the rapid rise of director remuneration for several years after 2000 has been taken as evidence of the collapse of the community firm. In the past, it was seen as undesirable to have a large gap between regular employee and director pay. Both rose together, and if employee pay had to be cut, directors took the lead in cutting their own pay first. But how big *is* the gap now, and how do employees perceive that gap?

Executive Careers

It is unclear just when internal careers leading to executive level became established in Japan. Aonuma (1965) estimates that around 1930, roughly 20 percent of executives had followed this path, with higher figures in leading banks and textile companies. The proportion increased sharply during World War II, and by 1962 had reached 46.4 percent. More recently, in early 1999 the proportion of executive directors fitting this description was 74.7 percent (Inagami and Rengo soken eds. 2000), suggesting a steady increase over forty years.

More recent data can be gained from Toyo keizai's *Director Quarterly* (2007) (of all listed companies). Taking companies with 3,000 + employees, and excluding those with the CCS or founded in the last ten years, we investigated directors (excluding auditors) in the remaining 238 companies. We found that three quarters (74.7%) of executives were internally promoted. There appears to have been no marked change in the past ten years. Figures for fifteen leading companies are given in Table 6.1. Here the ratios are even higher (84.6% overall), with the balance made up of external directors (10.0%) and those who joined as directors (5.4%).

As for those with the "company with committees" system, also with 3,000 + employees, the figure for Hitachi was eight out of thirteen (61.5%); the rest were external directors. For Toshiba, the figure was ten out of fourteen (71.4%), and for Mitsubishi Electric seven out of twelve (58.3%). With very few exceptions, corporate officers in these companies were all internally promoted. Even under this system, then, the majority of directors are internally promoted, and when it comes to corporate officers, including representative executives, almost all are internally promoted, as in the company with auditors system.

Table 6.1. Internal promotion rate of directors at fifteen major Japanese corporations (as of July 31 2007)

Company	Employees	Directors (Internal)[%]	Noninternally promoted
Toyota Motor	67,650	30 (27)[90.0%]	Three joined as directors ("j as d")
JR East	53,420	25 (23)[92.0]	Two external (Isuzu, university professor)
Matsushita Elec.	44,932	19 (16)[84.2]	One j as d, 2 external (Nissay, J Post)
Nippon Express	37,963	15 (15)[100.0]	
Fujitsu	36,561	10 (8)[80.0]	Two external (univ. professor, Fuji Electric)
TEPCO	35,984	19 (16)[84.2]	Two external (Daiichi Life, univ. prof)1 j as d
Denso	34,182	13 (9)[69.2]	Four j as d (including 3 from Toyota)
Mitsubishi HI	32,552	17 (14)[82.4]	Three external (M.bishi Corp, Aisin, METI)
Nissan Motor	32,489	10 (6)[60.0]	Two j as d (Renault) 2 external (Renault)
Honda	26,652	20 (18)[90.0]	Two external (BMTU MoFA)
JR West	26,038	13 (8)[61.5]	Five external (Sumitomo Elect, Osaka Gas, 2 prof + 1)
Sharp	22,793	26 (24)[92.3]	Two j as d (Cabinet Office, BMTU)
NEC	22,698	16 (11)[68.8]	Five external (SMBC, Daiwa Sec., Sumitomo Corp + 2)
Canon	20,377	27 (26)[96.3]	One j as d (Toshiba)
KEPCO	20,292	20 (16)[80.0]	Three external (Kintetsu, Daikin Ind., BTMU) 1 j as d

Note: Excludes companies with committees.

Source: Compiled from Toyo keizai shinposha (2007).

Changes to Executive Remuneration

Behind the marked rise in executive pay in the early twenty-first century were changes to the remuneration system itself, namely the abolition of the director's retirement gratuity, the introduction of annual remuneration, and performance-based remuneration. These changes began around 2002, with Nomura Holdings and Matsui Securities abolishing their directors' retirement gratuity and introducing a new performance-based pay system in that year, followed by Orix, Hoya, and thirteen others in 2003, and Odakyu Electric Railway, Omron, KDDI, and others in 2004. According to Pension Fund Association figures 133 companies scrapped the gratuity system in 2004, 131 in 2005, 114 in 2006, and seventy-eight in 2007. By 2007 almost half (47.9%) of first and second section TSE-listed companies had made this change (Nomura sogo kenkyujo 2007). The former gratuity money was redirected into directors' pay. According to a *Nikkei shimbun* survey of ninety-seven leading companies in 2006, directors' pay excluding the gratuity rose by 27 percent over the previous year to an average of ¥48.5 million, but averaged ¥60.3 million when the gratuity and stock option were included. In other words, the gratuity comprised up to 20 percent of the total.

As for performance-related pay, 44.3 percent of first and second section TSE-listed companies reported this system in 2004, 51.3 percent in 2005, 59.0 percent in 2006, and 49.5 percent in 2007 (Nomura soken 2007). As the performance of many companies improved in these years, directors' remuneration rose as well.

The Reality of Directors' Remuneration

Some data from ten years ago, before the marked rise in director remuneration, show that in first section TSE-listed companies the president on average earned 11.3 times a new recruit, and executives earned 9.2 times. If the starting wage for new recruits was ¥200,000 per month with an average bonus of five months that would make an annual total of 3.4 million yen, and the president's remuneration would be roughly ¥40 million (Inagami and Rengo soken eds. 2000). We actually have historical data for this ratio. In 1926, the average company president earned 100.7 times a male university graduate recruit.[17] The ratio had shrunk to 11.9 in 1963 and 9 times in 1973, and reached 7.5 times in 1980, symbolizing the "postwar revolution" (Table 6.2). The ratio of 11.3 in 1999 was close to the postwar high growth period figure.

Although the figures are not directly comparable, the average executive income of ¥31.3 million in 1999 and (excluding gratuity and stock options) 48.5 million in 2006 suggests an increase of around 55 percent, which is close to Dore's estimate of a 59 percent increase between 2001 and 2004. Taking individual companies, total director and auditor pay excluding

Table 6.2. President/new graduate recruit earnings ratio (¥1,000, a/b: multiple)

Year	a: President's earnings	b: New graduate recruit earnings	a/b
1926	151(165)	1.5 (1.5)	100.7 (110.0)
1963	3,013.5(6,082)	252.5 (257.9)	11.9(23.6)
1973	7,181.4 (15,676.7)	797.4 (825.5)	9 (19)
1980	11,543 (23,593)	1,546 (1,623)	7.5 (14.5)
1999	38,420	3,400	11.3
2006	[48,500]	3,400	[14.3]

Note: 1926–80 ( ) – pretax, others post-tax; [ ] 2006 average earnings of executives.

Source: 1926–80 – Nikkeiren (1982); 1999 – Inagami and Rengo Sogo kenkyujo eds. (2000); 2006 – *Nikkei shimbun* (August 28 2007).

[17] Executives also allegedly had non-legal earnings, and often didn't work very hard: cf. Ishiyama (1925), Ogata (1926), and Takahashi (1929).

bonuses at Toyota Motor in 2006 showed an increase of 40 percent over the previous year. (Bonuses increased by 30 percent; with stock options the average increase was 40 percent, from ¥53.6 million to ¥74.9 million: *Nikkei shimbun* June 8 2007). This increase reflects the reforms to executive remuneration at Toyota in 2006, as well as the company's exceptional performance. At Nissan, where the average was 3.7 times higher – probably the highest among listed companies – Carlos Ghosn declared: "We have made the responsibilities of directors clear. This figure is not high by world multinational standards" (*Nikkei shimbun* August 28 2007).

Returning to the ratio of executive to new recruit pay, this appears to have increased from roughly ten times in 1999 to fifteen times in 2006. Whether this marks the destruction of the community firm or not can be debated. One way of looking at it is to compare it with ratios in other countries. Another is to find out what employees think about it. Starting with the former, executive pay in the United States increased rapidly in the last quarter of the twentieth century. According to AFL-CIO PayWatch, total annual CEO pay for S&P500 companies, including stock options and incentives, was forty-two times the average worker in 1980, 107 times in 1990, 525 times in 2000, and 364 times in 2006. According to Economic Research Institute data for listed companies in the United States, the average remuneration of the highest paid executive in May 2008 was $17.2 million, up from $15.1 million in 1997. These figures – which often give rise to "fat cat" accusations – are an order of magnitude higher than Japanese figures.

As for employees' views of executive pay (in their company), according to JILPT (2006) figures for regular employees of large (3,000 +) employees) firms, half (50.7%) answered "don't know," a quarter (25.7%) answered "appropriate," 16.0 percent thought it was too high and 7.6 percent thought it was too low. Excluding the "don't knows," many of whom probably don't know how much their executives earn, this means that a third think executives earn too much, while two thirds think they earn an appropriate amount or too little. Although we cannot judge from this survey alone, it seems that many regular employees of large companies feel reasonably comfortable with the remuneration levels of their executives.

Summary and Conclusion

Let us summarize and conclude with the following comments. First, after the bursting of the bubble leading executives who were deeply concerned about the future of Japanese management also began to debate corporate governance. They probably envisaged a time-honored "Japanese spirit – Western technology" solution – importing Western practices while maintaining a Japanese essence or base. This included "shareholder emphasis."

Second, after many twists and turns, but clearly resonating with the vision of Kaneo Nakamura and colleagues in the early 1990s, in 2006 NK published its noteworthy *Interim Summary*, which clearly sets out the basic line for corporate governance reform in Japan. It claims that the corporation is not simply the property of the shareholders, but is also a public institution. It denies there is one "global standard" for corporate governance, demands appropriate ethics and accountability of shareholders, argues for valuing "genuine" shareholders and rejecting raiders, and declares that the Japanese auditor system should be recognized internationally as a sound system of governance.

Third, immediately prior to this publication NK also published *Toward Improving Internal Labour–Management Communication in a New Era*, which claimed that Japanese companies had been able to overcome their difficulties through joint labor–management effort, that the JPC'S Three Productivity Principles (employment stability, joint consultation and fair distribution) had undiminished significance, and that joint labor–management communication is a key source of competitiveness.

Fourth, one of the most widely noted institutional reforms of corporate governance has been the introduction of the CCS. However, comparatively few companies have actually adopted it, and the reality of those that have is not so different from those still using the company with auditors system.

Fifth, a negative side of corporate governance practice is corporate scandals. There are many causes for these, but a recent phenomenon has been the significant and often fatal damage resulting from wrongdoing, in addition to the resignation of executives. In addition to the strengthened legal framework, CSR awareness has spread, and executives are supposed to be exemplars of both high ethical standards and compliance, and are expected to expunge old, insular practices. Sixth, a further dimension of corporate governance practice is whom the company is run for. Partially reflecting a succession of corporate scandals, there has been a strong groundswell of support for emphasizing the public dimension of corporations. Extended to shareholder relations, this means that even today, relatively few executives see their job principally as agents of shareholders, charged with maximizing shareholder interests.

Seventh, however, Japan may well have experienced a subtle or "silent shareholder revolution," as Dore claims; in the twenty-first century, executives have grown fatter at the expense of their employees. There are undoubtedly grounds for this view, but this does not mean that the community firm has collapsed. Recognizing that without a viable business there is no community firm, on the contrary, in many cases executives and employees have cooperated to face serious challenges. A result of these efforts has been a greater emphasis of shareholder interests, and less of employee interests, but this does not mean that regular employees have been abandoned, and shareholders embraced by their "agents." Dore's thesis rightly raises the issue, however, of the balance of company, shareholder, executive, and employee interests, and how these may have changed and may change in the future.

Eighth, executive pay jumped in the early twenty-first century, from an average of ten times a new university graduate recruit to fifteen times. This does not necessarily mean that executives are no longer seen as employee "elders." In fact, the majority of employees appear to see their directors' remuneration as appropriate, or even low. The remuneration system for directors has undergone reform, and levels have risen. Their career paths, however, have not changed visibly. Three quarters are still internally promoted, mostly after working for many years in the company, as they were before the "silent shareholder revolution."

Bibliography

Aonuma, Y. (1965). *Nihon no keieisha – sono shusshin to seikaku (Japanese Executives: Origins and Nature)*. Tokyo: Nihon keizai shinbunsha.

Buchanan, J. and Deakin, S. (2008). "Japan's Paradoxical Response to the New 'Global Standard' in Corporate Governance." *Zeitschrift für Japanisches Recht*, 13(26): 59–84.

Dore, R. (1973). *British Factory – Japanese Factory: The Origins of National Diversity of Industrial Relations*. Berkeley: University of California Press.

—— (2006a). *Dare no tame no kaisha ni suruka (Who Is the Company to Be For?)*. Tokyo: Iwanami shoten.

—— (2006b). "Japan's Shareholder Revolution," in LSE Centre for Economic Performance. *CentrePiece*, Winter 2006/7: 22–4.

Department of Trade and Industry (1999). *Modern Company Law for a Competitive Economy: The Strategic Framework*. London: DTI.

European Commission (2001). *Promoting a European Framework for Corporate Social Responsibility: Green Paper*. Brussels: European Commission.

Inagami, T. (2000). "Joron: Shinnihongata korporeto gabanansu to koyo, roshi kankei" ("Preface: New Japanese-style Corporate Governance and Employment, Industrial Relations"), in T. Inagami and Rengo soken (eds.) *Gendai Nihon no korporeto gabanansu* (*Current Japanese Corporate Governance*). Tokyo: Toyo keizai shinposha.

—— (2007). "Soron: Kigyo no shakaiteki sekinin to roshi no taiyo" ("Overview: Corporate Social Responsibility and Labour-Management Response"), in T. Inagami and Rengo soken (eds.) *Rodo CSR* (*Labour CSR*). Tokyo: NTT Shuppan.

—— (2008). "Kaisha kyodotai no yukue" ("Whither the Community Firm"). *Ohara shakai mondai kenkyusho zasshi*, 599–600: 30–60.

—— and Rengo soken (2000) (eds.) *Gendai Nihon no korporeto gabanansu* (*Current Japanese Corporate Governance*). Tokyo: Toyo keizai shinposha.

—— and Whittaker, D.H. (2005). *The New Community Firm: Employment, Governance and Management Reform in Japan*. Cambridge: Cambridge University Press.

Ishiyama, K. (1925). *Gendai juyakuron* (*Current Debates about Executives*). Nagoya: Daiyamondo sha.

Japan Association of Corporate Auditors (JACA) – *see Nihon kansayaku kyokai*.

Japan Corporate Governance Forum (JCGF) – *see Nihon koporeto gabanansu foram*.

Japan Council for Economic Development (JCED) – *see Keizai doyukai*.

Japan Institute of Labour Policy and Training (JILPT) – *see Rodo seisaku kenkyu-kenshu kiko*.

Japan Management Association (JMA) – *see Nihon noritsu kyokai*.

Keizai doyukai (1947). *Kigyo minshuka shian: Shusei shihonshugi no koso* (*A Draft on Democratizing the Corporation: The Concept of Revised Capitalism*). Tokyo: Keizai doyukai.

—— (1992). *Dai 10 kai keizai hakusho: "Hito" sozo no keiei* (*10th Economic White Paper: Management Creating "People"*). Tokyo: Keizai doyokai.

—— (1994). *Dai 11 kai keizai hakusho: Henkakuki no kigyo keieisha* (*11th Economic White Paper: Company Executives in a Time of Reform*). Tokyo: Keizai doyukai.

—— (1998). *Dai 13 kai keizai hakusho: Shihon koritsu jushi keiei* (*13th Economic White Paper: Management Stressing Capital Efficiency*). Tokyo: Keizai doyukai.

—— (2003). *Dai 15 kai keizai hakusho: "Shijo no shinka" to shakaiteki sekinin keiei* (*15th Economic White Paper: "Market Evolution" and CSR Management*). Tokyo: Keizai doyukai.

Keizai doyukai Enterprise Trends Study Group (1994). "Atarashii koporeto gabanansu no kakuritsu" ("Establishing a New Corporate Governance"), in S. Shinagawa and J. Ushio (eds.) *Nihon no koporeto gabanansu o tou* (*Debating Japanese Corporate Governance*). Tokyo: Shoji homu kenkyukai.

Keizai koho senta (2008). *Dai 11 kai seikatsusha no "kigyokan" ni kansuru chosa kekka hokokusho* (*11th Survey Report on Views of Corporations*). Tokyo: Keizai koho senta.

Kobayashi, Y. (1992). "Introduction," in Keizai Doyukai, *Dai 10 kai keizai hakusho: "Hito" sozo no keiei* (*10th Economic White Paper: Management Creating 'People'*). Tokyo: Keizai doyukai.

Kosei rodosho (2007). *Heisei 19 nen ban rodo keizai hakusho* (*2007 White Paper on Labour Economy*). Tokyo: Zaimusho insatsukyoku.

—— (2008). *Heisei 19 nendo kobetsu rodo funso kaiketsu seido seko jokyo* (*2007 Individual Labour Dispute Resolution System Implementation*). Tokyo: Kosei rodosho shokugyo anteikyoku.

Ministry of Health, Labour and Welfare (MHLW) – *see Kosei rodosho*.

Mitarai, F. (2008). "Nihonteki keiei kara sekai e: Gurobaru keizaika no koporeto gabanansu no arikata" ("From Japanese Management to the World: Corporate Governance in a Globalised Economy"). *Gekkan kansayaku*, 542: 4–31.

—— and U. Niwa (2006). *Kaisha wa dare no tame ni* (*Who Is the Company for?*). Tokyo: Bungei shunju.

Naikakufu (2008). *Kigyo risku e no taioryoku ni tsuite no anketo chosa* (*Survey on Adaptability to Corporate Risk*). Tokyo: Naikakafu.

Nakamura, K. (1994). "Hajime ni" ("Introduction"), in Keizai doyukai, *Dai 11 kai keizai hakusho: Henkakuki no kigyo keieisha* (*11th Economic White Paper: Company Executives in a Time of Reform*). Tokyo: Keizai doyukai

—— (2000). "Koporeto gabanansu e no shiza" ("Perspective on Corporate Governance"), in S. Shinagawa and J. Ushio (eds.) *Nihon no koporeto gabanansu o tou* (*Debating Japanese Corporate Governance*). Tokyo: Shoji homu kenkyukai.

Nihon kansayaku kyokai (2003). *Kigyo fushoji to kansayaku no yakuwari.* (*Corporate Malfeasance and the Role of Auditors*). Tokyo: Nihon kansayaku kyokai.

—— (2008). *Kabunushi sokai zengo no yakuinto no kosei nado ni kansuru anketo shukei kekka: dai 8 kai intanetto anketo, iinkai sechikaisha ban* (*Survey Results of Director Composition at AGM Time, etc.: 8th Internet Survey, Company with Committees Edition*). Tokyo: Nihon kansayaku kyokai.

Nihon koporeto gabanansu foram (1998). *Koporeto gabanansu gensoku: Atarashii Nihongata kigyo tochi o kangaeru* (*saishu hokoku*) (*Corporate Governance Principles: Towards a New Japanese Style Corporate Governance* (*Final Report*)). Tokyo: Nihon koporetu gabanansu foram.

—— (2006). *Shin koporeto gabanansu gensoku* (*New Corporate Governance Principles*). Tokyo: Nihon koporetu gabanansu foram.

Nihon noritsu kyokai (2008). *Dai 11 kai shinnin yakuin no sugao ni kansuru chosa hokoku* (*11th Survey Report on New Directors*). Tokyo: Nihon noritsu kyokai.

Nikkeiren (1982). *Rodo mondai kenkyu iinkai hokoku: senshinkokubyo ni ochiiranai tameni* (*Labour Research Committee Report: How to Avoid Falling into Advanced Country Malaise*). Tokyo: Nikkeiren.

Nikkeiren kokusaitokubetsu iinkai (1998). *Nihon kigyo no koporeto gabanansu kaikaku no hoko: shihon shijo kara mo rodo shijo kara mo sentaku sareru kigyo o mezashite* (*Directions of Japanese Companies' Corporate Governance Reforms: Towards Firms Favoured by Both Capital and Labour Markets*). Tokyo: Nikkeiren.

Nippon Keidanren (2004). *Kigyo no shakaiteki sekinin suishin ni atatte no kihonteki kangaekata* (*Basic Thoughts on Promoting CSR*). Tokyo: Nippon Keidanren.

—— (2005). *Kigyo rinri, kigyo kodo ni kansuru anketo shukei kekka (gaiyo)* (*Survey Results of Corporate Ethics and Behaviour: Summary Version*). Tokyo: Nippon Keidanren.

—— (2006a). *Aratana jidai no kigyonai komyunikeshon no kochiku ni mukete* (*Towards Improving Labour-Management Communication in a New Era*). Tokyo: Nippon Keidanren.

—— (2006b). *Waga kuni ni okeru koporeto gabanansu seido no arikata* (*On the Ideal Way of the Japanese System of Corporate Governance*). Tokyo: Nippon Keidanren.

Niwa, U. (2006). "Keiei wa 'shinyo jutaku' dearu koto o wasureruna" ("Don't Forget That Management is 'Entrusted' "), in F. Mitarai and U. Niwa (eds.) *Kaisha wa dare no tame ni* (*Who is the Company For?*). Tokyo: Bungei shunju.

Nomura sogo kenkyujo (2007). *Nihon kigyo no yakuin shogu, jinzai kaihatsu ni kansuru anketo chosa* (*Survey on the Remuneration and HRD of Japanese Directors*). Tokyo.

Ogata, J. (1926). *Ginko hatan monogatari: Bokyu ginko juyaku no zangiroku* (*Tale of Bank Collapse: Confessions of Directors of Banks in Abeyance*). Tokyo: Bungado.

Rodo seisaku kenkyu kenshu kiko (2006). *Henkakuki no kinrosha ishiki* (*Worker Consciousness in an Age of Change*). Report No.49. Tokyo: Rodo seisaku kenkyu kenshu kiko.

—— (2008a). *Yusufuru rodo tokei* (*Useful Labour Statistics*). Tokyo: Rodo seisaku kenkyu kenshu kiko.

—— (2008b). *Dai 5 kai kinrosha seikatsu ni kansuru chosa: 2007* (*5th Survey on Workers' Living: 2007*). Tokyo: Rodo seisaku kenkyu kenshu kiko.

Shinagawa, S. and Ushio, J. (2000) (eds.) *Nihon no koporeto gabanansu o tou* (*Debating Japanese Corporate Governance*). Tokyo: Shoji homu kenkyukai.

Suzuki, T. (2000). "Maihama kaigi: Koporeto gabanansu yoranki ni keieisha wa nani o giron shitaka" ("The Maihama Conference: What Did Japanese Executives Debate in the Earliest Stages of Corporate Governance?"), in S. Shinagawa and J. Ushio (eds.) *Nihon no koporeto gabanansu o tou* (*Debating Japanese Corporate Governance*). Tokyo: Shoji homu kenkyukai.

Takahashi, K. (1929). *Kabushiki kaisha bokokuron* (*Stock Companies and Destruction of the Nation*). Tokyo: Banrikaku shobo.

Tokyo shoken torihikisho (TSE) (2007). *Tosho jojo kaisha koporeto gabanansu hakusho 2007* (*TSE-listed Company Corporate Governance White Paper 2007*). Tokyo: Tokyo Stock Exchange Inc.

Toyo keizai shinposha (2007). *Yakuin shikiho (zenjojo kaishaban), 2008 nen ban* (*Director Quarterly: All Listed Companies, 2008 Version*). Tokyo: Toyo keizai shinposha.

7

Whose Company Is It? Changing CEO Ideology in Japan

George Olcott

A number of influential commentators have pointed out that changes such as increasing dividends, more frequent and larger M&A transactions and increasing dialogue with shareholders point to a shift away from the communitarian ethic upon which Japanese postwar corporate governance framework has been based. Whether these changes have been caused by the leaders of Japanese firms embracing shareholder value as the guiding principle of a new Japanese capitalism, however, is open to question. In this chapter, I will examine shifting managerial ideology and the nature of Japanese leadership, based on a series of interviews carried out with a number of leading CEOs and former CEOs of Japanese firms. My conclusion is that despite evidence of changing practices, communitarianism as an ideology is far from delegitimized as a basis for enterprise organization.

In his book *Searching for a Corporate Saviour: the Irrational Quest for Charismatic CEOs* (2002), Rakesh Khurana describes the way in which the selection process for CEOs at large US corporations has changed since the beginning of the 1980s. His premise is that with the shifting of the foundations of American capitalism from one based on managerialism to a market-based investor-driven form, the very nature of the CEO's role has undergone a profound transformation (Khurana 2002). The shift in emphasis from managers to owners of American corporations had created a "liability of insiderness" where internal CEO candidates were, unless the company was performing particularly well, placed at an increasing disadvantage as he or she would be seen as favoring the status quo. Directors, who in managerialist organizations were more likely to feel a stronger allegiance to the CEO who had invited them to serve on the board in the first place, were suddenly under the sway of the leading investing institutions, often with the help of new intermediaries such as ISS taking a much more direct and often confrontational approach to company boards. Investment banking securities analysts have had an increasing influence on share prices through their published reports, often acting as judge and jury on corporate prospects, and many CEOs have gone to great lengths to cultivate them. During the period from 1980 to 2006, institutional ownership of US equities increased from 37 to 66 percent of total US equity markets (Conference Board 2008).[1]

This created a growing gap between CEOs and their boards, with a much higher likelihood at modern US boards that the outside directors will meet in "executive sessions" at each board meeting. "As CEOs and other management directors are excluded from executive sessions and forbidden from serving on key committees and as these committees have increased in importance," notes Marty Lipton, a renowned critic of shareholder activism, "it takes considerable effort to keep a board from becoming polarized and to maintain a shared sense of collegiality and a common understanding of all the issues facing the company" (Lipton 2008). CEO turnover has risen dramatically. According to research by Booz Allen Hamilton, the turnover rate of CEOs at major North American companies increased by over 50 percent between 1995 and 2005, with nearly half of these related to poor performance or mergers. During the same period, the firing of underperforming CEOs went up fourfold. "Boards of directors have become more responsive to shareholder and regulatory pressure, and are more proactive in ousting underperforming CEOs," they declare (Booz Allen Hamilton 2005: 3). In searching for a successor, boards have, according to Khurana, resorted increasingly to identifying candidates who will appear legitimate to institutional investors, analysts, and the business press. The key difference between the old business elite and the new was that the latter:

were no longer defined as professional managers but instead as *leaders*, whose ability to lead consisted in their personal characteristics or, more simply, their charisma (p. 69).

Two further developments worthy of note were, first the growth of intermediaries, particularly the executive search firms, who added "objectivity" to the process of recruitment, and the rapid rise in CEO compensation as the bargaining power of candidates who were perceived to possess the

---

[1] Institutions were defined as pension funds, investment companies, insurance companies, banks, and foundations.

elusive qualities that constitute "charisma" was greatly strengthened. Between 1980 and 2000, the earnings of the average US CEO rose from 42 times that of a blue collar worker to 531 times.

The Case of the Japanese CEO

While the term "managerialism" does not encapsulate the emphasis that exists in Japanese organizations on *all* of the company's employees, rather than just its managers, it is nevertheless an expression that is often used in the context of the Japanese corporate system. Fligstein, for example, refers to Japan as the "purest form of managerialism" (2001: 115): its legal framework described as "arguably the most managerialist of the principal corporate law jurisdictions" (Kraakman et al. 2004: 70). Insofar as Japanese management practices are criticized for the perpetuation of an internal elite that has usurped the control of corporations that should rightfully be exercised by shareholders, a trend identified by Berle and Means (1932) at US firms during the first decades of the twentieth century when ownership was "centrifugal" and management control was "centripetal," it is entirely appropriate to conceptualize Japanese firms in this way. Most writers, however, in trying to capture the more inclusive nature of Japanese organizations, have tended to use expressions such as "communitarian" or "organisation-oriented" (Dore 1973, 2000; Rohlen 1974).

While there are dangers in over-simplifying the consensual and collectivist nature of decision making in Japanese firms (cf. Clark 1979: 130–1), there is nevertheless strong evidence of a highly participative process with extensive delegation of responsibility to the lower reaches of the organization, underpinned by a long-term commitment to the organization by employees, slow promotion, and extensive job rotation (e.g., Aoki 1994). Consistent with the managerialist paradigm, Japanese firms have traditionally reinvested profits into the firm, rather than distributed them to shareholders in the form of dividends.[2] The mission of the management is the perpetuation of the firm and leadership in the context of the Japanese corporation is about "securing the continuation, development, and prosperity of the company as an ongoing community" (Inagami and Whittaker 2005: 26).

---

[2] In the postwar period Japanese firms consistently outspent their US counterparts in fixed capital investment (as a proportion of GDP) but in the last thirty years the productivity of its investment has lagged that of US firms (Smithers & Co. 2008).

Research has suggested that in keeping with the communitarian nature of Japanese organizations, Japanese corporate leaders have been seen as the senior members, the board as a "council of elders" (Dore 1973: 223), with the president as "chief elder." He (there are still very few female CEOs of Japanese companies) will almost certainly be an insider and among the firm's stakeholders is most likely to feel his allegiance belongs to his company colleagues than to shareholders. Asked to choose between cutting dividends or laying off employees in times of difficulty, he is much more likely than his US counterpart to choose the former course (Yoshimori 1995). His leadership is less about making the best decisions and more about "creating the atmosphere within the firm that ensures that all employees work as hard and as conscientiously and as co-operatively as possible so that *all* the decentralized decision-producing structures of the firm produce the best decisions" (Dore 1994: 381). He has not evidently been motivated by monetary considerations and there has in the past been little effort to align the interests of shareholders and corporate leaders through the incentive structure. Stock options schemes have only recently been introduced into the Japanese corporate lexicon, and, according to data from Towers Perrin, Japanese CEOs are likely to receive between a quarter and a fifth of the compensation of their US counterparts (Hymowitz 2004).[3]

Research suggests that the impact of CEO succession at Japanese corporations is both less immediate and more evolutionary than at US firms. A striking feature of Japanese CEO succession is the prevalence of the "apprentice model" in which the CEO nominates his successor, and then becomes chairman. While this is in line with "best practice" in that it ensures the separation of the roles of chairman and CEO, in practice the chairman often retains a great deal of influence.[4] This reduces the likelihood that a changing of the guard at the CEO level causes fundamental changes in direction for the company's strategy. A study by Ahn et al. (2004) suggests that even when the change in CEO is nonroutine, there is no discernible effect on firm performance or stock price.[5] Given the importance of expectations in share price determination, it is clear that in Japan, the expectation by the market that the firm's leader will make a

---

[3] In the international 2003 Survey by Towers Perrin cited by Hymowitz (2004), CEOs of companies with turnover of $500 million or more earned the following: US $2.25 million, Mexico $0.96 million, Germany $0.95 million, UK $0.83 million, South Africa $0.54 million, and Japan $0.46 million.

[4] See Booz Allen Hamilton (2005: 9).

[5] The study also reveals that of 3,250 CEOs in the data set, only twenty-six were CEOs of another firm previously, and of these, eight were intra-*keiretsu* moves.

difference is very low, particularly in comparison with the Anglo-Saxon economies. Another study (Sakano and Lewin 1999) shows that CEO succession at Japanese firms is not followed in the first two years by radical strategic or organizational changes of the kind that can be expected at US firms, in particular the kind of restructuring activity (e.g., disposal of non-core assets) that one might have expected given the extent of the downturn in the Japanese economy during the 1990s.

Recent Changes in Japanese Corporate Governance: Is Japan Shifting to Investor Capitalism?

There is little need to detail the pressures that the Japanese economy and Japanese organizations have been under since the bursting of the bubble. Suffice it to say for the purposes of this chapter that these pressures have caused intense debate as to the adequacies of the communitarian-based HR system, with many advocating a more market-oriented approach (e.g., Yashiro 1998). Although it appears to be the conclusion of most observers that the traditional organization-oriented Japanese model of capitalism is not fundamentally giving way to investor capitalism (e.g., Jacoby 2005; Rebick 2005; Vogel 2006) but merely undergoing an adjustment, there is evidence to suggest that Japanese management is paying a great deal more attention to shareholders.

One of the key changes that has taken place since the beginning of the 1990s is the marked increase in ownership of Japanese shares by foreign institutions, and there is evidence that increased foreign ownership is directly related to corporate restructuring and other shareholder-friendly actions by management (Ahmadjian and Robbins 2005). Large institutions such as CalPERS have actively engaged with Japanese management to improve in areas such as disclosure (Jacoby 2007). Dore (2006) has shown that dividend payments by Japanese firms and share buybacks are increasing at a dramatic rate, while wages have been stagnant. He also points to a considerable widening of the gap between the compensation of directors and ordinary company employees, possibly suggesting a closer link between executive pay and the interests of shareholders. It is certainly the case that the number of Japanese firms offering stock options to senior management has risen dramatically in the last decade (Robinson and Shimizu 2006).

The level of inequality in wider Japanese society has also steadily increased during the last twenty years, with income distribution now being less equal than most European countries (Economist 2006). This, some have argued, has led to a growing sense of alienation in the workforce (Genda 2005) and a sharp decline in worker morale (Nihon Keizai shimbun 2007). There has been, at least on the surface, considerable reform of Japanese corporate boards during the last ten years, reinforced by legal reforms such as the revision of the Commercial Code in 2002, which has enabled Japanese companies to adopt (voluntarily) the committee system (although few, in practice have). According to a study by Nippon Life, board sizes have been dramatically reduced and the average size of a TSE First Section listed company board falling from 17.65 directors in 1996 to 10.37 in 2004 (NLI Research 2007). During that period, the number of firms with more than 30 percent of their board members coming from outside the firm (not from banks or controlling shareholders) rose from 122 (10.7% of listed firms) to 293 (19.6%).

This has led to a change in the behavior of Japanese CEOs. In a study of Japanese CEO activity, Robinson and Shimizu (2006) found that substantial changes in CEO priorities had taken place during the past decade. In line with what one might expect of a corporate environment shifting from an organization orientation to one focused on shareholders, there was a considerable increase in the amount of CEO time devoted to investor and media relations and M&A, while the amount of time devoted to union and main bank relations declined.

Methodology

This chapter is part of a wider study into changing attitudes among key participants in the Japanese economic landscape in which a large number of corporate leaders, institutional investors, government officials, and other groups were interviewed by the author and Ron Dore, the full results of which are expected to be published during 2010. This paper focuses only on the CEO segment. Data was gathered through in-depth interviews with twenty two presidents,[6] chairmen, and former presidents, consisting of the following:

- Current presidents – ten
- Current chairmen (all former presidents) – eight
- Former chairmen/presidents – four
- Total – twenty-two

[6] The term "CEO" is slowly gaining currency in the language of the Japanese corporate hierarchy and is the equivalent of the more traditional expression "President."

Thus there were in effect three generations of Japanese corporate leader, ranging in age from former executives in their 80s who were CEOs in the late 1970s, to current CEOs in their late 40s. They represented a wide cross section of industries, from traditional manufacturing and financial firms, through to firms completely dependent on the newer technologies of the web and software development. The full list of interviewees appears in Appendix 1. I refer to the twenty-two companies where we carried interviews as the "interview firms."

The aim was to try to obtain a wide variety of perspectives of leaders of firms of various sizes, some of whom had started the firm or were part of the owning family, some of whom were exposed to intense global competition, and who were dependent to varying degrees on the capital markets (four of the companies were unlisted). An important aim was to establish any generational differences in ideology, and particular attention is paid to the different responses of the various age groups. Interviews were semi-structured and carried out over a period of just over one year between March 2007 and May 2008. They were carried out in Japanese and transcribed into English by the author. A questionnaire was sent in advance and designed to elicit responses which indicated the extent to which interviewees felt that various aspects of Japanese corporate governance had changed during the "lost decade" of the 1990s and early 2000s. For the purposes of this chapter, I focus in particular on the following five areas:

- The changing role of the Japanese CEO and causes of change
- Changing management objectives and the influence of the company's share price on the decision-making process
- Restructuring of Japanese boards, particularly the growing influence of outside directors
- Changing views on executive pay
- Attitudes toward the question "to whom does the company belong?"[7]

There are clearly problems related to this approach. First, there is the problem that the number of CEOs in the sample is small, and not necessarily representative. Second, the older generation will not have perfect recall of conditions pertaining to their time as CEO, with, in some cases, twenty years having elapsed since they were in charge. There is an in-built tendency for memory to be conditioned by current events and beliefs and

[7] This question is a popular way in which the corporate governance debate is currently framed in Japan in both academic circles and the mass media, centered around shareholder- vs. stakeholder-orientated poles.

correcting for this bias is not possible. Third, there are problems associated with the fact that the situations of each CEO may vary greatly, in terms of both the industry- and firm-specific characteristics within which they operate. Notwithstanding these drawbacks, it was felt that the opportunity to interview this number of Japanese corporate leaders using a systematic format would provide useful indicators as to changing managerial attitudes in important areas of governance.

The Changing Role of the Japanese CEO

There were two questions put to interviewees. First, did they feel that the role of the CEO had changed significantly during the last ten years, and second, if the answer was affirmative, what factors had been most important among the following:

- Changes in the market/intensification of competition/globalization
- Changes in the legal environment: particularly company law, rules regarding corporate governance, and corporate accounting
- Changes in relation to shareholders, particularly the rise in foreign ownership of Japanese shares
- Changes in relations with labor
- Others, particularly those that were company-specific.

There was generally a perception of great change across the three groups with all of the current presidents expressing the opinion that the role had changed greatly over the last ten years. There were some exceptions among current chairmen. As for the main contributing factors to change, the intensification of competition and the changing market place were cited as by far the most important.

The changes started with the way the president was selected, as an insider, by insiders, which strongly influenced the way decisions were reached. According to a company chairman:

During the last 10 years the role of the CEO has become a lot larger. Until then, the CEO position was more like the final station in one's career advancement, the place you'd get to after climbing the stairs of company life. The choosing of the CEO was a process of consensus and even when one became CEO it was not a matter of deciding everything by oneself, but you had to get consensus.

The web of senior figures that remained at the firm in one capacity or another presented a significant constraint to the decision-making powers of the new president (see also Bird 1990: 12–13). These senior figures were not motivated to stay on by financial considerations but, after a lifetime of commitment, the honor embedded in these positions was the reward they expected.[8] As one of the younger CEOs commented:

There's a real problem in the liquidity of management talent, so people cling on . . . the structure of large firms is such that in addition to the president, there are a lot of advisors, and a lot of his predecessors [*sempai*] above him. It's not good corporate governance: it doesn't lead to good corporate health . . . Another thing is that in this country it's not the money that's important, it's the honour. In a Japanese company, it's a matter of honour to go from President, to Chairman, to Advisor, to Supreme Advisor. That's what motivates them, not the money. And if you have these people around, they will interfere. They don't see any value in a 'beautiful retirement.' So if you have a company with a lot of these senior people around, when a company has to think in a global way, they can't respond swiftly to change.

However, globalization, increased competition, and the realization that the domestic market no longer provided sufficient options for long-term growth meant that CEOs had to act more decisively and quickly than before. Hatsuo Aoki, the chairman of Astellas, one of Japan's major pharmaceutical companies, illustrated the challenges facing the industry:

The pharmaceutical market has become much more global. At Astellas, about half of our sales are now overseas: it's the only part that is growing. Domestically the market is tightly controlled according to the needs of the national budget . . . . For the last ten years the growth rate has been around 1 or 2 per cent. We can't rely on the domestic market any more.

The result was more direct competition with overseas, rather than just domestic, firms. This necessitated a more top-down, unilateral approach to leadership. In consolidating global industries, firms were forced to concentrate to a much greater degree on their core businesses, which entailed disposing of noncore assets. This had been difficult in a consensus-oriented organization. As one chairman who had had to make a number of difficult decisions to change the direction of his company when he had been president, including the disposal of a number of subsidiaries, observed:

In Japan people don't want to sell. There are a lot of people involved in these companies. They don't want to know. People think of them as castles. And the president is the lord of the castle. We have to protect our castles. It's unthinkable to

---

[8] Although salaries associated with these positions were not high, a considerable number of perquisites (e.g., use of company car with driver, expense accounts, and so on) came with them.

pass them into the hands of others. That's part of the culture. Therefore unless I order it to be sold, it won't happen.

In dealing with new markets and new competitors, CEOs had to engage at a new level with their counterparts at competitor firms in a way they had not done previously. A CEO of a major manufacturing firm commented:

Only the president is able to carry this out. It's the CEO, one-to-one. Usually you don't have other people present, and no interpreters. With direct communication, you can get a better feel for the nuance, the facial expressions, their level of commitment. The entire body is used for communication.... This type of communication has increased a lot. It is very useful and was not available to the leaders of ten years ago. It's changed my role a lot.

There were a number of companies where change had taken place less due to changes in the external environment but more to specific company circumstances. Cybird and Matsui Securities, for example, were only listed within the last seven years (in 2001 and 2002, respectively) and had expanded rapidly. Lawson, on the other hand, while also recently listed (2000), was carved out of the financially troubled Daiei retail group and turned around by the injection of outside management. All three companies are still highly dependent on the domestic market. For Kazutomo Hori, the founder of Cybird,[9] Michio Matsui, the founder of the modern Matsui Securities,[10] and Takeshi Niinami, the CEO of Lawson who had been parachuted in from Mitsubishi Corporation to turn the company around, management issues were different from leaders of more stable, traditional companies dealing with the challenges of globalization.

Some firms, by the nature of the industry in which they operated, were evidently immune from short-term external influence. For example, Yoshiyuki Kasai, Chairman of Central Japan Railway Company ("JR Central"), while acknowledging that his successor as president was a very different type of leader to him, pointed out that stability of leadership and a long-term perspective were essential given the important role the railway industry played in the Japanese economy.

Railway companies in Japan have developed in an environment of stable employment, meticulously trained and disciplined employees with high morale who have worked with continuously improving technology. In that sense it's one of the industries that is most resistant to external influences.

---

[9] After our interview with Hori, Cybird completed a management buyout and is no longer listed.

[10] The current CEO of Matsui Securities transformed what was basically a traditional brokerage operation into one of Japan's largest online brokerage firms when he took the helm of the company in 1995.

Evolving Relationship with Shareholders

Despite the fact that few interviewees had listed "changing relationship with investors" as the key factor in influencing recent CEO behavior, its importance was emphasized almost universally. The one interviewee who cited governance as the main reason for the changing role was the chairman of a large manufacturing firm. He referred in particular to shifting perceptions of legitimacy in corporate attitudes toward shareholders:

Recently, the view has prevailed, some may call it the "western" way of thinking, that the system of cross-shareholdings is something to be avoided or undesirable. As a result, we have reduced our cross-shareholdings and those that we can really think of as stable shareholders have reduced...Previously, our communication with shareholders consisted only of trying to sail through the shareholders' meeting. Now we have to think constantly of how best we can deepen our shareholders' understanding of our company. This has become the president's personal responsibility, to explain to investors, including foreign investors, the company's strategy and results, and the outlook for the future.

The ability to communicate became a key strength of any modern CEO. This meant not only communicating with investors, but also the press, which was perceived by many as having a crucial mediating role between the company and both the financial community and the population at large. The level of scrutiny of Japanese managers by the media was felt to have grown far more intense during the last ten years, due principally to the increasing number of corporate scandals coming to light. Whereas in previous generations, relations with the press were handled at lower levels in the organization, now the CEO had to appear personally even for routine matters. One CEO remarked:

[What's] changed the most is that whereas before, in many situations the general manager or a director could have taken care of the media, now the President has to do it. Whether it's a press conference, or to deal with some problem, before a Deputy President, a director or a general manger might have taken care of it, now they all say "President! President!".

However, it was in the realm of investor relations (IR) in which the art of communication was seen to be of particular importance. It was widely acknowledged by the senior management of Japanese firms, particularly the older more established ones, that efforts to communicate with the owners of the firm had not been sufficient. A number of managers appeared to believe that the habit that existed in the "old days" of trying to rush the AGM through in half an hour (the so-called *shan-shan sokai*) was somehow embarrassingly symbolic of the prevailing attitude toward shareholders.

This had been remedied and firms now devoted far greater resources to IR. There was a strong sense that responsibility for investor communication ultimately lay with the CEO. One chairman noted:

What we need to do is to explain better the prospect of improved future returns in announcing large investment plans. If investors agree with us, we think they will buy our shares. In the last ten years, even though we were doing it before, IR has become very important, with the president himself going out and meeting investors and explaining the company's strategy and future investment plans.

Although managers were careful not to minimize the importance of domestic institutions, there was clearly a sense that it was the foreign institutions that had played a critical role in persuading Japanese managers to be more sensitive to the needs of shareholders. Many managers emphasized that they felt there was a clear distinction between the apparent short-term aims of the activist and hedge funds that had recently drawn a considerable degree of media attention (representing, as one chairman put it, the "short term demands of foreign capital," implying that it was inherently undesirable) and those foreign institutions with a more long-term perspective. The latter consisted principally of pension funds and mainstream institutional asset managers, who have been the focus of Japanese firms' IR efforts. However, even in the case of the "funds,"[11] some managers were prepared to acknowledge that they played a positive role. As one chairman noted:

even among our shareholders I don't deny that there are short term investors and we need to be constantly vigilant for their activities but they are fundamentally different in outlook from our company... [however] that gives rise to a tension in the good sense of the word.

Another chairman elaborated on the nature of the increased "tension" (*kinchōkan*) brought about by the funds:

Of course foreign investors have been present here for a long time but in the last 10 years the overall impact of various funds ... has been quite beneficial to the Japanese economy. Japan has always had money but we have lacked in various skills. Financial skills have recently become much more important and the funds have brought these skills and introduced an element of tension to Japanese management, even though among the funds there may be some extreme kinds. There may now be more

---

[11] I draw a distinction between "funds," a word often used by Japanese managers to denote activist and hedge funds, and the more mainstream institutions that have been active in Japanese equities for many decades. In practice the boundary between the two is extremely blurred but the distinction nevertheless exists strongly in the minds of management and the media.

hostile takeovers as a result but the overall impact in my view has been very favourable. There may been the Steel Partners type incidents but I feel the response has been exaggerated. It would be a mistake to see the tension it's brought to Japanese management as a negative.

He was not the only person to downplay the significance of the tussle between Steel Partners and Bull-Dog Sauce, emphasizing the minute scale of the company against the backdrop of the wider economy.

The ambivalent attitude toward the pressures that management felt from the new investor groups was well summed up by the president of a large manufacturing concern. He admitted that it would be difficult in practice to impose legal sanctions on the activities of hedge funds, other than for out-and-out greenmail.

Which part of their activities would you restrict? How do you define a hedge fund? We are operating in a capitalistic system so ideally we would permit most normal activity but for those exceptional cases such as greenmailing . . . Hedge funds do harm, but as I said at the same time they discipline managers. So it's not an easy thing.

He strongly criticized the "primitiveness" of the legal framework governing takeovers, which had been adapted inappropriately from US takeover laws. He also referred to the "childish" nature of the debate surrounding the recent "hostile" activity by the likes of Steel Partners and Murakami. We had not seen anything yet. It was, he said, "the beginning of a new age":

Real hostile takeovers are not like that. Really well-prepared hedge funds play to their strengths. They will explain clearly the logic of why they are taking over such and such a company and conduct a fair and open fight. These kinds of hostile acquirers have not yet appeared in Japan. The awareness isn't there. The discussions surrounding the recent attempt by Steel Partners to take over Bull-Dog were just emotional. There was no explanation from Bull-Dog as to why the current management running the company was going to add any more value that what Steel Partners were proposing. In that sense I am very concerned.

Changing Management Objectives and Sensitivity to the Share Price

Whereas in the past, senior management of Japanese firms had virtually no interest in the share price and other benchmarks of performance in which shareholders might have an interest (Abegglen and Stalk 1985: 187), there was ample evidence that management objectives had changed a great deal over the last ten-year period, and had become more geared toward satisfying shareholder requirements in terms establishing clearer quantitative goals and toward disclosure. While for some companies such as Cybird and Mitsubishi UBS Realty, these changes were more about these firms' stages of corporate development, for the majority, the new demands of the shareholders were the most important factor.

One of the older generation of leaders looked back at a time when he had "almost no interest in the share price" and when the share price did not appear to react to corporate events at all. Another identified a totally different attitude from the company's shareholders, which enabled the management to take a longer-term perspective:

I think investors in the old days were a little more sympathetic to the company and understood it more. They were more passive. I believe that the company is something that should exist in perpetuity, especially a company like [ours]. You don't pay shareholders short term rewards by jacking up the dividend temporarily. To ensure the long term existence of the company, you may have to endure periods when the dividend or the share price might go down. You have to invest. The company made some major investments during my time as president which took the company in new directions. The shareholders supported me. An investment might have an adverse effect in the short term on the bottom line. In the old days, investors accepted this. So I was able to make the necessary investments, which were considerable.

The CEO of a major manufacturing firm pointed out that the very concept of "equity" had changed substantially in recent years. If they had been asked about the share price ten years ago, he suspected that "they would have replied that it wasn't appropriate for them to take an interest in such a trifling subject!" This had prompted corporate leaders to take a much stronger interest in the usual benchmarks associated with increasing corporate value to shareholders. One chairman remarked:

The Japanese way was to emphasise sales and market share, and ordinary income [*keijo rieki*]. These were the three factors that most managers had in their heads. But market share has almost completely disappeared and instead concepts like ROI and ROA have come in and recently we have had more share-based profit measures coming in, such as dividend per share, payout ratio, or PER.

There was a fairly clear difference in the perception of the importance of more modern, shareholder-oriented, benchmarks. One of the younger executives was particularly withering about his industrial peers

... as far as this industry is concerned it's really hopeless. Very few CEOs know the meaning of ROE. They may know how to calculate it, but not what it means. The understanding of the concept of the cost of equity is very low.

The younger executives were generally very sensitive to the share price and more clearly benchmarked themselves against their peers in terms of earnings multiples or EBITDA.

For the older managers, while many felt that the possible effect on the share price acted as a constraint on investment decisions, there was an element of frustration that the emphasis on new benchmarks produced a focus on short-term performance which was not entirely welcome. One chairman noted that the management had a duty to discriminate between the short- and long-term shareholders.

When you say "shareholders" recently there are shareholders who hold the shares for about 30 seconds, or a week, or a month. Do we have to adjust our strategy for these shareholders? It doesn't make sense. Those shareholders who are interested in our long term prospects, who buy our shares on that basis: it may be too much to call them 'our real shareholders' but these are the shareholders we want to take care of. Those who sell after one week, those who buy only on the basis of price, the hedge funds: we do not manage our business for those people.

Interestingly, in this particular meeting, the chairman was joined by the former CFO of the firm who was still a director, who gave a slightly different perspective:

From the corporate governance perspective, the responsibilities of directors, or the relationship between the directors and auditors and the fundamental understanding of directors' relationship to shareholders, and the way the company operationalises this, has grown greatly in terms of its claims upon directors during the past 5 to 10 years, especially in the last 4–5 years. The responsibilities of directors have changed greatly, as well as how the company's structure accommodates this shift . . . We take a lot more care about the way our company's finances, its decision-making process is constructed and disclosed in a transparent way. This is demanded by our employees, the market and shareholders. In that way things have changed greatly. It's not just the share price that we look at, but it's one of the factors.

Some companies claimed they had not changed their stance at all in the past decade and not surprisingly, they tended to be in industries that were considered public services requiring large scale, long-term capital investments. Kasai, Chairman of JR Central, noted that the time scales involved in thinking about railway strategy were completely different from other industries:

The share price is not at all a constraint. It was that way 10 years ago and it's the same today. I should think my successor feels the same way. What we think most about today and every day, that is to say, the "present", is the passengers' safety and if we accumulate all the 'todays', we have a total of 44 years of operations of the Tokaido

Shinkansen. For us, the 'near future'means 20 years and for us to do something new may take that long before it's realised. If we go about our business every day looking at the share price, we couldn't run a railway. The 'future' means 50–100 years, and again, with this perspective, we are indifferent to daily stock price movements.

The former president and Chairman of Kansai Electric Power, Shoichiro Kobayashi, expressed similar sentiments. The overriding mission of the company was stable supply of power to its customers, and with pricing and competition strictly controlled by the government, short-term share price movements were irrelevant in his day, and, he thought, today. Both industries also enjoy de facto immunity from acquisition. This is in stark contrast to the situation facing railway and power companies in, say, the United Kingdom.[12]

What was clear in almost all cases was that the habit of paying "stable dividends" to shareholders had come to an end. As can be seen from Table 7.1, in all but two cases (MHI and Asanumagumi which made minor adjustments) during the three years 1996, 1997, and 1998, the dividends paid out by the firms whose executives we interviewed remained exactly the same, despite dramatically fluctuating economic conditions. Ten years later, the picture was very different, with a large increase in dividend volatility and, on the whole, a rising trend in dividend per share.[13]

It appears that companies are now prepared to see much more volatility in their dividend levels while trying to maintain a more stable payout ratio whereas the opposite was true ten years ago. The trading companies (Mitsubishi Corporation and Itochu), Olympus and Kikkoman are good examples of this.

While share buyback information for each individual company was not available, a number of companies, such as Astellas, had conducted annual buybacks. The pressure from shareholders to increase dividends was strongly felt. One chairman commented:

We kept our dividend very stable over a period of many years. Put more harshly, in the words of overseas investors, we didn't think much about our shareholders. That

[12] Notwithstanding the activist targeting of J-Power between 2006 and 2008. While this was not an attempted takeover as such, even if one had been made, it would almost certainly not have succeeded because of J-Power's position as an energy utility: see Chapter 2.

[13] The evidence on payout ratios paints a rather more complicated picture. In all but two cases (Chugai and MHI), the average payout ratio for the second period 2006–8 actually *decreased* over the 1996–8 period. The 1996–8 period was clearly a very difficult period for most Japanese firms with extreme pressure on profits but the stable dividend policy obliged them to maintain dividend levels to the extent that in some cases, dividend per share considerably exceeded earnings per share.

Table 7.1. Dividend/payout ratios of listed interview companies 1996–7 and 2006–7

Dividends	1996	1997	1998	Three year average	2006	2007	2008	Three year average
Itochu (¥)	6	6	6	6	9	14	18	13.67
payout ratio (%)	83	77	−58	383	10	12	13	12
Mitsubishi Corporation (¥)	8	8	8	8	35	46	56	45.67
payout ratio (%)	62	57	58	59	16	19	20	18
Chugai Pharm (¥)	11.5	11.5	11.5	11.5	34	30	30	31.33
payout ratio (%)	33	28	27	29	35	43	41	39
Nippon Sheet Glass (¥)	3	3	3	3	6	6	6	6
payout ratio (%)	73	86	115	88	34	27	8	16
Mitsubishi Heavy Industries (¥)	9	10	10	9.67	4	6	6	5.33
payout ratio (%)	33	30	40	34	45	41	33	38
Tokyo Electric Power (¥)	50	50	50	50	60	70	65	65
payout ratio (%)	140	87	51	79	26	32	−59	57
Kansai Electric Power (¥)	50	50	50	50	60	60	60	60
payout ratio (%)	102	112	74	93	35	38	65	42
Nippon Steel (¥)	2.5	2.5	2.5	2.5	9	10	11	10
payout ratio (%)	69	86	49	65	18	18	20	19
Olympus (¥)	13	13	13	13	22	35	40	32.33
payout ratio (%)	159	133	53	92	20	20	19	20
Kikkoman (¥)	7	7	7	7	12	15	15	14
payout ratio (%)	67	32	45	44	23	27	25	25
Hitachi (¥)	11	11	11	11	11	6	6	7.67
payout ratio (%)	69	32	45	44	98	−61	−34	N/A
Asanumagumi (¥)	8	8	7	7.67	5	2.5	0	2.5
payout ratio (%)	38	54	74	51	−46	−4	0	N/A
NYK (¥)	4	4	4	4	18	18	24	20
payout ratio (%)	182	66	111	101	24	34	26	27
Mizuho FG (¥)					4,000	7,000	10,000	7,000
payout ratio (%)					7	14	39	16
Matsui Securities (¥)					23.09	23	35	27.03
payout ratio (%)					30	46	74	46
Lawson (¥)					90	100	110	100
payout ratio (%)					42	50	51	47
Astellas (¥)					70	80	110	86.67
payout ratio (%)					38	33	31	33
JR Central (¥)					6,500	7,500	8,500	7,500
payout ratio (%)					13	11	11	12

Note: Income and balance sheet information in the "Japan Company Handbook," from which this data is taken, was shown on a parent only basis until 2000. All post-2000 data are shown on a consolidated basis. Therefore the comparisons between the 1996–8 and 2006–8 periods are not strictly like-for-like, but they are indicative, and therefore of some use. The companies at the bottom of the table were either not listed in the 1996–8 period or resulted from mergers that occurred after 1998.

was then. Now, I think we can say that finally, we have started to consider much more how to treat our shareholders.

A number of executives referred to the specific threat of hostile takeover if insufficient attention was paid to the share price. Although this was not a subject brought up by all executives, it is clear that the threat of takeover is an issue preying on the minds of Japanese management in a much bigger way than a decade ago. According to one CEO:

The action of trying to have your corporate value reflected in the share price, for defence against hostile takeover, or for making your own takeover, is a very meaningful thing. Unlike the past, the share price is a very precious management resource... it is very important. You have to have a share price strategy to create the virtuous circle of explaining properly to your investors what your strategy is, producing good performance, share price going up, and so on.

Board Size and the Role of External Directors

Table 7.2 shows the total number of directors and nonexecutive directors at the interview firms for the year 1998 and ten years later, in 2008. Of the companies that were listed in 1998, the average number of directors was over thirty and only four of the companies had outsiders on the board, with an average number of 0.62 outside members per board. Two of these were the Mitsubishi companies, who had a small number of executives (two in the case of Mitsubishi Corporation and one for MHI) from other Mitsubishi group companies on the board. By 2008, board sizes had been cut by more than half, and it was now firms *without* nonexecutive directors that were the minority, with only four out of the eighteen listed firms that had not appointed any. Average outside board members averaged 2.89, small by Anglo-Saxon standards but more than four times the level of ten years ago. Furthermore, many of the CEOs and chairmen that we interviewed sat on the boards of other firms. The tepid response to the "companies with committees" structure alluded to above (see also Chapter 2) is reflected in the group of companies in the sample, with only two firms – Hitachi and more recently Nippon Sheet Glass – having moved over to the new system. However, the more open board configuration is reflected not only in the increase in the number of firms with outside directors on their boards, but in firms that did not want to go all the way to the full committee system but nevertheless had set up either a Remuneration Committee (e.g., Cybird) or a Nomination Committee (e.g., Chugai) or both (e.g., Kikkoman).

Yuzaburo Mogi, the Chairman of Kikkoman, was the most outspoken of the corporate executives that were interviewed in his advocacy of an active role for outside directors, including, if necessary, the removal of poorly performing CEOs.

For example, when you are involved in a takeover, it's not good to rely on the private opinions of the management and there are a number of companies who have

Table 7.2. Board changes at interview companies, 1998–2008

	Number of directors 1998	NEDs 1998	Number of directors 2008	NEDs 2008
Itochu	45	0	13	0
Mitsubishi Corporation	45	2	15	5
Chugai Pharmaceutical	10	0	14	7
Nippon Sheet Glass	17	0	12	7
Mitsubishi Heavy Industries	37	1	19	3
Tokyo Electric Power	32	3	20	2
Kansai Electric Power	30	2	20	3
Nippon Steel	43	0	11	0
Olympus	20	0	15	3
Kikkoman	23	0	10	2
Hitachi	30	0	13	5
Asanumagumi	37	0	7	0
NYK	25	0	16	2
Mizuho FG			9	3
JR Central			21	3
Matsui Securities			8	0
Lawson			7	3
Astellas			7	4
Average	30.31	0.62	13.17	2.89

created independent committees. You need independent views in these situations. As a result, interest in independent directors has increased quite a lot in Japan during the last year, and especially since the approval of the setting up of the committee system there has been a sea change in Japanese corporate governance.

Like a number of other executives, he alluded to the problem of the lack of candidates for the position, but he urged his fellow business leaders to be more proactive in joining other boards. He said that it was his experience as an outside director of another firm, Teijin, which has set up an advisory board whose tasks include the deliberation of board succession and remuneration issues, that had influenced his views on corporate governance.

My own experience is that being an outside director is very educational. You participate in the management of other companies. It's a new challenge. It takes up a lot of time but it's useful for yourself and your company. It's OK to have academics, journalists and so on, but the main body has to be managers, or former managers. As much as time permits, current managers should do this and there are a lot of former managers around. They should get involved.

External directors were an antidote to the tendency of an internally focused board regime to develop "tunnel vision" and not check the power of the

CEO. This opinion was particularly strongly felt among the younger generation of CEOs, one of whom noted:

Rather than have people who have been brought up in the same culture discussing and deciding upon important matters, you need the perspectives of people from different cultures and who have had different experiences. Internal people can't disobey the president. Historically, it's the same everywhere – people at the top, the longer they stay there, the more they become like royalty. External directors are very important for both not letting the CEO run his own fiefdom and for enabling flexibility in thinking.

While a number of CEOs who had not yet appointed outside directors said they were starting to understand their value and were seriously considering bringing some on to their boards, not all were convinced. They tended to dismiss the growing popularity of outside directors as a legitimacy-seeking exercise.

It's a question of what outside directors are for. For most companies it's about appearances. It's a matter of "we have proper external auditing so we are a company that has credibility." The vast majority of cases are to assure a certain appearance of legitimacy... it's not possible for outside directors to make constructive suggestions about our business matters. We are thinking of these things every second of every day, year in year out. What we want from people like that is an honest statement of their opinion from an external perspective, even if it appears really simple. But for this we don't need outside directors, external auditors can fulfil this function.

The main arguments against the appointment of outside directors were, first, that they didn't know anything about the business, and second, that the auditors were able to fulfill the function of "representing the outside" perfectly adequately. Even among the companies that had appointed outside directors, very few of the managers saw them representing exclusively, or even predominantly, the shareholders. One company chairman observed:

The US system of corporate governance is well thought out from a theoretical standpoint. The CEO directs the affairs of the company. There are outsiders on the board who represent the shareholders. They express opinions on such matters as proper distribution of profit.... There are a lot of people saying that Japanese companies should appoint more external directors but they simply don't understand the meaning of external directors in Japan. We understand that the meaning is different here compared with the US. Traditional Japanese companies like ours are basically centred on the executive group. There may be a few external directors but they don't particularly represent the views of shareholders. They are there as experienced managers to give advice to the executive.

The idea of external directors representing an unbiased, "outside" view was common to virtually all the executives interviewed. While this perception of their role had more in common with that envisaged in the United Kingdom,[14] it is, as the chairman above notes, a far cry from the agency theory interpretation of directors acting primarily in the interests of the company's shareholders.

Executive Compensation

One of the key features of US executive pay has been the tendency to link increasingly large proportions of total compensation to corporate performance, particularly in the form of options linked to the company's share price. It is telling that, of the companies represented in the sample, only five had active share options schemes for directors. Remarkably, three companies had introduced options schemes and had subsequently terminated them. Even for the companies that had introduced option schemes, the value of the annual options granted amounted to, at maximum, an estimated 25 percent of total compensation. This is in contrast to the situation in the United States, where the value of options can amount to a multiple of annual base pay in many cases.

Although there is strong evidence that the gap between directors' and employees' pay is widening, almost all of the managers interviewed denied that this was occurring at their firms. If it was occurring, it was because of the following factors:

- Many firms had abolished the tradition of granting directors a retirement lump sum and folding in this element of remuneration into the directors' annual compensation. Retirement payments need to be ratified at the AGM and a number of managers pointed out that there had been a number of cases in recent years where media pressure had forced directors or CEOs to forgo their retirement pay if some sort of scandal had occurred during their watch, or if the company had performed poorly. Making these lump sum payments part of regular salary obviated the need to seek AGM approval, even if it did increase the

---

[14] Derek Higgs, in his 2003 report entitled *Review of Role and Effectiveness of Non-Executive Directors*, notes that a major contribution of the nonexecutive director is to bring wider experience and a fresh perspective to the boardroom (Higgs 2003: 35). The Combined Code does not specify the responsibilities of nonexecutive directors toward shareholders, although the latest version (2003) recommends as best practice active engagement between nonexecutive directors and institutional investors.

individual director's tax burden (as retirement payments benefit from considerably lower tax rates).[15]

- There has been, as we have seen above, a dramatic reduction in the size of Japanese boards during the last ten years. As the people who have left the board have been junior directors on lower salaries, board reduction will have had the effect of raising average directors' salaries.
- Many executives pointed out that during the lean years of the 1990s and early 2000s, board members had taken substantial pay cuts while leaving employee salaries unaffected, in the tradition, as one chairman put it, of the "bushido spirit" of leaders looking after their followers before taking care of themselves. Another chairman claimed in the ten years he had been a director, he had only once received a bonus. The fact that the economy had recovered during the last few years has meant that most CEOs and other directors have been able to restore bonuses, causing the pay gap between directors and other employees to widen.

Whether these factors can account for the entirety of the widening of the pay gap is uncertain, and would be worth further research. However, what was quite clear was that the majority of interviewees felt that the gap in real terms at their firms was not growing. As to whether that was a good thing, in other words as to whether the gap *should widen* was another matter. There were indeed some CEOs who thought that executive pay was too low compared to the greater responsibilities and risks they were supposed to bear. There appeared to be some generational differences here, with the younger CEOs particularly dissatisfied with executive compensation structures. One of the younger leaders pointed to the impact of Sarbanes–Oxley legislation, which places individual responsibility on internal controls and compliance on the directors, and particularly the CEO.

It's the extra care, the additional burden that we face to prevent these things from happening in the first place. There's a big difference between the two levels and I think the extra burden, including the psychological pressure, needs to be compensated . . . [In Japan] the multiple of CEO to employee salary is 20 times, maximum 30 times . . . I think it would be OK if it were 100 times [as in the US].

It is noteworthy, however, that of the three companies that had terminated option schemes for directors, two were run by younger CEOs and both for

---

[15] Some firms were making these payments to directors in the form of "¥1 options," where the strike price of the options was ¥1, which had the effect of linking retirement pay to the share price.

similar reasons, the apparently corrosive effect of large annual rewards on the motivation of senior management.

I don't want people who work in the organisation to put a priority on the amount of money they earn. So in answer to the question "why are you here" I don't want them to answer "because I'm well paid". I want them to be here because they are committed to [this company] achieving its goals or vision. Humans are weak after all, and if people understand what others are paid they begin to make comparisons. If that happens they start thinking in that crazy American way, that people with more money are somehow better. I don't like that.

It is also noteworthy that all of the advocates of higher pay for directors emphasized the need for increased responsibility and risk to be compensated: no one suggested a link between higher executive pay and tying the fates of directors closer to those of shareholders.

Many leaders referred to the inherent "egalitarian" nature of Japanese society and thought that executive pay was constrained first by the fact that the CEO's pay was determined by the HR Department which only looked at other firms (*yokonarabi*) to determine the appropriate level of pay for their own CEO, and second by the reactions of their own employees. When asked whether the individual pay of directors should be disclosed, one CEO replied:

The difficulty is that it's not really clear where the consensus is to receive the sort of salary I'm receiving. The analysts say I receive too little. [If I have increased the company's profitability], the analysts ask me "how much of that [difference] did you get? And how about the growth you're showing in the three year plan, how much of that are you getting?" I can't reply, as it's too low. But at Japanese companies, there is no sense as to how employees would react to full disclosure and that's a frightening thing. If we get 10 times or 20 times what they earn: what will they think? The real issue is how to motivate our employees. Our investors, or buy side or sell side analysts, say it's too low but there is a huge gap in the understanding. From an American perspective the gap is too small. But Japan is different. The tacit understanding might be that the president gets around ¥50 million [i.e. about $500,000]. That's probably what people think.

The idea that there is some sort of unwritten consensus between the employees of the firm and the senior management, an agreement that the CEO and other directors will not be excessively greedy, and that this is a key motivating factor for the company's employees, suggests that the debate about a closer link between executive pay and shareholders is being carried out on a different level in Japan compared with other countries, particularly the United States. Still, there appeared to be some "progress" compared with 20–30 years ago. One of the older generation of leaders noted that in his day:

Even if you became president, your pay wouldn't increase for the first two years. It would rise a little from the third year. Those first two terms were for "running in the new car" to check that it worked properly. It's a bizarre story but we used to do that in [those days]. These unique cultural traits must seem strange to the outside!

Whose Company Is It?

On this final question there was virtual unanimity. Only one interviewee was prepared to give an unambiguous shareholder-oriented response (oddly, from one of the most conservative leaders):

The company belongs to the shareholders. We used to treat the employees as the number one priority. With lifetime employment we couldn't fire anyone. Next came customers. These last ten years, we have come to treat customers as the priority, with employees as number three.

While most executives were prepared to acknowledge that the shareholders had made themselves much more keenly felt over the last decade, all of the leaders with the above exception responded along the lines of either "in theory the company belongs to the shareholders but..." or "it belongs to the stakeholders." There were no particular generational differences and the younger CEOs gave very similar responses. One said:

You can't say simply that it belongs to the shareholders. Of course theoretically it does. But it's not as simple as that. The employees come together and create knowledge and increase corporate value...they are my closest associates. They are very important. If they're unhappy, what's the point of the company? And there are our customers. I wouldn't say we only exist for them, but without them the company wouldn't exist.

There was little qualitative difference between that response, and the following, from one of the more traditional Japanese leaders:

It doesn't belong to any group in particular. It belongs to the shareholders, as they provide capital. It also belongs to society, also to customers, who are very important – because of them we provide products – and if we didn't have employees, we couldn't make those products...As I mentioned, in the past we didn't have to pay so much attention to shareholders but we now have to consider them as a very important element of the company. But from the point of view of actually managing the company I think the employees are the most important. If we didn't have employees, we couldn't make good products, we couldn't satisfy our customers. In the end, what we do is supply products to our customers; through this process we make a profit and we distribute this to our shareholders. If we over-emphasise shareholders, for a product oriented company such as ourselves, it may become very problematic. Furthermore, while the management of the company is an important element, it is the company that exists in perpetuity. It is for the continuity of the firm that the management, the employees and the shareholders need to work together in order to make products which satisfy our customers.

The requirement of the company to make contributions to all stakeholder groups, and the relationship between this requirement and the idea of the company as a body that should exist in perpetuity, was a common theme. There was a link between the persistence of the lifetime employment custom and the idea that employees and management shared a common destiny. This created a natural tendency, according to Japanese managers, to think long-term and resist as much as possible the short-term demands of shareholders. Hostile takeovers, in this scheme of things, were out of the question. As one CEO put it:

We read more and more in the newspapers about Livedoor, the Murakami Fund, and aggressive Anglo-Saxon ways of doing things. But we have a long history. Stories like Nippon Steel's anxiety about an approach from Mittal would have been unthinkable twenty years ago so it is becoming a real issue, but I don't think that there are many people around who really feel that the company belongs just to the shareholders. The employment system and the emphasis on lifetime employment is changing but it is still the basic assumption that when we recruit students from university, they want to work and develop here for their entire careers. It's true that the number of people leaving is growing but unless the employees perform, the company won't succeed. You can't fire people in Japan so we share a common destiny. It's difficult to respond to the short term demands of certain shareholders and I believe that the majority of shareholders understand this. There may be some extreme groups but they will see that you can't succeed with hostile takeovers. No one will benefit. Over time people will come to understand that the existing Japanese corporate culture and customs cannot be overcome.

Discussion and Conclusions

This chapter has examined the attitudes of both current and former CEOs of Japanese firms to ascertain whether certain underlying trends in executive compensation, board structure, and the distribution of corporate profit are indicative of a fundamental shift from an organization orientation to one favoring shareholders. In particular, I am trying to uncover through the interview process whether the communitarian managerial ideology is discredited in the eyes of the leaders of Japanese corporations, and the extent to which they embrace the commitment to the legal owners of the firm.

The visible data, the increase in dividend payments and the restructuring of Japanese boards, strongly suggest a shift toward a shareholder orientation. It is clear that most CEOs and former CEOs see great changes in the role of the leader of the modern Japanese corporation. While there were differing explanations as to whether the cause of these changes lies in increased competition and globalization or increased pressure from shareholders, in a sense this is a false dichotomy. Most managers talked of both being crucial ingredients and indeed inseparable. Globalization of the capital markets and the lowering of barriers to the movement of capital, and the increasing diversity of institutional investors with stakes in Japanese firms were significant factors in the rearrangement of relationships between Japanese corporate leaders and their shareholders.

Managers were on the whole more sensitive to their company's share price movements and had changed the benchmarks for corporate success to reflect a greater shareholder orientation. They were much more focused on IR and also saw the media as a crucial conduit through which messages to the company's financial stakeholders needed to pass. By contrast, very few interviewees saw industrial relations as a key issue, as they generally saw relations at their firms as being very harmonious.

Although Japanese companies have strengthened their IR and corporate communications functions, many CEOs increasingly saw their colleagues turning to them to take the lead in these areas. The influence of financial analysts and the larger institutional investors was such that CEOs felt they had no choice but to allocate significant amounts of time to this audience. Increasing reliance on M&A, not only as a way of entering new markets or consolidating positions in existing ones, but also as a means of exiting businesses, and the secrecy that is required in the process of buying or selling companies, has meant that CEOs have fewer colleagues to consult on important matters of strategy. Building broad internal consensus is not an option. One chairman who had made some important acquisitions during his time as president said:

For these big decisions, I made the decisions on my own. When it comes to M&A or big personnel decisions, there aren't actually any people with whom you can discuss things.

The need for the CEO to possess strong communication skills to appeal to the increasingly diverse stakeholder group has risen. Insofar as the leader is now making a greater number of decisions on his own and is required to convince his colleagues to support him, the importance of a commanding presence that instills the instinct to follow (which many would call "charisma") is also growing.

There is, however, strong evidence to suggest that despite all of the apparent moves made by Japanese managers to move toward a greater shareholder orientation, their fundamental guiding principles have not altered significantly. While some CEOs were prepared to admit that from a theoretical perspective the company was owned by shareholders, there was virtual unanimity in the expression of the stakeholder perspective of corporate governance, with the core employees of the company still occupying a prominent position in the minds of CEOs in considering who their main audience is and for what purpose they work. The idea of the enduring nature of the company's existence, its status as a permanent fixture of Japan's economic and social landscape, is still powerfully imprinted on the minds of Japanese managers. Anything that threatens its existence, however much it may benefit its owners or enriches the managers themselves, will be strongly resisted by them. Hostile M&A will for the time remain anathema for Japanese firms.

Japanese leaders acknowledge that the legitimacy of the communitarian model, and the practices upon which its foundations are built, have been eroded. But in expressing this view, they talked in terms of a prevailing mood, something changing "out there" but not subscribed to by themselves. They have appointed external directors not because they want the owners of the firm to be represented on the board, but because it now appears to be the legitimate thing to do to have an outside voice at board meetings (another example of *yokonarabi*). Most importantly, despite the fact that differentials between directors' and employees' pay may have widened somewhat, Japanese executives are not rewarding themselves in a way that aligns their interests significantly closer to shareholders, or causes them to boost the short-term performance of the firm. Equally significantly, the external market in CEOs is still to all intents and purposes nonexistent. While demand for charismatic leaders may have risen, the "irrational quest" for such CEOs will be strictly limited to internal candidates. The legitimacy of "insiderness" may be being undermined, but not to the extent that it is a liability.

I have observed in our interviews some generational differences. Particularly in areas such as executive pay, it would appear that some of the younger leaders have a more individualist and Anglo-Saxon attitude toward rewards. Even though they currently share with their older colleagues the same stakeholder-centered sense of corporate governance, it may be that the changing of the guard and the rise of the younger leaders who have been educated overseas (three of the four "younger generation" leaders received tertiary education in either the United States or the United Kingdom) will cause Japanese leaders to start identifying themselves much more closely with the interests of shareholders. For the current leadership of Japanese companies, increased pressure from shareholders has caused changes to behavior and an acknowledgment that surplus value needs to be reallocated in different ways. However, it is still far too early to say that this behavior amounts to a fundamental shift toward investor capitalism. The underlying ideology that underpins Japanese management practices is still infused with the communitarian ethic.

Appendix 1

List of interviewees (in alphabetical order)

Retired former Presidents and Chairmen
1. Shoichiro Kobayashi, Kansai Electric Power
2. Yotaro Kobayashi, Fuji Xerox
3. Jiro Nemoto, NYK
4. Toshiro Shimoyama, Olympus Optical

Current Chairmen
5. Hatsuo Aoki, Astellas Pharma
6. Yozo Izuhara, Nippon Sheet Glass
7. Yoshiyuki Kasai, Central Japan Railway
8. Yozaburo Mogi, Kikkoman
9. Takashi Nishioka, Mitsubishi Heavy Industries
10. Uichiro Niwa, Itochu
11. Nobutada Saji, Suntory
12. Etsuhiko Shoyama, Hitachi

Current Presidents
13. Kenichi Asanuma, Asanumagumi
14. Yuichi Hiromoto, Mitsubishi UBS Realty
15. Kazutomo Robert Hori, Cybird
16. Tsunehisa Katsumata, Tokyo Electric Power
17. Yorihiko Kojima, Mitsubishi Corporation
18. Terunobu Maeda, Mizuho Financial Group
19. Michio Matsui, Matsui Securities
20. Akio Mimura, Nippon Steel
21. Osamu Nagayama, Chugai Pharmaceutical
22. Takeshi Niinami, Lawson

Bibliography

Abegglen, J. C. and Stalk, G. (1985). *Kaisha, the Japanese Corporation*. New York: Basic Books.

Ahmadjian, C. L. and Robbins, G. E. (2005). "A Clash of Capitalisms: Foreign Shareholders and Corporate Restructuring in 1990s Japan." *American Sociological Review*, 70: 451–71.

Ahn, S., Bhattacharaya, U., Jung, T. and Nam, G. (2004). "Do Japanese CEOs Matter?" SSRN Working Paper Series Tokyo.

Aoki, M. (1994). "The Japanese Firm as a System of Attributes: A Survey and Research Agenda," in M. Aoki and R. Dore (eds.) *The Japanese Firm: Sources of Competitive Strength*. Oxford: Oxford University Press.

Berle, A. A. and Means, G. C. (1932). *The Modern Corporation and Private Property*. New York: MacMillan.

Bird, A. (1990). "Power and the Japanese CEO." *Asia Pacific Journal of Management*, 7: 1–20.

Booz Allen Hamilton (2005). "CEO Succession 2005: The Crest of the Wave." McLean, VA: Booz Allen Hamilton (www.strategy-business.com/media/file/sb43_06210.pdf).

Clark, R. (1979). *The Japanese Company*. New Haven: Yale University Press.

Conference Board (2008). *The 2008 Institutional Investment Report: Trends in Institutional Investor Assets and Equity Ownership of U.S. Corporations. Report No. 1433-08-RR*. New York: The Conference Board.

Dore, R. (1973). *British Factory–Japanese Factory: The Origins of National Diversity in Industrial Relations*. Berkeley: University of California Press.

—— (1994). "Equality-Efficiency Trade-Offs: Japanese Perceptions and Choices," in M. Aoki and R. Dore (eds.) *The Japanese Firm: Sources of Competitive Strength*. Oxford: Oxford University Press.

—— (2000). *Stock Market Capitalism: Welfare Capitalism – Japan and Germany versus the Anglo-Saxons*. Oxford: Oxford University Press.

—— (2006). *Dare No Tame No Kaisha Ni Suru Ka? (Who is the Company to Be For?)*. Tokyo: Iwanami Shoten.

Economist (2006). "The Rising Sun Leaves Some Japanese in the Shade." *The Economist*, June 17.

Fligstein, N. (2001). *The Architecture of Markets: An Economic Sociology of Twenty-First Century Capitalist Societies*. Princeton: Princeton University Press.

Genda, Y. (2005). *A Nagging Sense of Job Insecurity*. Tokyo: International House of Japan, Inc.

Higgs, D. (2003). *Review of Role and Effectiveness of Non-Executive Directors*. London: Department of Trade and Industry.

Hymowitz, C. (2004). "American CEOs Meet Resistance When Taking the Helm Overseas." *Wall Street Journal Online*, May 26.

Inagami, T. and Whittaker, D. H. (2005). *The New Community Firm: Employment, Governance and Management Reform in Japan*. Cambridge: Cambridge University Press.

Jacoby, S. (2005). *The Embedded Corporation: Corporate Governance and Employment Relations in Japan and the United States*. Princeton: Princeton University Press.

—— (2007). "Principles and Agents: Calpers and Corporate Governance in Japan," *Corporate Governance*, 15: 5–16.

Khurana, R. (2002). *Searching for a Corporate Saviour*. Princeton: Princeton University Press.

Kraakman, R., Davies, P., Hansmann, H., Hertig, G., Hopt, K., Kanda, H. and Rock, E. (2004). *The Anatomy of Corporate Law: A Comparative and Functional Approach*. Oxford: Oxford University Press.

Lipton, M. (2008). "Shareholder Activism and the 'Eclipse of the Public Corporation': Is the Current Wave of Activism Causing Another Tectonic Shift in the American Corporate World?" Address to the 2008 Directors Forum of the University of Minnesota Law School, June 25.

Nihon Keizai shimbun (2007). "Nemuru genseki: iyoku ni saitenka" ("Reigniting the Flame of Motivation"). *Nihon Keizai shimbun*, December 7.

NLI Research (2007). "The Diverse Evolution of Traditional Corporate Boards in Japan." www.nli-research.co.jp/english/pension_strategy/2007/str070329a.pdf. Accessed March 2007.

Rebick, M. (2005). *The Japanese Employment System*. Oxford: Oxford University Press.

Robinson, P. and Shimizu, N. (2006). "Japanese Corporate Restructuring: CEO Priorities as a Window on Environmental and Organizational Change." *Academy of Management Perspectives*, 20: 44–75.

Rohlen, T. P. (1974). *For Harmony and Strength: Japanese White-Collar Organization in Anthropological Perspective*. Berkeley: University of California Press.

Sakano, T. and Lewin, A. Y. (1999). "Impact of CEO Succession in Japanese Companies: A Coevolutionary Perspective." *Organization Science*, 10: 654–71.

Smithers & Co. (2008) *Japan: Shareholder Power, Cross-holdings and Over-Investment*. Report No 312, July 2. London: Smithers & Co.

Vogel, S. (2006). *Japan Remodeled: How Government and Industry Are Reforming Japanese Capitalism*. Ithaca: Cornell University Press.

Yashiro, N. (1998). *Jinjibu Wa Mou Iranai (Who Needs an HR Department Any More?)*. Tokyo: Kodansha.

Yoshimori, M. (1995). "Whose Company Is It? The Concept of the Corporation in Japan and the West." *Long Range Planning*, 28: 33–44.

8

Changes in Japan's Practice-Dependent Stakeholder Model and Employee-Centered Corporate Governance

Takashi Araki

Japan has long been regarded as an exemplar of a stakeholder model of corporate governance, emphasizing employee interests. Its model draws heavily on a number of customary practices, such as stable cross-shareholdings, appointment of senior managers through internal promotion, lifetime employment, and voluntary joint labor–management consultation. These practices are undergoing notable changes, however, making the model itself susceptible to change in a way that Germany's legally sanctioned stakeholder model, for example, may not be. A socio-economic system with closely interdependent institutions may be robust in normal times, but transformation is more likely in an era of disequilibrium when several institutions change simultaneously. This poses a question: will changes to Japanese practice lead to fundamental institutional changes that, in turn, will transform Japan's current stakeholder model into a shareholder-orientated model of governance?

This chapter addresses this question by focusing on employment and labor relations. First, it paints a contextual picture of how corporate practices have sustained its traditional system of stakeholder capitalism. Second, it reviews recent developments in shareholder ownership and management structures. Third, it explores shifts in employment, and the reactions to these shifts in labor–management relations.

Parts of this chapter are drawn from Araki (2007). The author expresses his deep gratitude to Leon Wolff for his invaluable comments on the draft paper.

Fourth, it examines changes in collective labor relations and their impact on Japanese corporate governance. The final section evaluates the impact of changes in practices, legislative developments, and thinking in Japanese corporate society, and outlines some implications for the future of Japan's corporate governance from the perspective of Japanese labor law.

Japan's Traditional Practice-Dependent Stakeholder Model

Until the early 1990s, Japan subscribed to a practice-dependent, employee-centered stakeholder model of corporate governance (Aoki 2007; Araki 2007; Jackson and Miyajima 2007). Its distinctive governance model was established under the following circumstances.

First, cross-shareholdings and long-term shareholdings featured prominently in the structure of ownership. The primary concern of shareholders was not share value but establishing and maintaining long-term relationships with trading partners. Thus, shareholders did not actively intervene in corporate governance. Indeed, banks rather than shareholders were the major suppliers of funds to Japanese companies. Yet even banks did not intervene in corporate governance so long as the firm maintained a level of performance sufficient to redeem its loans. This allowed management to prioritize the interests of employees, who were seen as members of a corporate "community" (Inagami and Whittaker 2005).

Second, the majority of managers in Japanese firms were promoted from within and, moreover, had close personal connections to trade unions.[1] In most large companies, management and a majority union concluded a union shop agreement, which required all hires to join the union on penalty of immediate dismissal. Under the practice of lifetime employment, this meant that current executives were members of the enterprise union in their 20s or 30s when they were rank-and-file white-collar workers.[2] Furthermore, according to a 1999 survey, 28.2 percent of top management had not only been former members of the enterprise union, but had been in a leadership position (Inagami and RIALS 2000: 339). In a

---

[1] According to Inagami and RIALS (2000), 75.6 percent of board members were internally promoted.

[2] Since enterprise unions in Japan organize workers in the same company irrespective of their jobs, both blue and white collar workers were organized in the same union.

sense, therefore, labor–management relations in Japanese enterprises were in fact relations between present and former union members, and collective bargaining was sometimes a process of negotiation between current and former union leaders. This created an environment under which both labor and management felt that they belonged to the same community, with shared views and common interests. This, in turn, promoted a consensual rather than an adversarial approach to solving workplace issues.

Third, under lifetime or long-term employment, management again understood employees to be members of a community rather than resources to be deployed in the interests of business. Labor and management voluntarily established forums for labor–management consultation, paving the way for a largely cooperative system of industrial relations.

The main pillars that have sustained Japan's stakeholder system as described above – cross-shareholdings, a stable body of shareholders, internal promotion of board members, long-term employment, and labor–management consultation – are simply practices or customs; they are not mandated by law. This explains why Japanese corporate governance is usually referred to as a "practice-dependent" stakeholder model, in contrast to Germany's "legally sanctioned" stakeholder model.[3]

Share Ownership and Management Structure: Changes and Persistence

These practices are currently undergoing significant change (Araki 2007; Jackson and Miyajima 2007). Yet despite this, the evidence still points to a persistence of traditional shareholding and management structures in Japan.

Following a shift in corporate financing away from banks in favor of capital markets from the late 1980s, traditional cross-shareholdings and long-term shareholdings gradually unraveled. After 1997, cross-shareholdings and long-term shareholdings, especially those between banks and their customer corporations, declined rapidly. Concomitantly with the decline of share ownership by financial institutions and business corporations, individuals emerged as important investors. A growing number of foreign investors, in particular, have put pressure on Japanese companies to embrace more shareholder-oriented governance systems.

---

[3] See Araki (2000: 87), Araki (2004), Dore (2000:182, 215), Milhaupt (2001: 2083); cf. also Aoki (2007: 440). The German stakeholder model is legally sanctioned by codetermination legislation both at the company level (Aufsichtsrat) and at the establishment level (Betriebsrat).

On the other hand, in the 2000s, the economic recovery and a rise in hostile takeover bids promoted a trend back to cross-shareholdings among industrial firms. Cross-shareholdings decreased up to 2005, but bounced back in 2006 and 2007 (*Mainichi shimbun*, July 1 2008). In the Bull-Dog Sauce case in 2007, where the target Bull-Dog Sauce took measures to protect itself against a takeover bid by Steel Partners, an American investment fund, the Supreme Court upheld the legality of Bull-Dog Sauce's defense measures (see Chapters 2 and 3). In this case, Bull-Dog Sauce's measures were supported by a large majority of the shareholders (83%). This Supreme Court decision further encouraged firms to rebuild cross-shareholdings to ward off the threat of hostile takeover bids, because cross-shareholdings were seen as the most assured way of securing support from shareholders for the approval of defense measures.

Management Structure: Symbolism and Reality

Corporate management structures underwent significant legal reform in 2002. Until 2002, Japan had a unique dual-monitoring system under which both the board of directors and auditors monitored corporate management. The problem with the board of directors monitoring the business decisions of representative directors is that the board simultaneously assumes a role in the conduct of the firm's business. In addition, many board directors are in fact subordinate to the representative director or president (*shacho*) and thus it is impractical to expect them to supervise their "boss."

To separate the business execution from the monitoring function, the 2002 revision to the Commercial Code and related laws introduced an American-style board of directors system utilizing external directors, called the "company with committees." In order to opt into this committee-based model, three committees – appointments, remuneration, and audit – must be established. Three or more directors must serve on each of these committees, and the majority must be external or nonexecutive directors. This new governance model, however, is entirely voluntary. Firms may choose to retain the traditional model of "company with auditors."

Under the 2002 revision, the new system with three committees was only available for large companies, capitalized at more than ¥500 million, or with total balance sheet debt of more than ¥20 billion, and for other companies otherwise deemed by law to be large companies. However, the Company Act of 2005, which came into effect in April 2006, made it possible for all companies to adopt the new model irrespective of their capital or debt size.[4] Thus, Japanese companies can either maintain the traditional dual-monitoring system or, by modifying their articles of incorporation, adopt the new committee-based model. As such, Japan has entered an era of competition between two different governance models (Egashira 2002: 412).

Although the 2002 revisions heralded a significant symbolic shift in Japanese corporate governance, the reality is that only a modest number of companies switched to the new governance model. According to a survey by the Japan Corporate Auditors Association, only 110 listed companies had adopted it as of July 8 2008 (JCAA 2008; see also Chapter 2). This number includes such leading corporations as Sony, Toshiba, Mitsubishi, Hitachi and Nomura, but most larger companies, including Toyota, Nissan, Honda, and Panasonic, maintain the traditional dual-monitoring governance model. In another survey conducted in April 2004 by the Japan Corporate Auditors Association, only 0.2 percent of the surveyed companies planned to adopt the new governance model and 1.4 percent of them were "considering" the matter; 86 percent of the surveyed companies expressed no intention of adopting the new model (JCAA 2004). Additionally, seventeen firms which initially adopted the "company with committees" model subsequently returned to the traditional model of "company with auditors."

Many managers prefer the traditional system on the grounds of managerial effectiveness because it permits a manager to exert his/her leadership, flexibly tailor decisions to suit the situation of the individual corporation, and pursue effective and expeditious corporate administration.[5] The scarcity of suitable candidates for the positions of outside director has further hindered the adoption of the new governance model. As a result, the majority of listed corporations continue to maintain the traditional corporate governance model.

Thus, changes have occurred to the legal framework, but traditional practices remain firmly in place. A similar trend is observable in the field of employment, the subject of the remainder of this chapter. Once again, significant transformations are taking place, but these have been counteracted in various ways which preserve the interests of employees.

---

[4] The Corporate Law of 2005 is an independent statute consisting of 979 articles providing comprehensive regulations on corporations and replacing the former Commercial Code chapters and other related laws regulating corporations.

[5] Ministry of Finance, Policy Research Institute (2003: table 3.24).

Changing Employment Relations

Japan is known for its lifetime or long-term employment system, with the employment security that it offers. For many years, Japan boasted a low unemployment rate, even following the two oil crises (Figure 8.1). However, after the collapse of the bubble economy in the early 1990s, the unemployment rate gradually – and after 1997, rapidly – increased and repeatedly reached new record levels, hitting a high of 5.4 percent in 2002.

Shrinking Stable Employment

The media have made much of the rise in unemployment (as well as the troubles of large corporations that traditionally guaranteed employment security), proclaiming the imminent demise of lifetime employment. This gave the misleading impression that Japanese employees had lost their employment security and could be easily dismissed. What was in fact occurring was that the share of permanent (regular) employees was shrinking and, in turn, the share of nonpermanent ("atypical" or "non-regular") employees, under fixed-term employment, part-time employment, temporary work, and so on, was increasing. In 1990, nonregular employees made up 20.2 percent of the Japanese workforce; by 2007 this had jumped to 33.5 percent (Figure 8.2).

The employment security of regular employees, however, has not been drastically diluted. On the contrary, it is precisely because the employment security of regular employees has been preserved that management

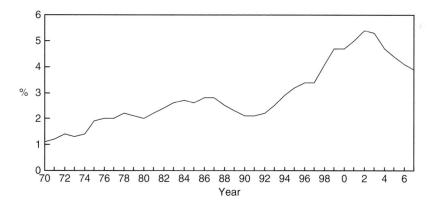

Figure 8.1. Unemployment trends in Japan
Source: Ministry of Internal Affairs and Communications, Statistics Bureau, Labor Force Survey.

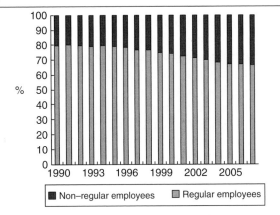

Figure 8.2. Ratio of regular/nonregular employees

Source: Ministry of Public Management, Home Affairs, Posts and Telecommunications, Labor Force Survey, respective years.

is increasingly resorting to hiring nonregular employees. The deregulation of labor market laws and regulations has facilitated this trend. This is a very important point to bear in mind when evaluating Japan's corporate governance and employment relations, and we will return to this later.

Labor Market Deregulation

Corporate restructuring from the 1990s increased the lateral (interfirm) mobility of regular employees. "Atypical" employees are also mobile. To cope with such increased labor mobility, and accelerate the flow of workers from declining industries to emerging new businesses, the Japanese government introduced a series of deregulatory measures to promote flexibility in the external labor market (Araki 1997: 5). From 1995 onward, the government explicitly identified a number of labor market regulations, in particular regulations on fee-charging placement services and worker dispatching agencies (or temporary employment agencies), as urgent targets for deregulation.

In line with international trends toward deregulation, regulations in the Employment Security Act (ESA) and the Worker Dispatching Act (WDA) were relaxed in 1999.[6] The ESA revisions abandoned the policy of a state

[6] Many European countries changed their regulatory attitude toward fee-charging placement services and temporary employment agencies from the late 1980s. On June 19 1997, the International Labour Organization adopted the Private Employment Agencies Convention (C-181, 1997) which dropped the state monopoly principle of employment placement services, and recognized the important role of private employment agencies in the labour market.

monopoly on employment placement, lifting the ban on private fee-charging placement services. The WDA revisions substantially relaxed regulations of temporary employment agencies. Previously the law was prima facie proscriptive, with a list of exceptions permitting a narrow range of activities by temporary employment agencies. By contrast, the 1999 revisions are prima facie permissive, with a list of prohibited temporary works (cf. Araki 1999). The 2003 revision of the WDA liberalized temporary work regulations even further. In particular, the prohibition on dispatching temporary workers to manufacturing jobs was removed (cf. Mizushima 2004).

Legislative Developments Promoting Corporate Restructuring

From the late 1990s, in response to Japan's prolonged economic slump, the government adopted a series of measures to promote corporate restructuring and market-orientated management. In 1997, it introduced a stock option system and revised the Anti-Monopoly Act by lifting the prohibition on genuine holding companies. In 1999, it enacted the Industrial Revitalization Special Measures Act, which encourages and supports business revitalization, and the Civil Rehabilitation Act, which has the aim of preventing bankruptcies and rehabilitating failing companies. In the same year, it created stock exchange and transfer systems to facilitate the formation of holding companies. And in 2000, it enacted a corporate division scheme to promote corporate reorganization. All these measures were designed to enable corporate restructuring, and they affected the employment security of workers.

New Interpretations of the Law Relaxing Restrictions on Economic Dismissal

Until 2003, Japanese legislation did not mandate just cause for dismissals. This was because the courts established a judicial standard preventing dismissals that constituted an "abuse of rights." In a line of cases, the courts would nullify a dismissal as an abuse of rights where they judged the dismissal lacked an objective rationale and was deemed socially inappropriate.

Applying this rule to dismissals during times of economic distress, the courts established a stringent four-part test: (*a*) there must be a business-based need for the reduction of the workforce; (*b*) the dismissals must be a last resort and thus the employer must exhaust all other avenues to cope with the economic difficulties;[7] (c) the selection of the workers to be dismissed must be made on an objective and reasonable basis; and (d) the employer must adopt proper procedures to explain the necessity of the dismissal, its timing, scale, and method to the labor union (or worker group if no union exists), and consult them regarding dismissals in good faith. Traditionally, the validity of economic dismissals rested on whether or not all four requirements were met. If one of four requirements was not satisfied, the dismissal was regarded as an abuse of the right to dismiss.

In 2000, the Tokyo District Court rejected this traditional interpretation and contended that there was no compelling reason in law for insisting that all four requirements had to be satisfied.[8] According to the Tokyo District Court, the relevant standard was simply whether or not a dismissal was abusive. The so-called "four-part test" merely provided four indicia that, together, identified an abuse. According to this view, if one of the four requirements (e.g., consultation) was not met, an economic dismissal could still be upheld as valid by taking all other factors surrounding the dismissal into consideration.

The majority of subsequent cases have upheld the four-indicia test. Even so, there is no evidence that courts, in practice, have relaxed the criteria for allowing economic dismissals. Most commentators observe that the courts still maintain a strict stance toward economic dismissals under the modified interpretive framework. Comparatively speaking, the legal restraint on economically motivated dismissals in Japan is still stringent.

Japanese Employment Relations: Flexible Responses to Environmental Changes

To understand current employment relations, it is worth dividing the workforce in Japanese firms into two: regular and nonregular employees. For regular employees, employment security remains largely intact. According to various surveys (see below), Japanese firms intend to maintain employment security for regular employees in the future. Yet even if management and employees want to uphold an employee-centered

---

[7] Before resorting to dismissals, employers were required to take other measures such as reductions in overtime, reductions in regular hiring or mid-term recruitment, implementation of transfers (*haiten*) or secondment (*shukko*) with respect to redundant workers, nonrenewal of fixed-term contracts, and solicitation of voluntary retirement.

[8] The *National Westminster Bank* case (3rd Provisional Disposition), 782 *Rodo Hanrei* 23 (Tokyo District Court, January 21 2000).

system of stakeholder governance and retain the lifetime employment system, will this be possible given enormous changes taking place in the Japanese corporate sector?

Lifetime employment – with its concomitant guarantee of employment security – implies numerical rigidity in terms of human resources deployment. Management therefore needs alternative forms of flexibility. One strategy is to use nonregular, nonpermanent employees, yielding *numerical flexibility*. Another strategy is to achieve *functional (or qualitative) flexibility* for regular employees by adjusting the terms and conditions of work. In combination, numerical and qualitative flexibility should enable Japanese firms to withstand external pressures while maintaining their commitment to traditional employment practices.

But how is qualitative flexibility possible? First, typical individual labor contracts in Japan do not specify in detail the terms and conditions of employment, particularly regarding the place and type of work. The Labour Standards Act (LSA) does require clarification of the place and type of work in a labor contract, but this is not construed as a specification of working conditions that cannot be subsequently modified without the employee's consent. In drafting work rules, employers normally reserve the right to transfer employees depending on business necessity. This might entail not only a change of work location, but also work tasks. Therefore, the employer can unilaterally order a change in the place and/or type of work without obtaining the employee's consent. Of course, the courts may review such a transfer order on the basis of whether it constitutes an abuse of right. However, since transfer orders are an important method of avoiding economically based dismissals, courts are generally reluctant to nullify them.

Second, the Supreme Court has established a unique rule governing the unfavorable adjustment of working conditions through the modification of work rules. This is that an unfavorable modification of the work rules has a binding effect on all workers, including those who opposed the modification, provided that such modifications are regarded as reasonable.[9] Work rules are sets of regulations set by an employer for the purpose of establishing uniform rules and conditions of employment in the workplace (LSA Art. 89; Araki 2002: 51ff). In drawing up or modifying the work rules, the employer is required to *ask* the opinion of a majority representative at the workplace. However, consent is not required. Even when the majority representative opposes the content of the work rules, the employer may submit them to the Labour Standards Inspection Office

---

[9] The *Shuhoku Bus* case, 22 *Minshu* 3459 (Supreme Court, December 25 1968).

with an opposing opinion and the submission will still be accepted. In this sense, the employer can *unilaterally* establish and modify work rules.

Third, the law now allows employers to modify work rules, even if they are less favorable than the terms stipulated in an individual worker's contract of employment. The LSA has always stated that labor contracts that stipulate working conditions inferior to those provided in the work rules are invalid and that such conditions are to be replaced by the standards set out in the work rules (LSA Art. 93). Until relatively recently, however, it made no reference to the opposite case: namely, the effect of work rules that set inferior standards to those in individual labor contracts. Yet this is precisely what many employers want to do when faced with a falling bottom line. Following legal challenges to unilateral and unfavorable modification of work rules, the Supreme Court controversially ruled that unfavorable modifications to work rules are permissible provided they are reasonable. Despite criticisms that it had no legal ground for reaching such an interpretation, the Supreme Court has adhered to this principle and repeatedly confirmed its position. In 2007, this judicial principle became legislatively enshrined in the Labour Contract Act (LCA Art. 9, 10).

Underlying this ruling are concerns over employment security and the necessity of adjusting working conditions. Traditional contract theory dictates that an employee who refuses modifications of future terms and conditions of employment may be discharged. However, under case law in Japan, such a dismissal may well be regarded as an abuse of the right to dismiss. On the other hand, because the employment relationship is a continuous contractual relationship, modification and adjustment of working conditions are inevitable. This rule gives priority to employment security, and in exchange for it, employees are expected to accept and be subject to reasonable changes in working conditions. This introduces internal or qualitative flexibility into the employment relationship, compensating for the lack of external or quantitative flexibility.

Compared to the American external flexibility model[10] and European security-oriented model,[11] Japan's employment system strikes a certain

---

[10] Even today, the US employment system is based on the principle of employment at will, where no just cause is required for dismissal. Of course, the United States has strict regulations preventing discriminatory dismissals and, in recent years, case law has been eroding the classic at-will doctrine by making dismissals that violate public policy or implied covenant of good faith and fair dealing illegal. Nevertheless, dismissal for economic reasons, for example, can be carried out more easily and quickly than in Europe or Japan. Accordingly, the United States adopts an employment system that is extremely strong on external or quantitative flexibility.

[11] European countries have traditionally restricted numerical flexibility and protected employment security by requiring just cause for dismissals, by strictly enforcing procedural regulations on dismissals, and by strictly limiting the use of fixed-term contracts. Regarding

balance between flexibility and security. This Japanese version of "flexicurity" might explain why lifetime or long-term employment has endured.

Countermeasures Protecting Employees' Interests

Maintenance of the stakeholder model of governance is also due to the countermeasures taken to protect employees given the disruptions caused by corporate reorganizations, the rise in unstable employment, the increase in labor mobility, and the widening gap between rich and poor.

Labour Contract Succession Act of 2000

First, amendments to the Commercial Code in 2000 introduced a "corporate division" scheme aimed at facilitating corporate restructures and reorganizations and, in turn, breathing some life into the sluggish Japanese economy.[12] However, it was feared that the scheme could easily be abused to downsize firms or streamline redundant workers, undermining employment security. To protect employee interests in the event of corporate division, the Labour Contract Succession Act (LCSA) was enacted taking effect from April 1 2001. Under the LCSA, under certain conditions employment contracts are automatically transferred to the newly established corporation (Yamakawa 2001: 6; Araki 2003: 27).

Since the LCSA prescribes automatic succession of employment relations to a newly established or successor company, it can be seen as a

---

the flexible adjustment of working conditions, because of the custom of employing a person for a particular job or post, there is a tendency to construe that the employee's job is specified in the labor contract, so that the employer cannot unilaterally change the place of employment or the content of the job without the individual's consent. In addition, social legislation traditionally provides generous employee protection. And collective bargaining agreements concluded at the sectoral or national level have wide coverage and provide protection for employees with normative effect.

[12] Prior to the 2000 revision of the Commercial Code, corporation division was carried out through transfers of business or undertakings. In order to transfer business, however, the transferor corporation had to obtain individual consent of all creditors as well as those workers transferred to the transferee corporation. Such procedures were thought to have hindered corporate restructuring and reorganization in Japan. The 2000 revision of the Commercial Code introduced simplified procedures for the division of corporation. When a corporation division plan is approved by special resolution at a shareholders meeting, corporation division becomes legally binding on all parties concerned without obtaining their individual consent, though dissenting creditors can express objection and seek liquidation.

Japanese version of the EC directive on transfers of undertakings. However, there are significant differences; the most important being that LCSA application is confined to divisions of corporations, whereas the EC directive covers not only the merger and division of corporations but also the transfer of undertakings. Unlike its EU counterpart, automatic and mandatory transfer of a labor contract is not required in the event of a transfer of undertakings.

Compared to the United States, in which no employment protection of this kind is provided in the event of a corporate restructuring (Schwab 2003: 183), it is notable that the Japanese legislature thought it necessary to provide such protection. It sought to strike a balance between the imperative of promoting corporate reorganization and the protection of employees, ultimately adopting a midway position between the EU and US approaches.

The 2003 Revision of the Labour Standards Act: Introduction of a Provision Nullifying Abusive Dismissals

Second, the 2003 revisions of the LSA introduced an explicit provision (Art. 18-2) on abusive dismissals: "in cases where a dismissal is not based upon any objectively reasonable grounds, and is not socially acceptable as proper, the dismissal will be null and void as an abuse of right." Labor unions and labor law scholars have long argued that regulation of unjust dismissals should be incorporated into legislation. This is because of the lack of transparency when statutory law does not require just cause to dismiss an employee but case law de facto does. However, their proposals had never been adopted in the past. The plan to revise the LSA to clarify the dismissal rules was raised by the Koizumi cabinet and its Council for Regulatory Reform, which intended to relax the case law rules which they saw as so rigid as to hinder structural changes enabling the mobilization of the workforce. Accordingly, the government and labor unions agreed to legislate on dismissals, but they did so from totally different perspectives.

Since the labor unions argued in favor of strengthening unfair dismissal regulations, they strongly opposed relaxing the case law rule in any statutory amendment. The Cabinet's Council for Regulatory Reform could also not reach agreement on a proposal put forward by management to resolve dismissal disputes with monetary settlements. As a result, the tripartite council agreed to codify the case law principle, namely that an abuse of the right to dismiss is null and void, without incorporating any rules on economically motivated dismissals or monetary settlements.

The government proposal (LSA Art. 18-2) originally stated that: "An employer may dismiss a worker where his right to dismiss is not restricted by this Law or other laws. However, a dismissal shall be treated as a misuse of that right and invalid where the dismissal lacks objectively rational grounds and is not considered to be appropriate in general societal terms." However, during deliberations in the Diet, the first part declaring the employer's right to dismiss was feared to have a presumptive effect of encouraging dismissals, and was deleted.

The overall effect of the revisions to the LSA – including the codification of the judicial rule on abusive dismissals, the omission of any declaration as to the employer's right to dismiss, and other revisions requiring clarification of the reasons for dismissal (Art. 89-3) and notification of them to the dismissed workers (Art. 22 para. 2) – was to counterbalance the increasing mobility of the workforce.[13] In 2007, LSA Art. 18-2 was moved from the LSA to the newly enacted LCA (LCA Art. 16).

The Whistleblowers Protection Act of 2004

A third important development was the enactment of the Whistleblowers Protection Act in 2004 (Sugeno 2005). Following scandals in the early 2000s involving illegal actions, fraud and noncompliance with regulations at large food corporations and an atomic power plant, the legislature moved to encourage whistleblowing in the interest of protecting life, property, and other relevant interests. Whistleblowers were to be protected against dismissals and other disadvantageous treatment where they acted in the public interest. Thus the Act explicitly prohibits dismissal for whistle-blowing in the public interest (Art. 3 para. 1) and other disadvantageous treatment such as demotion or wage deductions (Art. 5).

Although the Act aims to ensure compliance with the law and proper corporate governance, it is noteworthy that whistle-blowing in the public interest was added to the list of prohibited grounds for dismissal, and thereby strengthened employment security.

Establishment of a New Labor Tribunal System

Fourth, a new forum (*Rodo Shinpan* or Labor Tribunal) for individual labor dispute resolution was introduced in 2006. Japan has no labor

---

[13] Opinions as to the effect of the 2003 revision are divided. Compare Hanami (2004: 13) and Nakakubo (2004: 14).

courts.[14] Previously all labor and employment related lawsuits, including dismissal cases, had to be filed before the ordinary courts consisting solely of professional judges. Lay jurists, common in labor courts in European countries, did not exist in Japan until April 2006. There was no special procedure for labor litigation either. Partly because of this, the number of labor cases in Japan has been extremely small, about 3000 per year. However, because of increased labor mobility and corporate restructuring, the number of consultations filed with the government labor bureau had increased conspicuously.[15]

In 2004, as one of the significant achievements of the Judicial System Reform, a bill was passed to establish a labor tribunal system (Sugeno 2006), an embryonic form of a labor court system. The tribunal is not a new independent court but a forum newly created in the ordinary district courts. The tribunal consists of three judges: one professional judge and two lay judges, one each appointed by the labor side and management side. It is de facto a tripartite court, although the Act does not explicitly state this.

In principle, the Tribunal must adjudicate within three sessions. This means that a filed case must be handed down within four months. Since labor cases previously took a notoriously long time to reach judgment, both labor and management have welcomed the new expedited procedures. Parties dissatisfied with the adjudication may file an objection in which case the matter is automatically transferred to the ordinary courts. In brief, the establishment of the labor tribunal system is another factor furnishing better protection for employees in an era when corporate reorganization and restructuring place employees' rights and interests at stake.

Reinforcement of Labor Protection Regulations in 2007

Finally, in 2007 a series of labor statutes were passed to further protect employees. First, revisions to the Part-time Act (PTA) significantly reinforced protections for part-time employees. In particular, the amendments prohibit discrimination against part-time workers who perform similar work to regular employees (in terms of job description, responsibilities, and so on). They must not be discriminated against in relation to the manner of their utilization within the organization (the possibility of

---

[14] It has tripartite labor relations commissions, but they are administrative organs to adjudicate unfair labor practice cases involving labor unions.

[15] The number of consultations filed with the local labor bureau was 251,545 in 2001, 625,572 in 2002, and 734,257 in 2003: Ministry of Health, Labour and Welfare (2004a).

transfers, the scope of transfers, or their employment period, definite or indefinite). This was the first prohibition of discrimination against part-time employees in Japan. The PTA also introduces an open-ended duty on employers to "endeavor" to provide balanced treatment for part-time workers even if the part-time workers' job or performance is not the same as regular workers, seeking to narrow the gap between regular and nonregular employees.

Second, the 2007 revision of the Employment Measures Act prohibits age discrimination at the time of hiring, aiming to eliminate the practice of setting a maximum age for applicants and thereby denying older workers an opportunity to be interviewed for jobs. This is the first regulation concerning age discrimination in Japan, although the prohibition is confined to the hiring process and the Act allows various exceptions. Third, the 2007 revision of the Minimum Wages Act modernizes minimum wage regulation by abolishing minimum wages based on collective agreements that were not utilized in the past, and by taking into account public assistance available for a minimum standard for living.

Fourth, the long-awaited LCA was finally enacted in 2007. Previously, Japanese courts established various judicial standards governing individual labor contract issues. However, these remained unwritten law for years, and were problematic in terms of lack of transparency and general accessibility to the principles governing specific individual labor relations issues.[16] Though small in size, the 2007 LCA is a watershed in labor law in Japan. Compared to the traditional use of criminal and administrative sanctions in labor statutes, such as the LSA, Minimum Wages Act and the Industrial Safety and Health Act, the LCA is innovative in that it comprises only civil norms; it does not impose minimum working conditions but regulates the contractual relationship in areas which were formerly the subject of judicial interpretation. In this sense, it is a

---

[16] A study group chaired by Kazuo Sugeno of Meiji University established in the Ministry of Health, Labour and Welfare submitted a comprehensive proposal for a new act in 2005. However, the report was deliberately ignored by both the labor and management members in the working conditions subcommittee of the Labor Policy Council. The former dismissed as unacceptable proposals such as the prioritization of monetary settlements over reinstatement for dismissals, and the use of the labor–management committee as an employee representative organ. Management felt that the proposal contained too many interventionist norms, such as deeming a fixed term contract to be an indefinite contract if it did not have an express provision setting out the length of employment. Although the Council finally reached consensus on a draft bill, this draft only incorporated matters that both labor and management agreed upon; all other proposals, those generating disagreement, were omitted. Compared to the original proposal by the study group, the final version of the Labour Contract Act was a very modest statute containing only nineteen articles, and was mostly a restatement of the established case law.

fundamental law governing individual labor relations with a new regulatory style. The Act sets out fundamental principles of labor contracts, such as the establishment and modification of the employment relationship based on agreement between the parties, the prohibition of abusive exercise of employers' rights, and the employers' duty of care in relation to employees' safety, as well as important case law principles requiring reasonableness in any modification to the work rules. In conjunction with the labor tribunal system, the Act encourages employees to enforce their contractual rights through dispute resolution procedures.

In summary, therefore, although Japan may have placed increased stress on shareholder value and pursued a wide-ranging program of deregulation, a series of countermeasures protecting employee rights have attenuated the "marketization" of employment relations.

Industrial Relations, Employee Participation and Corporate Governance

Collective labor relations – marked by stable and cooperative industrial relations under enterprise unionism, widespread joint labor–management consultation practices and the promotion of management from within – have also sustained Japan's stakeholder model of corporate governance. This section focuses on recent changes to these practices. A continuing decline in the unionization rate and increasing diversification of the labor force are triggering a reconsideration of traditional enterprise unionism. Similarly, joint consultation has faced significant external pressures. Although collective labor relations have not undergone major legislative reform apart from the 2004 revisions to the Trade Union Act,[17] new channels for employee voice are emerging.

Changing Enterprise Unionism

More than 90 percent of labor unions in Japan take the form of enterprise-based unions.[18] Thus, most collective bargaining takes place at the enterprise or company level between the union and the individual employer.

---

[17] These strengthen the power of labor relations commissions, and expedite the remedial procedures of unfair labor practice cases. However the revision did not change any part of the representation mechanism.

[18] As of 1997, 95.7 percent of all labor unions in Japan were enterprise-based, and 91.2 percent of unionized workers belonged to enterprise-based unions.

The dominance of enterprise unionism in Japan is not attributable to the law[19] but due to institutional features of internal labor markets. Under the long-term employment system, dismissals are avoided at all costs. In exchange, workers accept the flexible adjustment of working conditions. As a result, they are particularly concerned about the working conditions within the firm which they work for. Industrial-level or national-level collective bargaining across an industry sector makes little sense in this context; enterprise unions and enterprise-level collective bargaining have been the most efficient means for responding to the needs of employees in their career at their particular firm.

Internally promoted managers, the majority of whom once belonged to the enterprise union, and the enterprise union usually negotiate in co-operative terms, identifying common interests such as the prosperity of the "community firm." The union agrees to productivity increases in return for management promises of employment security. Recent surveys confirm that firms with internally promoted management have lower dismissal rates than other firms (JILPT 2007: 91). When unions have their basis in a particular company, they tend to be more pragmatic than ideological, and more conscious about their own company's productivity and competitiveness than other forms of unions. On the other hand, enterprise unions are said to be weak in terms of bargaining power because their existence depends on the particular enterprise (Araki 2002: 164ff).

Japan's enterprise unions face both qualitative and quantitative challenges. Quantitatively, the unionization rate has been trending downward since 1975 (Figure 8.3). In 2007, the unionization rate hit a record low of 18.1 percent. Qualitatively, the increasing diversification of the workforce and increasing mobility cast doubt on the functional efficiency of enterprise unionism in the internal labor market.

Japan's enterprise unions have traditionally confined their membership to regular employees, although there are no legal obstacles to unionizing nonregular employees. This is because the interests of regular employees and those of nonregular employees differ and often conflict. Both management and enterprise unions see nonregular employees as "shock absorbers" against fluctuating economic circumstances, taking for granted that nonregular employees should be laid off in times of surplus labor, and that regular employees should be kept on.

[19] The Labour Union Act does not specify the form of labor union – in addition to enterprise unions, industrial or other types of unions seen in other countries are allowed. Indeed, general unions that organize employees across firms do exist in Japan.

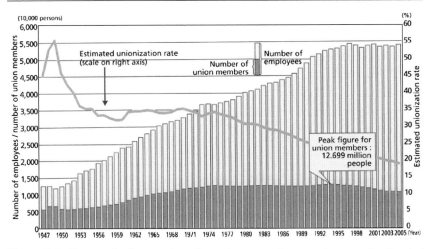

Figure 8.3 Changes in the number of employees, union members, and estimated unionization rate

Source: Japan Institute for Labour Policy and Training, Labour Situation in Japan and Analysis: General Overview 2006/2007: 67 (2006)

As already shown, however, nonregular employees have now grown to constitute one third of the work force. Their roles have also changed. More and more nonregular employees engage in similar jobs to those held by regular employees. In addition, nonregular workers include older employees who have reached the mandatory retirement age but have been rehired as part-timers; employees who are candidates for future management but are currently working part-time because of child-raising responsibilities; and foreign employees on fixed-term contracts. They can no longer be dismissed as peripheral to the labor force.

Employees promoted to middle management are supposed to leave their unions. However, corporate restructuring in the 1990s mostly targeted middle management. For them, enterprise unions could not provide adequate protection. Furthermore, Japanese labor laws give certain powers to a majority representative. Overtime work, for instance, is only possible when a majority representative of employees signs a labor–management agreement. When there is no majority union, an individual elected by a majority of employees becomes a majority representative. Whether such individuals can actually conduct substantive negotiations is highly questionable. These circumstances require analysis of alternative channels for representing employee interests beyond enterprise unions, as we shall see shortly.

Changes to Joint Labor–Management Consultation

Joint labor–management consultation has been an established practice in Japanese industrial relations. In many countries, labor–management consultation is not conducted on a voluntary basis, because employees' rights to information and consultation are legally established and enforced.[20] In Japan, by contrast, labor–management consultation is purely voluntary. A survey in 2004 showed that 37.3 percent of all surveyed establishments had joint consultation bodies (Ministry of Health, Labour and Welfare 2004*b*).

Voluntary joint labor–management consultation stems from the productivity movement promoted by the Japan Productivity Centre, which was established in 1955. Its three basic principles were (*a*) labor–management consultation to increase productivity; (*b*) productivity increases to enhance employment security, with surplus labor absorbed by transfers, and so on, rather than lay-offs; and (*c*) the fruits of increased productivity to be distributed fairly between the firm, employees, and customers.

Although left-leaning labor unions strongly opposed the productivity movement, moderate unions agreed to participate on condition that consultation was not used to bypass them and that their opinions should be fully respected. When management upheld their promise to treat unions as a partner, not to dismiss workers in a downturn, and to distribute the fruits of increased productivity fairly, the stance of the union movement shifted gradually, from being largely ideological and confrontational, to being more pragmatic and cooperative.

European countries (in particular German-influenced ones) typically have dual systems with industry-level collective bargaining by unions and company or plant level consultation by works councils. In Japan, this demarcation between joint consultation and collective bargaining is blurred. First, both joint consultation and collective bargaining take place at the same – plant or enterprise – level. Second, the parties involved are, in many cases, the same. According to the above 2004 survey, 78.9 percent of establishments with labor unions had union representatives serving as employee members on joint consultation bodies. Third, the subjects discussed in joint consultation and collective bargaining overlap. In the same survey, around 70 percent of joint-management consultation bodies discussed matters related to working conditions, such as working hours, holidays and vacations, changes in work method, health and safety,

---

[20] The standards set out in the EC Directive establishing a general framework for informing and consulting employees in the European Community (2002/14/EC, OJ L/2002/80/29) are an example of this kind of approach.

wages and bonuses, parental and family care leave, overtime premium rates, mandatory retirement systems, lay-offs, and retirement allowances.

The blurring of the distinction between collective bargaining and joint consultation has led to an informalization of collective bargaining. Normally, joint consultation occurs prior to collective bargaining, and the parties and subject-matter are similar in the two cases. When the parties reach an agreement through consultation, therefore, there is no need to proceed to collective bargaining, making joint consultation a replacement for collective bargaining. This shift from collective bargaining to joint consultation represents a shift from mandatory to voluntary, formal to informal, adversarial to cooperative, and *ex post* to *ex ante* styles of negotiation.

Although employers have a duty to bargain on mandatory subjects, they tend to reject bargaining over nonmandatory matters, in particular those they believe are managerial prerogatives. By contrast, joint consultation is a voluntary and informal procedure which is free of legal intervention. This encourages the parties to discuss any and all matters. Consequently, employers in Japan have developed strong communication networks with unions irrespective of whether the subjects being discussed are within the core of managerial prerogative. In joint consultation, especially with widespread prior consultations, employee representatives are regarded as partners rather than adversaries in managing employment-related issues. Through *ex ante* joint consultation, employers have been able to incorporate employee opinions into management policy, thereby preventing potential conflicts.

Joint labor–management consultation is still highly valued by both management and unions. Almost two thirds (61.3%) of establishments surveyed in 2004 viewed joint consultation as effective (Ministry of Health, Labour and Welfare 2004*b*). According to another survey, labor unions were satisfied with labor–management consultation because they had a strong voice in the consultation and their concerns were treated with respect by management (Rengo Soken, 2006: 11). However, these surveys also show evidence of waning support for joint consultation. The proportion of establishments with joint consultation bodies decreased from 41.8 percent in 1999 to 37.3 percent in 2004.[21] The Rengo Soken survey also acknowledges a weaker understanding of the nature of labor–management consultation among union members, and suggests that the union movement faces an uphill battle to combat increasing member apathy to union activities (Rengo Soken 2006: 12).

[21] Ministry of Labour (1999).

The Japan Productivity Center for Socio-economic Development (JPC-SED), the promoter of the productivity movement and joint consultation, points out that current joint consultation faces several challenges, including corporate reorganization resulting in the disappearance or marginalization of labor unions, increase in atypical employees, individualization of human resource management, declining human resources of both labor and management, and declining union density. To address these issues, JPC-SED (2006) publicized a new proposal entitled *For the New Development of Joint Labour–Management Consultation*, proposing a new framework for joint consultation to cope with these challenges, and to incorporate new values such as CSR, work-life balance, and individuals' rights consciousness, as well as cultivating experts in labor and employment relations.

Internal Promotion of Management

The practice of promoting executives from within the firm has greatly contributed to Japan's cooperative industrial relations and employee-centered corporate governance. In most larger companies, management and a majority union conclude a union shop agreement. As noted above, current executives were members of the enterprise union in their 20s and 30s when they were rank-and-file white-collar workers. Furthermore, a substantial minority had been leaders of the union, so labor–management relations are in a sense relations between present and former leaders. This has promoted a consensual approach to labor relations within the "community firm."

In Japan, junior directors promoted from managerial employee ranks have traditionally continued being employees. In the traditional governance model, nearly half of board members have been such directors-with-employee-functions. By accepting these employees as members of the board, Japanese corporations have established a channel which was capable of informally giving voice to employees' opinions in their dealings with corporate management. In the new (company with committees) governance system, by contrast, the majority of the committee members must be *outside* directors.[22] If widely adopted, the new governance model might have a significant impact on the internal promotion practice and labor and employment relations. So far, the number of firms adopting the

---

[22] This does not mean that the majority of board members must be outside directors. According to a recent survey of companies adopting the new system in 2004, the average number of board members was 10.31 and that of outside directors was 4.54: JCAA, 2004.

new model has been limited (110 in 2008). However, the practice of shrinking the size of boards and designating senior managers as executive officers, below board level, is becoming more widely adopted even in firms which have not opted into the company with committees structure (see Chapter 2). As this process continues, its effect may be to shut off a traditional, informal channel for the expression of employee voice within the firm.

New Channels for Employees' Voice?

Given the limitations of enterprise unionism and declining consultation, two new developments promoting employees' participation in corporate governance warrant attention. First, in the late 1990s when legislation was called for to promote corporate restructuring, labor unions insisted on establishing a forum to convey the employees' point of view. As a result, the 1999 Civil Rehabilitation Act introduced regulations to require an opinion on a rehabilitation plan by a majority union or a majority representative in the establishment. Similar regulations were adopted in the Revised Corporate Rehabilitation Act. The LCSA of 2000 also introduced regulations ordering the employer to consult with individual employees on a corporate division plan, and imposing a moral duty to consult with the majority union or majority representative, requesting employees' understanding and cooperation for the corporate division.

Second, with the growing diversity of the workplace, the representative legitimacy of enterprise unions solely representing the interests of regular employees has been called into question. There is also an argument that the majority representative system in the LSA is inappropriate because it gives an individual elected by the majority of employees the power to decide whether to conclude an agreement enabling an employer to deviate from minimum working conditions. In these contexts, a new representation system called a *roshi iinkai* (labor–management committee) was established as a result of 1998 revision to the LSA. Half of the members of this committee must be appointed by the labor union organized by a majority of workers at the workplace concerned, or with a person representing a majority of the workers where no such union exists. The labor–management committee is the first permanent organ with equal membership for labor and management that represents all the employees in the establishment. Thus, the labor–management committee can be regarded as an embryonic form of a works council, although its power is currently confined to the regulation of working hours.

The labor–management committee must be established when the employer intends to introduce a discretionary work scheme (management planning type),[23] which functions as a Japanese counterpart of the white-collar exemption from overtime regulations. Procedures to adopt the scheme were very complicated, but the 2003 revision of the Labour Standards Law simplified the procedure, changing the unanimity requirement to a four-fifths majority. Accordingly, the adoption rate of the management planning type discretionary scheme, which essentially means the ratio of establishing a labor–management committee, rose from 3.9 percent in 2002 to 6.3 percent in 2004 (MHLW General Survey on Wages 2004).

Further, in 2005, the study group for the LCA proposed that the labor–management committee should be involved in the modification of work rules and in the monetary settlement of dismissals. These proposals were flatly rejected by labor, but RENGO, the Japanese Trade Union Confederation, recognized the necessity for establishing a proper employee representation system, and submitted a bill on this in 2006. It remains to be seen whether the labor–management committee will become more common and entrench itself as a system of employee representation, or whether an alternative employee representation system will be created. However, the fact that there is serious discussion aimed at introducing or expanding employee representation indicates a growing perception of the importance of employee voice in corporate governance.

Conclusion: Erosion of the Practice-Dependent Stakeholder Model?

Japan's practice-dependent stakeholder model governance has faced significant changes. Cross-shareholdings have dissolved; stable shareholders have declined; the numbers of individual investors, and foreign investors have increased. Corporate scandals in the 1990s revealed dysfunctional aspects of the traditional system of Japanese governance based on insider managers, and calls were made for greater use of outside directors. The 2002 corporate law reform introduced the option of an American-style corporate governance model with committees, the majority of whose member had to be outsiders. The practice of internal promotion of management has also faced challenges. Lifetime employment has encountered an unprecedented prolonged economic slump and corporate

---

[23] There are two types of discretionary work scheme: professional work type and management planning type. Cf. Araki (2002: 94) and Shimada (2004: 56).

restructuring. Enterprise unionism faces qualitative and quantitative challenges. The effectiveness of joint labor–management consultation is being questioned.

Upon closer examination, however, the transformation of these practices is limited and traditional practices survive. Cross-shareholdings, having apparently been eroded away, are now on the increase again. Many firms are recognizing once again the merit of forming stable and long-term trading relations. In spite of the introduction of the US-style board with committees, a vast majority of Japanese firms are retaining the traditional governance model with auditors. And various surveys confirm that firms will still support lifetime employment while aiming to introduce more wage flexibility.

However, one important change continues unabated: the proportion of regular employees is shrinking, while the proportion of nonregular employees is rising.

Shareholder-Orientated Law Reforms and Countermeasures

Since the mid-1990s, corporate law reforms have aimed to promote corporate restructuring and orient corporate governance toward shareholder value. These legislative efforts have paved the way for the institutionalization of a shareholder model of governance.

In the area of labor law, however, various countermeasures have been adopted to safeguard employees' interests. As we saw, a typical example is the LCSA, enacted in 2000 at the same time as when the corporate division scheme was established in corporate law. Further, the 2003 revisions to the LSA explicitly proscribed abusive dismissals, reinforcing a governance system respecting employees. Recent legislative initiatives such as the Whistleblowers Protection Act of 2004, the Labour Tribunal Act of 2004, the Part-time Act of 2007, the Employment Measures Act of 2007, the Minimum Wage Act of 2007, and the LCA similarly strengthen labor protection. In collective labor relations, evidence of a decline in labor union participation and increased workforce diversification have led to calls for new forms of employee representation. In this respect, it will be interesting to see if the labor–management committee system introduced under the 1998 reforms evolves into a Japanese-style works council representing all employees in the establishment.

In sum, Japanese labor law has taken necessary countermeasures to the institutionalization of shareholder value in order to safeguard the interests of employees. Of course, these labor law developments are not equivalent to the institutionalized German stakeholder model, since the Japanese developments are confined to labor law, and are not directly connected to the corporate governance system as codetermination (in the sense of employee participation at board level) is in Germany. However, these developments in labor law have served to sustain the employee-centered stakeholder model, or, at least, to put a brake on radical transformation of the system into a shareholder value-based model.

Surveys Results Supporting the Stakeholder Model

Several surveys conducted in the 2000s prove that the stakeholder model is still widely supported in Japanese society despite some moves toward a shareholder-value model. According to a JPC-SED survey (2003), corporate planning directors and HRM directors – not just union leaders – support the view that profits should not be primarily distributed to shareholders but evenly distributed across shareholders, employees, internal reserves, and business investments. The same survey asked about "recent changes within your company in the last three years," to which 70 percent of the respondents indicated that their company had "adopted performance-based or achievement-based HRM" or had "adopted corporate restructuring or reorganization measures," but only 26 percent of them responded that their company "paid special consideration to the shareholders in management decision-making."

Another survey found that respondents rated banks and trading companies as less important and customers and shareholders as more important stakeholders between 1999 and 2002; employees, however, were still regarded as an equal stakeholder (MoF Policy Research Institute 2003). Indeed, there is evidence that their perceived importance is rising.[24] In relation to the external control of corporate governance, it is also notable that customers and product markets are seen as more important than the stock market.

In a JILPT survey in 2007, managers were surveyed as to whom they regarded as the more important stakeholders (Figure 8.4). The results reveal a declining importance attached to employees and an increasing concern for shareholder value; but even so, after customers management

[24] The Japan Management Association (2006) asked newly appointed directors as to whose interests they should prioritize. Until 2005, they stressed shareholders' interests; but in 2006, 42.3 percent said they would prioritize employee interests, compared to 25.1 percent for shareholders' interests.

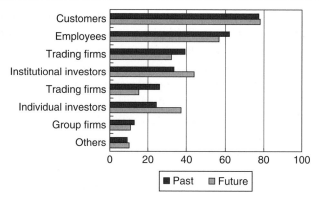

Figure 8.4. Important stakeholders for management
Source: JILPT 2007: 22.

still deems employees as the most important stakeholder (56.9%), ahead of institutional investors (44%) and individual investors (37.1%).

Social perceptions of the shareholder-value model also seem to have changed recently in Japan. Until 2001, the shareholder-value model was enthusiastically praised by some economists, business leaders, and business media like Nikkei-News. However, scandals both in the United States (especially Enron and WorldCom) and Japan, and the arrest of two shareholder-value heroes (Takafumi Horie, the president of Livedoor, an IT service company, and Yoshiaki Murakami, the most famous Japanese shareholder activist leading the Murakami Fund) in 2006 drew attention to the limitations of the shareholder-value model. Growing interest in corporate social responsibility reconfirmed the value of traditional Japanese-style management respecting employment. The resurgence of the economy also restored confidence in Japanese-style management.

Various surveys also confirm the maintenance of lifetime employment. A Ministry of Finance survey conducted in 2002 reported that 54.3 percent of firms maintain traditional lifetime employment and seniority pay, 29.8 percent utilize ability-based pay with lifetime employment and only 15.9 percent of surveyed firms utilize ability-based pay without lifetime employment (MoF Policy Research Institute 2003: 121). According to a METI Survey conducted in 2003, 85 percent of surveyed firms adopted lifetime employment – 8 percent with no merit pay, 34 percent with limited merit pay, and 43 percent with merit pay.[25] Only 12 percent of them utilized an employment system with merit pay but without lifetime

---

[25] METI Survey on the Corporate System and Employment 2003: see Jackson (2007: 285).

employment and 2 percent merit pay and limited lifetime employment. A JILPT survey conducted in 2005 shows the same trends. In principle, 59.5 percent of firms maintained lifetime employment; 27.4 percent thought that a partial revision of lifetime employment was inevitable; 6.5 percent thought that a fundamental revision of lifetime employment was needed; and 6.7 percent replied that they did not have lifetime employment (JILPT 2007: 65). Nearly 90 percent of firms said that they would maintain lifetime employment. As for employee attitudes, a 2008 JILPT survey demonstrates that even employees who once denounced lifetime employment now value and support it. Those supporting lifetime employment were 76.1 percent in 2001, and 77.8 percent in 2004; this rose to 86.1 percent in 2007 (JILPT 2008).

In terms of industrial relations, the JPC-SED (2003) survey shows that a majority of directors think labor–management consultation does not hinder management decision making. Moreover, 58.7 percent of management planning directors and 65.6 percent of HRM directors, as well as the majority of union leaders, responded that labor unions should be involved in management decision making in the future. There were few negative responses. This survey was conducted in July and August of 2001 when the Enron and WorldCom scandals had not yet come to light and US-style corporate governance was receiving its greatest accolades in the Japanese media. Even at such a time, labor and management recognized the value of union involvement. This seems to reflect the deep-rooted consciousness in Japan that employees are an important constituent of corporations.

Divided Employees and Corporate Governance

Survey data consistently demonstrates that Japanese firms intend to maintain employment security. However, given the remarkable increase in nonregular employees – part-time, fixed-term, and temporary workers – whose employment is unstable, it becomes questionable whether Japan's corporate governance can still be characterized as a truly employee-centered model. Nonregular employees now consist of one third of the labor force, hardly a peripheral number. For years, these nonregular employees have endured less protection and have been treated as "shock absorbers" to maintain the security of employment for regular employees. In the past, when nonregular employees were typically housewives or students, unstable employment and inferior working conditions were thought of as not very serious social problems because they were regarded as secondary earners who could depend on income from their partner or parents. Since the collapse of the bubble economy, however, many of the younger generation have been compelled to work as nonregular employees because they could not find any regular jobs. The deregulation of agency work also served to swell their numbers.

Regular and nonregular employees are divided into two groups within the firm, and mobility between them is very restricted. The expert meeting on labor market reform in the Council on Economic and Fiscal Policy, Cabinet Office, referred to this as one of the "barriers" that should be removed.[26] Although the 2007 PTA started to provide better protection for part-time workers, Japan's regulations on fixed-term contracts are much weaker than in Continental Europe. Employers do not need a reason to conclude a fixed-term contract and renewal of fixed-term contracts remains unregulated. According to case law, a repeatedly renewed fixed-term contract is regarded as the same as an open-ended contract, and so the prohibition on abusive dismissal rule applies *mutatis mutandis*. This is an important protection for fixed-term contract workers, but law reform deliberations could not reach a consensus to make this case law an explicit provision in the LCA of 2007.

Temporary workers, especially "daily temporary workers" who are hired and sent to a client on a daily basis, are now in the spotlight as the typical victims of deregulation policy. In 2008, a despairing young temporary worker killed seven innocent passers-by randomly in an inner-city Tokyo ward. Although no causal relationship was established between the incident and temporary work, the incident made politicians aware of the necessity to protect daily temps. In July 2008, the government changed its deregulatory policy and announced it would submit a bill prohibiting the practice of daily temporary work.

If nonregular employees continue to increase and remain less protected, the Japanese employment system will consist of two totally different types of groups: well-protected regular employees and nonregular employees vulnerable to the vicissitudes of the market. Clearly, the rights and interests of the latter group need better protection, but an employee-centered system of governance still focuses on regular employees' interests, with nonregular employees falling under a different regulatory system.

Policies for strengthening nonregular workers' protection have just started. The outcome of redressing the unfair gap between regular and nonregular employees is not clear. If total wage resources are fixed, it will imply a redistribution from regular to nonregular employees, which

---

[26] Agenda memo submitted by expert members from the private sector, December 20 2006.

would lead to a complete reconfiguration of the employment system. If total wage resources or wage shares are enhanced for such workers, then this is another story. Protections can still be maintained for regular employees. In this regard, the future of Japan's corporate governance will be influenced by such factors as the extent of any reinforcement of nonregular employees' protections, the redistribution of resources between regular and nonregular employees, and the overall distribution between labor and capital.

However, given the aforementioned countermeasures for protecting employees' interests, the survey results supporting the stakeholder model, and the increasing negative perception of shareholder-value model among the general population, it is not likely that the current stakeholder model will completely convert into a shareholder-value model. Shareholder value has certainly become an important management indicator for governance. However, it is not an absolute, just as employment security is no longer an absolute. At least for the time being, Japanese society must look for a better balance between the shareholder and employee value. To that end, diversity in corporate governance will increase and competition between the different governance models will take place. The competition will not be for more profit for shareholders, but for a better balance between shareholder and employee interests.

Bibliography

Aoki, M. (2007). "Conclusion: Whither Japan's Corporate Governance?" in M. Aoki, G Jackson, and H. Miyajima (eds.), *Corporate Governance in Japan: Institutional Change and Organisational Diversity.* Oxford: Oxford University Press.

Araki, T. (1997). "Changing Japanese Labour Law in Light of Deregulation Drives: A Comparative Analysis." *Japan Labour Bulletin*, 36(5): 5–10 (http://www.jil.go.jp/bulletin/year/1997/vol36-05/06.htm).

—— (1999). "1999 Revisions of Employment Security Law and Worker Dispatching Law: Drastic Reforms of Japanese Labour Market Regulations." *Japan Labour Bulletin*, 38(9): 5–12 (http://www.jil.go.jp/bulletin/year/1999/vol38-09/06.htm).

—— (2000). "A Comparative Analysis: Corporate Governance and Labour and Employment Relations in Japan." *Comparative Labor Law and Policy Journal*, 22: 67–95.

—— (2002). *Labour and Employment Law in Japan.* Tokyo: Japan Institute of Labour.

—— (2003). "Corporate Restructuring and Employment Protection: Japan's New Experiment," in R. Blanpain and M. Weiss (eds.), *Changing Industrial Relations and*

Modernisation of Labour Law – Liber Amicorum in Honour of Professor Marco Biagi, 27. The Hague: Kluwer Law International.

——(2007). "From Employee-Centered to Shareholder-Centered Governance?: Corporate Governance Reforms and the Future of Japan's Practice-Based Stakeholder Model," in U. Jürgens, D. Sadowski, F. Schuppert, and M. Weiss (eds.), *Perspectiven der Corporate Governance*. Baden–Baden: Nomos.

Dore, R. (2000). *Stock Market Capitalism: Welfare Capitalism*. Oxford: Oxford University Press.

Egashira, K. (2002). *Kabushiki gaisha, yugen gaisha-ho, dai-nihan (Laws of Stock Corporations and Limited Liability Companies)*. Tokyo: Yuhikaku.

Hanami, T. (2004). "The Changing Labour Market, Industrial Relations and Labour Policy." *Japan Labour Review*, 1(1): 4–16 (http://www.jil.go.jp/english/documents/JLR01_hanami.pdf).

Inagami, T. and RIALS (2000) (eds.), *Gendai Nihon no koporeto gabanansu (Corporate Governance in Contemporary Japan)*. Tokyo: Toyo keizai.

—— and Whittaker, D. H. (2005) *The New Community Firm: Employment, Governance and Management Reform in Japan*. Cambridge: Cambridge University Press.

Jackson, G. (2007). "Employment Adjustment and Distributional Conflict in Japanese Firms," in M. Aoki et al. (eds.), *Corporate Governance in Japan: Institutional Change and Organizational Diversity*. Oxford: Oxford University Press.

—— and Miyajima, H. (2007). "Introduction: The Diversity and Change of Corporate Governance in Japan," in M. Aoki et al. (eds.), *Corporate Governance in Japan: Institutional Change and Organizational Diversity*. Oxford: Oxford University Press.

Japan Corporate Auditors Association (2004). *Nihon kansayaku kyokai, iinkaito-setchi-gaisha eno ikou to koporeto gabanansu ni kansuru anketo shukei kekka (Survey Results on Corporate Governance Including Trends Towards Companies with Three Committees)* (http://www.kansa.or.jp/PDF/enquet4_040514.pdf).

——(2008). "Iinkaito setchi-gaisha iko-gaisha risuto" ("Companies which Changed into the Companies with Three Committees") (http://www.kansa.or.jp/PDF/iinkai_list.pdf).

Japan Management Association (2006). *Dai 9 kai shin-nin yakuin no sugao ni kansuru chosa (The 9th Survey of the Real Face of Newly Appointed Directors)* (http://www.jma.or.jp/release/data/pdf/20060802.pdf).

JILPT (2007). *Kigyo no Koporeto Gabanansu, CSR to jinjisenryaku ni kansuru chosha kenkyu hokokusho (Japan Institute for Labour Policy and Training, Report on Corporate Governance, CSR and HRM Strategy)*, Rodo seisaku kenkyu hokokusho No. 74. Tokyo: JILPT.

——(2008). *The 5th Survey of Working Life* (http://www.jil.go.jp/press/documents/20080324.pdf).

JPC-SED (2003). *21 seiki: kigyo keiei no henka to roshi kankei: Wagakuni ni okeru koporeto gabanansu no henyo o fumaete (Changes in Corporate Management and Labour–Management Relations in the 21st Century: Responding to Transformations in Corporate Governance in Japan)*. Tokyo: Japan Productivity Center for Socio-Economic Development, Labour–Management Relations Committee.

—— (2006). *Roshi kyogi-sei no aratana tenkai o mezashite* (*For the New Development of Joint Labour–Management Consultation*). Tokyo: Japan Productivity Center for Socio-Economic Development, Labour–Management Relations Committee.

Milhaupt, C. (2001). "Creative Norm Destruction: The Evolution of Nonlegal Rules in Japanese Corporate Governance." *University of Pennsylvania Law Review*, 149: 2083–129.

Ministry of Finance, Policy Research Institute (2003). *Shinten suru koporeto gabanansu kaikaku to Nihon kigyo no saisei* (*Developing Corporate Governance and Regeneration of Japanese Corporations*). Tokyo: Ministry of Finance, Policy Research Institute (http://www.mof.go.jp/jouhou/soken/kenkyu/zk063/cg.pdf).

Ministry of Health, Labour and Welfare (2004a). *Implementation and Current Situation of the Individual Labour Disputes Resolution System*. Tokyo: Ministry of Health, Labour and Welfare.

—— (2004b). *Heisei 16 nen Roshi Komyunikeshon Chosa* (*Survey of Communication Between Labour and Management in 2004*). Tokyo: Ministry of Health, Labour and Welfare (http://www.mhlw.go.jp/toukei/itiran/roudou/roushi/jittai/jittai04/yousi.html].

Ministry of Labour (1999). *Survey of Communication Between Labour and Management in 1999*. Tokyo: Ministry of Labour (http://www.jil.go.jp/kisya/daijin/20000619_02_d/20000619_02_d.html).

Mizushima, I. (2004). "Recent Trends in Labour Market Regulations." *Japan Labour Review* 1(4): 6–26 (http://www.jil.go.jp/english/documents/JLR04_mizushima.pdf).

Nakakubo, H. (2004). "The 2003 Revision of the Labour Standards Law: Fixed-Term Contracts, Dismissal and Discretionary-Work Schemes." *Japan Labour Review*, 1 (2): 4–25 (http://www.jil.go.jp/english/documents/JLR02_nakakubo.pdf).

Rengo Soken (2006). *Rodosha sanka, roshi komyunikeshon ni kansuru chosa* (*Survey of Worker Participation and Labour–Management Communication*). Tokyo: Rengo Soken (http://www.rengo-soken.or.jp/dio/no214/dio214.pdf).

Shimada, Y. (2004). "Working Hour Schemes for White-Collar Employees in Japan." *Japan Labour Review*, 1(4): 48–69.

Sugeno, K. (2005). "A New Law to Protect Whistle-Blowing: Changing Legal Consciousness in Japanese Industrial Society," in A. Höland, C. Hohmann-Dennhardt, M. Schmidt, and A. Seifert (eds.), *Employee Involvement in a Globalising World – Liber Amicorum Manfred Weiss*. Berlin: Berliner Wissenschafts-Verlag.

—— (2006). "Judicial Reform and the Reform of the Labour Dispute Resolution System." *Japan Labour Review*, 3(1): 4–12.

Schwab, S. (2003). "United States." *Bulletin of Comparative Labour Relations*, 47: 177–96.

Yamakawa, R. (2001). "Labour Law Issues Relating to Business Reorganization in Japan." *Japan Labour Bulletin*, 40(2): 6–13.

9

Management Innovation at Toshiba: The Introduction of the Company with Committees System

Hisayoshi Fuwa

Introduction

This chapter considers how a Japanese high-tech company, Toshiba Corporation (subsequently "Toshiba"), established a scheme to improve its corporate governance with an emphasis on its management organization structure. It also considers how, as a direct result of this, Toshiba embarked on a program of management innovation with a view to becoming a much more open company, better equipped to operate as an international business.

The two issues of corporate governance and management innovation are closely related to one another. By transforming its corporate governance, and by linking this directly to management innovation, Toshiba metamorphosed and at the same time reinforced the visibility and message of the Toshiba brand in order to become more attuned to its stakeholders. Even before these developments, Toshiba had already established its key management policies, in readiness for these changes to its corporate governance and management style. This chapter considers this process of management innovation and the resulting new direction in a characteristically Japanese management system. First, however, I will provide a brief profile of the company.

One of Japan's leading high technology corporations, Toshiba is a diversified manufacturer and marketer of advanced electronic and electrical products. Toshiba products delivered worldwide range from information and communications equipment and systems, Internet-based solutions and services, through electronic components and materials, power systems, industrial and social infrastructure systems, and household appliances.

Toshiba's early history has two roots. One comes from the establishment of Tanaka Seizo-sho (Tanaka Engineering Works), Japan's first manufacturer of telegraphic equipment, founded in 1875. The founder, Hisashige Tanaka (1799–1881), was well known for his inventions, which included mechanical dolls and a perpetual clock. Under the name Shibaura Seisaku-sho (Shibaura Engineering Works) his company became one of Japan's largest manufacturers of heavy electrical apparatus. Hakunetsu-sha & Co., Ltd. was Toshiba's second early root. Founded in 1890, it was Japan's first plant for electric incandescent lamps. In 1899, the company was renamed Tokyo Denki (Tokyo Electric Co.). In 1939, these two companies merged to start an integrated electronic and electrical equipment manufacturer, Tokyo Shibaura Denki (Tokyo Shibaura Electric Co., Ltd.). The company was soon popularly known as "Toshiba," which became its official name in 1978.

Toshiba expected sales of ¥6.7 trillion for the financial year to March 2009. As of March 31 2008, Toshiba reported total assets of ¥5.9 trillion, with shareholder equity of ¥1.0 trillion. It had about 375,000 shareholders and 197,000 employees among its stakeholders.

Changes to Toshiba's Corporate Governance Scheme

In June 2003, Toshiba reorganized its structure of management and corporate governance and became a company with committees. It introduced a new scheme with a revised board of directors and three committees, in accordance with options permitted by the 2002 revision to Japan's Commercial Code (effective from April 2003). The operation of the new structure is shown in Figure 9.1.

The board of directors now consists of fourteen directors, of whom seven are nonexecutives. These nonexecutive directors comprise:

– Four outside directors
– The chairman of the board of directors

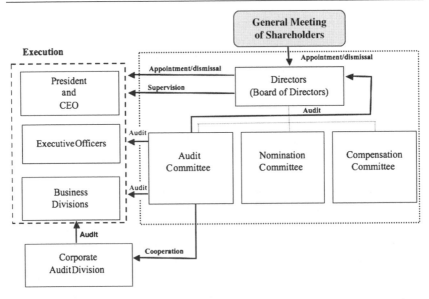

Figure 9.1. Structure of supervision under Toshiba's corporate governance from 2003

– Two internally appointed directors who are audit committee members

There are three committees next to the board, which are

– The Nomination Committee
– The Compensation Committee
– The Audit Committee

Each of the three committees has a majority of outside directors, and the Nomination Committee and the Compensation Committee are both chaired by outside directors. The Nomination Committee is customarily responsible for appointment and dismissal of directors, but at Toshiba the Nomination Committee is endowed with greater authority to appoint and dismiss the president and members of the committees. The outside directors receive prior explanations on matters to be resolved at board meetings from the staff in charge of the relevant business areas. They also attend the monthly liaison conferences of executive officers in order to oversee Toshiba's management.

The executive officers comprise an empowered executive layer immediately beneath the board of directors, responsible for normal business management. The general scope of their authority and responsibility, and the duties of individual executive officers, are clearly stated in organization manuals. This process of clarification means not only that the executive officers know the extent and limits of their authority, but also that the board of directors has a clear idea of what it is supposed to supervise and is able to create an internal check system to oversee the entire company.

Lead-Up to the New Structure for Management Execution and Supervision

Prior to the introduction of the company with committees system in 2003, Toshiba had already adopted a system of "Managing Officers" in 1998. Managing Officers (essentially with the same functions as the later "executive officers"[1]) were constituted as the highest of the hierarchical positions for employees, but were not members of the board of directors. The board of directors required Managing Officers to fully understand the company's corporate responsibility and corporate governance policies and to fulfill their duties in their own operations in accordance with these.

Thus, Managing Officers at that time were on a different level from the board of directors, the supervising authority, but their status was the highest among employees. Managing Officers were responsible for day-to-day operations in an assigned field, and were given the primary authority in management execution, with powers of delegation. These officers controlled management execution, and took responsibility for activities delegated to subordinate managers. Specifically, Managing Officers were responsible to the board of directors for controlling activities such as sales, bringing new products to market, and directing research and development by foreseeing future market changes.

Most Managing Officers would probably have become directors under the old system. As Managing Officers, however, they were now able to focus on specific responsibilities in their specialized fields, such as being in charge of a semiconductor company, or responsible for formulating divisional management strategy. They no longer needed to express opinions on a wide range of general management issues as members of the board of directors, in situations where their judgment tended anyway to be focused on narrower considerations. Effectively, they became free from the strain

---

[1] The Japanese term is *shikkoyaku* (normally translated as "executive officer"), as opposed to *shikkoyakuin* (normally translated as "corporate executive officer"), who has the same role outside the company with committees system.

of trying to separate their positions as directors from their parallel executive positions within the company organization.

This change greatly accelerated management decision making and the issuing of prompt and effective instructions. Secondly, it enabled the company to appoint a much larger number of Managing Officers than directors, whose appointment required the approval of shareholders, and gave Managing Officers substantial responsibility for management. Thirdly, it played an important role in changing the company's culture regarding management organization. When employees who had been in charge of their fields were appointed Managing Officers, they usually made even greater efforts than before to cultivate a manager's viewpoint and style of judgment. They saw themselves not as ordinary employees, but as persons with responsibility, and the possibility of promotion to "Higher Managing Officer" and then "Director."

Experience following this change gave Toshiba confidence in operating a management system in which execution of management was independent of supervision. This enabled Toshiba to shift smoothly to a company with committees structure in which execution of managerial decisions is clearly demarcated from supervision, which rests with the board. Toshiba's transition to the new system was smooth, since most senior managers had a better knowledge than those in other companies about the responsibility and authority given to the new position of executive officer, and also about the mission and authority of the board of directors that stood above the executive officers as the supervising authority.

Improved Speed and Flexibility of Management

Toshiba adopted the company with committees system in order to improve its speed and flexibility of management, to reinforce the supervision of management, and to increase transparency. All of these should improve management efficiency, but they are also intended to improve the efficiency of the whole organization. They will only be considered successful if they translate into a revitalization of Toshiba's businesses and stakeholder relationships. Thus they should be seen in the context of major efforts by Toshiba's senior management to bring about a much wider transformation.

When he became President and CEO of Toshiba in 2005, Atsutoshi Nishida expressed his desire to change Toshiba's management to increase flexibility and make the company more attuned to all its stakeholders. His goal as president was "to create a lively, more clearly defined Toshiba Group that channels ceaseless innovation into achieving sustained growth with profit across Toshiba businesses." As an important aspect of this, he committed himself to reinforcing the visibility and message of Toshiba's corporate brand, both externally and internally. To these ends, in 2006, Toshiba announced a new brand tag line: "TOSHIBA Leading Innovation." Three elements of the initiatives are as follows.

A Toshiba for Tomorrow

First, Toshiba's operations span electronic devices and components, digital products, infrastructure systems, and home appliances but particular emphasis has been placed on promoting capital investments and channelling significant resources into specific key businesses that will sustain further growth and add to profitability. This can be seen in the investments in new semiconductor facilities, particularly for NAND flash memory, and the drive for leadership in the AV market through products such as next-generation TVs. Toshiba acquired the nuclear power systems manufacturer Westinghouse, which has significant expertise in nuclear power generation and nuclear fuel, and a worldwide market presence. This business has an important role to play in taking Toshiba's energy systems business to the global level.

Multiplier Effect of Innovations

Second, Toshiba is aiming for much faster growth than before. To do this, it needs wide-ranging innovation in its ways of doing business. Mr Nishida introduced a new program known internally as "i cube" to Toshiba and its group, which aims to promote innovation in development, manufacturing, and sales, generating a multiplier effect by applying these advances throughout the company and the group's operations. The objective is to take the company beyond conventional methods of incremental improvements. The "i cube" program aims to empower each business unit to develop its capabilities to the full, and bring a "sense of urgency" to their work and to the development of business processes.

CSR-Based Management

Third, Toshiba's approach also requires that management is grounded in CSR (corporate social responsibility), at the core of its business. This approach prioritizes respect for life, safety, and legal compliance in all activities, and regards CSR as an integral part of the activities of every business unit and employee. Mr Nishida has also stated that he wants the company to earn the trust of its stakeholders, and the wider community, through outreach programs and voluntary activities. Protection of the global environment is particularly important. The "Toshiba Environmental Vision 2010" initiative and its voluntary environmental action plan are intended to double Toshiba Group's overall eco-efficiency by fiscal 2010.

To Whom does the Company Belong?

One of the basic issues of corporate governance discussed in Japanese companies, as in other countries, is "To whom does the company belong?" or "Who are the company's stakeholders?" Toshiba's stance on these basic issues was clarified in its proposal to its shareholders' meeting in 2006, for countermeasures to any large-scale acquisitions of the company's shares (the "Plan"). Based on shareholders' approval for the basic concept at the Ordinary General Shareholders' Meeting held in June 2006, the Plan was introduced "for the purpose of protection and enhancement of the corporate value of the company and the common interests of shareholders." It seeks to protect and enhance the corporate value of Toshiba and its group and the common interests of its shareholders by explicitly setting out the procedures to be followed when a large-scale acquisition of the company's shares is made, ensuring that shareholders are provided with necessary and adequate information and sufficient time to make appropriate decisions, and securing the opportunity for the board of directors to negotiate with the acquirer.

More specifically, if an acquirer starts or plans to start an acquisition or a takeover bid that would result in the acquirer holding 20 percent or more of Toshiba's total outstanding shares, the Plan will require the acquirer to provide any pertinent information in advance to the board of directors. The board will then establish a Special Committee that will, at its discretion, obtain advice from outside experts, evaluate and consider the details of the acquisition, disclose to Toshiba's shareholders the necessary information regarding the acquisition, as well as any alternative proposal prepared by Toshiba's CEO, and then negotiate with the acquirer. If the acquirer does not comply with the procedures under the Plan, or if the Special Committee decides that the acquisition would damage Toshiba's corporate value or the common interests of its shareholders, the Special Committee will recommend to the board that it implement countermeasures, such as a gratis allotment of stock acquisition rights (*Shinkabu yoyakuken no musho wariate*), a condition of which will be that they cannot be exercised by acquirers or the like, in order to protect the corporate value of Toshiba and the common interests of its shareholders.

Here, we can clearly see Toshiba's views regarding the question "to whom does the company belong?" Toshiba respects its existing stakeholders, including customers, shareholders and investors, employees, local communities, and suppliers. In all its activities, encompassing development, production, sales, after-sales service, and all other aspects, Toshiba seeks communication and engagement with its stakeholders, in order to respect their concerns, satisfy their needs, and respond to their aspirations, not least through clear and timely explanations. Toshiba itself is a balance of all these interests, generating value for them all, and the purpose of the Plan is to protect that balance.

Internal Control Systems: Ensuring the Function of the Board

Toshiba considers that corporate governance can be effectively implemented only when there exists the right scheme of internal controls, basic policies known to all, and standards of conduct for day-to-day operations. This means striving to ensure compliance with laws and regulations, social norms and ethics, and internal rules throughout Toshiba's worldwide operations. In practice, Toshiba's people are requested to accord the highest priority to human life and safety, and to observe regulatory compliance in everything they do, while promoting business activities through fair competition and serving the interests of customers to the best of their ability.

Already in 1990, Toshiba had established the Toshiba Group Standards of Conduct to govern business activities within the Toshiba Group. Every year since then, priority themes for compliance have been set in the light of business circumstances, and actively promoted. By implementing a Plan-Do-Check-Act (PDCA) cycle of self-assessment, not only at Toshiba itself but also at group companies worldwide, a follow-up process has been put in place to promote efforts to ensure compliance.

Mr Nishida's guiding principle – "Be truthful in thought, word and deed" – means striving to express what one really thinks in truthful words, putting those words into action, and then taking responsibility for those actions. By adhering to this principle and diffusing it throughout the Toshiba Group, Toshiba and its group companies are resolved to fulfil their responsibility to their stakeholders.

In response to the Financial Instruments and Exchange Law (sometimes known as "J-Sox"), promulgated in 2006 (which required formalization of internal control systems), Toshiba's board of directors further formalized its basic policies on the internal control system in April 2006. Group companies in Japan were requested to adopt the same basic policies on internal control systems by resolutions of their respective boards of directors, in order to reinforce internal control systems throughout the Toshiba Group. These measures were taken to ensure the integrity of corporate governance at the group level, and to ensure that the various companies' boards are functioning properly. They are supported in this by Toshiba, through establishment of prototype models of basic policies and rules covering internal control systems.

Additionally, in 2007, Toshiba set compliance with antitrust legislation worldwide and the prevention of bribery overseas as priority themes. It established new guidelines and strict mechanisms for ensuring compliance, including education, monitoring, and measures designed to preclude violations.

Risk-Compliance Management Systems Implemented Below Board Level

Toshiba's Risk-Compliance Committee is chaired by the Chief Risk-Compliance Management Officer (CRO), one of the senior class of executive officers. It acts in cooperation with the divisions concerned to determine and implement measures to deal with major risks, and prevent recurrence of any problems identified. Failure to respond appropriately to large-scale disasters, such as earthquakes, typhoons, floods, etc., could result in long-term closure of operations, resulting in a great financial loss and a large impact on stakeholders. In addition to measures to ensure the safety of employees and their families, support recovery of devastated areas, and maintain business sites and factories in the event of natural or other disasters, Toshiba established a Business Continuity Plan (BCP) in 2006. This covers those businesses that have large social and economic impacts in order to minimize any interruption in the supply of products and services. Furthermore, Toshiba introduced a whistle-blower system in 2000, the "Risk Hotline," whereby employees can report their concerns or seek advice via the intranet or phone, so that internal risk information is rapidly obtained and any breach of compliance is either prevented or nipped in the bud.

The Supervisory Function of the Board in Relation to Corporate Strategy and Decision Making

Effective implementation of the supervisory function of the board of directors was demonstrated in the course of certain strategic decision-making processes in 2006, when Toshiba moved to change its business portfolio. Instead of providing a comprehensive evaluation of the company's management systems, a concrete example will serve to show how the system helped (*a*) to achieve the strategic objectives of management; (*b*) to clarify the responsibility for execution in accordance with the strategic objectives; and (*c*) to foster strong leadership at the executive management level.

As the highest executive within Toshiba, Mr Nishida has placed a high priority on speed in decision making. The following example demonstrates this in practice. In 2007, Toshiba withdrew from the music and recording business after nearly fifty years of involvement. When EMI, Toshiba's music joint venture partner in Japan, expressed a wish to take full control of the Japanese business, Toshiba agreed to sell. EMI was due to start procedures for a change in its own ownership structure, and offered advantageous terms in return for a speedy negotiation of the conditions. Toshiba did not miss this opportunity. In essence, it took only three days (and nights) from when the conditions were proposed for Toshiba to reach agreement. That was probably an unprecedented speed of negotiation by a Japanese company in an M&A transaction. Other examples may also be given in which prompt decisions and negotiations saved time and generated advantages, including the sale of a majority equity stake in an asset-holding company, and withdrawal from a joint manufacturing business for SED (Surface-conduction Electron-emitter Displays) with Canon.

While withdrawing from noncore activities through a chain of business transfers and share sales, Toshiba has also bought major businesses. In order to secure an advantageous positioning in the nuclear power generation sector, where it was already a leading player in manufacturing BWR (Boiling Water Reactor) plants, it bought out the competing business of Westinghouse, which manufactures plants using the alternative PWR (Pressurized Water Reactor) technology. In this case, the buyout price was approximately ¥600 billion, roughly 30 percent of Toshiba's approximate aggregate market value at that time of ¥2 trillion. Hitherto, nuclear power systems manufacturers had specialized in either BWR or PWR. No company had ever attempted to offer development, manufacture, and maintenance of both types of system.

Japan is the only country in the world that has been the victim of a nuclear attack. Although the nuclear technology in this case is for peaceful use only, it was expected that Toshiba would face strict safety requirements from the Japanese government and public opinion. Toshiba foresaw that a major investment would be necessary for the development of processes to meet such requirements and to enhance the technology so that it could offer better reliability.

In the decision-making process for this series of divestitures and investments, Mr Nishida and his executive management on the one hand, and the board of directors on the other, took care to exercise their respective functions of management execution and supervision. They communicated closely through frequent board meetings during the period of these M&A negotiations. The board members were closely involved in each case and received reports of valuation based on business plans and the status of negotiations with the counterparties. All of these were important cases of how supervision of decision making and management execution combined to implement a strategy. They were also a demonstration of how an electronics manufacturer such as Toshiba could ensure that the governance of a Japanese company with committees functions properly.

The Reputation of Toshiba's Corporate Governance and Internal Control Systems

There are a number of indicators of the reputation Toshiba has established with regard to its corporate governance and internal control practices. Toshiba was ranked top in the JCGIndex Survey conducted by the Japan Corporate Governance Research Institute, Inc. (October 2007). In addition, Toshiba's stock was selected for the Corporate Governance Fund of the Pension Fund Association.[2] Toshiba has been a fixture on the Dow Jones Sustainability Indexes (DJSI) of the world's 300 leading companies for eight consecutive years since 2000. The DJSI, compiled by Dow Jones of the United States and Sustainable Asset Management (SAM) of Switzerland, is an influential ranking system that seeks to promote socially responsible investment. DJSI assesses the sustainability performance of the world's 2,500 largest companies and selects the top 10 percent for

[2] The Pension Fund Association (PFA) is a major Japanese pension fund which has established a reputation for insistence on high standards of governance at companies in which it invests.

the index. Toshiba was also selected as one of four leading companies among thirty-nine in "Diversified Industrials" of "DJSI World 2007."

Conclusion

Toshiba does not see its conversion to a company with committees as a sudden and radical change. It had been developing its Managing Officers system for some years before the change to the company with committees structure took place, and the new structure complemented its plans to empower executive management and make the distinction between supervision and execution more transparent. The company with committees system is often described as a "US-style" model, but Toshiba does not consider its corporate governance to be particularly American, although the concept of separating supervision from execution is clearly a common element.

What Toshiba's experience shows is that corporate governance is about much more than just the behavior of the board of directors. If it is to be effective, it needs to have a comprehensive approach that covers all considerations of board structure, the supervisory role of the board, management systems and execution, internal controls, attention to stakeholders, and CSR. Moreover, it must penetrate the thinking of the entire company, at all levels. It is often said that good corporate governance does not translate automatically into good performance. Toshiba feels that it should and is trying to ensure that it does, by combining its principles of governance with management systems innovation, leading to improved quality of execution by empowered managers under the supervision of the board.

10

Corporate Governance, Institutions, and the Spirits of Capitalism

D. Hugh Whittaker and Simon Deakin

Introduction

This concluding chapter has two main aims. First, we would like to provide a context for interpreting some of the key findings of the individual chapters. To do this, we have to broaden our discussion from corporate governance to include the wider institutions, practices, and ideologies which shape the processes of corporate governance. This context is both historical and comparative. Second, by doing so we situate our findings in relation to the extensive debates about varieties of capitalism and institutional change. In trying to explain our findings, we are forced to recognize the importance not just of formal institutions, but of norms, informal practices and ideology. These are interrelated, but not as tightly as some accounts assume.

What key findings do we seek to explain? Many of the chapters have looked at executives of Japanese corporations. They tell a largely consistent story. First, that executives' behavior has changed. Their allocation of time has changed. They spend more time than in the past thinking about share prices and relating to shareholders (Chapter 2). Top executives now have to front up in investor relations activities; in fact they have to assume a much more visible leadership role which is strategic in addition to

We are grateful for comments on an earlier draft from Ronald Dore, Takeshi Inagami and Sanford Jacoby. The usual disclaimers apply.

representational (Chapter 7). Their governance and decision-making bodies have changed too, whether they have adopted the (US-inspired) company-with-committees system or not. The changes are in part attributable to the widespread institutional reforms over the past decade and a half, spearheaded by legislation and deregulation, as well as persistent pressure from vocal shareholders (or at least the demonstration effect of a few well-publicized court cases), backed up by a sympathetic business media. They have also been driven by changes in competition and product markets.

On the other hand, an equally consistent finding of the chapters which focus on executives is of less than enthusiastic support for the shareholder primacy model. Rather, executives show continued support for the community firm, albeit with modification. For some, this may be a nostalgic wish to return to the good old days, untroubled by shareholder distractions, or new competitive pressures (to paraphrase a *Financial Times* editorial cited in Chapter 3). In many cases, however, it is the very result of executives grappling with new pressures, and crafting positions which they think are best for their firms going forward. Chapter 9, which describes the implementation of new governance structures in Toshiba not in terms of shareholder relations, but revitalizing management, speeding up decision making and ensuring internal accountability, provides a graphic example.

In fact, there is an underlying tension between the changes pursued by the executives, or changes they accede to, and those envisaged by the shareholder primacy model and related views. This is neatly encapsulated in the heavy industry executive's discussion with a financial analyst on how to restore profitability, related by METI vice minister Kitabata (Chapter 5). The "dialogue of the deaf" goes nowhere because, according to the executive, the analyst's logic misses the "practical realities of management" – ongoing relational contracting – but it also exposes a fundamentally different logic about how value is created, captured, and distributed. Another encounter between an executive and an analyst is related by Olcott (Chapter 7); in response to the analyst's enquiry about how much of the profit of the three year growth plan he will receive, the executive says: "I can't reply, as it's too low... Our investors, or buy side or sell side analysts, say it's too low, but there is a huge gap in understanding."

While generally rejecting what they see as a "US" corporate governance logic, executives do believe they need to solicit wider opinions for their decision making, and some comment that increased interaction with investors, and increased merger and acquisition activity – some of it hostile – has introduced a tension to their job which is more beneficial than damaging. Overall, however, there appear to be two underlying narratives about corporate governance change, one characterized by the "US" logic, or the logic of finance (clearly expressed by CalPERS representatives interviewed by Jacoby, Chapter 4), and the other, expressed cogently in the peak business organization publications discussed by Inagami in Chapter 6, particularly Nippon Keidanren's 2006 *Interim Report* (and its companion publication, which upholds the crucial role of management–labor cooperation). This narrative, we suggest below, expresses the logic of Japanese producer capitalism.

This book has highlighted the latter narrative (or path) through a focus on executives' perspectives. The first task in this chapter is to place this narrative in a broader historical and comparative context. We do this not by focusing on formal institutions so much as norms and practice, and ultimately ideas and ideologies. There can, in fact, be a considerable discrepancy between these. This observation is not new; the discrepancy between the concept of ownership enshrined in Japanese law and the informal institutions which embody a different sense of ownership, for instance, has long been noted. The growing tension between them, and their interaction, however, needs recognition, as does continuity in norms, ideas, and ideologies in the face of significant formal institutional change.

Having created this context, and argued the importance of norms and practice, ideas, and ideology, we discuss the two narratives, or paths of change within Japan. We characterize the positions on reform of the main proponents, and discuss the outcomes. Finally, we relate the discussion of context and change (and continuity) to recent writing on varieties of capitalism and institutional change. As we do so, we are mindful of the unfolding global financial crisis, and the possibility of a new tide of institutional change, particularly in those countries which have most fully embraced neoliberal marketization, financialization, and expansion of credit. Japan will not be unaffected, but our analysis gives reason to believe there will not be a dramatic swing in corporate governance norms and practices.

Goodwill and the Spirits of Capitalism

In his classic article "Goodwill and the Spirit of Market Capitalism," Dore (1983, 1987) set out what he saw as a central feature of Japanese capitalism, namely the extensive use of goodwill in stakeholder relations, which he ultimately attributed to an inability on the part of the Japanese to believe in Adam Smith despite their fascination with him, and to Confucian benevolence.[1] Citing the definition from Palgrave's 1923 dictionary of economics, he noted that "in the old Marshallian days" goodwill meant much the same thing to economists as it did to those in commerce, but that in the intervening half century its definition had been "extended to cover not just the benefits accruing to the purchaser of a business from the affectionate or inertial habits of its customers, but also those accruing out of his consequent shift from the position of price-taker to that of price-maker – his enhanced ability to hold those customers up to ransom" (Dore 1987: 171).

In fact, the shift occurred in the nineteenth century, with the transition from small owner-managed businesses to large corporations, according to an economist keen to use the concept as it was employed in commerce shortly after the turn of the century. Veblen (1904: 140) noted that goodwill's meaning had "been gradually extended to meet the requirements of modern business methods. Various items, of very diverse character, are to be included under the head of 'good-will'; but the items included have this much in common that they were 'immaterial wealth,' 'intangible assets'; which, it may parenthetically be remarked, signifies among other things that these assets are not serviceable to the community, but only to their owners."

Intangible assets, Veblen argued, had become central in the capitalization of the modern corporation, which in turn was central to the modern business system. The basis of share price valuation had shifted from material assets to future earnings capability, or pecuniary assets (cf. Raines and Leathers 1996). Fluctuating share prices reflected "variations in confidence on the part of investors, on current belief as to the probable policy or tactics of the businessmen in control . . . and on the indeterminable, largely instinctive, shifting movements of public sentiment and apprehension" (Veblen 1904: 149). The "folk psychology" (ibid) nature of share prices, which included perceptions of the businessmen at the helm of their corporation, could also be manipulated by them:

It follows . . . that under these circumstances the men who have the management of such an industrial enterprise, capitalized and quotable on the market, will be

---

[1] "The Japanese . . . have never managed actually to bring themselves to *believe* in the invisible hand. They have always insisted – and teach in their schools and their 'how to get on' books of popular morality – that the butcher, the baker, and the brewer *need* to be benevolent as well as self-interested" (Dore 1987: 181, emphasis in original).

able to induce the putative and actual earning-capacity, by expedients well known and approved for the purpose, partial information, as well as misinformation, sagaciously given out at a critical juncture, will go far toward producing a favourable temporary discrepancy of this kind, and so enabling the managers to buy and sell securities of the concern with advantage to themselves (Veblen 1904: 156–7).[2]

Veblen portrayed such manipulation as based on self-interest and predatory motives. Businessmen, he argued, could win favor in financial markets through improving productive capacity, to be sure, but also through the disruption of production (or "sabotage"), or manipulation of goodwill in the sense lamented by Dore. In Veblen's view, they had become increasingly indifferent as to which of these they used. Modern corporations were built on the industrial system, but as manufacturing capabilities expanded to the point that further expansion did not necessarily equate with profit, and as functional and particularly hierarchical specialization increased, so the businessmen at the top became increasingly divorced from the logic of industry.[3,4] Writing later, Veblen noted how many engineers, too, had either become inured to the capitalization of industry, or were willing to serve as "lieutenants" to businessmen and the "captains of industry." A few – mainly younger – engineers, however, were critical of "habitual mismanagement by ignorance and commercial sabotage" (1921: 73).

There are other views of US capitalism in the early twentieth century, of course, and there were other currents. Jacoby (1997) highlighted the emergence of "welfare capitalism" in the same period that Veblen was

---

[2] Also cited in Ganley (2004: 398–9).

[3] "Addiction to a strict and unremitting valuation of all things in terms of price and profit leaves them by settled habit, unfit to appreciate those technological facts and habits that can be formulated only in terms of tangible mechanical performance; increasingly so with every further move into a stricter addiction to businesslike management..." (Veblen 1921: 39).

[4] Max Weber, whose book *The Protestant Ethic and the Spirit of Capitalism*, is indirectly reflected in this chapter's title, also noted two types of capitalism. Writing at the same time as Veblen, he contrasted rational, ascetic, bourgeois capitalism with "adventurer captialism": "The capitalism of promoters, large-scale speculators, concession hunters, and much modern financial capitalism even in peace time, but, above all, the capitalism essentially concerned with exploiting wars, bears this stamp even in modern Western countries, and some, but only some, parts of large-scale international trade are closely related to it, today as always. But in modern times the Occident has developed, in addition to this, a very different form of capitalism which has appeared nowhere else: the rational capitalistic organization of (formally) free labour" (Weber 1904–5/1930: 21). Despite his comment about financial capitalism, Weber's and Veblen's evolutionary schemes are very different. Cf. Swedberg (1998) on Weber's types of capitalism.

observing, particularly in founder-run firms grappling with the growing labor movement, and in the new science-based electrical and chemical industries. Its core became the Special Conference Committee, formed in 1919 by leading executives to coordinate labor and personnel policies. John D. Rockefeller Jr. summed up a central theme: "the only solidarity natural in history is the solidarity which unites those in the same business establishment" (Jacoby 1997: 21). "Welfare capitalism" no doubt encompassed a broad range of motives, from tactical positioning to head off organized labor, to genuine belief in coprosperity. Generally, however, the attention of executives was turned toward the affairs of their "manors" rather than stock markets, and toward productive activity rather than sabotage or the manipulation of goodwill.

Both currents, however, were submerged by new developments in the 1930s following the Wall Street crash in October 1929, depression and the New Deal. Finance capitalism was brought to heel – most jarringly by the Glass-Steagall Act and related legislation of 1933–34 – and "big government" and "big labor" (Jacoby's terms) became increasingly influential. Jacoby argues that welfare capitalism reemerged in the 1960s and 1970s with the transformation of work and workers, and a growing emphasis on commitment. "Thus was modern welfare capitalism transformed into the 'new' nonunion model of today" (Jacoby 1997: 9).

But finance capitalism – or "investor capitalism" (Useem 1996; Kharuna 2007) – also reemerged in the 1970s and 1980s. The Glass-Steagall Act was progressively eroded long before it was formally replaced in 1999, the year after the bailout of Long-Term Capital Management (the first nonbank bailout by the Federal Reserve), and shortly after the creation of Citigroup through the merger of Travelers Insurance and Citibank (see Geisst 2005).

Not surprisingly Veblen's long-neglected theories of finance capitalism and capitalization have enjoyed a resurgence in the wake of a succession of crashes and scandals, from the 1987 stock market crash, to Enron and WorldCom (e.g., Raines and Leathers 1996; Cornehls 2004; Ganley 2004) and prospectively to the current global financial meltdown. The job of executives, according to Cornehls, has been to maximize putative earnings capability, to secure more capital or finance for expansion, and beat down competitors slow to adopt similar tactics. Systemically, the result has been a huge growth in the volume of credit, with boom followed by eventual bust, and a redistribution of assets from debtors to creditors. Bust is typically followed by new regulations, which executives and their lawyers then find new ways to get around.

They have a strong incentive to do so, for they are rewarded by their boards of directors and even by their stockholders if they are successful in increasing the market price of the stock. To do this they must play the game of financial expansion, according to the dictates of the capitalist system described by Veblen (Cornehls 2004: 45).

The "irrational exuberance" of the stock market bubble of the 1990s based on *projections* of earnings growth while price-earnings ratios were steadily rising, and the massive rise in executive compensation increasingly disconnected from real performance, both sometimes cloaked in smoke and mirrors by creative accounting, spin and complicit professionals (and compounded in the 2000s by similar irrational exuberance in housing – Shiller 2000, 2008; Bogle 2005) indeed suggest a full flowering of Veblenian finance capitalism.[5] The spirit of this capitalism reached Japan exogenously through the rise of foreign investors in the 1990s, as well as endogenously, as we shall see.

Japan in the late nineteenth and early twentieth century faced the prior task of securing a place for commerce and industry in the new post-feudal order. Seeking to overturn the (neo)-Confucian mistrust of commerce, people like the influential bureaucrat-turned-businessman Eiichi Shibusawa declared that businessmen "must be nothing less than moral exemplars."[6] To do this, they had to engage in "respectable" business practices as opposed to "abusive" or "speculative" business practices.[7] As Chapter 6 indicates, such "respectable" capitalism was far from dominant, even in the 1920s.

Second, most new enterprises in the late nineteenth and early twentieth centuries were owner-managed. Salaried managers were relatively rare in top management until the late Meiji, pre-World War I period, and as there was typically a chronic shortage of both capital and management talent, boards of joint stock companies were often dominated by representatives of the former. Friction between the two groups is depicted by Sanji Muto

---

[5] The term "irrational exuberance" originated in a dinner speech given by Alan Greenspan in December 1996, when he asked rhetorically: "But how do we know when irrational exuberance has unduly escalated asset values, which then become subject to unexpected and prolonged contractions as they have in Japan over the past decade?" Immediately following the speech, stock markets around the world plunged by 2–4 percent. (http://www.irrationalexuberance.com/definition.htm, accessed November 4 2008).

[6] Shibusawa attempted to create a philosophy combining the Analects and the abacus (*Rongo sorobanshugi*; Kinzley 1991: 15). See also the arguments deployed by business leaders opposed to factory legislation in the same period: Dore (1969).

[7] Note the echoes in recent corporate governance debates, and the Tokyo High Court view of Steel Partners in the Bull-Dog Sauce case, discussed in several chapters in this volume.

(from the latter camp), who was once forced to resign his job as a top manager in Kanegafuchi Cotton Spinning Co.:

In Japan, there are capitalists who buy up stock for speculative reasons, control the future course of the company, make imprudent plans to increase stock, attempt to raise the market value of stock, and then sell their shares of stock to make big profits. Those who bought stock at high prices not only try to cut operating expenses but even discontinue welfare facilities for employees. Such avaricious capitalists keep the employees in a miserable state and endanger the basis of the existence of the company.[8]

Morikawa (1989: 41, 43) argues that in the post-World War I slump the managerial limitations of such capitalists were exposed; companies with salaried managers in top posts continued to grow, while many of those dominated by financiers went bankrupt. Third, in the 1920s, new science-based industries were emerging in Japan as well, and under the "domestic production" (*kokusanka*) movement there was a strong management emphasis on building up technological capabilities. One champion was Masatoshi Okochi, a graduate of Tokyo Imperial University's engineering department who became director of Riken (Institute of Physical and Chemical Research), which spawned many businesses. A strong advocate of "science-based industry," he denounced "capitalistic industry":

The defect found naturally in capitalistic industry, apparent already in its history, is that capital controls industrial management and authority. Not only does science come under its control as well, but managers do not recognize its value nor do they succeed in understanding it because they lack the knowledge . . . Or, even if managers more or less understand a proposal, their first concern is how much money it will cost. Then they usually try to postpone a decision until they have accumulated more profits.[9]

Ultimately, "capitalistic industry" or Veblenian finance capitalism was suppressed in Japan as well. Welfare capitalism, however, was not. The Cooperation and Harmony Society (Kyochokai), also founded in 1919, might be seen as a functional equivalent of the (U.S.) Special Conference

---

[8] Cited in Morikawa (1989: 42).

[9] Cited in Cusumano (1989: 280). Okochi distinguished between "passive capitalism" exemplified by the United Kingdom, and "positive capitalism" of the United States, where businessmen did appear willing to invest in new technology and industry, although (in a striking resemblance to Veblen's views) "firms in the United States still exhibited 'passive' tendencies whenever production exceeded demand. Their response to surplus capacity was usually to reduce output [Veblen's sabotage], raising unit costs and encouraging the formation of cartels to maintain high prices by setting production limits for entire industries" (Cusumano 1989: 281).

Committee (cf. Kinzley 1991). In addition to addressing Japan's growing "social problem" – vividly expressed in the 1918 Rice Riots – and the growing labor movement, it also established the influential Industrial Efficiency Institute. Here we see a strong and enduring link established between welfare and industrial capitalism, backed by scientific management. We refer to this as producer capitalism. Instead of going underground in the 1930s, it evolved in the context of wartime mobilization, and was not dislodged after the war by the Occupation's democratization and New Deal reforms which legalized unions and collective bargaining.[10]

Indeed, it really began to flower in the reconstruction and high growth years under the banner of the productivity movement (see Chapters 6 and 8). Here the crucial link between industrial and welfare capitalism can be seen; labor was to cooperate in increasing productivity on condition that employment security was not undermined as a result, and the fruits of productivity increases were to be shared (spelled out in the Japan Productivity Centre's Three Productivity Principles). The principal mechanism for sharing the fruits, moreover, was also established in 1955 – the *shunto* spring wage offensive, led by leading unions in leading sectors.

In sum, the "solidarity which unites those in the same business establishment" was very deliberately nurtured, with all the nuances and contradictions noted by Jacoby.[11] Relatedly, this evolutionary path maintained much of Veblen's industrial capitalism, and suppressed the emergence of finance capitalism.[12] It might be argued that the latter reemerged endogenously in the second half of the 1980s in the spectacular asset bubble, but at the same time, producer capitalism was still in its heyday.

[10] The basis of industrial relations, however, shifted from paternalism to negotiated settlement. On the history of scientific management in prewar and postwar Japan, and indirectly the formation of Japan's industrial/welfare capitalism, see Tsutsui (1998). For a critical view of how the burgeoning postwar labor movement took the contours of enterprise unionism, see Kawanishi (1992). And on how, comparatively speaking, the logic of union organization in the United States worked against producer capitalism, see Cole (1979).

[11] "Liberals focus on workplace conflict, while conservatives emphasize the harmony between labor and capital. But in reality, workers and managers simultaneously have opposing *and* shared interests" (Jacoby 1999: 6; cf. Gordon 1998). Jacoby's view of welfare capitalism in Japan, and parallels with the United States, can be found in Jacoby (1993).

[12] Strictly speaking, we see Japan's producer capitalism as a type of industrial capitalism. Another type would feature scientific management with market/market power emphases in employment relations. On the restrictions placed on capital market activity, and dividends, especially during the late 1930s and early 1940s, see Okazaki (1994), cf. also Okazaki and Okuno-Fujiwara (1999). After World War II the mechanisms were largely informal. They included stable or reciprocal shareholding, and the main bank system and "convoy" system, which limited competition in the financial sector. See our discussion in Chapter 1.

Under these circumstances goodwill retained much of its original meaning, and indeed became a central feature of Japanese producer capitalism. Dore (1987: 170) sees it as "sentiments of friendship and the sense of diffuse personal obligation which accrue between individuals engaged in recurring contractual economic exchange." Beginning with those inside the same establishment, it was also applied to other stakeholders, such as suppliers, group companies, financial institutions, and customers. In other words, it is the essence of "relational contracting" between the stakeholders of Japanese businesses, and its diffusion is based on risk-sharing, duty and a preference for Parsonian affectivity rather than affective neutrality in relationships (Dore 1987: 182). Stock markets are less central to this variety of capitalism, and such goodwill is not necessarily reflected in share prices (although it was sometimes used to justify share prices with enormous price-earnings ratios during the bubble years). In particular, it is not recognized by the representatives of US funds who came to do more and more of the share trading on Japan's stock markets from the late 1990s.

One further "spirit" related to relational contracting in Japan should be noted. In a recent study, Whittaker et al. (2009) identified different types of entrepreneurship in high-tech manufacturing in the United Kingdom and Japan, which they called project entrepreneurship and lifework entrepreneurship, respectively. Underlying project entrepreneurship was a logic of *choice*. This was associated with increasing marketization, financialization, and projectification from the 1980s.[13] Needless to say, investor choice is expanded by marketization, financial market deregulation, auditing, and information disclosure; management choice is expanded by outsourcing and casualization of workforces.[14]

This was contrasted with the Japanese entrepreneurs, whose business became a lifework, with adjustments typically made *within* it. Here a logic of commitment was apparent. In fact, commitment was necessary in order to secure customers and stakeholder buy-in, which they needed to do business. Although they have projects and project managers, Japanese organizations are characteristically based on a longer-term set of commitments to stakeholders. Commitments secure higher levels of participation;

---

[13] On projectification, see, for example, Lundin and Söderholm (1995), Davies and Hobday (2005), and Ekstedt et al. (1999). On marketization and financialization, see below.
[14] Recent advisor to the UK Conservative Party, and trenchant critic of both Thatcherism and New Labour, Phillip Blond claims: "The idea of choice has destroyed our cultural legacy" (cited in *Times Higher Education*, October 9 2008, p. 24).

insistence on the right to exercise choice undermines it. Commitments, as well as goodwill, form the basis of relational contracting.

Reforming Producer Capitalism

Japan's producer capitalism was partly a product of formal institutional arrangements which changed over time, but was strongly influenced by norms and informal practices. These sought to reconcile two sets of issues – efficiency and innovation on the one hand (industrial capitalism) and fairness and stability, evolving from earlier notions of paternal obligation and attempts to tame the labor movement, on the other (welfare capitalism). For convenience we shall refer to them simply as efficiency and equity, recognizing potential tensions within as well as between them. The views of executives in the 1920s, and the formulation of the Three Productivity Principles, suggest that they were strongly linked. Despite their fascination with Adam Smith, noted by Dore, most Japanese, including business leaders, never accepted Smith's neat device of resolving these two sets of tensions through "interests," specifically the pursuit of self-interest.[15]

Second, the strong preference of business leaders was to resolve these tensions within their "manor." The parameters may have been set by public debate, and formal or quasi-formal institutions such as the spring wage offensive, but the actual resolution of production issues, integration, communication, and distribution, was to take place within the "manor," or in this case, the community firm (cf. Inagami and Whittaker 2005). The result was a kind of decentralized (but coordinated) "micro-corporatism" which, in addition to the rejection of Adam Smith, may help to explain Japan's relative stability in terms of norms and underlying ideology. Despite major political, legal, and other institutional changes, Japan did not experience the Polanyian "double movement" and "reverse double movement" swings of some other industrialized countries, including the United States, in the twentieth century.[16]

[15] On Smith's successful collapsing of the "passions" into avarice, and avarice into self-interest, the pursuit of which promotes economic and social progress, see Hirschman (1977).

[16] In Polanyi's view, "the advance of capitalism and the commoditization of labor created 'embedded' markets. In reaction to this, labor mobilized and demanded protection from the state against the strictures of the market. This was Polanyi's great insight, the double movement. Those dislocated by the market will use the state to protect themselves, the consequence of which is large-scale institutional change" (Blyth 2002: 3 and 4). See also Swenson (2002).

While less susceptible to endogenous instability, Japan's micro-corporatist producer capitalism nonetheless came under intense pressure from the 1990s, some of it, in fact, deriving from stability. A breakdown of changes in the distribution of Hitachi's gross value added, for example, gives some indication of a slow time bomb ticking internally. In the late 1950s, almost half went to operating profits, just over a third to labor and about one eighth to investment (measured by depreciation). By the late 1970s and early 1980s, operating profit had declined to a quarter, while the labor share had risen to 60 percent, with investment rising slightly. By the mid to late 1990s, operating profit had dropped to single figures, the labor share had risen to 70 percent, and investment had climbed to over 20 percent (Inagami and Whittaker 2005: 134). Shareholders got stable dividends of 11–16 percent of paid in capital over the same period, and while rising share prices (until 1990) reduced dividend yields, they produced potential capital gains. However, with the labor share set to rise further with an aging workforce, it was apparent that something had to give. Change was precipitated by Hitachi's first ever loss, in 1998–99, of over $3 billion.

Giants like Hitachi were caught between new competitive models emerging in the United States, which featured a powerful combination of modularity, IT-mediated outsourcing (on a global scale), and venture capital-backed specialist startups on the one hand, and the rise of Asian challengers who had absorbed Japanese production and quality techniques – and indeed many of its technologies – on the other. These Asian challengers often aligned themselves with US manufacturers (or retailers) in global value chains. Such challenges came on top of prolonged post-bubble domestic recession and financial problems, at a time when responsiveness was impaired by slower decision making and other problems associated with "large firm malaise."[17] Increased expenditure on R&D in these circumstances did not improve performance, and a growing number of companies then began to curtail R&D, and in some cases closed central R&D labs.

Thus the somewhat vague sense of crisis expressed by the authors of the Keizai Doyukai's 10th and 11th Economic White Papers in 1992 and 1994 (and summed up by Yotaro Kobayashi of Fuji Xerox: "Japanese companies have to set sail with neither a marine chart nor a model to emulate": Chapter 6) was not simply alarmist. For many companies the postwar

[17] See, for example, Cole and Whittaker (2006), and other contributions in the same volume.

growth formula appeared to have run its course. Some of Hitachi's managers opined that the company had been very good at "how" to make its products, but had not focused sufficiently on "what" to make, a view echoed in Porter et al.'s *Can Japan Compete?* (2000). They envisaged a greater emphasis on strategy, and decision making at the top level, involving restructuring, and the establishment of a holding company, legalized in 1997.

Into this context came calls for corporate governance reform. Under producer capitalism, the governance concerns of executives are primarily inward and stakeholder-oriented, as Chapter 9 neatly illustrates. Some of the advocates of reform, however, sought to reorient executives outward, toward shareholders, with a mutual focus on the market valuation of the firm, expressed in the share price. The result was at times a "dialogue of the deaf," but the path of reform of producer capitalism became increasingly intertwined with demands emanating from finance capitalism. Let us briefly survey these, and their proponents.

Two Paths of Reform

The path of reform of producer capitalism, as the preceding discussion suggests, is characterized by a reluctance to sever the link between efficiency and equity, industry and welfare. But pressures from resurgent (mainly United States-based) finance capitalism, in association with domestic proponents, pointed to a different path, favored by those much closer in spirit to Adam Smith, if not Veblen's businessmen and captains of industry. This path, of course, is that of financialization and marketization, and associated emphases on unshackled opportunity, choice, and openness.[18]

Japan began its postindustrial transition (in terms of employment composition) in the early 1990s, a transition which, in the United Kingdom and United States, was infused with financialization and marketization, triggered in part by declining profitability in manufacturing and rising demands by investors for better returns after initial diversification

[18] Financialization is "the increasing role of financial motives, financial markets, financial actors, and financial institutions in the operation of the domestic and international economies" (Epstein 2005; Dore 2008: 1097–8). Marketization is the increasing use of markets for the allocation of resources and exchange, promoted by privatization, deregulation, and techniques to assign monetary value to goods, services, intellectual property, processes, and so on.

strategies only made matters worse (e.g., Useem 1996). Some thought it natural that Japan also follow this path. Not surprisingly, advocates were more visible outside the manufacturing sector, in financial services, the media, and in some cases bureaucracy and government. In practice, the two paths were not identified as such, but may be seen as currents in the larger, turbulent debates of reform. Let us look briefly at some of the main participants and their arguments.

Fund Managers, Shareholders

The most visible pressure for change along the financialization path came as mentioned from fund managers and the financial services sector. Here, however, there were in fact a range of actors, with a range of stances. The most voluble proponents of change were a small number of investment and pension funds, both foreign (largely United States) and domestic. Foreign ownership of Japanese stocks rose from under 10 percent in the early 1990s to reach 28 percent in 2007, with higher proportions in many companies. Foreign shareholders – or their fund managers – accounted for around 60 percent of trades, so their influence was direct and considerable. They had the support of the Office of the US Trade Representative, seeking to "level the investment playing field." Some large Japanese players also became more assertive, notably the Pension Fund Association, with some ¥4 trillion invested in Japanese stocks in 2007. Arguments for change (explicitly or implicitly) advanced by this group of actors include:

- Japanese executives have to pay more attention to the legal "owners" of their businesses.
- Japanese companies shielded from market and investor pressure, with executive entrenchment, will stagnate.
- The US system of corporate finance, and governance, and executive incentives, must be superior because of superior US economic performance in the 1990s and early 2000s.
- It is unfair not to have a level playing field in investment, indicated by higher levels of foreign direct investment into Japan.
- Japan will be bypassed by global finance unless it plays by open rules which are investor-friendly and do not discriminate against foreigners.

Jacoby (in Chapter 4), however, shows that not all investors acted in concert. Aggressive assertion of shareholder rights, moreover, whether by foreign or domestic funds, typically came at a reputation/brand cost. Some attempts at coordination were made, for instance, through the Japan Corporate Governance Forum, which issued its guidelines in 1997 (allowing CalPERS to issue its own shortly after), and which, with the Tokyo Stock Exchange and Pension Fund Association, hosted the 2001 International Corporate Governance Network meeting in Tokyo. Such efforts, however, did not provide a coherent articulation of interests, and some financial sector managers continued to believe that finance should play a supporting role to industry, or that mutuality should be respected.[19]

Lawmakers and Bureaucrats

The postwar Liberal Democratic Party (LDP) politicians as well as bureaucrats were an integral part of the developmental state, which helped to create and consolidate Japan's producer capitalism (Johnson 1982). By the mid-1990s, however, some had decided that the developmental state itself, as well as Japanese capitalism, needed a fundamental overhaul. Bureaucrats were under fire for failure to counter recession and deflation, and for protecting their own interests, and wanted to be seen to do something to restore competitiveness, and produce change and openness. Some politicians were keen to wrest control over policy from the bureaucrats. The slow pace of administrative reform has been the subject of many books,[20] but as many of the chapters in this book note, there have been important changes to the legal and regulatory framework for business and finance over the past ten to fifteen years. This in itself is significant, given the "bureaucratic informalism" in Japan since the 1920s, which sought to limit the use of law and litigation as a driver of social change (Upham 1987).

The legal and regulatory reforms were informed by a range of motives. Second generation urbanites, some of them US educated, were visible among the academics, lawyers, and others who made up the consultative bodies whose opinions informed the bills. Some of the lawmakers and bureaucrats themselves fitted this description, and the overall thrust of

---

[19] Vogel (1999) has written a perceptive account of why Japanese consumer organizations were reluctant to act in their own apparent interests to undermine Japan's producer-oriented capitalism, to the bewilderment of US trade negotiators, merchants, and academics. Preferences, he points out, do not always coincide with interests. Here we may substitute consumers with investors, and indeed executives, who would benefit financially from closer alignment with shareholder interests. Interests, ideas, and institutions are not interchangeable.

[20] See, for example, Lincoln (2001), George-Mulgan (2003), and Carlile and Tilton (1998). For different evaluations, see Pempel (1998) and Vogel (2006).

their policies was to seek to remove or erode the institutional features which made Japan "different" and move it toward an internationally accepted, postdevelopmental state. As Araki notes, however, legal changes and deregulation which might push Japanese executives toward favoring shareholders, and weakening the community firm, were countered to some extent by other laws and measures, such as the revisions to the Labour Standards Act, and mandating employee voice in certain work-related areas. In the rulings reported by Hayakawa and Whittaker, moreover, it appears that the judiciary has sought to strike a similar balance.

Media

The mass media play an obvious role in shaping the ideological climate, none more than the Nikkei business media group and its flagship *Nikkei shimbun*. In the 1990s, the stance of the business media toward Japanese management practices changed visibly. Until the early 1990s, companies like Hitachi would have been criticized for laying off workers, but by the end of that decade they were being severely criticized for jeopardizing current and future employment by failing to take bold restructuring measures. Thus the business media by and large supported corporate restructuring, and legislative and deregulatory measures to promote it. In general they were sympathetic to the Koizumi reform agenda for similar reasons.

Regarding corporate governance and shareholder relations, they by and large supported the overlapping arguments that (*a*) increased responsiveness to shareholders and profit emphasis will reinvigorate companies; (*b*) it will force them to specialize more, freeing up space and resources for new participants; (*c*) companies should move away from reciprocal shareholding and similar measures which might insulate managers from shareholder pressure and market forces; and (*d*) the Japanese economy risks closing itself off from global trends and interaction if it does not become more investor friendly.

Thus, while not necessarily favoring strongly changes such as the company-with-committees system, or stock options for executives, the business media promoted restructuring, profit emphasis (or restoration), greater information disclosure, and other investor-friendly measures, and a form of "global standards." It also favored greater media visibility of top corporate executives, and hence implicitly a new style of leadership. On the other hand, while it supported the assault on "bad"

281

egalitarianism,[21] it echoed or even amplified concern over increasing wealth differentials. And it supported the technology management movement and other means of strengthening industry.

Business Executives

We have touched on the views of corporate executives, at least in the manufacturing sector, and they have featured throughout this book. In the deepest gloom of 1998–2000, when corporate failures spread from the financial sector into manufacturing, and the United States was at the height of its own dot-com bubble, many seriously wrestled with how much of the past model they could afford to keep, and how radical their reforms should be. Their ideological compass wavered somewhat. Pressures on them intensified if anything in the wake of the dot-com bubble burst, and came not just from the media, financial analysts or shareholders, but from product markets as well. By and large, however, most sought reform along a path consistent with producer capitalism.

Unions

The year 1989 saw the formation of "8 million Rengo" (the Japanese Trade Union Confederation, with almost 8 million members), almost unifying the labor movement, and enhancing the prospect of national level "neo-corporatism," albeit largely informal and supplementary to the corporate level. The prospect soon faded in the 1990s with deep recession, restructuring, membership attrition, constantly changing alliances of political parties, and the policy shift toward deregulation. As in other countries, organized labor was on the back foot. Unions were forced to acquiesce in – or actively support – management reforms, at considerable pain to themselves, but they did play a role in keeping executives from straying too far from the producer capitalism path in the late 1990s and early 2000s. They appealed to fairness, and noted the dangers to employee morale of drastic restructuring, and to social cohesion of widening wealth differentials. These arguments had some resonance, not just among executives, but among some lawmakers and bureaucrats as well. On the other hand, they found themselves representing a shrinking group of regular employees – 18.2 percent in 2006,

---

[21] This was seldom defined, but generally referred to an emphasis on outcome equality by various means, including opportunity constriction.

and less in the private sector – and were under pressure to do something about organizing nonregular workers.[22]

The Outcome: Change and Its Interpretation

Out of the turbulence of prolonged recession and deflation, crisis in the financial sector, changing competition, business restructuring and social sustainability issues, and a cacophony of prescriptions as to what should be done, what emerged? Dore claims that the advocates of financialization and marketization have gained ideological ascendancy, with the backing of legal and other formal institutional changes. The grounds for his argument, in addition to the seductiveness of finance (or stock market) capitalism's missionaries and Japan's loss of confidence in the 1990s, are structural and essentially twofold. First, there is generational change. The children and grandchildren of the first postwar generation have been brought up in urban affluence without forging interclass ties through postwar hardship and state schooling. Some of the most vociferous and self-confident have studied in the United States, and increasingly dominate the business media, government panels, ministries, and government itself (Dore 1999). To this he adds, again in the words of METI vice minister Kitabata in this volume, the irrepressible growth of capital and funds, sweeping the globe and changing the rules of capitalism: "We are shifting from a real world economy to a world in which finance dominates the economy, which cannot but have implications for the corporation" (cf also Dore 2008).

To be sure, there has been movement along the path of marketization and financialization. The deregulation movement gained momentum under Prime Minister Koizumi (2001–6), industrial restructuring accelerated, mergers and acquisitions increased, reciprocal and other stable shareholdings continued to fall, emphasis on profit increased, and even employment relations were marketized in the senses of performance-based management for regular employees, and increasing numbers of nonregular employees on fixed term or agency contracts. Consolidated management, quarterly accounting, stock options, defined contribution pensions (or portions of pensions) and the professionalization of the company–investor interface all fit the picture of change in this direction.

---

[22] Less than 5 percent of nonregular workers are organized. A few unions – notably UI Zensen Domei, and Jichiro, as well as Zenroren affiliates – have been active in organizing them, but most Rengo affiliates' efforts have been lukewarm at best.

And yet, as noted in the beginning of this chapter, much of the evidence in this book is actually of muted movement along this path, despite the deregulation movement, despite growing pressure from investors through stock markets and, increasingly, shareholder meetings, and despite media pressure. Indeed a strong case can be made for the movement along the path in which executives seek to adapt producer capitalism to new circumstances. This occurred after some vacillation. Hitachi appeared to be poised in 1999 after its massive loss to take advantage of legislation permitting holding companies, and spinning out its operating units as separate companies, which could have destroyed the union, but in the end opted for less drastic restructuring solutions. Its medium term plans announced bold exit targets, aimed at reassuring investors and analysts, but these were revised in the face of the realities of relational contracting. Its HRM reforms, after debate, focused on stimulating the creativity/performance of white collar university graduates, rather than cutting overall wage costs (although there was restructuring, with movement of employees to outer tier companies, as well as voluntary redundancies). Stock options were introduced for seventy-one senior managers, but were largely symbolic. The company-with-committees system was adopted, but none of the four external board members could be considered a direct representative of investor interests. Rather, it reflected a perceived need to keep abreast of rapid changes in the external environment.[23]

In fact, another interpretation is possible of Japan's fascination with marketization, financialization and "global standards" of corporate governance, namely that these are used to stimulate change which is difficult to bring about endogenously. They are held in tension with existing norms and practices, debated and partially absorbed, but in the process are changed to maintain underlying continuity in the internal balances and implicit contracts of producer capitalism (efficiency/innovation and fairness/stability). Japan has a very long history of such adaptive absorption; the Meiji catch phrase "Japanese spirit and Western learning/technology" (*wakon yosai*) rephrased an earlier tradition of "Japanese spirit and Chinese learning/technology."

The corporate governance debates mark new institutional borrowing and reshaping to address multiple issues. These include relations with investors, speeding up decision making and strengthening its strategic elements, introducing mechanisms to absorb external views directly into this decision making, and clarifying mechanisms of social accountability,

---

[23] For details, see Inagami and Whittaker (2005).

to prevent corporate wrongdoing. At a broader level, the debates have provided a focus for exchanging views and creating common understandings of just what elements of producer capitalism should be changed, and what should be maintained. "Global standards" are often seen as an attempt to align Japan's producer capitalism with US-led financial capitalism, but they may also be seen as a means of representing a dialectical "other" in order to promote adaptive change.[24]

As a result of adaptive absorption practices, moreover, there has long been a gap between formal institutions such as legal codes, and informal norms and practices. The discrepancy between the formal ownership of the Commercial Code and that implicit in the stakeholder relations of Japan's producer capitalism is an obvious example. Thus when considering change, it is not enough to focus on formal institutions. We must also look at informal practices, norms, and the ideologies behind these. The increase of nonregular workers, for example, may be seen as the "marketization of employment relations," but it may also be seen as an attempt to preserve the community firm in the face of growing external challenges and volatility. Which of these is more accurate matters if we wish to interpret other executive behavior, or predict what executives will do in different circumstances. With these comments in mind, let us draw out the implications of this analysis for institutional research.

As Streeck and Thelen (2005: 1) argue, if we reject the notion of convergence toward a single model of capitalism, "we notice that many arguments in support of distinctive and stable national models lack the analytic tools necessary to capture the changes that are indisputably going on in those countries." The result is a tendency either to understate the amount of change, or to see it as simply adaptive. Without tools to explain gradual change, resort is made to punctuated equilibrium models which see long periods of relative stability punctuated by sharp change triggered by an exogenous force. Their volume describes various types of gradual change, including stability in formal and semiformal institutions, but different uses made of those institutions. Instead of being dismantled, for instance, corporate networks in Japan have been used for downsizing and increasing labor market flexibility (Vogel 2005). Thus "formal institutions do not fully determine the uses to which they may be put. This is one

---

[24] This interpretation risks imposing greater intentionality than warranted by the evidence. As Buchanan and Deakin argue in Chapter 2, executive behavior has been varied, and some of it has been defensive, but it fits with their "characteristic reaction" of executives seeking to recognize shareholder rights, "absorbing and co-opting them into the structures of the community firm."

important reason why major change in institutional practice may be observed together with strong continuity in institutional structures" (Streeck and Thelen 2005: 17).

But the reverse may apply as well: institutions (in the sense used by Streeck and Thelen – formalized rules which may be enforced by calling on a third party) may change without corresponding changes to informal practices and norms. Such loose coupling is seen in the relatively small empirical difference in corporate governance practices between companies adopting the company-with-committees system and those with the company-with-auditors system, as it has come to be called. This, too, shows that formal institutions and practices and norms are not tightly coupled, and changes may occur in either, or in their interaction, over time.[25]

A further difficulty in institutionalist and varieties of capitalism writing has been recognition of agency or actors (Crouch 2005). People will support, circumvent, negotiate or seek to change institutions which establish "rules of the game," not just for the sake of maintaining the status quo (path dependence) or maximizing personal utility, but for a variety of reasons and motives, which are socially shaped but not necessarily institutionally stamped, and here ideas and ideology matter.[26] The central concerns of Japanese producer capitalism, embedded in norms and practice, are ideological, and concern how value is – should be – created, captured, and distributed. We contrasted these with the concerns of Veblenian finance capitalism, in which actors have very different views.

Recognition of the ideological dimension of change is necessary if we wish to understand the reception of US-derived corporate governance practices in Japan. It may well be that the ideology of financialization and especially marketization is more coherently articulated than the micro-corporatist efficiency-equity ideology of producer capitalism, and that the ideological compass of Japanese executives has wavered somewhat, but it does not appear to be broken.

After initially being feted by some financial and political leaders, it is no coincidence that Japan's most prominent would-be norm changers – Yoshiaki Murakami and Takafumi Horie – became linked by the media to

---

[25] Streeck and Thelen identify five types of gradual institutional change – displacement, layering, drift, conversion, and exhaustion. Examples of most of these can be found in relation to Japan. Sako (2007), for example, gives examples of conversion and layering in financial and labor markets in Japan, which is one cause of increasing institutional diversity.

[26] See, for example, constructivist institutionalism (e.g., Blyth 2002; Hay 2006) and actor-centered institutionalism (e.g. Scharpf 1997; Mantazavinos 2001).

increasing wealth differentials, a new social ill.[27] The logic that they used, the logic of finance capitalism, was associated with a "winner take all" approach to business which was abhorrent to industry-dominated organizations like the Nippon Keidanren.[28]

In conclusion, ideological preferences account for at least some of the resistance of the Japanese executives to aligning themselves more closely with their shareholders, and the reception of corporate governance in Japan. Despite ambivalence and vacillation, and some sensitivity to claims that they have neglected shareholder interests in the past, at heart they believe that shareholders must also demonstrate commitment to deserve greater attention, and that any such realignment should not apply to "abusive" or speculative shareholders. Moreover, they do not feel that shareholder interests should be prioritized at the expense of other stakeholders, particularly those directly involved in the industry tasks of designing and making goods, or consumers. Disclosure, yes, but as a demonstration of sincerity and effort, rather than a commitment to foster choice, or to prevent share prices from sliding rather than to manipulate for financial chess. Stock options to show that shareholders and share price are considered important, but not to ratchet up their own earnings, and so on.

While pressure from actors using the logic of finance capitalism may be deflated along with global asset prices,[29] on the other hand, tensions in corporate governance and investor relations will continue. An array of unresolved challenges will ensure that pressures for change are unabated. These include systemic problems – a tendency to overproduce, insider–outsider dualism, with heavy demands placed on members of the community firm and disadvantages for nonmembers (notably women and

---

[27] When grilled over his investment in the Murakami Fund, Bank of Japan Governor Toshihiko Fukui "said he regrets he could not restrain his feelings to support young people like Murakami, whom he said had been expected to stand up and break new ground in a society gasping for fresh air after years of recession" (*Japan Times*, June 21 2006). Horie was encouraged by Koizumi to stand against an "old guard" politician in the 2005 general election.

[28] Hiroshi Okuda, then Chairman of Toyota and of the Nippon Keidanren criticized Takafumi Horie's famous "there is nothing money can't buy" credo as being bad for Japanese society. He drew a parallel with the actions of T. Boone Pickens in acquiring shares in Koito Manufacturing, a supplier to Toyota, in 1989, which were fiercely resisted. Horie responded to criticisms of his style with: "If you see a loophole and you don't use it, someone else will use it against you," and "Time is money. You have to consider the lost earnings on the money that's just lying around. There was nothing to be gained by just letting the NBS shares lie" (cited in *Japan Echo*, 32/4 August 2005: "Friction with the Neighbours"). Another "dialogue of the deaf."

[29] The apostasy of long-time neo-liberal policy proponent Iwao Nakatani in late 2008 (Nakatani 2008) might mark the beginning of this trend.

youth in recent years), calling the equity or fairness of the system into question. Inequality will probably continue to rise.[30] They also include a succession of corporate scandals referred to in Chapter 6, which frequently stem from attempts to preserve an inner core of relationships at the expense of other stakeholders, especially consumers, under increasing market pressure. And they include competitive challenges, including innovation and entrepreneurship in fast moving and newly emerging industries, and strengthening universities in the national innovation system. The effectiveness of the postwar productivity solution will continue to be challenged as work becomes increasingly service-based and carried out by white collar "creative knowledge workers." But the probability is high that the changes will continue to be driven along the producer capitalism path, in which the link between efficiency and equity is not broken, in which goodwill retains much of its original meaning, commitment is not overridden by choice, and Adam Smith remains a source of inspiration, but a foreign one.

Bibliography

Aoki, M., Jackson, G. and Miyajima, H., eds. (2007). *Corporate Governance in Japan: Institutional Change and Organizational Diversity*. Oxford: Oxford University Press.

Blyth, M. (2002). *Great Transformations: Economic Ideas and Institutional Change in the Twentieth Century*. Cambridge: Cambridge University Press.

Bogle, J. (2005). *The Battle for the Soul of Capitalism*. New Haven: Yale University Press.

Carlile, L. and Tilton, M., eds. (1998). *Is Japan Really Changing Its Ways? Regulatory Reform and the Japanese Economy*. Washington DC: Brookings Institution.

Cole, R. (1979). *Work, Mobility and Participation: A Comparative Study of American and Japanese Industry*. Berkeley: University of California Press.

——and Whittaker, D.H. (2006). "Introduction," in D.H. Whittaker and R. Cole, eds., *Recovering from Success: Innovation and Technology Management in Japan*. Oxford: Oxford University Press.

Cornehls, J. (2004). "Veblen's Theory of Finance Capitalism and Contemporary Corporate America." *Journal of Economic Issues*, 38: 29–58.

Crouch, C. (2005). *Capitalist Diversity and Change: Recombinant Governance and Institutional Entrepreneurs*. Oxford: Oxford University Press.

---

[30] On Japan's rising Gini coefficient, see Minami (2008), and other articles in the same volume. Minami shows how the Gini coefficient also rose in interwar Japan, when the foundations for Japan's producer capitalism – and political instability – were being laid.

Cusumano, M. (1989). " 'Scientific Industry': Strategy, Technology and Entrepreneurship in Prewar Japan," in W. Wray, ed., *Managing Industrial Enterprise: Cases from Japan's Prewar Experience*. Cambridge, MA: Harvard University Press.

Davies, A. and Hobday, M. (2005). *The Business of Projects*. Cambridge: Cambridge University Press.

Dore, R. (1969). "The Moderniser as a Special Case: Japanese Factory Legislation, 1882–1912." *Comparative Studies in Society and History*, 11: 433–50.

—— (1983/1987). "Goodwill and the Spirit of Market Capitalism." *British Journal of Sociology*, 34/iv, reprinted in R. Dore, *Taking Japan Seriously: A Confucian Perspective on Leading Economic Issues*. Stanford: Stanford University Press.

—— (1999). "Japan's Reform Debate: Patriotic Concern or Class Interest? Or Both?" *Journal of Japanese Studies*, 25: 65–89.

—— (2008). "Financialisation of the Global Economy." *Industrial and Corporate Change*, 17: 1097–112.

Ekstedt, E., Lundin, R., Söderholm, A. and Wirdenius, H. (1999). *Neo-Industrial Organizing: Renewal by Action and Knowledge Formation in a Project-Intensive Economy*. Routledge: London.

Epstein, G. ed. (2005). *Financialisation and the World Economy*. Aldershot: Edward Elgar.

Ganley, W. (2004). "The Theory of Business Enterprise and Veblen's Neglected Theory of Corporation Finance." *Journal of Economic Issues*, 38: 397–403.

Geisst, C. (2005). *Undue Influence: How the Wall Street Elite Puts the Financial System at Risk*. Hoboken, NJ: John Wiley.

George-Mulgan, A. (2003). *Japan's Failed Revolution: Koizumi and the Politics of Economic Reform*. Canberra: Asia Pacific Press.

Gordon, A. (1998). *The Wages of Affluence: Labour and Management in Postwar Japan*. Cambridge, MA: Harvard University Press.

Hall, P. and Soskice, D., eds. (2001). *Varieties of Capitalism: The Institutional Foundations of Comparative Advantage*. Oxford: Oxford University Press.

Hay, C. (2006). "Constructivist Institutionalism," in R. Rhodes, S. Binder and B. Rockman, eds., *The Oxford Handbook of Political Institutions*. Oxford: Oxford University Press.

Hirschman, A. (1977). *The Passions and the Interests: Political Arguments for Capitalism Before Its Triumph*. Princeton: Princeton University Press.

Inagami, T. and Whittaker, D.H. (2005). *The New Community Firm: Employment, Governance and Management Reform in Japan*. Cambridge: Cambridge University Press.

Jacoby, S. (1993). "Pacific Ties: Industrial Relations and Employment Systems in Japan and the United States Since 1900," in N. Lichtenstein and H.J. Harris, eds., *Industrial Democracy in America: The Ambiguous Promise*. Cambridge: Woodrow Wilson Centre Press and Cambridge University Press.

—— (1997). *Modern Manors: Welfare Capitalism Since the New Deal*. Princeton: Princeton University Press.

Johnson, C. (1982). *MITI and the Japanese Miracle*. Stanford: Stanford University Press.

Kawanishi, H. (1992). *Enterprise Unionism in Japan*. London: Kegan Paul International.

Kharuna, R. (2007). *From Higher Aims to Hired Hands: The Social Transformation of American Business Schools and the Unfulfilled Promise of Management as a Profession*. Princeton: Princeton University Press.

Kinzley, W.D. (1991). *Industrial Harmony in Modern Japan: The Invention of a Tradition*. New York: Routledge.

Lincoln, E. (2001). *Arthritic Japan: The Slow Pace of Economic Reform*. Washington DC: Brookings.

Lundin, R. and Söderholm, A. (1995). "A Theory of the Temporary Organization." *Scandinavian Journal of Management*, 11: 437–55.

Mantzavinos, C. (2001). *Individuals, Institutions, and Markets*. Cambridge: Cambridge University Press.

Minami, R. (2008). "Income Distribution of Japan: Historical Perspective and Its Implications." *Japan Labor Review*, 5: 5–20.

Morikawa, H. (1989). "The Increasing Power of Salaried Managers in Japan's Large Corporations," in W. Wray, ed., *Managing Industrial Enterprise: Cases from Japan's Prewar Experience*. Cambridge, MA: Harvard University Press.

Nakatani, I. (2008). *Shihonshugi wa naze jikai shita no ka: Nihon saisei e no teigen (Why Did Capitalism Self Destruct? Proposals for Japan's Renewal)*. Tokyo: Shueisha.

Okazaki, T. (1994). "The Japanese Firm under the Wartime Planned Economy," in M. Aoki and R. Dore, eds., *The Japanese Firm: Source of Competitive Strength*. Oxford: Oxford University Press.

——and Okuno-Fujiwara, M., eds. (1999). *The Japanese Economic System and Its Historical Origins*. Oxford: Oxford University Press.

Pempel, T.J. (1998). *Regime Shift: Comparative Dynamics of the Japanese Political Economy*. Ithaca: Cornell University Press.

Porter, M., Takeuchi, H. and Sakakibara, M. (2000). *Can Japan Compete?* Basingstoke: Macmillan.

Raines, J.P. and Leathers, C. (1996). "Veblenian Stock Markets and the Efficient Markets Hypothesis." *Journal of Post Keynesian Economics*, 19: 137–51.

Sako, M. (2007). "Organizational Diversity and Institutional Change: Evidence from Financial and Labour Markets in Japan," in M. Aoki, G. Jackson and H. Miyajima, eds., *Corporate Governance in Japan: Institutional Change and Organizational Diversity*. Oxford: Oxford University Press.

Scharpf, F. (1997). *Games Real Actors Play*. Oxford: Westview Press.

Shiller, R. (2000). *Irrational Exuberance*. Princeton: Princeton University Press.

——(2008). *The Subprime Solution: How Today's Global Financial Crisis Happened, and What to Do about It*. Princeton: Princeton University Press.

Streeck, W. and Thelen, K. (2005). "Introduction: Institutional Change ·in Advanced Political Economies," in W. Streeck and K. Thelen, eds., *Beyond

Continuity: Institutional Change in Advanced Political Economies. Oxford: Oxford University Press.

Swedberg, R. (1998). *Max Weber and the Idea of Economic Sociology*. Princeton: Princeton University Press.

Swenson, P. (2002). *Capitalists against Markets: The Making of Labour Markets and Welfare States in the United States and Sweden*. New York: Oxford University Press.

Tsutsui, W. (1998). *Manufacturing Ideology: Scientific Management in Twentieth Century Japan*. Princeton: Princeton University Press.

Upham, F. (1987). *Law and Social Change in Postwar Japan*. Cambridge MA: Harvard University Press.

Useem, M. (1996). *Investor Capitalism: How Money Managers Are Changing the Face of Corporate America*. New York: Basic Books.

Veblen, T. (1904). *The Theory of Business Enterprise*. New York: Charles Scribner's Sons.

—— (1921). *The Engineers and the Price System*. New York: Augustus M. Kelley.

Vogel, S. (1999). "When Interests Are Not Preferences: The Cautionary Tale of Japanese Consumers," in *Comparative Politics*, 31, pp. 187–207.

—— (2005). "Routine Adjustment and Bounded Innovation: The Changing Political Economy of Japan," in W. Streeck and K. Thelen, eds., *Beyond Continuity: Institutional Change in Advanced Political Economies*. Oxford: Oxford University Press.

—— (2006). *Japan Remodeled: How Government and Industry Are Reforming Japanese Capitalism*. Ithaca: Cornell University Press.

Weber, M. (1904–5/1930). *The Protestant Ethic and the Spirit of Capitalism*. New York: Harper Collins.

Whittaker, D.H., with Byosiere, P., Momose, S., Morishita, T., Quince, T. and Higuchi, J. (2009). *Comparative Entrepreneurship: The UK, Japan and the Shadow of Silicon Valley*. Oxford: Oxford University Press.

Witt, M. (2006). *Changing Japanese Capitalism: Societal Coordination and Institutional Adjustment*. Cambridge: Cambridge University Press.

INDEX

Figures, tables and notes are indexed in bold. US spelling has been used.